AUSTIN-HEALEY SPRITE AND MG MIDGET

1958 to 1971

OWNER'S HANDBOOK AND SERVICE MANUAL

948 c.c. - 1098 c.c. - 1275 c.c.

By
Technical Editors of
Clymer Publications

Originally Published by Floyd Clymer
This 2015 Revised & Updated Edition
Published by:
www.VelocePress.com

INTRODUCTION

Welcome to the world of digital publishing ~ the book you now hold in your hand, while unchanged from the original edition, was printed using the latest state of the art digital technology. The advent of print-on-demand has forever changed the publishing process, never has information been so accessible and it is our hope that this book serves your informational needs for years to come. If this is your first exposure to digital publishing, we hope that you are pleased with the results. Many more titles of interest to the classic automobile and motorcycle enthusiast, collector and restorer are available via our website at www.VelocePress.com. We hope that you find this title as interesting as we do.

NOTE FROM THE PUBLISHER

The information presented is true and complete to the best of our knowledge. All recommendations are made without any guarantees on the part of the author or the publisher, who also disclaim all liability incurred with the use of this information.

TRADEMARKS

We recognize that some words, model names and designations, for example, mentioned herein are the property of the trademark holder. We use them for identification purposes only. This is not an official publication.

INFORMATION ON THE USE OF THIS PUBLICATION

This manual is an invaluable resource for those interested in performing their own maintenance. However, in today's information age we are constantly subject to changes in common practice, new technology, availability of improved materials and increased awareness of chemical toxicity. As such, it is advised that the user consult with an experienced professional prior to undertaking any procedure described herein. While every care has been taken to ensure correctness of information, it is obviously not possible to guarantee complete freedom from errors or omissions or to accept liability arising from such errors or omissions. Therefore, any individual that uses the information contained within, or elects to perform or participate in do-it-yourself repairs or modifications acknowledges that there is a risk factor involved and that the publisher or its associates cannot be held responsible for personal injury or property damage resulting from the use of the information or the outcome of such procedures.

WARNING!

One final word of advice, this publication is intended to be used as a reference guide, and when in doubt the reader should consult with a qualified technician.

FOR A COMPLETE LIST OF ALL OUR AUTOMOBILE & MOTORCYCLE BOOKS
PLEASE VISIT OUR WEBSITE AT
www.VelocePress.com

ANNOUNCEMENT

The old axiom that racing improves the breed was never better illustrated than with the progress of the Austin Healey *Sprite* and its new twin, the MG *Midget*. The Sprite caught on instantly as a vehicle which could be raced competitively on a small budget and was still highly enjoyable to drive on the street. Like the famous MG TD, it became everyman's sports car and, without any doubt, a large percentage of new car sales derived exclusively from the impression that *Sprites* created on club circuits. The factory changes and model modifications from year to year and the optional equipment reflect the same bias.

Thus the *Sprite* or *Midget* owner drives a better-performing automobile and a safer one than would be the case if the model improvements all derived from the styling department as is so often the rule.

By the same token, the owner of these cars is a great deal more interested in the mechanical and performance aspects than the average, and, in our experience, is more vitally concerned with the care and upkeep of his automobile.

It is to this person that the SPRITE-MG MIDGET OWNER'S HANDBOOK is directed. He may never want to as much as adjust the idling speed of the engine, but he will, after reading the book, have a thorough understanding of the complete car and a knowledge of how all maintenance and repair should proceed. It is not a shop manual, nor intended to replace the shop manual, but covers comprehensively the data encompassed in factory literature. In an emergency, or at the owner's discretion, he can effect repairs which would otherwise perhaps leave him stranded. It is therefore recommended that this volume be kept in the vehicle at all times.

That the average owner will want to avail himself of genuine BMC parts and the services of BMC dealers and authorized service garages is well understood and recommended. There is no substitute for original equipment and competent, trained personnel.

I hope that *Sprite* and *Midget* owners will receive as much satisfaction from this Handbook as we have gained in being able to publish it.

Floyd Clymer
Publisher

CONTENTS

Model Identification Chart 4
General Data (All Models) 5
Wiring Diagrams (All Models) 291

SECTION I   948 c.c. Engine   31-198

Ignition 32
Fuel System 48
Mk. II & Midget Carburetors 60
Electrical System 68
Engine 95
Cooling System 131
Clutch 137
Gearbox 144
Driveshaft 157
Rear Axle 161
Suspension 167
Steering 175
Brakes 178
Wheels & Tires 191

SECTION II   1098 c.c. Engine Supplement   199-262

SECTION III   1275 c.c. Engine Supplement   263-290

CONTENTS
SECTION II AND III

SECTION II — 1098 c.c. Engine Supplement — 199-262

Performance Maintenance	200
Ignition	202
Fuel System	205
Electrical System	211
Engine	219
Cooling System	232
Clutch	235
Gearbox	237
Drive Shaft	241
Rear Axle	242
Suspension	244
Steering	247
Brakes	247

SECTION III — 1275 c.c. Engine Supplement — 263-290

Ignition	264
Fuel System	264
Electrical	266
Engine	266
Clutch	274
Rear Axle	277
Rear Suspension	277
Brakes	278
Exhaust Emission Control Data	280
Exhaust Emission Control	283
Increasing Power & Performance	311

MODEL CHART

VEHICLE NAME AND ENGINE SIZE	CHASSIS SERIAL NUMBER RANGE	ENGINE SERIAL NUMBER RANGE	BOOK SECTION AND MAJOR CHANGES
AUSTIN-HEALEY SPRITE MK I 948cc	H-AN5-501 to 50116 "Bug-Eye"	9C/U/H 101 to 49201	Section I (1958-1961) Data Sheet - pages 6-12
AUSTIN-HEALEY SPRITE MK II 948cc	H-AN6-101 to 24731	9CG/Da/H 101 to 36711	Section I (1961-1962) New Body Styling
M.G. MIDGET MK I 948cc	G-AN1-101 to 16183		Data Sheet - pages 13-18
AUSTIN-HEALEY SPRITE MK II 1098cc	H-AN7-24732 to 38828	10CG/Da/H 101 to 21048	Section II (1962-1964) Disc Brakes
M.G. MIDGET MK I 1098cc	G-AN2-16184 to 25787		'A' Type Gears* Data Sheet - pages 19-21
AUSTIN-HEALEY SPRTE MK III 1098cc	H-AN8-38829 to 64734	10CC/Da/H-101 to 12CC	Section II (1964-1966) 'A' Type Gears 10CC * /DA H-101 through H-4641. 'B' Type Gears 10CC/DA H-4642 on. Roll-Up Windows
M.G. MIDGET MK II 1098cc	G-AN3-25788 to 52389		Data Sheet - page 22
AUSTIN-HEALEY SPRITE MK IV 1275cc	H-AN9-52390 to 72033 USA	12CC/Da/H-101 to 12CD (to year 1967)	Section III (1966-1968) 'B' Type Gears * Folding Top
M.G. MIDGET MK III 1275cc	G-AN4-52390 to 60440 USA		Data Sheet - pages 23-27
AUSTIN-HEALEY SPRITE MK IV 1275cc	H-AN9-72034 on USA	12CD/Da/H- on (year 1968 on)	Section III (1968-1971) Exhaust Emission Control
M.G. MIDGET MK III 1275cc	G-AN4-60441 on USA		Negative Ground Electrical System Safety Dashboard Data Sheet - pages 28-29

*Refers to type of gears used in the gearbox. When ordering gearbox parts, specify the laygear part number (stamped on the laygear).

There are numerous running charges not covered by the above MAJOR CHANGES. It is necessary to refer to the manufacturer's parts list using the exact serial number of the car and engine concerned.

DATA SHEETS

1958-1961
948cc AUSTIN-HEALEY SPRITE MKI
Pages 6-12

1961-1962
948cc AUSTIN-HEALEY SPRITE MKII & MG Midget MKI
Pages 13-18

1962-1964
1098cc AUSTIN-HEALEY SPRITE MKII & MG MIDGET MKI
Pages 19-21

1964-1966
1098cc AUSTIN-HEALEY SPRITE MKIII & MG MIDGET MKII
Page 22

1966-1968
1275cc AUSTIN-HEALEY SPRITE MKIV & MG MIDGET MKIII
Pages 23-27

1968-1971
1275cc AUSTIN-HEALEY SPRITE MKIV & MG MIDGET MKIII
Pages 28-29

TUNING DATA FOR 1968-1971 CARS FITTED WITH EMISSION CONTROL
Page 30

SPRITE GENERAL DATA

ENGINE

Number of cylinders	Four
Capacity	57·87 cu. ins. (948 cc.)
B.H.P.	43 b.h.p. at 5,200 r.p.m.
Torque	52 lbs./ft. at 3,300 r.p.m.
Bore	2·478 in. (62·9 mm.)
Stroke	3·00 in. (76·2 mm.)
Compression ratio	8·3 : 1
First oversize bore	·010 in. (·254 mm.)
Second oversize bore	·020 in. (·508 mm.)
Third oversize bore	·030 in. (·762 mm.)
Fourth oversize bore	·040 in. (1·016 mm.)
Firing order	1, 3, 4, 2
Piston type	Aluminium split skirt
Piston clearance at skirt	·0006 in. (·015 mm.) to ·0012 in. (·03 mm.)
Piston ring gap (fitted)	·007 in. (·178 mm.) to ·012 in. (·30 mm.)
Piston rings:	
1st ring (Top)	Plain compression
2nd ring	Taper compression
3rd ring	Taper compression
4th ring (Oil control ring)	Slotted scraper
Width of plain and taper	·069 in. (1·753 mm.) to ·070 in. (1·778 mm.)
Width of oil control ring	·124 (3·15 mm.) to ·125 (3·175 mm.)
Oil capacity, sump	6 pints approx. (fill to dipstick) + 1 pint for filter if changed.
Oil pressure (normal) running	60 p.s.i. (4·2 kg./sq. cm.) approx.
Oil pressure (normal) idling	15 p.s.i. (1·05 kg./sq. cm.) min.
Oil filter	Full-flow type with renewable element
Gudgeon pin type	Clamped in con. rod
Gudgeon pin diameters	·6244 in. (15·860 mm.) to ·6246 in. (15·865 mm.)
Fit in piston	·0001 in. (·00254 mm.) tight to ·0003 in. (·0076 mm.) slack
Crankpin diameter (standard)	1·6254 in. (41·285 mm.) to 1·6259 in. (41·298 mm.)
Connecting rod length between centres	5¾ in. (146·05 mm.)
Connecting rod—type of bearing	Steel-backed copper—lead (thinwall)
Connecting rod—side clearance	·008 in. (·203 mm.) to ·012 in. (·305 mm.)
Connecting rod—diametral clearance	·001 in. (·025 mm.) to ·0025 in. (·063 mm.)
Number of main bearings	Three
Type	Steel-backed white metal (thinwall)
Standard Journal diameter	1·7505 in. (44·463 mm.) to 1·751 in. (44·475 mm.)
Regrind sizes:	
1st undersize	1·7405 in. (44·209 mm.) to 1·741 in. (44·221 mm.)
2nd undersize	1·7305 in. (43·955 mm.) to 1·731 in. (43·967 mm.)
Length of main bearings	1¾₆ in. (30·16 mm.)
Main bearing running clearance	·0005 in. (·0127 mm.) to ·002 in. (·0508 mm.)
Crankshaft end thrust taken on	Centre main bearing
Number of camshaft bearings	Three
Camshaft bearing type	Front—steel-backed white metal. Centre and rear—direct in crankcase
Camshaft bearing clearance–front	·001 in. (·0254 mm.) to ·002 in. (·0508 mm.)
Camshaft bearing clearance—centre—rear	·00125 (·032 mm.) to ·00275 in. (·07 mm.)
Camshaft end thrust taken on	Front end

SPRITE GENERAL DATA

Camshaft end float	·003 in. (·0762 mm.) to ·007 in. (·178 mm.)
Camshaft drive type	Single roller chain ⅜ in. (9·52 mm.) pitch, 52 pitches, endless with synthetic rubber tensioner rings on camshaft gear
Valve timing marking	Adjoining gear teeth are marked
Exhaust valve:	
Throat diameter	0·908 in. (23·06 mm.)
Head diameter	1·00 in. (25·4 mm.)
Stem diameter	0·2788 in. (70·81 mm.) to 0·2793 in. (7·094 mm.)
Inlet valve:	
Throat diameter	$\frac{31}{32}$ in. (24·6 mm.)
Head diameter	1$\frac{3}{32}$ in. (27·8 mm.)
Stem diameter	0·2793 in. (7·094 mm.) to 0·2798 in (7·107 mm.)
Valve seat angle	45°
Timing:	
Inlet valve opens	5° before T.D.C.
Inlet valve closes	45° after B.D.C.
Exhaust valve opens	40° before B.D.C.
Exhaust valve closes	10° after T.D.C.
Valve clearance for timing	0·019 in. (·48 mm.)
Inlet valve working clearance (cold)	0·012 in. (·3 mm.)
Exhaust valve working clearance (cold)	0·012 in. (·3 mm.)
Valve guides	Removeable and interchangeable
Valve lift	·28 in. (7.14 mm.)

with 0·019 in. (·48 mm.) valve rocker clearance (for checking purposes only).

IGNITION

Type	Lucas 12 volt coil
Distributor type	Lucas DM2 PH4
Direction of rotation	Clockwise at rotor arm
Contact breaker gap	0·014 in. (·356 mm.) to 0·016 in. (·406 mm.)
Static setting	5° before T.D.C.
Coil type	Lucas LA12
Sparking plug type	Champion N5
Sparking plug gap	·024 in. to ·026 in. (·6196 mm. to ·6604 mm.)

COOLING SYSTEM

Capacity	10 pints (5·68 litres, 12 U.S. pints)
Circulation	Pump and thermostat

FUEL SYSTEM

Fuel delivery	A.C. Sphinx. 'Y' Type. Mechanical
Carburetter type	Two S.U. H.I. Semi down draught
Needle (normal)	GG
Tank capacity	6 gallons (27·3 litres, 7·2 U.S. gallons)
Air cleaner	Twin 'Pancake'

CLUTCH

Make	Borg and Beck
Type	Single dry plate
Diameter	6¼ in. (16 cm.)
Total frictional area	15·05×2 sq. in. (97·072×2 cm.²)
Thickness of linings	⅛ in. (3·175 mm.)
Release bearings	Special carbon graphite or copper carbon graphite

SPRITE GENERAL DATA

Number of springs	Six
Total axial spring pressure	540 to 600 lbs. (245 to 272 kg.)
Thrust plate travel to full release	0·24 in. to 0·27 in. (6·2 to 6·8 mm.)
Pedal free movement	$\frac{5}{32}$ in. (3·969 mm.)

GEARBOX

Type	Synchromesh on 2nd, 3rd and top
Type of gear	Helical constant mesh
Gear ratios:	
First	3·627:1
Second	2·374:1
Third	1·412:1
Top	1·0:1
Reverse	4·664:1
Layshaft bearing:	
Type	Needle rollers
Length	0·7795 in. (19·8 mm.)
Housing diameter	0·8296 in. to 0·8301 in. (2·1072 to 2·1085 cm.)
Inside diameter	0·6315 in. to 0·6320 in. (1·6040 to 1·6053 cm.)
Number of rollers	23
Diameter of rollers	0·0984 in. (2·5 mm.)
Gearbox bearings:	
Make	R. & M. 2/LJ16—3 dot
Type	Ball journal (light)
Size	$1 \times 2\frac{1}{4} \times \frac{·623 \text{ in}}{·625 \text{ in}}$
Oil capacity	2¼ pints (1·325 litres, 2·807 U.S. pints)

REAR AXLE

Type	¾ floating
Ratio	9/38
Oil capacity	1¾ pints (1·0 litres, 2·1 U.S. pints)
Final drive	Hypoid
Bearings:	
Pinion Front:	
Make	Timken or Skefco
Type	Taper roller
Size	1 × 2·3125 × ·594 × ·762 in.
Pinion rear:	
Make	Timken or Skefco
Type	Taper roller
Size	1·125 × 2·745 × ·75 × ·745 in.
Differential:	
Make	R. & M.
Type	LJT 35—3 dot
Size	35 × 72 × 17 mm.
Hub:	
Make	R. & M.
Type	LJ 35—3 dot
Size	35 × 72 × 17 mm.

REAR SPRINGS

Type	$\frac{1}{4}$ elliptic
Number of leaves	15
Thickness of leaves	5 at $\frac{5}{32}$ in. (3·97 mm.), 10 at $\frac{1}{8}$ in. (3·18 mm.)
Width	$1\frac{3}{4}$ in. (44·45 mm.)
Laden camber	$\frac{21}{32} \pm \frac{1}{8}$ in. (16·67 ± 3·18 mm.) positive
Working load	375 lb. (170 kg.)
Average load rate	97·8 lb. in. (1·13 kg. m.)
Alternative heavy duty type:	
Number of leaves	10
Thickness of leaves	$\frac{3}{16}$ in. (4·76 mm.)
Width of leaves	$1\frac{3}{4}$ in. (44·45 mm.)
Laden camber	$\frac{21}{32} \pm \frac{1}{8}$ in. (16·67 ± 3·18 mm.) positive
Working load	375 lb. (170 kg.)
Average load rate	118 lb. in. (1·357 kg. m.)

STEERING

Type	Rack and pinion
Ratio	$2\frac{1}{4}$ turns, lock to lock
Track toe in	0 in. to $\frac{1}{8}$ in. (0 mm. to 3·175 mm.)

FRONT SUSPENSION

Type	Independent by coil springs and wishbones
Spring:	
Free length	9·4 in. (23·8 cm.)
Fitted length	6·625 in. (16·85 cm.) at 750 lbs. (340 kilos) load
Solid length	4·25 in. (10·8 cm.)
Inside diameter of coil	3·125 in. (7·94 cm.)
Number of working coils	7
Diameter of wire	0·5 in. (1·27 cm.)
Spring rate	271 lbs./in. (19 kg./cm.)
Castor Angle	3°
Camber Angle	1°
Swivel pin inclination	$6\frac{1}{2}$°
Shock Absorbers	Lever Hydraulic

BRAKES

Make	Lockheed
Footbrake	Hydraulic
Handbrake	Mechanical on rear wheels only
Drum diameter	7 ins. (17·78 cm.)
Total Friction Area	67·5 sq. in. (435·37 sq. cm.)
Shoe Lining Length	6·75 in. (17·14 cm.)
Shoe Lining Thickness	0·203 to 0·193 in. (5·1562 to 4·9022 mm.)
Shoe Lining Width	$1\frac{1}{4}$ in. (3.175 cm.)
Pedal Free Movement	$\frac{5}{32}$ in. (3·969 mm.)

ELECTRICAL

Battery:	
Type	BT7A
Type (export only)	BTZ7A (dry-charged)
Voltage	12.
Capacity:	
20 hour rate	43 amp.hr.

SPRITE GENERAL DATA

Initial charging current	2·5 amps.
Normal recharge current	4·0 amps.
Cell electrolyte capacity	⅜ pint (·43 litre)
Generator:	
Type	Lucas C39 PV2 with extended drive for tachometer
Cutting in speed	1,050 to 1,200 r.p.m.
Maximum output	13·5 volts 19 amps.
Field resistance	6·1 ohms.
Starting Motor:	
Type	Lucas M35 G1
Control Box:	
Type	Lucas RB 106/2
Regulator setting at:	
10°C (50°F)	16·1 to 16·7 volts.
20°C (68°F)	15·8 to 16·4 volts.
30°C (86°F)	15·6 to 16·2 volts.
40°C (104°F)	15·3 to 15·9 volts.
Cut-in voltage	12·7 to 13·3 volts.
Drop off voltage	9 to 10 volts.
Reserve Current	3 to 5 amps.
Windscreen wiper:	
Type	Lucas DR2
Normal running current	2·3 to 3·1 amp. at 12 volts.
Stall current (Motor hot)	8 amp.
Stall current (Motor cold)	14 amp.
Armature resistance (adjacent commutator segments)	·34 to ·41 ohms.
Field resistance	12·8 to 14·00 ohms.
Fuse Unit	
Type (2 live, 2 spare fuses)	Lucas SF6
Fuses	2 × 35 amp.
Sidelamps	
Type	Lucas model 52338A
Headlamps	
Type	Lucas model F700
Stop Tail Lamps	
Type	Lucas model 53330
Number Plate Illumination	
Type	Lucas model 052410
Bulbs	
Headlamps, R.H.D. vehicles	
Type	Lucas No. 414 B.M.C. No. 13H140
Voltage	12 volts.
Wattage	50/40 watts.
L.H.D. Vehicles (not Europe)	
Type	Lucas No. 415 B.M.C. No. 13H141
Voltage	12 volts.
Wattage	50/40 watts.
L.H.D. Vehicles (France)	
Type (from Car No. 7782)	Lucas No. 411 B.M.C. No. 13H139
Voltage	12 volts.
Wattage	45/40 watts.

SPRITE GENERAL DATA

L.H.D. vehicles (Europe except France)
    Type ..   Lucas No. 370   B.M.C. No. 3H921
    Voltage   12 volts.
    Wattage   45/40 watts.
    Type (from Car No. 10489)   Lucas No. 410   B.M.C. No. 13H138
    Voltage   12 volts.
    Wattage   45/40 watts.

R.H.D. vehicles (Sweden)
    Type (from Car No. 21118)   Lucas No. 370   B.M.C. No. 3H921
    Voltage   12 volts.
    Wattage   45/40 watts.

Side Lamps and Flasher
    Type ..   Lucas No. 380   B.M.C. No. 1F9026
    Voltage   12 volts.
    Wattage   21/6 watts.

Number Plate Illumination
    Type ..   Lucas No. 989   B.M.C. No. 2H4817
    Voltage   12 volts.
    Wattage   6 watts.

Rear Flasher
    Type ..   Lucas No. 382   B.M.C. No. 1F9012
    Voltage   12 volts.
    Wattage   21 watts.

Stop and Tail Lamp
    Type ..   Lucas No. 380   B.M.C. No. 1F9026
    Voltage   12 volts.
    Wattage   21/6 watts.

Headlamp main beam warning lamp
Flashing indicator warning lamp
Instrument illumination lamps
    Type ..   Lucas No. 987   B.M.C. No. 2H4732
    Voltage   12 volts.
    Wattage   2·2 watts.

Flashing Indicator Unit (FL5)
    Type   Lucas No. 35010A

TYRE SIZES AND INFLATION PRESSURES

Tyre sizes ..   5.20 × 13 Tubeless
Pressures:
    Front   18 lbs./sq. in. (1·27 kg.cm²)
    Rear ..   20 lbs./sq. in. (1·41 kg.cm²)

WHEELS

Type ..   13 in. ventilated steel disc with 4 stud fixing

TORQUE SPANNER DATA

Cylinder head stud nuts   40 lb. ft. (5·5 kg. m.)
Connecting rod big end bolts   35 lb. ft. (4·8 kg. m.)
Main bearing set screws   60 lb. ft. (8·3 kg. m.)
Flywheel set screws   40 lb. ft. (5·5 kg. m.)
Rocker bracket nuts   25 lb. ft. (3·4 kg. m.)
Gudgeon pin clamp screws   25 lb. ft. (3·4 kg. m.)
Road wheel nuts   37 to 39 lb. ft. (5·02 to 5·4 kg. m.)
Steering wheel nut   25 lb. ft. (3·4 kg. m.)

SPRITE GENERAL DATA

LEADING DIMENSIONS

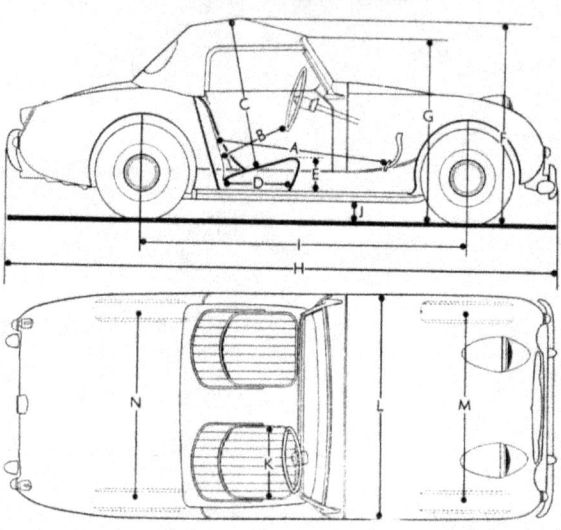

Pedal to seat squab	A	3 ft. 3¼ in. (1·00 m.)
		3 ft. 7¼ in. (1·10 m.)
Steering wheel to seat squab	B	1 ft. 2 in. (0·36 m.)
		1 ft. 5 in. (0·43 m.)
Height over seat	C	2 ft. 10½ in. (0·88 m.)
Seat cushion depth	D	1 ft. 7 in. (0·48 m.)
Seat cushion above floor	E	7¾ in. (0·20 m.)
Overall height (hood up)	F	4 ft. 1¾ in. (1·26 m.)
Overall height (hood down)	G	3 ft. 8⅛ in. (1·12 m.)
Overall length	H	11 ft. 5¼ in. (3·49 m.)
Wheelbase	I	6 ft. 8 in. (2·03 m.)
Minimum ground clearance	J	5 in. (0·13 m.)
Seat cushion width	K	1 ft. 5 in. (0·43 m.)
Overall width	L	4 ft. 5 in. (1·35 m.)
Track (front)	M	3 ft. 9¾ in. (1·16 m.)
Track (rear)	N	3 ft. 8¾ in. (1·14 m.)
Turning Circle		31 ft. 6 in. (9·60 m.)
Approximate weight—(Kerbside)		13 cwt. (660 kg.)

SPRITE MK. II & MIDGET GENERAL DATA

ENGINE
Type	9CG.
Number of cylinders	4.
Bore	2·478 in. (62·94 mm.).
Stroke	3·00 in. (76·2 mm.).
Capacity	57·87 cu. in. (948 c.c.).
Firing order	1, 3, 4, 2.
Compression ratio	9 : 1.
Capacity of combustion chamber (valves fitted)	24·5 c.c.
Valve operation	Overhead by push-rod.
B.M.E.P.	135 lb./sq. in. (9·50 kg./cm.^{2}) at 4,000 r.p.m.
Torque	52 lb. ft. (7·19 kg. m.) at 4,000 r.p.m.
Oversize bore: 1st	·010 in. (·254 mm.).
Max.	·040 in. (1·016 mm.).

CRANKSHAFT
Main journal diameter	1·7505 to 1·7510 in. (44·46 to 44·47 mm.).
Minimum regrind diameter	1·7105 in. (43·45 mm.).
Crankpin journal diameter	1·6254 to 1·6259 in. (41·28 to 41·30 mm.).
Crankpin minimum regrind diameter	1·5854 in. (40·27 mm.).
Main bearings	
Number and type	3 shell type.
Material: Bottom half	Steel-backed, lead-indium-lined.
Top half	Steel-backed, lead-indium-lined.
Length	1·312 in. (33·32 mm.).
End-clearance	·002 to ·003 in. (·051 to ·076 mm.).
End-thrust	Taken by thrust washers at centre main bearing.
Running clearance	·0005 to ·002 in. (·0127 to ·0508 mm.).

CONNECTING RODS
Length between centres	5·75 in. (14·605 cm.).
Big-end bearings	
Material: Bottom half	Steel-backed, lead-indium-lined.
Top half	Steel-backed, lead-indium-lined.
Bearing side clearance	·008 to ·012 in. (·203 to ·305 mm.).
Bearing diametrical clearance	·001 to ·0025 in. (·025 to ·063 mm.).

PISTONS
Type	Flat crown, aluminium alloy, anodized.
Clearances: Bottom of skirt	·0016 to ·0022 in. (·040 to ·559 mm.).
Top of skirt	·0036 to ·0042 in. (·0914 to ·1067 mm.).
Oversizes	+·010 in., +·020 in., +·030 in., +·040 in. (+·254 mm., +·508 mm., +·762 mm., +1·02 mm.).

PISTON RINGS
Compression: Plain	Top ring.
Tapered	Second and third rings.
Width (plain)	·069 to ·070 in. (1·75 to 1·78 mm.).
Thickness	·103 to ·109 in. (2·62 to 2·78 mm.).
Fitted gap	·007 to ·012 in. (·178 to ·30 mm.).
Clearance in groove	·0015 to ·0035 in. (·038 to ·089 mm.).
Oil control type	Slotted scraper.
Width	·124 to ·125 in. (3·15 to 3·175 mm.).

SPRITE MK. II & MIDGET GENERAL DATA

Thickness	·103 to ·109 in. (2·62 to 2·78 mm.).
Fitted gap	·007 to ·012 in. (·178 to ·30 mm.).
Clearance in groove	·0015 to ·0035 in. (·038 to ·089 mm.).

GUDGEON PIN

Type	Semi-floating.
Fit in piston	·0001 to ·00035 in. (·0025 to ·009 mm.).
Fit in connecting rod	·0001 to ·0006 in. (·0025 to ·015 mm.).
Diameter (outer)	·6244 to ·6246 in. (15·86 to 15·865 mm.).

VALVES AND VALVE GEAR

Valves

Seat angle: Inlet and exhaust	45°.
Head diameter: Inlet	1·151 to 1·156 in. (29·23 to 29·36 mm.).
Exhaust	1·000 to 1·005 in. (25·4 to 25·53 mm.).
Stem diameter: Inlet	·2793 to ·2798 in. (7·094 to 7·107 mm.).
Exhaust	·2788 to ·2793 in. (7·081 to 7·094 mm.).
Valve lift	·285 in. (7·24 mm.).
Valve stem to guide clearance: Inlet	·0015 to ·0025 in. (·038 to ·063 mm.).
Exhaust	·002 to ·003 in. (·051 to ·076 mm.).
Valve rocker clearance: Running (hot)	·012 in. (·305 mm.); ·015 in. (·381 mm.) for competition work.
Timing	·029 in. (·725 mm.).
Timing markings	Dimples on timing wheels.
Chain pitch and number of pitches	⅜ in. (9·52 mm.). 52 pitches.
Inlet valve: Opens	5° B.T.D.C. ⎫ With
Closes	45° A.B.D.C. ⎬ ·021 in. (·533 mm.)
Exhaust valve: Opens	51° B.B.D.C. ⎨ clearance at
Closes	21° A.T.D.C. ⎭ valve.

VALVE GUIDES

Length: Inlet and exhaust	1·687 in. (42·86 mm.).
Diameter—inlet and exhaust: Outside	·4695 to ·470 in. (11·92 to 11·94 mm.).
Inside	·2813 to ·2818 in. (7·145 to 7·177 mm.).
Fitted height above head	19/32 in. (15·1 mm).

VALVE SPRINGS

Free length	1·75 in. (44·45 mm.).
Fitted length	1·291 in. (32·79 mm.).
Number of working coils	4½.
Pressure: Open	88 lb. (39·9 kg.).
Closed	52 lb. (23·6 kg.).

TAPPETS

Type	Bucket.
Diameter	·8120 in. (20·62 mm.).
Length	1·505 in. (38·23 mm.).

SPRITE MK. II & MIDGET GENERAL DATA

CAMSHAFT

Journal diameters
- Front .. .. 1·6655 to 1·666 in. (42·304 to 42·316 mm.).
- Centre .. .. 1·62275 to 1·62325 in. (41·218 to 41·231 mm.).
- Rear .. .. 1·3725 to 1·3735 in. (34·862 to 34·887 mm.).

End-float .. .. ·003 to ·007 in. (·076 to ·178 mm.).
Bearing: number and type .. .. 3. Steel-backed white metal.
Inside diameter (reamed in position): Front .. .. 1·667 to 1·6675 in. (42·342 to 42·355 mm.).
                                  Centre .. .. 1·6245 to 1·6255 in. (41·261 to 41·287 mm.).
                                  Rear .. .. 1·3748 to 1·3755 in. (34·914 to 34·937 mm.).

ENGINE LUBRICATION SYSTEM

Oil pump
Type .. .. Eccentric rotor or vane type.
Relief pressure valve operates .. .. .. 50 lb./sq. in. (3·52 kg./cm.^{2}).
Relief valve spring: Free length .. .. .. 2·860 in. (72·63 mm.).
                   Fitted length .. .. 2·156 in. (54·77 mm.).

Oil filter
Type .. .. Tecalemit or Purolator.
Capacity .. .. 1 pint (·57 litre).

Oil pressure
Normal running .. .. 60 lb./sq. in. (4·22 kg./cm.^{2}).
Idling (minimum) .. .. 15 lb./sq. in. (1·05 kg./cm.^{2}).

TORQUE WRENCH SETTINGS

Cylinder head nuts .. .. 40 lb. ft. (5·5 kg. m.).
Main bearing nuts .. .. 60 lb. ft. (8·3 kg. m.).
Connecting rod set screws .. .. 35 lb. ft. (4·8 kg. m.).
Flywheel securing bolts .. .. 40 lb. ft. (5·5 kg. m.).
Steering-wheel nut .. .. 40 lb. ft. (5·5 kg. m.).
Road wheel nuts .. .. 45 lb. ft. (6·22 kg. m.).
Rear damper bolts .. .. 25 lb. ft. (3·4 kg. m.).

FUEL SYSTEM

Carburetters
Make and type .. .. S.U. Twin HS2 semi-downdraught.
Diameter .. .. 1¼ in. (31·75 mm.).
Jet .. .. ·090 in. (2·29 mm.).
Needle .. .. V3.

AIR CLEANER
Type .. .. Paper element.

FUEL PUMP
Make and type .. .. A.C. 'Y' type. Mechanical.
Delivery rate .. .. 40 pints/hr. (22·8 litres/hr.).
Delivery pressure .. .. 1·5 to 2·5 lb./sq. in. (·105 to ·175 kg./cm.^{2}).

COOLING SYSTEM
Type .. .. Pressurized radiator. Thermo-siphon, pump- and fan-assisted.
Thermostat setting .. .. 149 to 158° F. (65 to 70° C.).

SPRITE MK. II & MIDGET GENERAL DATA

IGNITION SYSTEM

Sparking plugs	Champion N5.
Size	14 mm.
Plug gap	·024 to ·026 in. (·625 to ·660 mm.).
Coil	Lucas Type LA12.
Distributor	Lucas Type DM2P4.
Distributor contact points gap	·014 to ·016 in. (·35 to ·40 mm.).
Static ignition timing	4° B.T.D.C.

CLUTCH

Make and type	Borg & Beck. Single dry plate.
Diameter	6¼ in. (16 cm.).
Facing material	Wound yarn.
Pressure springs	6.
Colour	Yellow and dark green.
Damper springs	4.
Colour	Light grey.
Release lever ratio	3·6 : 1.

GEARBOX

Number of forward speeds	4.
Synchromesh	Second, third, and top gears.
Ratios: Top	1·0 : 1.
Third	1·357 : 1.
Second	1·916 : 1.
First	3·200 : 1.
Reverse	4·114 : 1.
Overall ratios: Top	4·22 : 1.
Third	5·726 : 1.
Second	8·975 : 1.
First	13·504 : 1.
Reverse	17·361 : 1.
Speedometer gear ratio	5/13.

STEERING

Type	Rack and pinion.
Steering-wheel turns—lock to lock	2¼.
Steering-wheel diameter	16 in. (40·6 cm.).
Camber angle	1°.
Castor angle	3°.
King pin inclination	6½°.
Toe-in	0 to ⅛ in. (0 to 3·175 mm.).

FRONT SUSPENSION

Type	Independent. Coil springs.
Free length	9·4 in. (23·8 cm.).
Mean coil diameter	3·625 in. (9·2 cm.).
Number of effective coils	7.
Working load	750 lb. (340 kg.).
Spring rate	271 lb. in. (3·127 kg. m.).
Dampers (front)	Lever arm type.

SPRITE MK. II & MIDGET GENERAL DATA

REAR SUSPENSION

Type	Quarter-elliptic.
Spring details: Number of leaves	15.
Width of leaves	5 at $\frac{9}{32}$ in. (3·97 mm.), 10 at $\frac{1}{8}$ in. (3·18 mm.).
Working load	375 lb. (170 kg.).
Free camber	$3\frac{7}{32}$ in. (81·76 mm.).
Dampers (rear)	Lever arm type.

PROPELLER SHAFT

Type	Tubular. Reverse spline.
Make and type of joints	Hardy Spicer. Needle-roller.
Propeller shaft length (between centres of joints)	26¼ in. (66·6 cm.).
Diameter	1¾ in. (44·45 mm.).

REAR AXLE

Type	Three-quarter-floating.
Ratio	9/38 (4·22 : 1).

ELECTRICAL EQUIPMENT

System	12-volt. Positive earth.
Charging system	Compensated voltage control.
Battery	Lucas BT7A (BT27A Export).
Battery capacity	43 amp./hr. (at 20-hour rate).
Starter motor	Lucas 4-brush M35G/1.
Dynamo	Lucas C40.
Control box	Lucas RB106/2.
Cut-out: Cut-in voltage	12·7 to 13·3.
Drop-off voltage	8·5 to 11·0.
Reverse current	5·0 amps. (max.).

Regulator RB106/2 (at 1,500 r.p.m. dynamo speed):
Open-circuit setting at 68° F. (20° C.) .. .. 15·4 to 16·4 volts.
For ambient temperatures other than 60° F. (20° C.) the following allowances should be made to the above settings:
For every 18° F. (10° C.) above 68° F. (20° C.) subtract ·1 volt.
For every 18° F. (10° C.) below 68° F. (20° C.) add ·1 volt.

BRAKES

Type	Lockheed hydraulic.
Front	Two leading shoes.
Rear	Single leading shoe.
Drum size	7 in. (17·78 cm.).
Lining dimensions: Front and rear	6¾ in. × 1¼ in. (17·14 cm. × 3·175 cm.).
Total lining area	67·5 sq. in. (435·37 cm.²).

WHEELS

Type	Ventilated disc. 4-stud fixing.

TYRES

Size	5·20—13.
Tyre pressures—normal and fully loaded: Front	18 lb./sq. in. (1·27 kg./cm.²).
Rear	20 lb./sq. in. (1·41 kg./cm.²).

SPRITE MK. II & MIDGET GENERAL DATA

CAPACITIES

	Imp.	U.S.	Litres
Engine sump (including filter)	6·5 pts.	7·8 pts.	3·7
Gearbox	2·25 pts.	2·7 pts.	1·3
Rear axle	1·5 pts.	1·8 pts.	·85
Cooling system	10 pts.	12 pts.	5·68
Fuel tank	6 gal.	7·2 gal.	27·3

GENERAL DIMENSIONS

Wheelbase	6 ft. 8 in. (2·03 m.).
Overall width	4 ft. 5 in. (1·35 m.).
Overall height	4 ft. 1¾ in. (1·25 m.).
Ground clearance	5 in. (12·7 cm.).
Turning circle: Left lock	32 ft. 1½ in. (9·79 m.).
Right lock	31 ft. 2½ in. (9·51 m.).
Track: Front	3 ft. 9¾ in. (1·16 m.).
Rear	3 ft. 8¾ in. (1·14 m.).

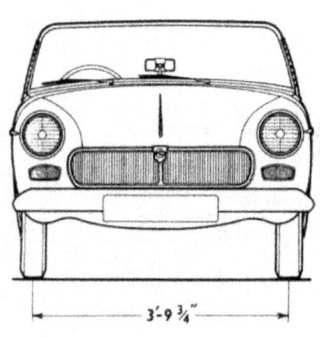

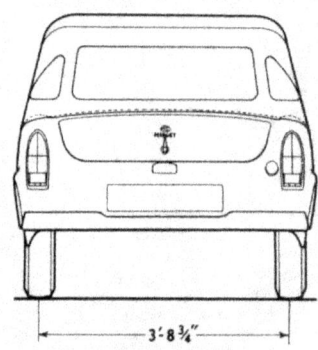

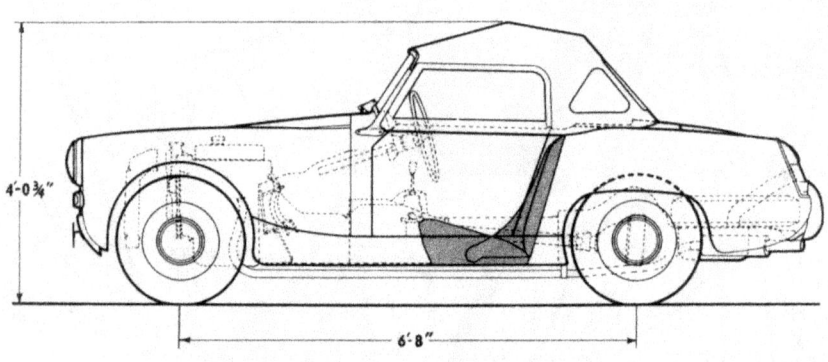

GENERAL DATA
(1098 c.c.)

The following information is applicable to the 1098-c.c.-engined car and should be used in conjunction with the preceding specification for the 948-c.c.-engined car.

ENGINE
Type	10CG.
Bore	2·543 in. (64·58 mm.).
Stroke	3·296 in. (83·72 mm.).
Capacity	67 cu. in. (1098 c.c.).
Compression ratio	8·9 : 1 (or 8·1 : 1).
Capacity of combustion chamber (valves fitted)	1·8 cu. in. (28·2 c.c.).
Valve operation	Overhead by push-rod.
Oversize bore: 1st	+·010 in. (·254 mm.).
Max.	+·020 in. (·508 mm.).
Torque	H.C. 62 lb. ft. (8·6 kg. m.) 3,250 r.p.m.
	L.C. 61 lb. ft. (8·4 kg. m.) 3,250 r.p.m.

Main bearings
Length .. 1 1/16 in. (27 mm.).

Pistons
Type	Solid skirt.
Clearances: Bottom of skirt	·0005 to ·0011 in. (·013 to ·028 mm.).
Top of skirt	·0021 to ·0037 in. (·053 to ·094 mm.).
Oversizes	+·010 in., +·020 in. (+·254 mm., +·508 mm.).

Piston rings
Compression: Type: Top ring	Plain, internally chamfered (chrome-faced).
Second and third rings	Tapered.
Width: Top ring	·062 to ·0625 in. (1·575 to 1·587 mm.).
Second and third rings	·0615 to ·0625 in. (1·558 to 1·587 mm.).
Thickness	·106 to ·112 in. (2·69 to 2·84 mm.).
Clearance in groove	·002 to ·004 in. (·051 to ·102 mm.).
Oil control: Type: Early engines	Slotted scraper.
Thickness	·106 to ·112 in. (2·69 to 2·84 mm.).
Type: Later engines	Wellworthy-Duraflex 61.
Fitted gap: Rails	·012 to ·028 in. (·31 to ·7 mm.).
Side spring	·10 to ·15 in. (2·54 to 3·81 mm.).

Gudgeon pin
Type	Fully floating.
Fit in piston	Hand push fit.

Valves
Head diameter: Inlet .. 1·213 to 1·218 in. (30·81 to 30·94 mm.).

FUEL SYSTEM
Carburetters
Needles: Standard	GY.
Weak	GG.
Rich	M.
Piston spring	Blue.

COOLING SYSTEM
Thermostat setting
Standard	82° C. (180° F.).
Hot climates	74° C. (165° F.).
Cold climates	88° C. (190° F.).

GENERAL DATA—continued
(1098 c.c.—continued)

IGNITION SYSTEM
Distributor
- Type .. 25D4.
- Serial number .. 40919.
- Rotation of rotor .. Anti-clockwise.
- Cam closed period .. 60°±3°.
- Cam open period .. 30°±3°.
- Automatic advance .. Centrifugal and vacuum.
- Automatic advance commences .. 400 r.p.m.
- Maximum advance (crankshaft degrees) .. 32° at 5,500 r.p.m.
- Vacuum advance (crankshaft degrees) .. 20° at 13 in. (33·3 cm.) Hg.
- Decelerating check (crankshaft degrees, engine r.p.m.) .. 32° at 5,500 r.p.m.
  28° at 4,400 r.p.m.
  16° at 1,800 r.p.m.
  4° at 1,200 r.p.m.
  1° at 800 r.p.m.
- Contact point gap setting .. ·014 to ·016 in. (·35 to ·4 mm.).
- Breaker spring tension .. 18 to 24 oz. (510 to 680 gm.).
- Condenser capacity .. ·22 mF.
- Timing marks .. Pointer on timing chain case and notch on crankshaft pulley.
- Static ignition setting: High compression .. 5° B.T.D.C.
  Low compression .. 3 to 5° B.T.D.C.
- Stroboscopic timing .. 8° B.T.D.C. at 600 r.p.m. (engine).

CLUTCH
- Diameter .. 7¼ in. (184 mm.).
- Pressure springs .. 6.
- Colour .. Red.
- Damper springs .. 4.
- Colour .. Black/light green.
- Clutch fluid .. Lockheed Disc Brake Fluid (Series II).

GEARBOX
- Ratios: Reverse .. 4·120 : 1.
- Overall ratios: Reverse .. 17·32 : 1.

ELECTRICAL EQUIPMENT
- Battery .. Lucas N9 or NZ9.
- Capacity .. 43 amp.-hr. (at 20-hour rate).
- Electrolyte to fill one cell .. ¾ pint (430 c.c., ⅞ U.S. pint).
- Dynamo .. Lucas C40/1.
- Maximum output .. 22 amps.
- Field coil resistance .. 6·0 ohms.
- Control box .. Lucas RB 106/2.

BRAKES
- Type .. Lockheed hydraulic; disc front, drum rear; leading and trailing shoes.
- Brake fluid .. Lockheed Disc Brake Fluid (Series II).

Front
- Disc diameter .. 8·25 in. (209·5 mm.).
- Pad area (total) .. 18 sq. in. (116·1 cm.²).
- Swept area (total) .. 135·28 sq. in. (871 cm.²).
- Lining material .. Ferodo DA3.
- Minimum pad thickness .. 1/16 in. (1·59 mm.).

GENERAL DATA—continued
(1098 c.c.—continued)

Rear

Drum diameter	7 in. (177·8 mm.).
Lining dimensions	6·68 in. × 1·25 in. × ·187 in. (169·8 mm. × 37·5 mm. × 4·75 mm.).
Swept area (total)	55 sq. in. (342 cm.²).
Lining material	Ferodo AM8.

GENERAL DIMENSIONS

Track: Front	3 ft. 10 1/16 (1·16 m.) (static unladen condition)
Rear	3 ft. 8¾ in. (1·14 m.).
Vehicle weight (dry)	1,466 lb. (665 kg.).

WEIGHTS OF COMPONENTS

Engine	253 lb. (114·7 kg.).

TORQUE WRENCH SETTINGS

Rocker bracket nuts	25 lb. ft. (3·4 kg. m.).
Sump to crankcase	6 lb. ft. (·8 kg. m.).
Cylinder side covers	2 lb. ft. (·28 kg. m.).
Timing cover—¼ in. UNF. bolt	6 lb. ft. (·8 kg. m.).
Timing cover—5/16 in. UNF. bolt	14 lb. ft. (1·9 kg. m.).
Water pump	17 lb. ft. (2·3 kg. m.).
Water outlet elbow	8 lb. ft. (1·1 kg. m.).
Oil filter	16 lb. ft. (2·2 kg. m.).
Oil pump	9 lb. ft. (1·2 kg. m.).
Manifold to cylinder head	15 lb. ft. (2·1 kg. m.).
Rocker cover	4 lb. ft. (·56 kg. m.).
Crankshaft pulley nut	70 lb. ft. (9·6 kg. m.).
Distributor clamp bolt: Fixed nut type	50 lb.in. (·576 kg.m.).
Fixed bolt type	30 lb.in. (·345 kg.m.).

Suspension and steering

Steering lever to hub bolts	30 to 35 lb. ft. (4·1 to 4·8 kg. m.).
Steering-wheel nut	41 lb. ft. (5·76 kg. m.).
Road wheel nuts	60 to 63·5 lb. ft. (8·3 to 8·7 kg. m.).
Disc to hub	40 to 45 lb. ft. (5·5 to 6·2 kg. m.).
Front swivel hub to calliper	45 to 50 lb. ft. (6·2 to 7 kg. m.).

GENERAL DATA
SPRITE (Mk. III) and MIDGET (Mk. II)

The following information is applicable to the Sprite (Mk. III) and Midget (Mk. II) and should be used in conjunction with the preceding specifications.

ENGINE
Type .. .. 10CC.
Torque .. .. H.C. 65 lb. ft. (8·9 kg. m.) at 3,500 r.p.m.
                                                                            L.C. 64 lb. ft. (8·8 kg. m.) at 3,250 r.p.m.

Crankshaft
Main journal diameter .. .. 2·0005 to 2·0010 in. (50·79 to 50·80 mm.).

FUEL SYSTEM
Carburetters
Needles .. . . Standard AN. Rich H6. Weak GG.

Fuel pump
Make and type .. .. S.U. (electrical) Type AUF200.
Delivery rate .. .. 56 pints/hr. (67 U.S. pints/hr., 32 litres/hr.)
Delivery pressure .. .. 2·5 to 3·0 lb./sq. in. (·17 to ·21 kg./cm.^{2}).

FRONT SUSPENSION
Spring free length .. .. 9·59 in. (24·4 cm.).

REAR SUSPENSION
Type .. .. Semi-elliptic.
Spring details: Number of leaves .. .. 5.
              Thickness of leaves .. .. $\frac{11}{64}$ in. (4·37 m.n.).
              Width of leaves .. .. $1\frac{1}{2}$ in. (38·10 mm.).
              Working load .. .. 375 lb. (170 kg.).
              Free camber .. .. 4·437 (112·7 mm.).

TYRES
Tyre pressures—for sustained speeds in excess of 80–85 m.p.h.
(129–136 km.p.h.) increase pressure to: Front .. .. 22 lb./sq. in. (1·55 kg./cm.^{2}).
                                                             Rear .. .. .. 24 lb./sq. in. (1·69 kg./cm.^{2}).

WEIGHTS
Vehicle weight (dry) .. .. 1,490 lb. (676 kg.).

TORQUE WRENCH SETTINGS
Cylinder side cover (deep pressed type) .. .. .. 5 lb. ft. (·7 kg. m.).

GENERAL DATA
SPRITE (Mk. IV) and MIDGET (Mk. III)

The following information is applicable to the Sprite (Mk. IV) and Midget (Mk. III) and should be used in conjunction with the preceding specifications.

ENGINE

Type	12CC.
Number of cylinders	4.
Bore	2·78 in. (70·61 mm.).
Stroke	3·2 in. (81·28 mm.).
Capacity	77·8 cu. in. (1274·86 c.c.).
Firing order	1, 3, 4, 2.
Valve operation	Overhead by push-rod.
Compression ratio: H.C.	8·8 : 1.
L.C.	8·0 : 1.
B.M.E.P.: H.C. (Standard)	139 lb./sq. in. (9·77 kg./cm.^{2}) at 3,000 r.p.m.
L.C. (Standard)	127 lb./sq. in. (8·93 kg./cm.^{2}) at 3,000 r.p.m.
Torque: H.C. (Standard)	72 lb. ft. (9·96 kg. m.) at 3,000 r.p.m.
L.C. (Standard)	64·5 lb. ft. (8·91 kg. m.) at 3,000 r.p.m.
Cranking pressure: H.C.	120 lb./sq. in. (8·44 kg./cm.^{2}) at 350 r.p.m.
L.C.	
Engine idle speed	650 to 700 r.p.m.
Oversize bore: 1st	·010 in. (·254 mm.).
Max.	·020 in. (·508 mm.).

Crankshaft

Main journal diameter	2·0005 to 2·0010 in. (50·813 to 50·825 mm.).
Min. regrind diameter	
Crankpin journal diameter	1·6254 to 1·6259 in. (41·28 to 41·29 mm.).
Min. regrind diameter	
Crankshaft end-thrust	Taken by thrust washers at centre main bearing.
Crankshaft end-float	·002 to ·003 in. (·051 to ·076 mm.).

Main bearings

Number and type	3 thin-wall; split shells, steel backed: copper-lead-indium.
Material	VP3 lead-indium or NFM/3B.
Length	·975 to ·985 in. (24·765 to 25·019 mm.).
Diametrical clearance	·0010 to ·0027 in. (·0254 to ·067 mm.).
Undersizes	

Connecting rods

Type	Horizontally split big-end, plain small-end.
Length between centres	5·748 to 5·792 in. (145·99 to 145·101 mm.).

Big-end bearings

Type and material	Steel-backed lead-indium plated.
Length	·840 to ·850 in. (21·336 to 21·590 mm.).
Diametrical clearance	·0010 to ·0025 in. (·0254 to ·063 mm.).
Undersizes	
End-float on crankpin	·006 to ·010 in. (·15 to ·254 mm.).

Pistons

Type	Aluminium solid skirt dished crown.
Clearance in cylinder: Top of skirt	·0029 to ·0037 in. (·074 to ·095 mm.).
Bottom of skirt	·0015 to ·0021 in. (·038 to ·054 mm.).
Number of rings	4 (3 compression, 1 oil control).
Width of ring grooves: Top, second, and third	·0484 to ·0494 in. (1·229 to 1·255 mm.).
Oil control	·1578 to ·1588 in. (4·008 to 4·033 mm.).
Gudgeon pin bore	·8125 to ·8129 in. (20·638 to 29·647 mm.).

GENERAL DATA—continued
(SPRITE (Mk. IV) and MIDGET (Mk. III)—continued)

Piston rings
Compression:
  Type: Top .. .. Internally chamfered chrome.
    Second and third .. .. Tapered cast iron.
  Width: Top .. ..
    Second and third .. } ·0615 to ·0625 in. (1·558 to 1·583 mm.).
  Fitted gap: Top .. .. ·011 to ·016 in. (·279 to ·406 mm.).
    Second and third .. ·008 to ·013 in. (·203 to ·330 mm.).
  Ring to groove clearance: Top .. ..
    Second and third .. } ·0015 to ·0035 in. (·038 to ·088 mm.).

Oil control
  Type .. .. .. Duaflex 61.
  Fitted gap: Rails ..
    Side spring .. } ·012 to ·028 in. (·305 to ·70 mm.).

Gudgeon pin
  Type .. .. .. Pressed in connecting rod.
  Fit in piston .. .. Hand push-fit.
  Diameter (outer) .. .. ·8123 to ·8125 in. (20·63 to 20·64 mm.).
  Fit to connecting rod .. .. ·0008 to ·0015 in. (·020 to ·038 mm.) interference.

Camshaft
  Journal diameters: Front .. 1·6655 to 1·6660 in. (42·304 to 42·316 mm.).
    Centre .. 1·62275 to 1·62325 in. (41·218 to 41·231 mm.).
    Rear .. 1·37275 to 1·37350 in. (34·866 to 34·889 mm.).
  Bearing liner inside diameter (reamed after fitting): Front 1·6670 to 1·6675 in. (42·342 to 42·355 mm.).
    Centre 1·62425 to 1·62475 in. (41·256 to 41·369 mm.).
    Rear 1·3745 to 1·3750 in. (34·912 to 34·925 mm.).
  Bearings: Type .. .. White-metal lined, steel backed.
  Diametrical clearance .. .. ·001 to ·002 in. (·0254 to ·0508 mm.).
  End-thrust .. .. Taken on locating plate.
  End-float .. .. ·003 to ·007 in. (·076 to ·178 mm.).
  Cam lift .. .. ·250 in. (6·35 mm.).
  Drive .. .. Duplex chain and gear from crankshaft.
  Timing chain .. .. ⅜ in. (9·52 mm.) pitch × 52 pitches.

Tappets
  Type .. .. .. Bucket.
  Outside diameter .. .. ·81175 to ·812 in. (20·618 to 20·64 mm.).
  Length .. .. .. 1·495 to 1·505 in. (37·973 to 38·23 mm.).

Rocker gear
  Rocker shaft:
    Diameter .. .. ·5615 to ·5625 in. (14·262 to 14·287 mm.).
  Rocker arm:
    Bore .. .. ·686 to ·687 in. (17·424 to 17·449 mm.).
    Rocker arm bush inside diameter .. ·5630 to ·5635 in. (14·3 to 14·313 mm.).

Valves
  Seat angle: Inlet and exhaust .. 45°.
  Head diameter: Inlet .. 1·307 to 1·312 in. (33·198 to 33·21 mm.).
    Exhaust .. 1·1515 to 1·1565 in. (29·243 to 29·373 mm.).
  Stem diameter: Inlet .. ·2793 to ·2798 in. (7·094 to 7·107 mm.).
    Exhaust .. ·2788 to ·2793 in. (7·081 to 7·094 mm.).
  Stem to guide clearance: Inlet and exhaust .. ·0015 to ·0025 in. (·0381 to ·0778 mm.).
  Valve lift: Inlet and exhaust .. ·318 in. (8·076 mm.).

GENERAL DATA—continued
(SPRITE (Mk. IV) and MIDGET (Mk. III)—continued)

Valve guides
Length: Inlet .. 1·6875 in. (42·87 mm.).
Exhaust
Fitted height above seat: Exhaust .. ·540 in. (13·72 mm.).
Inlet

Valve springs

	Outer	Inner
Free length	1·828 in. (46·474 mm.).	1·703 in. (43·259 mm.).
Fitted length	1·383 in. (35·128 mm.).	1·270 in. (32·258 mm.).
Load at fitted length	51 lb. (23·1 kg.).	25 lb. (11·3 kg.).
Load at top of lift	87 lb. (39·5 kg.).	44 lb. (20 kg.).
Valve crash speed	6,750 r.p.m.	

Valve timing
Timing marks .. .. Dimples on timing gears.
Rocker clearance: Running (Standard) .. ·012 in. (·305 mm.) cold.
    (Competition work) .. ·015 in. (·381 mm.) cold.
    Timing .. ·029 in. (·725 mm.).
Inlet valve: Opens .. 5° B.T.D.C.
    Closes .. 45° A.B.D.C.
Exhaust valve: Opens .. 51° B.B.D.C.
    Closes .. 21° A.T.D.C.

Lubrication
System pressure: Running .. 40 to 70 lb./sq. in. (2·81 to 4·92 kg. cm.^{2}).
    Idling .. 20 lb./sq. in. (1·4 kg. cm.^{2}).
Oil pump .. Gear type: splined drive from camshaft.
Oil filter .. Full-flow type; renewable element: differential pressure switch.
Oil pressure relief valve .. 50 lb./sq. in. (5·3 kg. cm.^{2}).
Relief valve spring: Free length .. 2·86 in. (72·64 mm.).
    Fitted length .. 2·156 in. (54·77 mm.).
    Load at fitted length .. 13 to 14 lb. (5·90 to 6·35 kg.).

IGNITION SYSTEM
Coil .. Lucas 11C 12.
  Resistance at 20° C. (68° F.) primary winding .. 3 to 3·4 ohms.
  Consumption: Ignition switch on .. 3·5 to 4 amps.
    At 2,000 r.p.m. .. 1 amp.

Distributor .. Lucas 23D4.
  Rotation of rotor arm .. Anti-clockwise.
  Cam closed period .. 60°±3°.
  Cam open period .. 30°±3°.
  Automatic advance .. Centrifugal.
  Serial number .. 40819H.
  Automatic advance commences* .. 600 r.p.m.
  Maximum advance* .. 30°.
  Decelerating check .. 24°–28° at 6,000 r.p.m.
    22°–26° at 5,200 r.p.m.
    11°–15° at 2,000 r.p.m.
    10°–14° at 1,600 r.p.m.
    6°–12° at 1,000 r.p.m.
    0°–3° at 600 r.p.m.
  Contact point gap setting .. ·014 to ·016 in. (·35 to ·40 mm.).
  Breaker spring tension .. 18 to 24 oz. (510 to 680 gm.).
  Condenser capacity .. ·18 to ·24 mF.
  Timing marks .. Pointer on timing chain case and notch in crankshaft pulley.

*Crankshaft degrees and r.p.m.

GENERAL DATA—continued
(SPRITE (Mk. IV) and MIDGET (Mk. III)—continued)

Static ignition timing: H.C.	7° B.T.D.C.
L.C.	7° B.T.D.C.
Stroboscopic ignition timing	22° at 1000 r.p.m.

Sparking plugs — Champion UN12Y.
- Size — 14 mm.
- Gap — ·024 to ·026 in. (·62 to ·66 mm.).

COOLING SYSTEM

Thermostat settings: Standard	82° C. (180° F.).
Hot countries	74° C. (165° F.).
Cold countries	88° C. (190° F.).
Pressure cap	7 lb./sq. in. (·49 kg./cm.²).

FUEL SYSTEM

Carburetter	Twin S.U. Type H.S.2.
Choke diameter	1·25 in. (31·75 mm.).
Jet size	·090 in. (2·29 mm.).
Needles	Standard AN; Weak GG; Rich H6.
Piston spring	Light blue.

CLUTCH

Make and type	Borg & Beck; diaphragm-spring type.
Clutch plate diameter	6·5 in. (165 mm.).
Facing material	Wound yarn.
Number of damper springs	4.
Damper spring colour	2 lavender, 2 white and violet.
Clutch release bearing	Carbon pad.
Clutch fluid	Lockheed Disc brake (Series II).

BRAKES
Front:

Pad lining material	Ferodo 2424F.
Brake fluid	Lockheed Disc Brake (Series II).

WHEELS

Size and type (Standard)	3·5D × 13 Disc.
(Optional extra)	4J × 13 Wire.

TYRES

Sizes and type — 5·20—13 Dunlop C41 Gold Seal (Nylon) Tubeless.
5·20—13 Heavy-Duty (6-ply) Tubeless.
145—13 SP 41—Tubed.

Tyre pressures (set cold):

	Dunlop C41 Gold Seal (Nylon); Heavy Duty	SP41
Normal:		
Front	18 lb./sq. in. (1·3 kg./cm.²).	22 lb./sq. in. (1·6 kg./cm.²).
Rear	20 lb./sq. in. (1·4 kg./cm.²).	24 lb./sq. in. (1·7 kg./cm.²).
For sustained speeds in excess of 80–85 m.p.h. (129–137 km.p.h.):		
Front	22 lb./sq. in. (1·6 kg./cm.²).	22 lb./sq. in. (1·6 kg./cm.²).
Rear	24 lb./sq. in. (1·7 kg./cm.²).	24 lb./sq. in. (1·7 kg./cm.²).

GENERAL DATA—continued
(SPRITE (Mk. IV) and MIDGET (Mk. III)—continued)

DIMENSIONS

	Wire wheels	Disc wheels
Track: Front	3 ft. 10 $\frac{9}{16}$ in. (1·16 m.).	3 ft. 10 $\frac{9}{16}$ in. (1·16 m.).
Rear	3 ft. 9¼ in. (1·15 m.).	3 ft. 8¾ in. (1·14 m.).
Overall width	4 ft. 8½ in. (1·5 m.).	4 ft. 6⅞ in. (1·4 m.).
Overall height	4 ft. ⅝ in. (1·22 m.).	

WEIGHT

Dry weight .. .. 1,510 lb. (685 kg.).

TORQUE WRENCH SETTINGS

Oil pump securing bolts .. .. 12 lb. ft. (1·66 kg. m.).
Cylinder head nuts .. .. 50 lb. ft. (6·91 kg. m.).
Connecting rod bolts .. .. 45 lb. ft. (6·22 kg. m.).
Steering-column pinch bolt .. .. 10 lb. ft. (1·38 kg. m.).

GENERAL DATA
SPRITE (Mk. IV) and MIDGET (Mk. III)
(WITH EXHAUST EMISSION CONTROL)

The following information is applicable to the Sprite (Mk. IV) and Midget (Mk. III) and should be used in conjunction with the preceding specifications.

Engine
- Engine type .. .. 12CD (4-cylinder overhead valve)
- Bore .. .. 2·78 in. (70·61 mm.)
- Stroke .. .. 3·2 in. (81·28 mm.)
- Cubic capacity .. .. .. 77·8 cu. in. (1274·86 c.c.)
- Compression ratio .. .. .. 8·8 : 1
- Firing order 1, 3, 4, 2
- Valve rocker clearance (cold) .. ·012 in. (·3 mm.)
- Idle speed .. .. 1,000 r.p.m.
- Fast idle speed .. .. .. 1,100 r.p.m. to 1,200 r.p.m.
- Oil pressure:
  - Normal (approx.) .. .. 40 to 70 lb./sq. in. (2·81 to 4·92 kg./cm.^{2})
  - Idling (approx.) .. .. .. 20 lb./sq. in. (1·4 kg./cm.^{2})

Ignition
- Sparking plugs .. .. .. Champion N.9.Y
- Sparking plug gap .. .. .. ·024 to ·026 in. (·62 to ·66 mm.)
- Stroboscopic ignition timing .. 10° B.T.D.C. at 1,000 r.p.m.
- Contact breaker gap .. .. ·014 to ·016 in. (·35 to ·40 mm.)

Fuel system
- Carburetters .. .. Twin S.U. type HS2
- Carburetter needle .. .. .. AN.
- Pump .. .. S.U. (Electric) type AUF 206

Transmission
- Rear axle ratio .. .. .. 4·22 : 1
- Overall gear ratios: First .. .. 13·504 : 1
- With synchromesh
  - Second .. 8·085 : 1
  - Third .. 5·726 : 1
  - Fourth .. 4·22 : 1
- Reverse .. 17·395 : 1

Wheels and tyres
- Wheel size .. .. Disc—3·5D × 13; wire—4J × 13
- Tyre size and type .. .. .. 5·20—13 Dunlop C41 Gold Seal (Nylon) Tubeless
  - 5·20—13 Heavy-Duty (6-ply) Tubeless
  - 145—13 SP41—Tubed
- Tyre pressures (set cold):

	Dunlop C41 Gold Seal (Nylon); Heavy Duty	SP41
Normal:		
Front	18 lb./sq. in. (1·3 kg./cm.^{2})	22 lb./sq. in. (1·6 kg./cm.^{2})
Rear	20 lb./sq. in. (1·4 kg./cm.^{2})	24 lb./sq. in. (1·7 kg./cm.^{2})
For sustained speeds in excess of 80–85 m.p.h. (129–137 km.p.h.):		
Front	22 lb./sq. in. (1·6 kg./cm.^{2})	22 lb./sq. in. (1·6 kg./cm.^{2})
Rear	24 lb./sq. in. (1·7 kg./cm.^{2})	24 lb./sq. in. (1·7 kg./cm.^{2})

GENERAL DATA—continued

(with exhaust emission control)

(SPRITE (Mk. IV) and MIDGET (Mk. III)—continued)

	Wire wheels	Disc wheels
Dimensions		
Track: Front..	3 ft. $10\frac{8}{16}$ in. (1·16 m.)	3 ft. $10\frac{5}{16}$ in. (1·16 m.)
Rear ..	3 ft. $9\frac{1}{4}$ in. (1·15 m.)	3 ft. $8\frac{3}{4}$ in. (1·14 m.)
Turning circle: Left lock ..	32 ft. $1\frac{1}{2}$ in. (9·79 m.)	
Right lock	31 ft. $2\frac{1}{2}$ in. (9·51 m.)	
Front wheel alignment ..	Parallel to $\frac{1}{8}$ in. toe-in (0 to 3·2 mm.)	
Wheelbase	6 ft. 8 in. (2·03 m.)	
Overall length	11 ft. $5\frac{3}{8}$ in. (3·49 m.)	
Overall width: Disc wheels	4 ft. $6\frac{7}{8}$ in. (1·4 m.)	
Wire wheels	4 ft. $8\frac{1}{4}$ in. (1·5 m.)	
Overall height	4 ft. $\frac{5}{8}$ in. (1·22 m.)	
Ground clearance	5 in (12·7 cm.)	
Weight Dry weight	1,519 lb. (689 kg.)	
Capacities Fuel tank	6 gallons (7·2 U.S. gallons, 27·3 litres)	
Engine sump (including filter)	$6\frac{1}{2}$ pints (7·8 U.S. pints, 3·7 litres)	
Gearbox	$2\frac{1}{4}$ pints (2·7 U.S. pints, 1·3 litres)	
Rear axle	$1\frac{3}{4}$ pints (2·1 U.S. pints, ·99 litre)	
Cooling system (with heater)	6 pints (7 U.S. pints, 3·4 litres)	

TUNING DATA

MODEL: SPRITE (Mk. IV)/MIDGET (Mk. III)

ENGINE
Type	12CD
Firing order	1, 3, 4, 2
Capacity	1274·86 c.c. (77·8 cu. in.)
Compression ratio	8·8 : 1
Compression pressure	120 lb./sq. in. (8·44 kg./cm.²)
Idle speed	1,000 r.p.m.
Fast idle speed	1,100 r.p.m. to 1,200 r.p.m.
Valve rocker clearance	·012 in. (·305 mm.) set cold
Stroboscopic ignition timing	5° B.T.D.C. at 1,000 r.p.m. (vacuum pipe
Static ignition timing	T.D.C. disconnected)
Timing mark location	Pointer on timing case, notch on crankshaft pull

DISTRIBUTOR
Make	Lucas
Type	25D4
Serial number	41211
Contact breaker gap	·014 to ·016 in. (·35 to ·40 mm.)
Rotation of rotor	Anti-clockwise
Dwell angle	57° to 63°
Condenser capacity	·18 to ·24 mF
Centrifugal advance	
Crankshaft degrees (vacuum pipe disconnected)	0° at 500 to 700 r.p.m.
	20° at 2,100 to 2,300 r.p.m.
	30° ± 2° at 4,000 r.p.m.
Vacuum advance	
Starts	5 in. Hg
Finishes	8 in. Hg
Total crankshaft degrees	6° ± 2°

SPARKING PLUGS
Make	Champion
Type	N-9Y
Gap	·024 to ·026 in. (·625 to ·660 mm.)

IGNITION COIL
Make	Lucas
Type	11C12
Resistance—primary	3 to 3·4 ohms at 20° C. (68° F.)
Consumption	
Ignition on—standing	3·5 to 4 amps.
at 2,000 r.p.m.	1 amp.

CARBURETTER(S)
Make	S.U.
Type/Specification	Twin HS2/AUD 266
Choke diameter	1¼ in. (31·75 mm.)
Jet size	·090 in. (2·28 mm.)
Needle	AN
Piston spring	Blue
Initial jet adjustment	11 flats from bridge

EXHAUST EMISSION
Exhaust gas analyser reading:
At engine idle speed	3 to 4% CO (provisional)
Air pump test speed	1,200 r.p.m. (engine)

SECTION I

948 c.c. Engined Cars

1958-1962

IGNITION

The ignition system consists of two circuits — primary and secondary. The primary circuit includes the battery, ignition switch, the primary or low-tension circuit of the coil and the distributor contact breaker and capacitor (Condenser). The secondary circuit includes the secondary or high-tension circuit of the coil, the distributor rotor and cover segments, the high-tension cables and the spark plugs.

The ignition coil, which is mounted on the right-hand side of the engine, consists of a soft iron core around which is wound the primary and secondary windings. The coil carries at one end a centre high-tension terminal and two low-tension terminals marked (SW) (switch) and (CB) (contact breaker) respectively.

The ends of the primary winding are connected to the (SW) and (CB) terminals and the secondary winding to the (CB) terminal and the high-tension terminal.

The distributor is mounted on the right-hand side of the engine and is driven by a shaft and helical gear from the camshaft. Automatic timing control of the distributor is controlled by a centrifugal mechanism and a vacuum-operated unit each opening entirely independently of each other. The centrifugal mechanism regulates the ignition advance according to engine speed, while the vacuum control varies the timing according to engine load. The combined effect of the two mechanisms gives added efficiency over the full operating range of the engine. A micrometer adjuster is provided to give a fine timing adjustment to allow for the engine condition and the grade of fuel used.

A keyed moulded rotor with a metal electrode is mounted on top of the cam. Attached to the distributor body above the centrifugal advance mechanism is a contact breaker plate carrying the contact breaker points and a capacitor connected in parallel. A cover is fitted over the distributor body and retained by two spring clips attached to the body.

Inside the cover is a center electrode and spring-loaded carbon brush which makes contact with the rotor. The brush is of composite construction, the top portion being made of a resistive compound, while the lower portion is made of softer carbon to prevent wear of the rotor electrode. Under no circumstances must a short non-resistive brush be used to replace this long resistive type. A measure of radio interference suppression is given by this brush.

Spaced circumferentially around the centre electrode are the spark plug high-tension cable segments. The distributor is secured in position on the cylinder block by a clamp plate.

The spark plugs are located on the right-hand side of the engine and have a 14 mm. thread with a ¾ in. reach.

When the ignition is **switched on**, the current from the battery flows through the primary circuit, and a magnetic field is built up around the core of the coil. When the contact breaker points are opened by rotation of the distributor cam, the current flow is interrupted, causing a high voltage to be induced in the secondary winding of the coil by sudden collapse and consequent change in the magnetic field. The high-tension current thus generated in the secondary winding of the coil is conveyed by the coil high-tension cable to the centre terminal of the distributor cover. From here the current passes through the carbon brush to the rotor, where the high-tension current passes along the rotor electrode and is distributed to the segments and thence to the spark plugs via the high-tension cables.

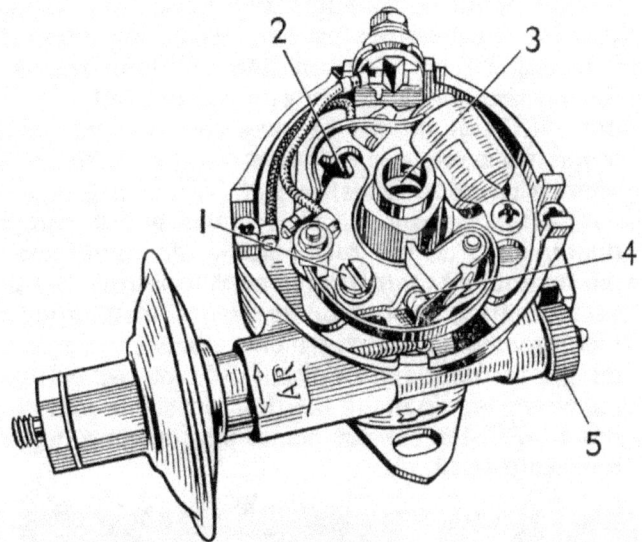

1. *Contact adjusting screw.*
2. *Contact adjusting slot.*
3. *Cam and drive shaft oiling point.*
4. *Contact points.*
5. *Micrometer adjuster.*

ADJUSTMENTS IN THE VEHICLE

The purpose of the following adjustments is to maintain efficient engine performance and economical running.

(1) Adjust the spark plugs at the recommended intervals as follows:

The gap of the plug points should be within the limits of .024 to .026 in. (.61 to .66 mm.).

Gap adjustment should be made by bending the side electrode only. Never bend the central electrode.

(2) Adjust the contact breaker points at the recommended intervals as follows:

Remove the distributor cover and rotor. Turn the engine using a wrench on the crankshaft pulley securing nut until the contacts are fully open. Slacken the fixed contact plate securing screw '1' (See Illustration). Insert a screwdriver in the slot '2' and move the plate until the gap gauge is a sliding fit between the contacts (.014 to .016 in. or .356 to .406 mm.) and then fully tighten the securing screw. Recheck the gap. Replace the rotor and cover.

(3) Adjust the ignition timing if the distributor has been disturbed.

Remove the valve rocker cover so that the valve action can be observed. Rotate the engine using a wrench on the crankshaft pulley securing nut until No. 1 Piston is at the top of its compression stroke (i.e. the exhaust valve of No. 4 cylinder is just closing and the inlet valve just opening). Turn the crankshaft until the recess in the crankshaft pulley flange is in line with the largest pointer (TDC) on the timing case cover. If the timing cover has been removed, align the timing marks on the camshaft and crankshaft wheels. No. 1 and 4 piston are now at T.D.C. Set the micrometer adjustment on the distributor in its central position. The crankshaft should now be rotated backwards 5° to obtain its correct position before setting the distributor points, this setting is correct for premium grade fuels only. With the cover removed the distributor body should be rotated until the rotor arm is pointing to the position of No. 1 electrode in the cover. With the contact points just opening, tighten the clamp plate bolt.

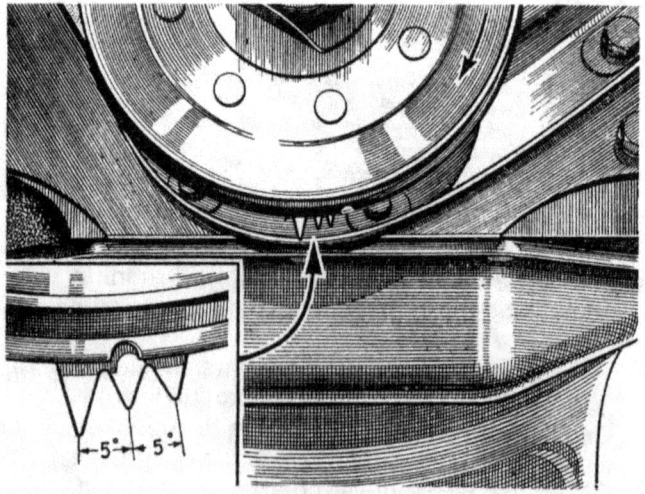

Finer adjustment can be obtained under road conditions, by means of the micrometer adjustment. **Note:** this adjustment should not be used for initial setting of the ignition; it is only altered if the main setting requires adjustment to meet the characteristics of the grades of fuel being used. There is a considerable amount of latitude for adjustment but only extremely small movements of the adjustment knob should be made at one time.

Replace the distributor cover and cylinder head cover.

TO TEST IN THE VEHICLE

If the ignition system fails, or misfiring occurs, first make sure that the trouble is not due to defects in the engine, carburetor or fuel supply. Faults should be diagnosed by applying the following tests:

(1) Examine the high-tension cables, i.e. the cables from the coil to the distributor, and from the distributor to the plugs. If the rubber insulation shows signs of deterioration or cracking, the cable should be renewed.

(2) Test the plugs and high-tension cables by removing the plugs in turn and allowing them to rest on the cylinder head or other convenient earthing point, and observing whether a spark occurs at the points when the engine is turned by hand. It should, however, be noted that this is only a rough test, since it is possible that a spark may not take place when the plug is under compression. If necessary, clean and test the plugs, using a plug cleaning and testing machine.

(3) To trace a fault in the low-tension circuit, release the instrument panel from the dash, switch on the ignition, and turn the engine until the distributor contacts are opened. Refer to the wiring diagram, and, with the aid of a voltmeter (0 to 20), check the circuit as follows:

   (a) **Cable — Battery to starter switch**
   Connect the voltmeter between the supply terminal of the starter switch and an earthing point. No reading indicates a faulty cable or loose connection.

   (b) **Cable (brown) — Starter switch to two-way fuse unit A.1 terminal**
   Connect the voltmeter between the fuse unit A.1 terminal and earth. No reading indicates a faulty cable or loose connection.

   (c) **Control box**
   Connect the voltmeter between the control box terminal (A.1) and earth. No reading indicates a faulty control box.

   (d) **Cable (brown and blue) — Control box to lighting and ignition switch**
   Connect the voltmeter between the lighting switch terminal (A) and earth. No reading indicates a faulty cable or loose connection.

(e) **Ignition switch**
Connect the voltmeter between the ignition switch (white cable terminal) and earth. No reading indicates a faulty ignition switch.

(f) **Cable (white) — Ignition switch to fuse unit A.3 terminal**
Connect the voltmeter between the fuse unit A.3 terminal and earth. No reading indicates a faulty cable or loose connection.

(g) **Cable (white — Fuse unit A.3 terminal to ignition coil**
Connect the voltmeter between the ignition coil terminal (SW) and earth. No reading indicates a faulty cable or loose connection.

(h) **Ignition coil**
Connect the voltmeter between the ignition coil terminal (CB) and earth. No reading indicates a faulty ignition coil.

(i) **Cable (white and black) — Ignition coil to distributor**
Connect the voltmeter between the distributor terminal and earth. No reading indicates a faulty cable or loose connection.

(j) **Distributor**
Connect the voltmeter across the distributor contacts. If no reading is given, remove the capacitor and test again. If a reading is given, the capacitor is faulty.

(4) If, after carrying out the foregoing tests, the fault has not been located, remove the high-tension cable from the terminal of the distributor. Switch on the ignition and crank the engine until the contacts close. Flick the contact breaker lever open while the high-tension cable from the ignition coil is held about 3/16 in. (5 mm.) away from the cylinder block. If the ignition equipment is in order a strong spark should be obtained. If no spark is given, it indicates a faulty ignition coil.

IGNITION COIL

To remove

(1) Disconnect the high-tension cable from the coil center terminal.

(2) Disconnect the low-tension cables from the (SW) and (CB) terminals of the coil.

(3) Unscrew the bolts fastening the coil to the generator strap, and remove the coil.

To replace

The installation of the ignition coil is a reversal of the procedure 'To remove'.

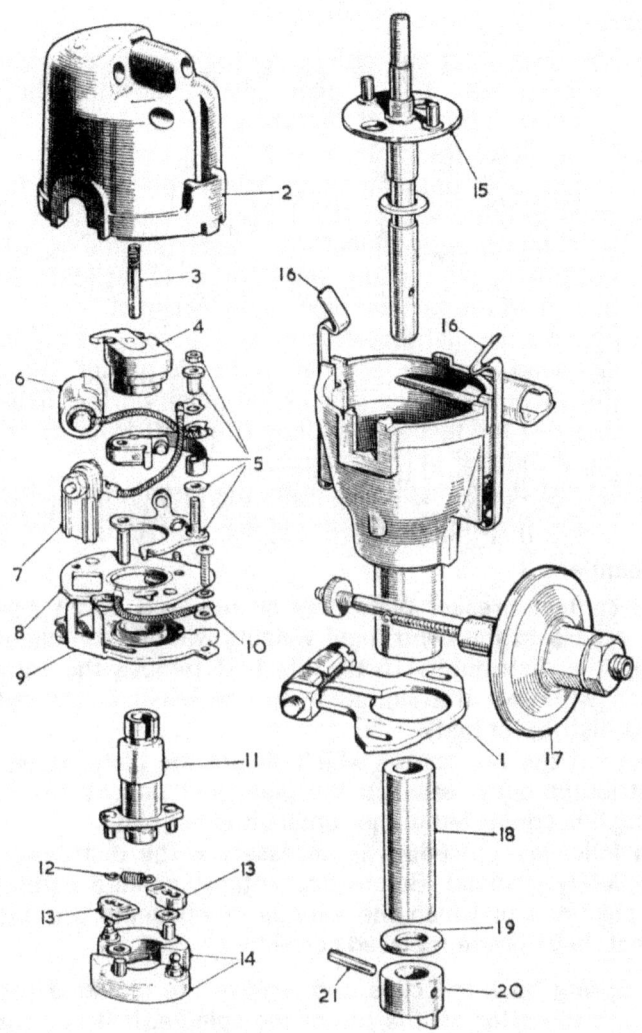

The components of the DM2P4 distributor

1. Clamping plate.
2. Moulded cap.
3. Brush and spring.
4. Rotor arm.
5. Contacts (set).
6. Capacitor.
7. Terminal and lead (low-tension).
8. Moving contact breaker plate.
9. Contact breaker base plate.
10. Earth lead.
11. Cam.
12. Automatic advance springs.
13. Toggles.
14. Weight assembly.
15. Shaft and action plate.
16. Cap-retaining clips.
17. Vacuum unit.
18. Bush.
19. Thrust washer.
20. Driving dog.
21. Taper pin.

DISTRIBUTOR

To remove

(1) The distributor can be removed and replaced without interfering with the ignition timing, provided the clamp plate pinch-bolt is not disturbed.

(2) To facilitate the replacement of the distributor, turn the engine over until the rotor arm is pointing to the segment in the cover for No. 1 cylinder plug lead to provide a datum for replacement. Also, ascertain the approximate position of the vacuum unit in order to facilitate the connection of the vacuum pipe on replacement.

(3) Remove the distributor cover and disconnect the low-tension lead from the terminal on the distributor. Disconnect the suction advance pipe at the union on the distributor.

(4) Unscrew the tachometer drive (if fitted) from its connecting at the rear of the generator.

(5) Extract the two bolts securing the distributor clamp plate to the distributor housing and withdraw the distributor.

To dismantle

The contact breaker plate may be removed as an assembly to give access to the centrifugal weights without completely dismantling the distributor. To do this first remove the rotor arm and then withdraw the slotted nylon low-tension terminal post from the distributor body.

Take out the two screws which secure the plate assembly to the distributor body, ease up the plate and unhook the flexible actuating link connected to the contact breaker plate.

The following procedure is necessary if the distributor is to be completely stripped. Before dismantling, make a careful note of the positions in which the various components are fitted in order that they may be replaced correctly.

(1) Spring back the clips and remove the moulded cap.

(2) Lift the rotor off the top of the spindle. If it is a tight fit it must be levered off carefully with a screwdriver.

(3) Remove the nut and washer from the moving contact anchor pin. Withdraw the insulating sleeve from the capacitor lead and low-tension lead connectors, noting the order in which they are fitted. Lift the moving contact from the pivot pin and remove the large insulating washer from the anchor pin.

(4) Take out the screw, spring and flat washer, securing the fixed contact plate, and remove the plate.

(5) Take out the securing screw and remove the capacitor (condenser).

(6) Extract the two screws securing the base-plate to the distributor body, noting that one also secures the earthing lead, and lift out the base-plate.

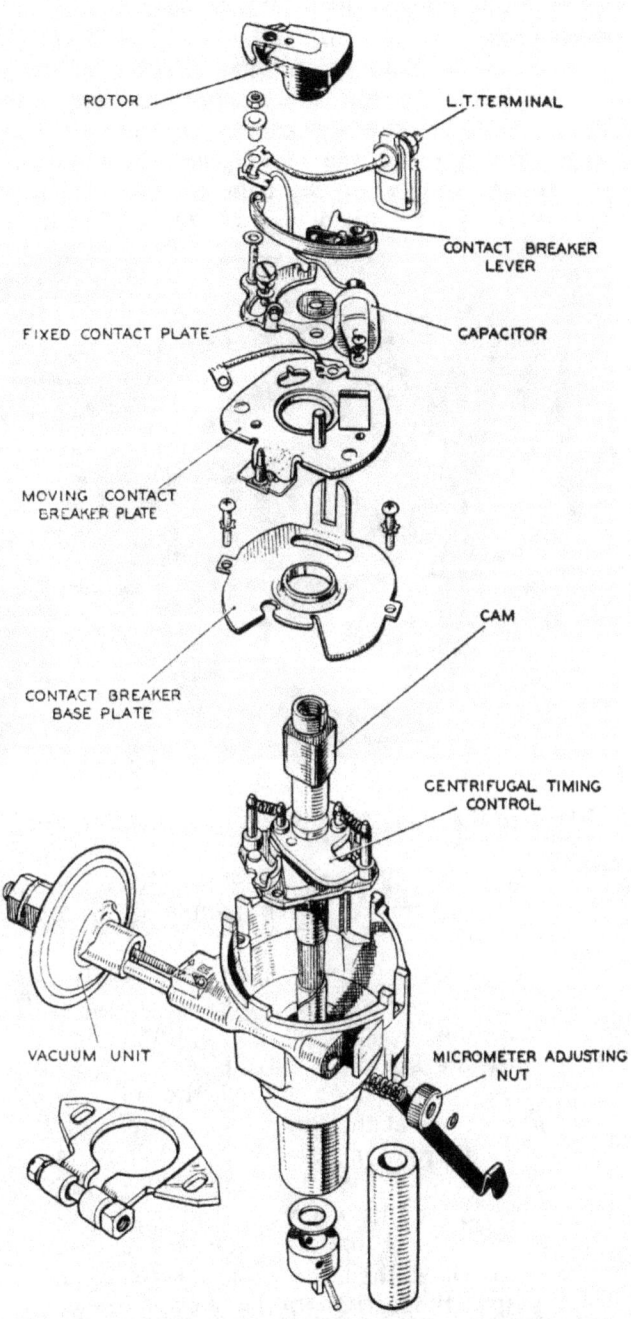

The component parts of the DM2 distributor.

Unhook the flexible actuating link connecting the diaphragm in the vacuum unit with the moving contact breaker plate.

Important — Note the relative position of the rotor arm drive slot in the cam spindle and the offset drive dog at the driving end of the spindle, to ensure that the timing is not 180° out when the cam spindle is engaged with the centrifugal weights during assembly. (See illustration.)

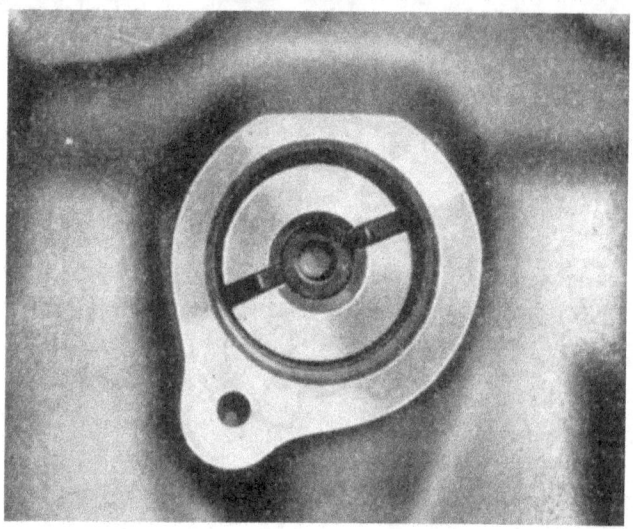

(7) Take out the cam retaining screw and remove the cam spindle.

(8) Take out the centrifugal weights. These may be lifted out as two assemblies, each complete with a spring and toggle.

(9) To release the vacuum advance unit, remove the circlip, adjusting nut and spring. Withdraw the unit. Take care not to lose the adjusting nut lock spring clip.

(10) To release the spindle from the body, drive out the parallel driving pin passing through the collar of the driving tongue member at the lower end of the spindle.

(11) Clean the distributor cover and examine it for signs of cracks and evidence of 'Tracking', i.e. a conducting path may have formed between adjacent segments. This is indicated by a thin black line between the segments, when this has occurred the cover should be renewed.

(12) Ensure that the carbon brush moves freely in the distributor cover.

(13) Examine the attachment of the metal electrode to the rotor moulding. If slack or abnormally burned, renew the rotor.

(14) The contact face of the contact breaker points should present a clean, greyish, frosted appearance. If burned or blackened, renew the contact set or polish the contact face of each point with a fine oil stone, working with a rotary motion. Care should be taken to maintain the faces of the points flat and square, so that when reassembled full contact is obtained. Clean the points thoroughly in fuel.

(15) Check that the movable contact arm is free on its pivot without slackness.

(16) Check the centrifugal timing control balance weights and pivot pins for wear and renew the cam assembly or weights if necessary.

(17) The cam assembly should be a free sliding fit on the driving shaft. If the clearance is excessive, or the cam face is worn, renew the cam assembly or shaft as necessary.

(18) Check the fit of the shaft in the body bearing bushes. If slack, renew the bushes and shaft, as necessary.

Press out the old bushes. The new bushes should be allowed to stand completely immersed in thin engine oil for twenty-four hours, or alternatively for two hours in oil which has been heated to 212°F (100°C), before pressing them into the distributor body.

To reassemble

Reassembly is a direct reversal of the dismantling procedure, although careful attention must be given to the following points:

(1) As they are assembled, the components of the automatic advance mechanism, the distributor shaft, and the portion of the shaft on which the cam fits must be lubricated with thin, clean engine oil.

(2) Turn the vacuum control adjusting nut until it is in the half-way position when replacing the control unit.

(3) When engaging the cam driving pins with the centrifugal weights, make sure that they are in the original position. When seen from above, the small offset of the driving dog must be on the right, and the driving slot for the rotor arm must be in the six o'clock position.

(4) Adjust the contact breaker to give a maximum opening of .014 to .016 in. (.36 to .40 mm.).

To Install

Replacing the distributor is the reverse of the procedure 'To Remove', noting the following points:

(1) Insert the assembled distributor, with its cap removed, into the spindle housing, and turn the rotor arm until the driven dog on the distributor engages with the slot in the housing.

(2) Screw in the two setpins securing the distributor clamp plate to the distributor housing.
(3) Position the distributor so that the vacuum control unit is in the same position as noted before removal.
(4) Check the contact breaker gap and ignition timing.

DISTRIBUTOR DRIVING SPINDLE

Removal
(1) Remove the distributor as described.
(2) By using a 5/16 in. U.N.F. bolt approximately 3½ in. long, screwed into the tapped end of the driving spindle, the spindle may be withdrawn.
(3) Examine the drive gear for worn teeth.

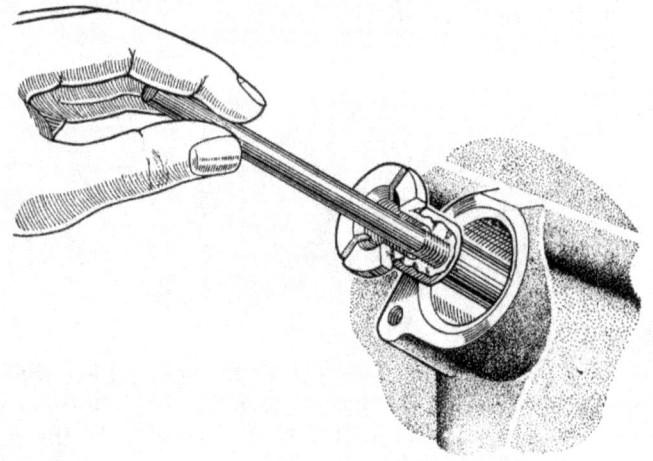

To Replace
(1) Remove the valve gear cover.
(2) Crank the engine until No. 1 Piston is at the top of its compression stroke (i.e. the exhaust valve of No. 4 cylinder is just closing and the inlet valve just opening).
(3) Turn the crankshaft until the recess in the crankshaft pulley flange is in line with the (T.D.C.) indicating pointer on the timing chain cover.
(4) Screw the 5/16 in. U.N.F. bolt into the threaded end of the distributor drive and replace the drive into its housing so that the off-set slot takes up the position in illustration.
(5) Replace the distributor following the instructions given above.

SPARK PLUGS

Inspect, clean, adjust and renew spark plugs at the recommended mileage intervals.

When plugs are removed from the engine their gaskets should be removed with them and replaced on the plugs, which should be placed in a suitable holder. It is advisable to identify each plug with the number of the cylinder from which it was removed so that any faults revealed on examination can be traced back to the cylinder concerned.

When examining the plugs, place a new plug of the same type beside the others to afford a ready comparison of the relative condition of the used plugs.

Examine for signs of oil fouling. This will be indicated by a wet, shiny, black deposit on the insulator. This is caused by oil pumping due to worn cylinders and pistons or gummed-up or broken rings. Under such conditions, oil from the cylinder walls is forced up past the rings on the suction stroke of the piston, and is eventually deposited on the plugs.

A permanent remedy for this cannot be effected, the only cure being the fitting of a new piston and rings, or, in extreme cases, a rebore may be necessary.

Next examine the plugs for signs of petrol (gasoline) fouling. This is indicated by a dry, fluffy, black deposit which is usually caused by over-rich carburation, although ignition system defects such as a run-down battery, faulty distributor, coil or condenser defects, or a broken or worn-out cable may be additional causes. If the plugs appear to be suitable for further use, proceed to clean and test them.

First remove the plug gaskets and examine them for condition. A large proportion of the heat of the plug is normally dissipated to the cylinder head through the steel gasket between the plug and the head. Plugs not screwed down tightly can thus easily become over-heated so that they operate out of their proper heat range, thus producing pre-ignition, short plug life and 'pinking'. On the other hand, it is unnecessary and unwise to tighten up the plugs too much. What is required is a reasonably good seal between the plug and the cylinder head and the use of a torque wrench is recommended to tighten the plugs to a figure of 30 lb. ft. (4.15 kg. m.).

If the plugs require cleaning it is preferable to make use of a proper plug cleaner of the type recommended by the plug manufacturers, and the makers' instructions for using the cleaner should be followed carefully.

Occasionally a blistered insulator or a badly burnt electrode may be noticed when examining the plugs.

If the plug is of the type normally recommended for the engine and it was correctly installed (down tightly on the gasket), this condition may have been brought about by a very lean mixture or an overheated engine. There is, however, a possibility that a plug of another type is required, but as a rule the recommended plug should be adhered to.

After cleaning carefully, examine the plugs for cracked insulators and wear of the insulator nose due to excessive previous cleaning. In such cases the plugs have passed their useful life, and new plugs should be installed.

Examine the insulator for deposits underneath the side electrode which have possibly accumulated and which act as a 'hot spot' in service.

After cleaning the plugs in a special cleaner, blow all surplus abrasive out of the body recesses, and off the plug threads, by means of an air-blast. Next examine the threads for carbon. Any deposits can be removed and the threads cleaned with a wire brush. A wire buffing wheel may also be utilized, but reasonable care must be used in both methods in order not to injure the electrodes or the tip of the insulator. The thread section of the plug body is often neglected when cleaning the plugs, owing to the fact that it is not generally realized that, like the gaskets, the threads are a means of heat dissipation and that when they are coated with carbon it retards the flow of the heat from the plug, producing overheating. This simple procedure will also ensure absence of binding on the threads on replacement and also avoid unnecessary use of the plug wrench .

When replacing a plug, always screw it down by hand as far as possible and use the torque wrench for final tightening only. Whenever possible use a socket to avoid possible fracture of the insulator.

Examine the electrodes for the correct gap. (See 'General Data'.) Avoid an incorrect reading in the case of badly pitted electrodes.

Remember that electrode corrosion and the development of oxides at the gap area vitally affects the sparking efficiency. The special cleaner can remove the oxides and deposits from the insulator, but the cleaner stream does not always reach this area with full effect owing to its location, and cannot necessarily deal with corrosion effectively as this sometimes requires too strong a blast for proper removal.

When plugs appear worthy of further use it is good practice to dress the gap area on both center and side electrodes with a small file before resetting them to the correct gap. The intense heat, pressure, explosion shock, and electrical and chemical action to which the plugs are submitted during miles of service are so intense that the molecular structure of the metal points is eventually affected. Plugs then reach a worn-out condition and resetting the points can no longer serve a good purpose. When points are burnt badly, it is indicative that the plug has worn to such an extent that its further use is undesirable and wasteful.

Before replacing the plug in the engine, test it for correct functioning under air pressure in a plug tester, following out the instructions issued by the makers of the plug tester. Generally speaking, a plug may be considered satisfactory for further service if it sparks continuously under a pressure of 100 lb./sq. in. (7 kg./cm.^{2}) with the gap between the points set at .022 in. (.56 mm.). It is essential that the plug point should be reset to the recommended gap before the plug is refitted to the engine. (See 'General Data'.)

While the plug is under pressure in the tester, it should be inspected for leakage by applying oil round the terminal. Leakage is indicated by the production of air bubbles, the intensity of which will serve to indicate the degree of leakage. The leakage gases have a 'blow-torch' effect when the engine is running which rapidly raises the temperature of the plug, raising it above its designed heat range, thus producing overheating, pre-ignition, and rapid electrode destruction.

The top half of the insulator is frequently responsible for poor plug performance due to the following faults: splashes; accumulation of dirt and dust; cracked insulators, caused by a slipping wrench; overtightness of the terminals.

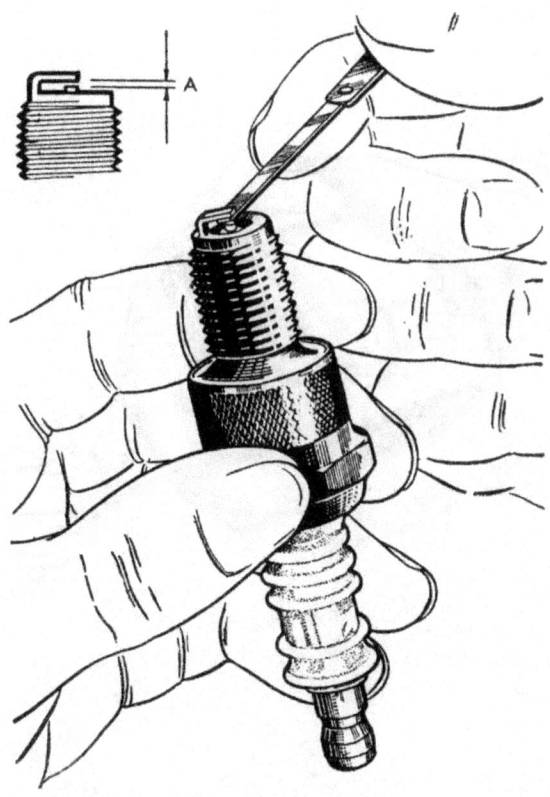

HIGH-TENSION CABLES

To remove
  (1) Obtain access to the high-tension cables by raising the bonnet.
  (2) Pull the high-tension cables off the spark plugs.
  (3) Unscrew the moulded terminal to release the cable from the coil.
  (4) Straighten out the bare strands of cable, remove the brass washer and withdraw the cable from the moulded terminal.
  (5) Release the screw securing the cable in the distributor cover and withdraw the cable.

To replace
  (1) Thread the cable through the moulded terminal and brass washer and bend back the bare strands of the cable against the brass washer.
  (2) Push the other end of the cable into the distributor cover and secure it with the pointed screw.
  (3) Install the cables in the coil and distributor cover and onto the spark plugs in the correct order. The firing order is 1, 3, 4, 2 following **round in** an anti-clockwise direction.

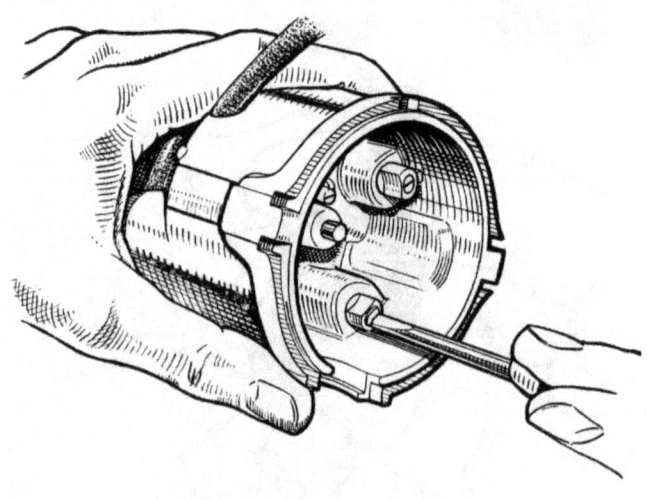

FAULT DIAGNOSIS

Symptom	No.	Possible Fault
(a) Engine will not fire	1	Battery discharged
	2	Distributor contact points dirty, pitted or out of adjustment
	3	Distributor cover 'tracked' or cracked
	4	Distributor carbon brush not in contact with cover
	5	Loose connection in low-tension circuit
	6	Distributor rotor arm cracked
	7	Coil faulty
(b) Engine misfires	1	Distributor contact points dirty, pitted or out of adjustment
	2	Contact breaker spring weak
	3	Distributor cover 'tracked' or cracked
	4	Coil faulty
	5	Loose connection in low-tension circuit
	6	High-tension cables cracked or perished
	7	Sparking plug loose
	8	Sparking plug insulation cracked
	9	Sparking plug gap incorrect
	10	Ignition timing too far advanced

FUEL SYSTEM

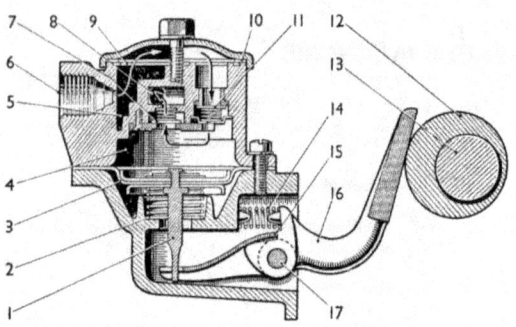

1. Diaphragm pull-rod.
2. Diaphragm return spring.
3. Diaphragm.
4. Pump chamber.
5. Sediment chamber.
6. Inlet union.
7. Delivery valve.
8. Delivery port.
9. Gauze filter.
10. Cork sealing washer.
11. Inlet valve.
12. Crankshaft eccentric.
13. Camshaft.
14. Anti-rattle spring.
15. Connecting link.
16. Rocker arm.
17. Rocker arm pivot pin.

FUEL PUMP

Description

The fuel pump is an AC-Sphinx 'Y' type mechanical pump operated off an eccentric on the engine camshaft. The illustration shows a sectional view of the pump.

As the engine camshaft (13) revolves, the eccentric (12) lifts the pump rocker arm (16) which is pivoted at (17). The rocker arm pulls the pull-rod downwards (1) together with the diaphragm (3) against the pressure of the spring (2), thus creating a vacuum in the pump chamber (4). Fuel is drawn from the tank and enters at (6) into the sediment chamber (5), through filter gauze (9), suction valve (11) into the pump chamber (4). On the return stroke the pressure of the spring (2) pushes the diaphragm (3) upwards, forcing fuel from the pump chamber (4) through the delivery valve (7) and port (8) into the carburetor.

When the carburetor bowl is full the float will shut the needle valve, thus preventing any flow of fuel from the pump chamber (4). This will hold the diaphragm (3) downward, against the pressure of the spring (2) and will remain in this position until the carburetor requires further fuel and the needle valve opens. The rocker arm (16), operates the connecting link by making contact at (15) and this construction allows idling movement of the rocker arm when there is no movement of the fuel pump diaphragm.

Spring (14) keeps the rocker arm (16) in constant contact with the pushrod and eccentric (12) to eliminate noise.

SERVICING THE PUMP

To Remove from Engine

Start by disconnecting the pipe unions and then remove the two set screws which hold the petrol pump to the engine crankcase. The fuel pump will now readily come away.

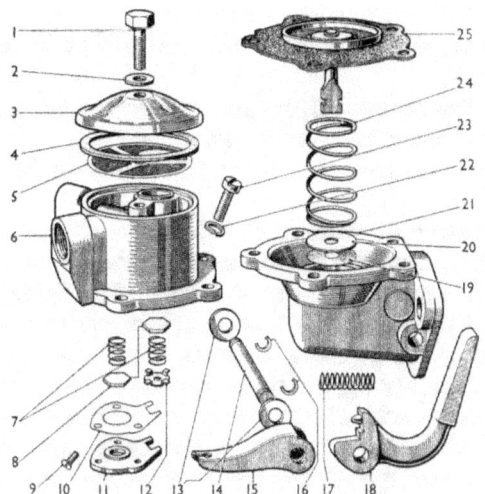

1. Cover retaining screw.
2. Fibre washer.
3. Cover.
4. Cork sealing washer.
5. Gauze filter.
6. Upper casting.
7. Valve springs.
8. Inlet and delivery valves.
9. Valve plate screw.
10. Valve plate gasket.
11. Valve plate.
12. Retainer.
13. Packing washers.
14. Rocker arm pivot pin.
15. Connecting link.
16. Retaining clips.
17. Anti-rattle spring.
18. Rocker arm.
19. Fibre washer.
20. Metal washer.
21. Pump body.
22. Spring washer.
23. Upper chamber securing screws.
24. Diaphragm return spring.
25. Diaphragm assembly.

To Dismantle the Pump

(1) Unscrew the set bolt (1) and lift off the cover (3).
(2) Lift off the filter gauze (5) and cork sealing washer (4).
(3) Unscrew the five upper chamber securing screws (23) and separate the two halves of the pump body (6 and 21).
(4) Unscrew the three screws (9) and remove the valve plate (11), inlet and delivery valves (8), valve plate gasket (10) springs (7), and delivery valve spring retainer (12).
(5) Remove the diaphragm and pull rod assembly (25) by rotating it through 90° and pulling it out. This will release the diaphragm spring (24).
(6) Remove the metal washer (20) and fibre washer (19).
(7) Remove the two retaining circlips (16) and washers (13), push out the rocker arm pivot pin (14) which will release the rocker arm (18), link (15) and spring (17).

Re-assembling the Fuel Pump

The following procedure should be adopted, dealing with the upper portion of the pump first.

All valves should be clean before re-assembly. Apart from the cleaning effect this improves the sealing between the valve and seat.

(1) Place the delivery valve (8) on its spring (7).
Place the inlet valve (8) on the valve seat located in the upper casting.
(2) Put valve spring (7) on the center of the inlet valve (8).
(3) Position retainer (12) on top of the inlet valve spring (7) — this retainer is a small four-legged pressing which retains the inlet valve spring — taking care not to distort the legs.
(4) Lay valve plate gasket (10) in position.
(5) Locate valve plate (11) in position and secure it with three screws (9).

(6) Now use a piece of wire to ensure that the valves work freely.
(7) Place the gauze filter screen (5) in position on top of the casting, making certain that it fits snugly.
(8) Fit the cork sealing washer (4), cover (3), fibre washer (2) and retaining screw (1).
(9) To assembly the lower half proceed as follows:
Assembly link (15), packing washers (13), rocker arm (18) and rocker arm spring (17) in the body (21). Insert rocker arm pin (14) through the hole in the body, at the same time engaging the packing washers (13), link and the rocker arm. Then, spring the retaining clips (16) into the grooves on each end of the rocker arm pin. The rocker arm pin should be a tap fit in the body, and if due to wear it is freer than this, the ends of the holes in the body should be burred over slightly.

Note: The fitting of the rocker arm pin can be simplified by first inserting a piece of .240 in. (6.096 mm.) diameter rod through the pin hole in one side of the body far enough to engage the rocker arm washers and link, then pushing in the rocker arm pin from the opposite side, removing the guide rod as the pin takes up its proper position.

(10) To fit the diaphragm assembly to the pump body: Insert fabric washer (19), metal washer (20) and place the diaphragm spring (24) in position in the pump body.
Place the diaphragm assembly (25) over the spring, the pull rod being downwards, and center the upper end of the spring in the lower protector washer.
Press downwards on the diaphragm, at the same time turning the assembly to the left in such a manner, that the slots on the pull rod will engage the fork in the link, ultimately turning the assembly a complete quarter turn to the left. This will place the pull rod in the proper working position in the link and at the same time permit the matching up of the holes in the diaphragm with those in the pump body flanges. When first inserting the diaphragm assembly into the pump body, the locating 'tab' on the outside of the diaphragm should be at the 12 o'clock position. After turning the diaphragm assembly a quarter of a turn to the left, the 'tab' should be at the 9 o'clock position. **Note:** Under certain conditions it is possible to insert the diaphragm pull rod too far through the slot in the operating link, with the result that the connecting link instead of engaging the two small slots in the pull rod, rides on the pull rod shoulder.
The diaphragm is correctly fitted when the slot in the link engages with the two slots in the diaphragm pull rod

after the diaphragm has been turned through 90°.
Correct assembly can be checked by measuring the distance from the top of the pump body to the upper diaphragm protector, when the diaphragm is held at the top of its stroke by the return spring. A measurement of approximately 9/16 in. (14.29 mm.) indicates correct assembly, whereas one of 3/16 in. (4.76 mm.) proves that the assembly is unsatisfactory.

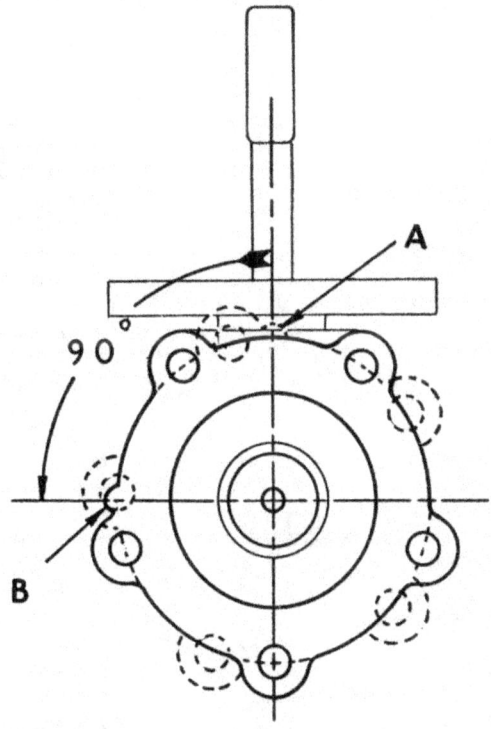

When fitting the diaphragm to the pump body, the locating tab (A) should be in the position shown. Turn the diaphragm to the left, so that the pull rod slots engage in the connecting link fork, until it arrives at position (B).

(11) The two sub-assemblies of the pump are now ready for fitting together and this is carried out as follows:
Push the rocker arm towards the pump until the diaphragm is level with the body flanges.
Place the upper half of the pump into the proper position, as shown by the mark made on the flanges before dismantling.
Install the cover screws and lockwashers and tighten only until the heads of the screws just engage the washers. Use a screwdriver to hold the rocker arm at its outward position and while so held, securely tighten the cover screws diagonally.

SPRITE (H.I.) CARBURETORS

The two S.U. type H.I. carburetors are of the variable-jet type, fitted with twin 'Pancake' air cleaners.

A damper is provided in each carburetor, consisting of a plunger and non-return valve attached to the oil cap nut, and operates in the hollow piston rod which is partly filled with oil. Its function is to give a slightly enriched mixture on acceleration by controlling the rise of the piston and to prevent piston flutter.

No.	Description.
1.	Body—bare—front.
1A.	Body—bare—rear.
4.	Suction chamber and piston assembly.
5.	Oil damper assembly.
8.	Fibre washer—oil damper cap.
10.	Securing screw—suction chamber.
11.	Spring washer—D/C—screw.
12.	Jet needle.
13.	Jet needle locking screw.
15.	Jet with head.
16.	Jet sealing nut.
17.	Jet adjusting nut.
19.	Jet adjusting lock spring.
20.	Jet sealing ring—brass.
21.	Jet sealing ring—cork.
22.	Jet bearing copper washer—bottom half bearing
23.	Jet bearing—bottom half.
24.	Jet gland washer—cork.
25.	Jet gland washer—brass.
26.	Jet gland spring.
27.	Jet bearing—top half.
28.	Jet bearing copper washer—top half bearing.
29.	Jet return spring.
34.	Jet lever.
35.	Jet link.
37.	Nut (2 BA).
38.	Washer.
39.	Pivot pin—short.
39A.	Pivot pin—jet link.
41.	Pivot pin—jet lever to stirrup.
41A.	Screw—cable clamp.
41B	Starlock washer—jet link.
41C.	Starlock washer—link rod.
42.	Split pin.
45.	Link rod.
45A.	Stirrup—connecting jet lever.
46.	Float-chamber—bare—front.
46A.	Float-chamber—bare—rear.

No.	Description.
47.	Float-chamber lid.
48.	Float-chamber lid washer.
49.	Overflow pipe—front.
49A.	Overflow pipe—rear.
50.	Serrated fibre washer—cap nut.
51.	Aluminium packing washer.
52.	Float.
53.	Float needle and seat assembly.
55.	Float hinged lever.
56.	Float hinged lever pin.
64.	Cap nut—float lid.
66.	Holding-up bolt—float—chamber.
68.	Washer—steel—holding-up bolt.
68A.	Rubber grommet—holding-up bolt.
81.	Throttle spindle—front.
81A.	Throttle spindle—rear.
82.	Throttle disc.
83.	Throttle disc screw.
86.	Return spring—throttle—front.
87.	End clip.
88.	Anchor plate.
89.	Throttle lever.
90.	Bolt (2 BA).
91.	Taper pin.
92.	Throttle stop—front.
92A.	Throttle stop—rear.
93.	Adjusting screw.
94.	Lock spring—screw.
95	Rocker lever—front.
96.	Bolt—pivot—front.
96A.	Spring washer—pivot bolt.
96B.	Aluminium washer—cam.
99.	Coupling—folded.
100.	Connecting rod—throttle.
101.	Bolt (4 BA).
102.	Nut (4 BA).
103.	Washer (4 BA).

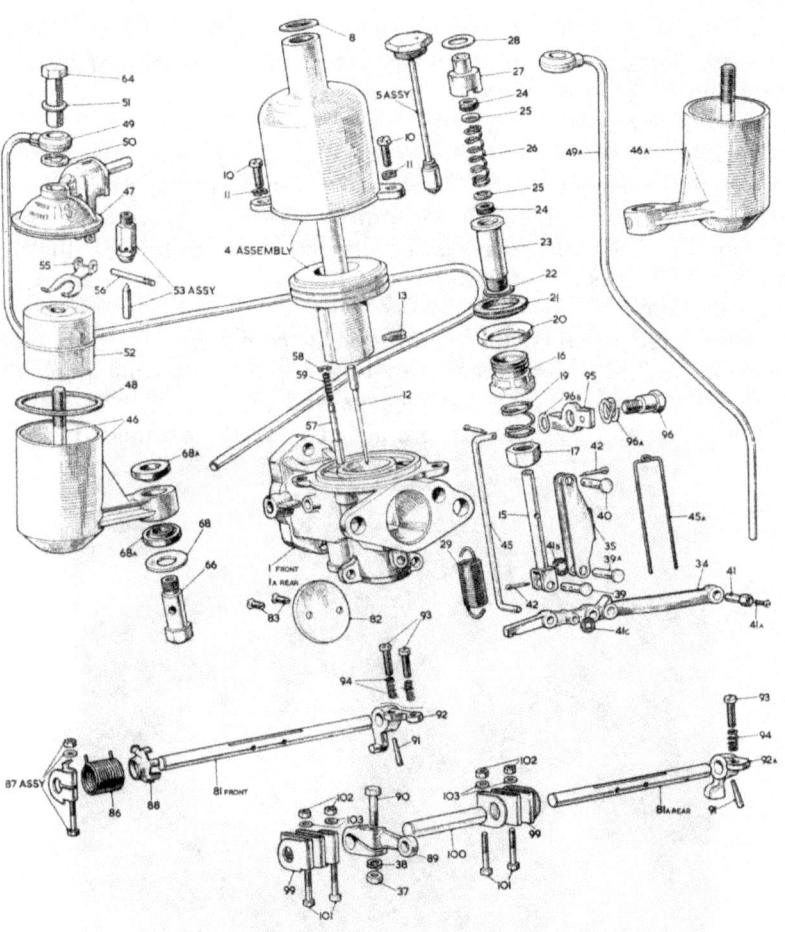

ADJUSTMENT

It is first essential to run the engine until it has attained its normal running temperature before commencing any mixture or slow-running adjustments.

The slow-running is governed by the setting of the jet adjusting screws and the throttle stop screws, all of which must be correctly set and synchronized if satisfactory results are to be obtained.

The throttles are interconnected by a coupling shaft and spring coupling clips which enable them to be correctly synchronized when adjustments take place.

Before blaming the settings for bad slow-running make quite sure that it is not due to badly set contact points, faulty plugs, bad valve clearance setting or faulty valves and valve springs.

Good slow-running cannot be obtained if the setting for the jets is incorrect. It is therefore advisable to commence any adjustments at this point.

In order to adjust the carburetors successfully it is necessary to remove the air cleaners and intake pipe assembly from the carburetors and engine valve cover and make sure the pistons work freely and the jets are properly centered (see below).

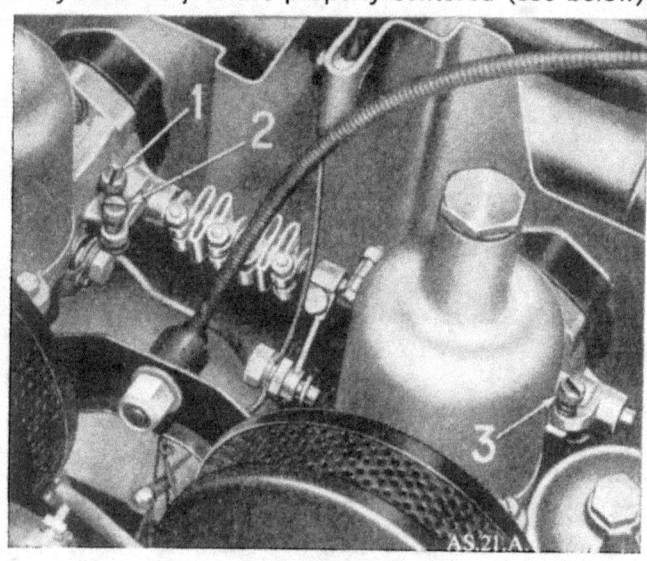

1 & 3. *Slow running adjustment screws.* 2. *Throttle mixture control interconnecting lever adjustor.*

Adjusting the Jets

(1) Slacken off the pinch-bolt of one of the spring coupling clips locating the interconnecting shaft to the throttle spindles and also release the two screws securing the choke spring to the jet levers, so that each carburetor can be operated independently.

(2) Release the throttle lever adjusting screws until both throttles are completely closed.

(3) Turn the throttle lever adjusting screw for the rear carburetor clockwise until it is just touching the web on the body and then give it one full turn. This will set the rear carburetor for fast idling and leave the front one out of action. This can be ensured further by lifting the front carburetor piston a matter of ½ in. (13 mm.).

(4) With the engine running, set the jet adjusting screw for the rear carburetor so that a mixture strength is obtained which will give the best running speed for this throttle opening, taking care to see that the jet head is kept in firm contact with the adjusting nut the whole time.

(5) The correctness or otherwise of this setting can be checked by raising the suction piston with a small screwdriver, or similar instrument to the extent of 1/32 in. (.8 mm). This should cause a very slight momentary increase in the engine speed without impairing the evenness of running in any way.

If this operation has the effect of stopping the engine it is an indication that the mixture setting is too weak (lean). If an appreciable speed increase occurs and continues to occur when the piston is raised as much as ¼ in. (6 mm.) it is an indication that the mixture is too rich.

(6) When the rear carburetor mixture setting has been carried out correctly release its throttle adjusting screw so that it is clear of the stop and the throttle is completely closed, and lift the piston ½ in. (13 mm.) to render it inoperative. Then repeat the jet-adjusting operations on the front carburetor.

(7) When both carburetors are correctly adjusted individually for mixture strength the throttles of each should be set so as to give the required slow-running and synchronization.

Slow-running and Synchronization

Screw each throttle lever adjusting screw so that its end is only just making contact with the web on the body, then give each screw one full turn exactly.

Start the engine, which will now idle on the fast side.

Unscrew each throttle lever adjusting screw an equal amount, a fraction of a turn at a time until the desired slow-running speed is achieved.

Correct synchronization can be checked by listening at each carburetor air intake in turn through a length of rubber tube and notice of the noise produced by the incoming air is the same in both. Any variation in intensity of the sound indicates that one throttle is set more widely open than the other — the louder sound indicates the throttle with the greater opening.

When the same intensity of sound is produced by both carburetors the intercoupling shaft clip should be tightened up firmly to ensure that the throttles work in unison.

Since the delivery characteristics, when both carburetors are operating together, vary somewhat from those existing when each is working separately it will be found necessary to check them again for correctness of mixture strength by lifting the pistons in turn as described in 'Adjusting the jets,' making such adjustments of the jet adjusting nuts as are required to balance the mixture strength and to ensure that it is not too rich.

Another method of synchronization is to employ a visual vacuum indicator such as the "Unisyn", available at sportscar accessory houses or parts departments of many dealerships. These units are simple in construction and adjustable over a wide range of vacuum. The technique is to place the base of the instrument firmly against the intake of the first carburetor and regulate the flow through the base by means of an adjusting screw until the float is centered in the tube. Then move the instrument to the second carburetor. If the float changes relative position, up or down, it indicates that the throttle setting is at variance with that of the first carburetor. Regulating the throttle lever adjusting screw to bring the float back to center accomplishes synchronization.

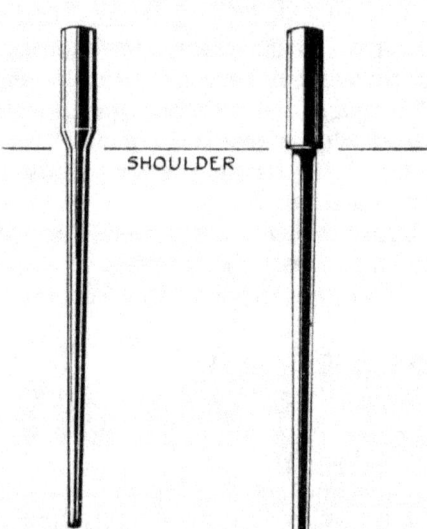

The shoulder of the needle should be flush with the underface of the piston. Two types of shoulder are in use and the correct datum point for each is shown.

Fitting New Needles

If the road performance is not satisfactory after the above adjustments have been made, larger or smaller needles may be necessary.

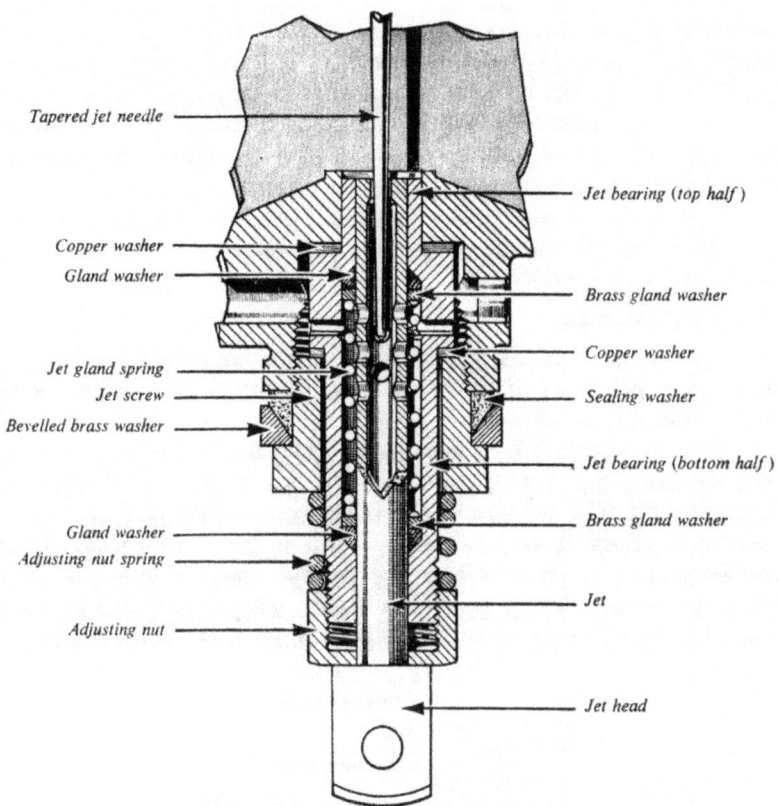

To change the needles, remove the screws and lift off the suction chambers, having marked them to ensure refitting to their respective units. Remove the pistons.

Unscrew the screw at the side of each piston tube and withdraw the needles.

Fit the new needles: a needle should be fitted with its shoulder flush with the face of the piston.

Centering a Jet

First remove the clevis pin at the base of the jet which attaches the jet head to the jet operating lever; withdraw the jet completely, and remove the adjusting nut and adjusting nut spring. Replace the adjusting nut without its spring and screw it up to the highest position. Slide the jet into position until the jet head is against the base of the adjusting nut. When this has been done, feel if this piston is perfectly free by lifting it up with the finger with the dashpot piston removed. If it is not, slacken the jet sealing nut and manipulate the lower part of the assembly, including the projecting part of the bottom half jet bearing, adjusting nut and jet head. Make sure that this assembly is now slightly loose. The piston should then rise and fall quite easily as the needle is now able to move the jet into the required central position. The jet sealing nut should now be tightened and a check made to determine that this piston is still quite free. If it is not found to be so, the jet sealing nut should be slackened again and the operation repeated. When complete freedom of the piston is achieved the jet adjusting nut should be replaced. The adjusting nut should now be screwed back to its original position.

Experience shows that a large percentage of carburetors returned for correction have had jets removed and incorrectly centered on replacement.

The Float-chamber

The position of the forked lever in the float-chamber must be such that the level of the float (and therefore the height of the fuel at the jet) is correct.

This is checked by inserting a 7/16 in. (11.11 mm.) round bar between the forked lever and the machined lip of the float-chamber lid. The prongs of the lever should just rest on the bar when the needle is on its seating. If this is not so, the lever should be reset at the point where the prongs meet the shank. Care must be taken not to bend the shank which must be perfectly flat and at right angles to the needle when it is on its seating.

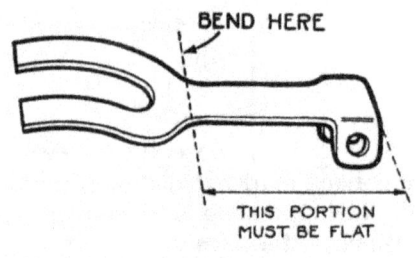

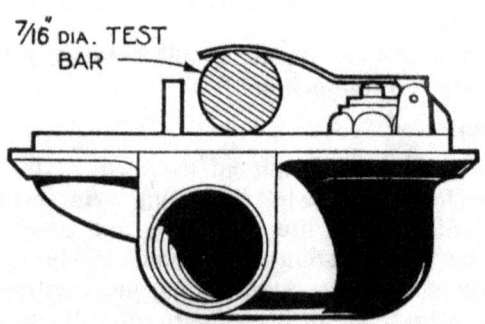

SOURCES OF TROUBLE

Piston Sticking

The piston assembly comprises the suction disc and the piston forming the choke into which is inserted the hardened and ground piston rod which engages in a bearing in the center of the suction chamber and in which is, in turn, inserted the jet needle.

The piston rod running in the bearing is the only part which is in actual contact with any other part, the suction disc, piston, and needle all having suitable clearances to prevent sticking. If sticking does occur the whole assembly should be cleaned carefully and the piston rod lubricated with a drop of thin oil. No oil must be applied to any other part except the piston rod. A sticking piston can be ascertained by removing the dashpot piston damper, inserting a finger in the air intake and lifting the piston, which should come up quite freely and fall back smartly onto its seating when released.

Water or Dirt in the Carburetor

When this is suspected lift the piston: the jet can then be seen; flood the carburetor and watch the jet; if fuel does not flow through freely there is a blockage. To remedy this, start the engine, open up the throttle, and block up the air inlet momentarily without shutting the throttle, keep the throttle open until the engine starts to race. This trouble seldom arises with the S.U. owing to the size of the jet and fuel ways. When it does occur the above method will nearly always clear it. Should it not do so, the only alternative is to remove the jet.

Float-chamber Flooding

This can be revealed by fuel flowing over the float-chamber and dripping from the air inlet, and is generally caused by grit between the float chamber needle and its guide. Remove the float chamber top and withdraw the float lever by extracting its pivot pin. The needle valve will now drop out of its seating and can be checked for cleanliness. If there is no grit or foreign matter on the needle or its seating make certain that the needle is not unduly worn. Should this be the case a new needle valve and seating must be fitted.

Float Needle Sticking

If the engine stops, apparently through lack of fuel when there is plenty in the tank and the pump is working properly, the probable cause is a sticking float needle. An easy test for this is to disconnect the pipe from the fuel pump to the carburetor, turn the engine with the starter motor to check if the fuel is being delivered: if it is starvation it has almost certainly been caused by the float needle sticking to its seat, and the float chamber lid should therefore be removed, the needle and seat cleaned, and refitted. At the same time it will be advisable to clean out the entire fuel system, as this trouble is caused by foreign matter in the fuel, and unless this is removed it is likely to recur. It is of no use whatever renewing any of the component parts of the carburetor, and the only cure is to make sure that the fuel tank and pipe lines are entirely free from any kind of foreign matter or sticky substance capable of causing this trouble.

THE AIR CLEANERS

Remove the units and wash the gauze in petrol (gasoline) every 6,000 miles (9600 km.) or every 3,000 miles (4800 km.) in exceptionally dusty conditions.

When the gauze is clean and dry, re-oil it with engine oil and allow it to drain before refitting to the engine.

MODIFIED CARBURETOR DAMPER ASSEMBLIES

To allow the carburetor pistons to lift more freely avoiding restriction of performance, new hydraulic damper assemblies have been fitted in model production. The damper pistons of the new assemblies were shortened from .378 in. (9.596 mm.) to .308 in. (7.823 mm.).

These hydraulic damper assemblies (part number AUC8114) are identified by the letter 'O' stamped on the brass hexagon caps. They can be fitted, with advantage, to earlier carburetors in pairs. Alternatively, the original damper pistons may be modified be machining .070 in. (1.78 mm.) off their lower faces.

MK II AND MIDGET CARBURETORS

Construction

The HS2 carburetors are of the automatically expanding choke type in which the size of the main air passage (or choke) over the jet, and the effective area of the jet, are variable according to the degree of throttle opening used on the engine against the prevailing road conditions (which may differ widely from light cruising to heavy pulling).

To serve the complete throttle range a single jet is used, being a simple metal tube sliding in a single bearing bush, fed by fuel along a small-diameter nylon tube leading direct from the base of the float-chamber. The jet is varied in effective area by a tapered fuel metering needle sliding into it.

Piston sticking

The piston assembly comprises the suction disc and the piston forming the choke, into which is inserted the hardened and ground piston rod which engages in a bearing in the center of the suction chamber and in which is inserted the jet needle. The piston rod running in the bearing is the only part which is in actual contact with any other part, the suction disc, piston and needle all having suitable clearances to prevent sticking. If sticking does occur the whole assembly should be cleaned carefully and the piston rod lubricated with a spot of thin oil. No oil must be applied to any part except the piston rod. A sticking piston can be ascertained by removing the piston damper and lifting the piston by pressing the piston lifting pin; the piston should come up quite freely and fall back smartly onto its seating when released. On no account should the piston return spring be stretched or its tension be altered in an attempt to improve its rate of return.

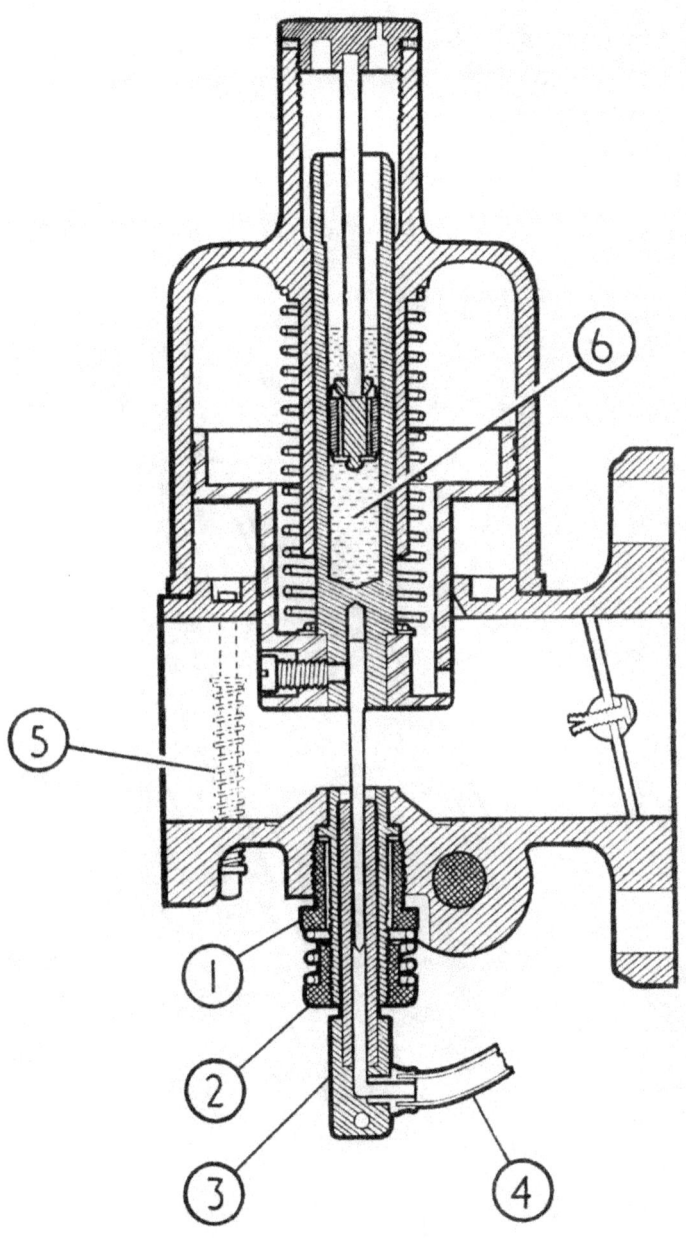

1. Jet locking nut.
2. Jet adjusting nut.
3. Jet head.
4. Nylon fuel pipe.
5. Piston lifting pin.
6. Piston damper oil well.

Water and dirt in the carburetors

Float-chamber flooding

Float needle sticking

Adjustments

For these conditions, see same headings under Sprite, H.I. Carburetor.

Slow-running and synchronization

Slacken the pinch-bolt of the delayed-action lever coupling the rear throttle spindle to the interconnecting shaft. This will permit each carburetor throttle to be set independently of the other.

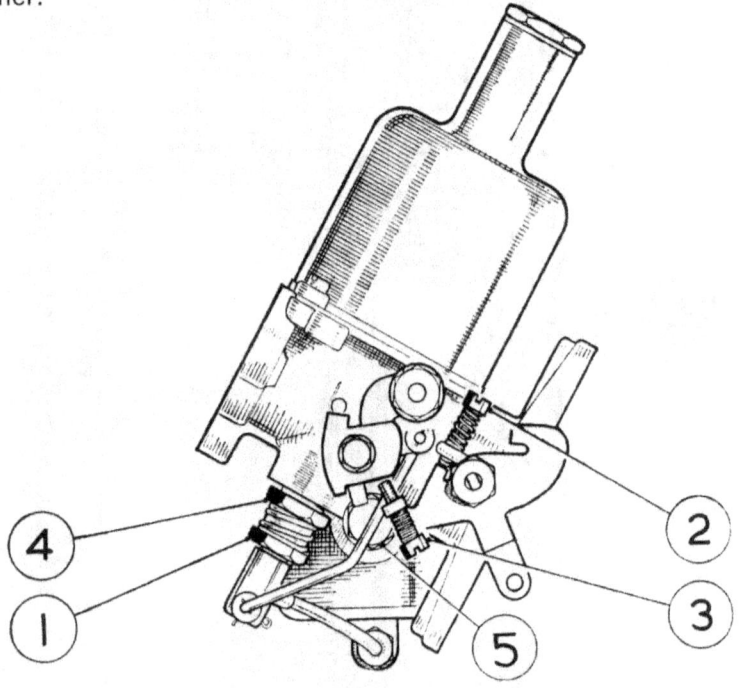

1. Jet adjusting nut.
2. Throttle adjusting screw.
3. Fast-idle adjustment screw.
4. Jet locking nut.
5. Float-chamber bolt.

Unscrew the throttle adjusting screws and screw these back until they will just hold a thin strip of paper between the end of the screw and the fixed stop web on the butterfly arm when the throttle disc is fully shut; then screw them in one complete turn.

The engine may now be started and left running until thoroughly warmed up, when it may be found necessary to readjust the throttle adjusting screws by equal amounts in either direction according to whether a higher or lower speed is required. To check for exact matching of the throttle openings it is best to listen to the air intake hiss, after first removing the air cleaners. This is most easily done by holding one end of a piece of rubber tubing against the ear and the other end against the intake of each carburetor in turn, when the intensity of the intake hiss can be gauged. The larger the throttle opening, the more intense is the intake hiss, and with this as a guide the necessary adjustments for matching can readily be made after a little experience.

Also, see "Using the Unisyn" above.

Adjusting the jets

When the degree of throttle opening has been dealt with, slacken the pinch-bolt on one of the coupling levers on the interconnecting shaft and adjust the mixture strength by moving both jet adjusting nuts the same amount. Move upwards for weakening or downwards for enriching until a satisfactory engine beat has been found which should give **the fastest idling speed consistent with even firing.**

When this has been found it may be necessary to lower the idling speed by slackening off slightly both throttle adjusting screws an equal amount.

Note that a weak idling mixture gives a 'splashy', irregular type of misfire, with a colourless exhaust, whilst a rich idling mixture gives a 'ryhthmical' or regular misfire, with a blackish exhaust.

When the mixture strength is correct on both carburetors lifting the piston by the special piston lifting pin on the side of the body casting will give uneven firing from excessive weakness on that particular carburetor.

If lifting this piston of one carburetor stops the engine and lifting that of the other does not, this indicates that the mixture on the first is set weaker than that on the second, and therefore the mixture strength on the first one should be enriched by unscrewing the jet adjusting nut one or two flats of the hexagon.

There is one occasion when the above check does not give a correct indication, and that is the rare condition when the throttle on one carburetor is set open a generous amount coupled with a weak setting of the jet adjusting nut, and the second is set the opposite way, with a rich setting of the jet adjusting nut coupled with a slight throttle opening. The overall effect will probably give a fair idling performance for the complete unit; but lifting the piston on the second carburetor will stop the engine although it is actually running rich — thus contradicting the original instruction. Also, lifting the piston on the first carburetor will not stop the engine although it is actually running weak; the lifting of the piston in this case only slightly weakens off an already markedly weak mixture and is not enough to stall the engine.

The obvious cure for such a combination of extremes is to make sure firstly (possibly by using the simple rubber stethoscope already described) that both throttles are open the same amount for idling, giving approximately the same suction on each jet.

Make sure that the jets are hard up against the bottom face of the adjusting nuts after any movement of the latter; also check the same point when reconnecting the link shaft between the jet units.

Although it is advisable, before the actual start of the tuning operation, to check that the jet adjusting nuts are all screwed the same amount downwards from the top-most position, later, when a satisfactory setting for each nut has been found giving a correct slow run, it may be that this finalized position is not exactly similar for each nut — that is, one may be two turns down and another two and a half turns down.

This apparent discrepancy is well within normal variation, and even on new carburetors may be as much as one full turn, depending on such factors as exactly similar positioning of each jet needle in the piston, etc. On worn units, where there is also the influencing factor of unequal wear on individual parts, then the variation in jet nut position may be greater, and up to two full turns down.

The throttle couping lever pinch-bolt may now be tightened, taking care to see that light pressure is put on the head of each throttle stop screw and setting the throttle opening delaying mechanism as the bolt is tightened.

Setting the throttle opening delaying mechanism

To ensure smooth acceleration when initially opening the throttle the linkage between the throttle spindles is designed to delay slightly the opening of the front carburetor throttle. This delaying mechanism is incorporated in the throttle spindle connecting rod rear coupling levers.

Connection between the two levers is made by a pin secured to the front lever operating in a hole drilled in the rear lever slightly larger in diameter than the pin, and it is this difference in diameter which allows a limited amount of free movement between the two levers to delay the opening of the front throttle.

To set this mechanism, slacken the front lever pinch-bolt and push the pin end of the lever towards the engine until the pin is just bearing against the engine side of the hole in the rear lever. Hold the levers in this position and tighten the pinch-bolt, ensuring that both throttle stop screws are bearing on the stop webs of the butterfly levers.

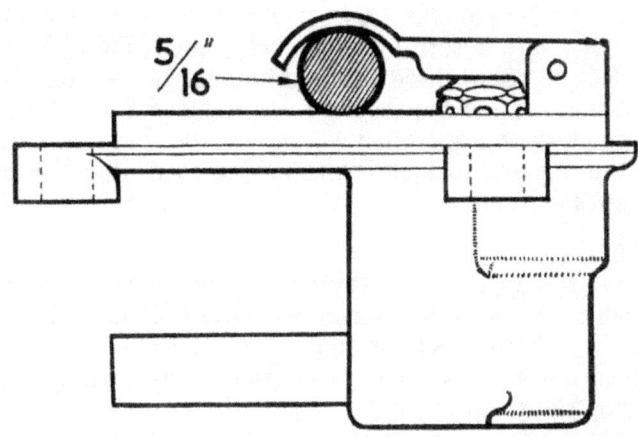

Float-chambers

The position of the float lever in the float-chamber must be such that the level of the float (and therefore the height of the fuel at the jet) is correct.

This is checked by inserting a 5/16 in. (7.94 mm.) round bar between the float lever and the machined lip of the float-chamber lid. The forked end of the lever should just rest on the bar when the needle is on its seating. If this is not so, the lever should be reset at the point where the forked end meets the shank.

Do not bend the shank, which must be perfectly flat and at right angles to the needle when it is on its seat.

Centering the jet

When the suction piston is lifted by the spring-loaded piston lifting pin it should fall freely and hit the inside jet bridge with a soft, metallic click — that is, with the jet adjusting nut (2) in its topmost position.

If this click is not audible, but is so when the test is repeated with the jet in the fully lowered position, then the jet unit requires recentering on the needle, as described below.

Disconnect the rod between the jet lever and the jet head.

Unscrew the union holding the nylon feed tube into the base of the float-chamber, and withdraw the tube and jet together. Unscrew the jet adjusting nut and remove the lock spring. Replace the adjusting nut and screw it right up to its topmost position, then replace the jet and feed tube.

Slacken off the large jet locking screw (1) until the jet bearing is just free to rotate by finger pressure.

With the damper removed and using a pencil on top of the piston rod, gently press the piston and needle down onto the jet bridge.

Tighten the jet locking screw, observing that the jet head is still in its correct angular position.

Lift the piston and check that it falls freely and evenly, hitting the jet bridge with a soft, metallic click. Then fully lower the jet and re-check to see if there is any difference in the sound of the impact; if there is and the second test produces a sharper impact sound, the centering operation will have to be repeated until successful, the nut and lock spring being replaced after the conclusion of the operation.

Removing

Remove the air cleaners. Disconnect the mixture and throttle control cables, the vacuum advance pipe, and the fuel delivery hose from their respective positions on the carburetors.

Release the interconnecting coupling tension springs and the throttle stop return spring.

Remove the nuts and spring washers securing the carburetors to the manifold flanges. Lift off the assemblies as one unit. The interconnecting couplings are fitted in sleeved nuts, and when the assemblies are removed the couplings can be lifted away from both carburetors.

It should be noted that the heat shield fitted between the carburetors and the manifold flanges has gaskets, which should be renewed if the shield has been removed.

Refitting

Reverse the removal procedure when refitting.

AIR CLEANERS

Removing

Remove the center-securing nut and washer on the tie bracket.

Remove the through-bolts and lift away the air cleaners from the carburetor assemblies.

NOTE: Servicing of the paper-element-type air cleaners should be carried out every 12,000 miles (19200 km.), at which stage a new element should be fitted.

In countries where dusty operating conditions exist this operation should be carried out at more frequent intervals.

Do not disturb the air cleaner covers or remove the elements at any other time.

Refitting

Refitting is a reversal of the removal procedure

FAULT DIAGNOSIS

Symptom	No.	Possible Fault
(a) Leakage or insufficient fuel delivery	1 2 3 4 5 6 7 8	Air vent restricted. Lines restricted or partially clogged. Air leakage at pipe connections. Fuel pump or carburetor filter gauze clogged. Fuel pump gasket damaged. Fuel pump diaphragm damaged. Fuel pump valves sticking or seating improperly. Fuel vaporizing in line.
(b) Excessive fuel consumption	1 2 3 4 5 6 7 8 9	Carburetor out of adjustment. Fuel leakage. Carburetor controls sticking. Air cleaners dirty. Excessive engine temperature. Brakes dragging. Under-inflated tyres. Excessive idling. Vehicle overloaded.
(c) Fast idling	1 2 3	Rich fuel mixture. Carburetter controls sticking. Slow-running screws incorrectly adjusted.
(d) Fuel pump noise	1 2 3 4	Pump mountings loose. Air leak on suction side. Obstruction in line. Filter obstructed.
(e) Air leak on suction side of pump	1 2 3	Suction pipes, pump inlet or pump filter unions loose. Insufficient fuel in the tank. Faulty pipe.

ELECTRICAL SYSTEM

The 12-volt electrical equipment incorporates compensated voltage control for the charging circuit. The positive earth system of wiring is employed.

Battery details may be found in 'General Data'.

The generator is mounted on the right of the cylinder block and driven by an endless belt from the crankshaft pulley. A rotatable mounting enables the bolt tension to be adjusted.

The voltage control unit adjustment is sealed and should not normally require attention. The fuses are carried in external holders mounted in an accessible position on the right-hand side of the engine compartment together with spare fuses.

The starter motor is mounted on the flywheel housing on the right-hand side of the engine unit and operates on the flywheel through the usual sliding pinion device.

BATTERY

The battery is a 12-volt lead-acid type, having six cells, each cell consisting of a group of positive and negative plates immersed in a solution of sulphuric acid (electrolyte).

The battery has three functions:

(1) To supply current for starting, ignition and lighting.
(2) To provide a constant supply of current to the electrical equipment under normal operating conditions and when the consumption of the electrical equipment exceeds the output of the generator.
(3) To control the voltage of the electrical supply system.

The purpose of the following operations is to maintain the performance of the battery at its maximum:

(1) The battery and its surrounding parts should be kept dry and clean, particularly the tops of the cells as any dampness could cause a leakage between the securing strap and the battery negative terminal, resulting in a partially discharged battery. Clean off any corrosion from the battery bolts, strap and tray with diluted ammonia, afterwards painting the affected parts with antisulphuric paint.
(2) Remove the vent plugs and check they are not perished or cracked, otherwise leakage of electrolyte will occur. Clean out the vent holes if necessary with a piece of wire.
(3) The electrolyte levels should be maintained just above the tops of the separators by adding distilled water. Never add acid.
(4) Check the terminal posts. If they are corroded remove the cables and clean with diluted ammonia. Smear the posts with petroleum jelly before remaking the connections and ensure that the cable terminal clamp screws are secure.

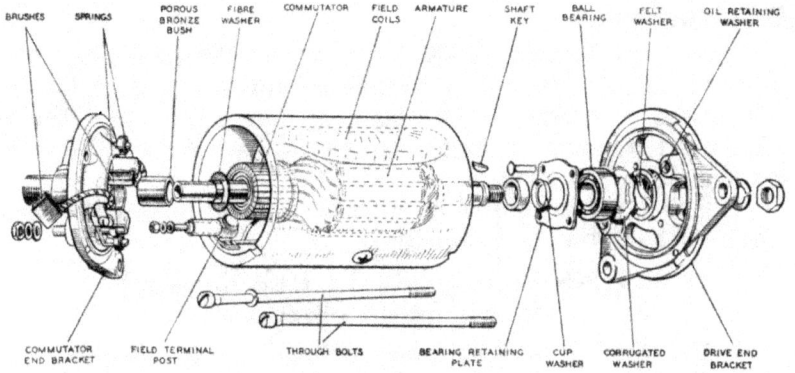

GENERATOR

The generator is a shunt wound two-pole, two-brush machine, arranged to work in conjunction with a compensated voltage control regulator unit. A fan integral with the driving pulley draws cooling air through the generator, inlet and outlet holes being provided in the end brackets of the unit.

The output of the generator is controlled by the regulator and is dependent on the state of charge of the battery and the loading of the electrical equipment in use. When the battery is in a low state of charge the generator gives a high output, whereas if the battery is fully charged, the generator gives only sufficient output to keep the battery in good condition without any possibility of overcharging. In addition an increase in output is given to balance the current taken by lamps and other accessories when in use. Further, a high boosting charge is given for a few minutes immediately after starting up, thus quickly restoring to the battery the energy taken from it by the electric starting motor.

MAINTENANCE

Lubrication

Every 12,000 miles (19200 km.) unscrew the cap of the lubricator on the side of the bearing housing, lift out the felt pad and spring and about half-fill the lubricator cap with high melting point grease. Replace the spring and felt pad and screw the lubricator cap back into position.

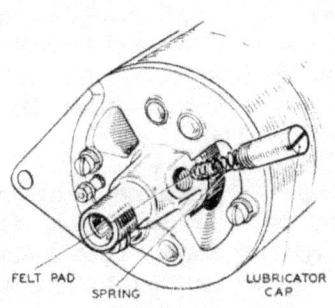

Belt Adjustment

Every 3,000 miles (4800 km.) inspect the generator drive belt and adjust if necessary to take up any undue slackness by turning the generator on its mounting. Care should be taken to avoid overtightening the belt which should have sufficient tension to drive without slipping.

See that the generator is properly aligned, otherwise undue strain will be thrown on the bearings.

TESTING IN POSITION TO LOCATE FAULT IN CHARGING CIRCUIT

In the event of a fault in the charging circuit, adopt the following procedure to locate the cause of the trouble:

(1) Inspect the driving belt and adjust if necessary.
(2) Check that the generator and control box are connected correctly. The larger generator terminal must be connected to the control box 'D' terminal, and the smaller generator terminal to control box 'F' terminal. Check the control box terminal 'E' and associated earthing cable for tightness.
(3) Switch off all lights and accessories, disconnect the cables from the generator terminals and connect the two terminals with a short length of wire.
(4) Start the engine and set to run at normal idling speed.
(5) Clip the negative lead of a moving coil voltmeter, calibrated 0 to 20 volts, to one generator terminal, and the other lead to a good earthing point on the yoke.
(6) Gradually increase the engine speed, when the voltmeter reading should rise rapidly without fluctuation. Do not allow the voltmeter reading to reach 20 volts, and do not race the engine in an attempt to increase the voltage. It is sufficient to run the generator up to a speed of 1,000 r.p.m. If there is no reading check the brushgear as described below.

If there is a low reading of approximately. $\frac{1}{2}$ to 1 volt, the field winding may be at fault (see 'Field Coils'). If there is a reading of 4 to 5 volts, the armature winding may be at fault (see 'Armature').

(7) If the generator is in good order, leave the link between the terminals in position and restore the original connections, taking care to connect the larger generator terminal to control box terminal 'D', and the smaller terminal to control box 'F'.
(8) Remove the lead from the (D) terminal on the control box and connect the voltmeter between this cable and a good earthing point on the vehicle. Run the engine as before. The reading should be the same as that measured directly at the generator. No reading on the volt-

meter indicates a break in the cable to the generator. Carry out the same procedure for the (F) terminal, connecting the voltmeter between cable and earth. Finally remove the link from the generator. If the reading is correct test the control box.

GENERATOR ASSEMBLY

To Remove

(1) Disconnect the two leads to the generator.
(2) Disconnect the high tension lead and the two low tension leads to the coil.
(3) Slacken the nut securing the sliding link and the two hinge bolts holding the generator to the crankcase and water pump.
(4) Push the generator downwards to slacken the fan belt so that the latter can then be removed.
(5) Remove the set pin from the upper end of the sliding link, and take out the two generator hinge bolts, and lift the generator clear of the engine.
(6) Unscrew the nut securing the coil to its bracket on the generator and remove the coil.

To Dismantle

(1) Take off the driving pulley.
(2) Remove the nut, spring washer and flat washer from the smaller terminal (i.e. field terminal).
(3) Unscrew the two through bolts at the commutator end and remove the bracket from the generator yoke. The driving end bracket together with the armature can now be removed from the generator yoke.
(4) The driving end bracket need not be separated from the shaft unless the bearing is suspect and requires examination, or the armature is to be replaced, in this event the armature should be removed from the end bracket by means of a hand press.

INSPECTION AND OVERHAUL

Brushgear

Lift the brushes up into the brush boxes and secure them in position by positioning the brush spring at the side of the brush. Fit the commutator end bracket over the commutator and release the brushes. Hold back each of the brush springs and move the brush by pulling gently on its flexible connector. If the movement is sluggish, remove the brush from its holder and ease the sides by lightly polishing it on a smooth file. Always refit the brushes in their original positions. If the brushes are badly worn, new brushes must be fitted and bedded to the commutator. The minimum permissible length of brush is 11/32 in.

Test the brush spring tension using a spring scale. The tension of the springs when new is 22 to 25 oz. In service it is permissible for this value to fall to 15 oz. before performance may be affected. Fit new springs if the tension is low.

Commutator

A commutator in good condition will be smooth and free from pits or burnt spots. Clean the commutator with a solvent-moistened cloth. If this is ineffective carefully polish with a strip of fine emery paper while rotating the armature.

To remedy a badly worn commutator mount the armature, with or without the drive end bracket, in a lathe, rotate at high speed, then take a light cut with a very sharp tool. Do not remove more metal than is necessary. Polish the commutator with very fine emery paper. Undercut the insulators between the segments to a depth of 1/32 in. (.8 mm.) with a hacksaw blade ground to the thickness of the insulator.

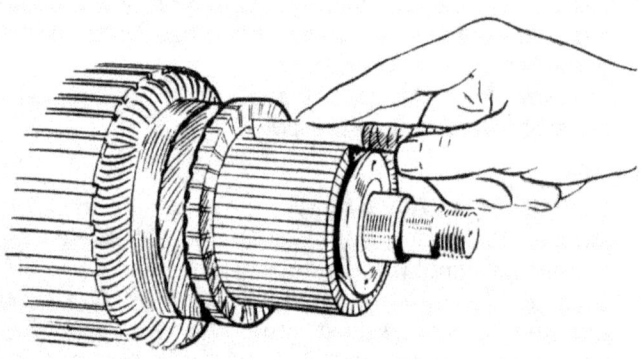

The most common armature faults are usually confined to open- or short-circuited windings. Indications of an open-circuited armature winding is given by burnt commutator segments. A short-circuited armature winding is easily identified by discolouration of the overheated windings and badly burnt commutator segments.

If armature testing facilities are not available, an armature can be tested by substitution.

Field Coils

Measure the resistance of the field coils, without removing them from the generator yoke, by means of an ohmmeter connected between the field terminal and the yoke.

The ohmmeter should read 6 ohms approximately.

If an ohmmeter is not available connect a 12-volt D.C. supply with an ammeter in series between the field terminal and generator yoke. The ammeter reading should be approximately 2 amperes. Zero on the ammeter or 'Infinity' ohmmeter reading indicates an open-circuit in the field winding.

If the current reading is much more than 2 amperes or the ohmmeter reading much below 6 ohms it is an indication that the insulation of one of the field coils has broken down.

ASSEMBLING AND REPLACING

In the main the reassembly of the generator is a reversal of the dismantling procedure. Before refitting the generator, however, inject S.A.E. 30 oil into the commutator end bracket as previously described. The replacement is the reverse of the procedure 'To Remove'. Check the fan belt adjustment.

THE STARTER

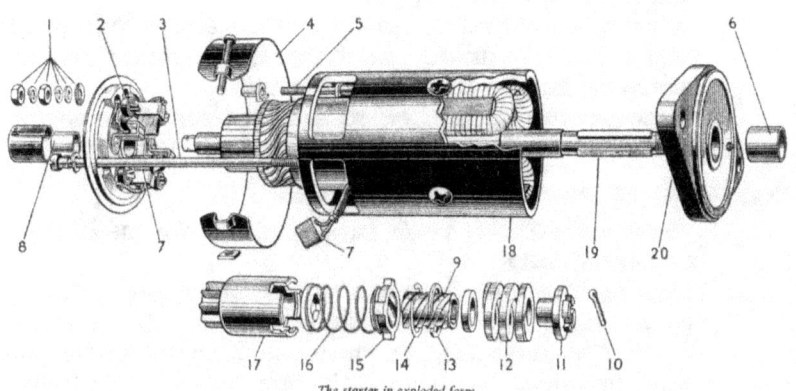

The starter in exploded form.

1. Terminal nuts and washers.	8. Bearing bush.	15. Control nut.
2. Brush spring.	9. Sleeve.	16. Restraining spring.
3. Through bolt.	10. Split pin.	17. Pinion and barrel.
4. Cover band.	11. Shaft nut.	18. Yoke.
5. Terminal post.	12. Main spring.	19. Armature shaft.
6. Bearing bush.	13. *Retaining ring.*	20. Driving end bracket.
7. Brushes.	14. Corrugated washer.	

Testing on the Vehicle

In the following test it is assumed that the battery is in a charged condition:

(1) Switch on the lamps and operate the starter control. If the lights go dim, but the starter is not heard to operate, an indication is given that the current is flowing through the starter motor windings but that for some reason the armature is not rotating; possibly the starter pinion is meshed permanently with the geared ring on the flywheel. This could be caused by the starter being operated while the engine is still moving. In this case, the starter motor must be removed from the engine for examination.

(2) Should the lamps retain their full brilliance when the starter switch is operated, check that the switch is functioning. Next if the switch is in order, examine the connections at the battery, starter switch, and also examine the wiring joining these units. Continued failure of the starter to operate indicates an internal fault in the starter, which must be removed for examination.

Sluggish or slow action of the starter is usually caused by a poor connection in the wiring which causes a high resistance in the starter circuit. Check the wiring as described above.

SERVICING THE STARTER

To Remove and Replace
(1) Remove the distributor.
(2) Release the starter cable from the terminal and unscrew the top starter securing bolt.
(3) Working beneath the vehicle release and withdraw the dirt deflector situated under the starter motor and unscrew the bottom starter securing bolt.
(4) Maneuver the starter forward and lift clear of the engine.
(5) Installation is the reversal of the removal procedure.

Examination of Commutator and Brush Gear
(1) Remove the starter cover band and examine the brushes and commutator.
(2) Hold back each of the brush springs and move the brush by pulling gently on its flexible connector. If the movement is sluggish remove the brush from its holder and ease the sides by lightly polishing with a smooth file. Always replace brushes in their original positions. If the brushes are worn so they no longer bear on the commutator, or if the brush flexible lead has become exposed on the running face, they must be renewed.
(3) If the commutator is blackened or dirty, clean it by holding a solvent-moistened cloth against it while the armature is rotated.
(4) Secure the body of the starter in a vice and test by connecting it with heavy-gauge cables to a 12-volt battery. One cable must be connected to the starter terminal the other held against the starter body or end bracket. Under these light load conditions the starter should run at a very high speed.

If the operation of the starter is still unsatisfactory, it should be dismantled for detail inspection and testing.

To Dismantle
(1) Take off the cover band at the commutator end, hold back the brush springs and take out the brushes.
(2) Extract the split pin at the driving end.
(3) Unscrew the nut (R.H. thread) and take off the main spring. The complete drive can now be removed from the splined shaft by withdrawing it with a rotary movement.
(4) Remove the terminal nuts and washers from the terminal post on the commutator end bracket. Unscrew and withdraw the two through-bolts and take off the commutator

end bracket.

(5) Remove the driving end bracket complete with armature end bracket.

Brushes

(1) Test the brush springs with a spring balance. The Correct tension is 25 to 15 ozs. (.7087 to .4252 kg.). Fit a new spring if the tension is low.

(2) If the brushes are worn so that they no longer bear on the commutator, or if the flexible connector has become exposed on the running face, they must be renewed. Two of the brushes are connected to terminal eyelets attached to the brush boxes on the commutator end bracket. The other two brushes are connected to tappings on the field coils.

The flexible connectors must be removed by unsoldering and the connectors of the new brushes secured in their place by soldering. The brushes are pre-formed so that bedding of the working face to the commutator is unnecessary.

Drive

(1) If the pinion is tight on the screwed sleeve, wash away any dirt with paraffin (kerosene).

(2) If any parts are worn or damaged they must be replaced.

(3) Unscrew the nut (R.H. thread) and take off the main spring.

(4) The complete drive can now be removed for the splined shaft by pulling it off with a rotary movement. Unscrew the screwed sleeve from the barrel assembly.

(5) Further dismantling of the barrel assembly is carried out by removing the large retaining ring.
Note: If the screwed sleeve is worn or damaged it is essential that it is replaced together with the control nut. Reassemble by reversing the above procedure.

Commutator

A commutator in good condition will be smooth and free from pits and burnt spots. Clean the commutator with a cloth moistened with petrol (gasoline). If this is ineffective, carefully polish with a strip of fine emery paper while rotating the armature. To remedy a badly worn commutator, dismantle the starter drive as described above and remove the armature from the end bracket. Now mount the armature in a lathe, rotate it at high speed and take a light cut with a very sharp tool. Do not remove any more metal than is absolutely necessary, and finally polish with very fine emery-paper.

The mica on the starter commutator **must not be undercut.**

Field Coils

The field coils can be tested for an open circuit by connecting a 12-volt battery having a 12-volt bulb in one of the leads to the tapping point of the field coils to which the brushes are connected and the field terminal post. If the bulb does not light there is an open circuit in the wiring of the field coils.

Lighting of the bulb does not necessarily mean that the field coils are in order, as it is possible that one of them may be earthed to a pole shoe on to the yoke. This may be checked by removing the lead from the brush connector and holding it on a clean part of the starter yoke. Should the bulb now light it indicates that the field coils are earthed.

Should the above tests indicate that the fault lies in the field coils they must be renewed.

Armature

Examination of the armature will in many cases reveal the cause of failure, e.g. conductors lifted from the commutator due to the starter being engaged while the engine is running and causing the armature to be rotated at an excessive speed. A damaged armature must in all cases be renewed — no attempt should be made to machine the armature core or to true a distorted armature shaft.

Bearings (Commutator End)

Bearings which are worn to such an extent that they will allow excessive sideplay of the armature shaft must be renewed. To renew the bearing bush proceed as follows:

Press the new bearing bush into the end bracket, using a shouldered mandrel of the same diameter as the shaft which is to fit into the bearing.

Note: The bearing bush is of the porous phosphor-bronze type, and before fitting, new bushes should be allowed to stand completely imemrsed for twenty-four hours in thin engine oil in order to fill the pores of the bush with lubricant.

Reassembly

The reassembly of the starter is a reversal of the operations described in this section.

THE CONTROL BOX

This unit contains the cut-out and voltage regulator.

The regulator controls the generator output in accordance with the load on the battery and its state of charge. When the battery is discharged, the generator gives a high output, so that the battery receives a quick recharge which brings it back to its normal state in the minimum time.

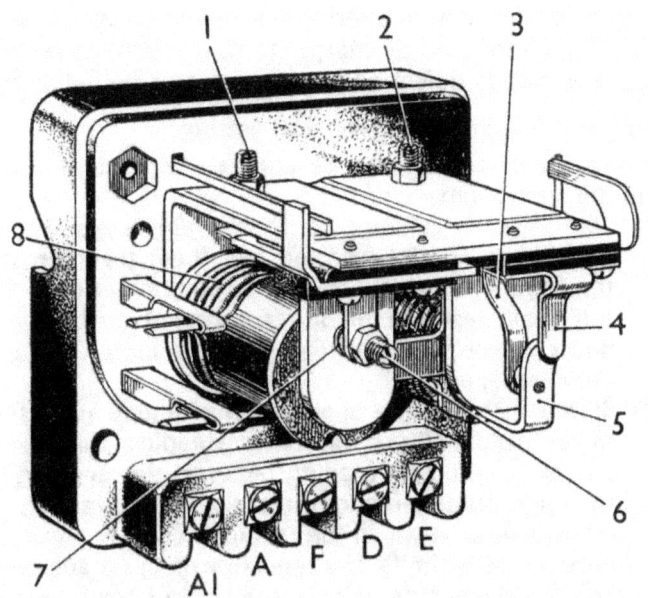

1. *Regulator adjusting screw.*
2. *Cut-out adjusting screw.*
3. *Fixed contact blade.*
4. *Stop arm.*
5. *Armature tongue and moving contact.*
6. *Regulator moving contact.*
7. *Fixed contact.*
8. *Regulator series windings.*

On the other hand, if the battery is fully charged the generator is arranged to give only a trickle charge, which is sufficient to keep it in good condition without any possibility of causing damage to the battery by overcharging.

The regulator also causes the generator to give a controlled boosting charge immediately after starting up, which quickly restores to the battery the energy taken from it when starting. After about 30 minutes running, the output of the generator has fallen to a steady rate best suited to the particular state of charge of the battery.

The cut-out is an automatic switch for connecting and disconnecting the battery with the generator. This is necessary because the battery would otherwise discharge through the generator when the engine is stopped or running at a low speed.

Regulator Adjustment

The regulator is carefully set before leaving the works to suit the normal requirements of the standard equipment, and in general it should not be necessary to alter it. If, however, the battery does not keep in a charged condition, or if the generator output does not fall when the battery is fully charged, it may be advisable to check the setting and if necessary to readjust.

It is important, before altering the regulator setting when the battery is in a low state of charge, to check that its condition is not due to a battery defect or to the generator belt slipping.

Checking and Adjusting the Electrical Setting

The regulator setting can be checked without removing the cover of the control box.

(1) Withdraw the cables from the terminals marked 'A' and 'A1' at the control box and join them together. Connect the negative lead of a moving coil voltmeter (0 to 20 volts full scale reading) to be 'D' terminal on the generator and connect the other lead from the meter to a convenient chassis earth.

(2) Slowly increase the speed of the engine until the voltmeter needle 'flicks' and then steadies; this should occur at a voltmeter reading between the limits given for the appropriate temperature of the regulator.

If the voltage at which the reading becomes steady occurs outside these limits, the regulator must be adjusted.

(3) Shut off the engine, remove the control box cover, release the locknut (1) (see photo), holding the adjusting screw (2) and turn the screw in a clockwise direction to raise the setting or in an anti-clockwise direction to lower the setting. Turn the adjustment screw a fraction of a turn and then tighten the locknut.

When adjusting, do not run the engine up to more than half throttle because, while the generator is an open circuit, it will build up to a high voltage if run at a high speed and in consequence a false voltmeter reading would be obtained.

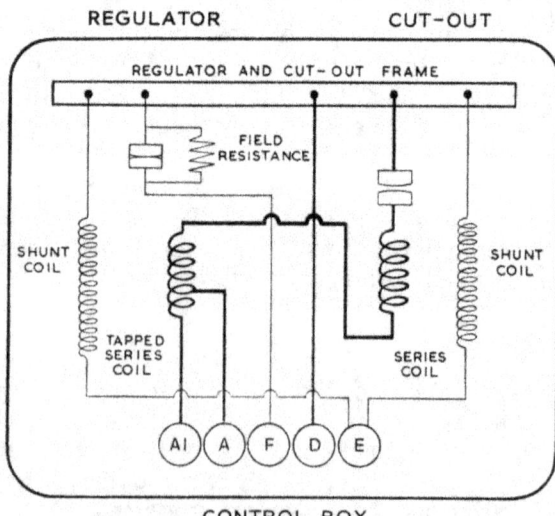

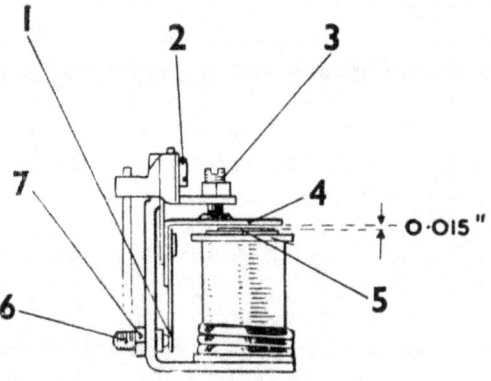

1. *Armature tension spring*
2. *Armature securing screws.*
3. *Fixed contact adjustment screw.*
4. *Armature.*
5. *Core face and shim.*
6. *Voltage adjusting screw.*
7. *Locknut.*

Mechanical Setting

The mechanical settings of the regulator are accurately adjusted before leaving the factory and provided that the armature carrying the moving contact is not removed these settings should not be tampered with. If however, the armature has been removed, the regulator will have to be reset. To do this proceed as follows:

(1) Slacken the fixed contact locking nut and unscrew the contact until it is well clear of the armature moving contact. Slacken the two armature assembly securing screws. Slacken the voltage adjusting screw locking nut and unscrew the adjuster until it is well clear of the armature tension spring. Slacken the two armature assembly securing screws.

(2) Insert a .015 in. (.381 mm.) feeler gauge between the armature and core shim. Take care not to turn up or damage the edge of the shim. Press the armature squarely down against the gauge and re-tighten the two armature assembly securing screws.

(3) With the gauge still in position, screw the adjustable contact down until it just touches the armature contact. Tighten the locknut and remove the feeler gauge. Reset the voltage adjusting screw as described under 'Electrical Setting'.

Cleaning Regulator Contacts

After periods of long service it may be found necessary to clean the regulator contacts. Fine carborundum stone or fine emery cloth may be used. Carefully wipe away all traces of dust or other foreign matter, using a clean fluffless cloth moistened with alcohol.

Cut-Out Electrical Setting

If the regulator is correctly set but the battery is still not being charged, the cut-out may be out of adjustment. To check the voltage at which the cut-out operates remove the control box cover and connect the voltmeter between the terminals 'D' and 'E'. Start the engine and slowly increase its speed until the cut-out contacts are seen to close, noting the voltage at which this occurs. This should be 12.7 to 13.3 volts.

If operation of the cut-out takes place outside these limits, it will be necessary to adjust. To do this, slacken the locknut of (2), (see photo), securing the cut-out adjusting screw and turn the screw in a clockwise direction to raise the voltage setting, or in an anti-clockwise direction to reduce the setting. Turn the screw a fraction at a time and then tighten the locknut. Test after each adjustment by increasing the engine speed and noting the voltmeter readings at the instant of contact closure. Electrical settings of the cut-out, like the regulator, must be made as quickly as possible because of temperature rise effects. Tighten the locknut after making the adjustment.

Adjustment of the drop-off voltage is effected by carefully bending the fixed contact blade. If the cut-out does not operate there may be an open circuit in the wiring of the cut-out and regulator unit, in which case the unit should be removed for examination or renewal.

Cut-out Mechanical Setting

If for any reason the cut-out armature has to be removed from the frame, care must be taken to obtain the correct air gap settings on reassembly. These can be obtained as follows:

(1) Slacken the adjusting screw locking nut and unscrew the adjusting screw until it is **well clear** of the armature tension spring. Slacken the **two armature** assembly securing screws.

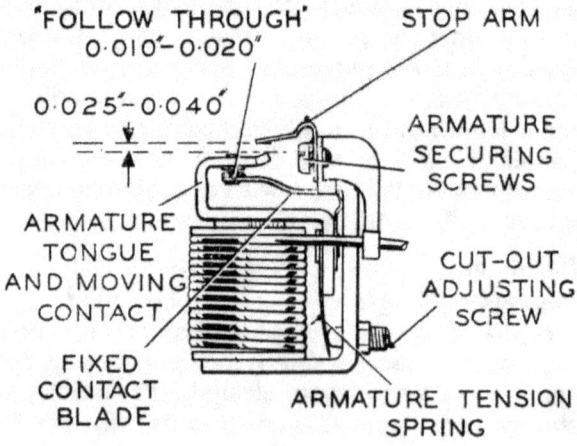

(2) Press the armature firmly down against the copper sprayed core face and re-tighten the two armature assembly securing screws.

(3) Using a pair of round-nosed pliers, adjust the gap between the armature stop-arm and armature tongue by bending the stop-arm. The gap must be .025 to .040 in. (.635 to 1.016 mm.) when the armature is pressed squarely down on the core face.

(4) Similarly the insulated contact blade must be bent so that when the armature is pressed squarely down against the core face there is a 'follow through' or contact deflection of .010 to .020 in. (.254 to .508 mm.). Reset the cut-out adjusting screw as described under 'Cut-out Electrical Setting'.

Cleaning Cut-out Contacts

If the contacts appear rough or burnt place a strip of fine glass paper between, and with them closed by hand draw the paper through. This should be done two or three times with the rough side towards each contact. Wipe away all dust or other foreign matter, using a clean fluffless cloth moistened with alcohol.

FUSE UNIT

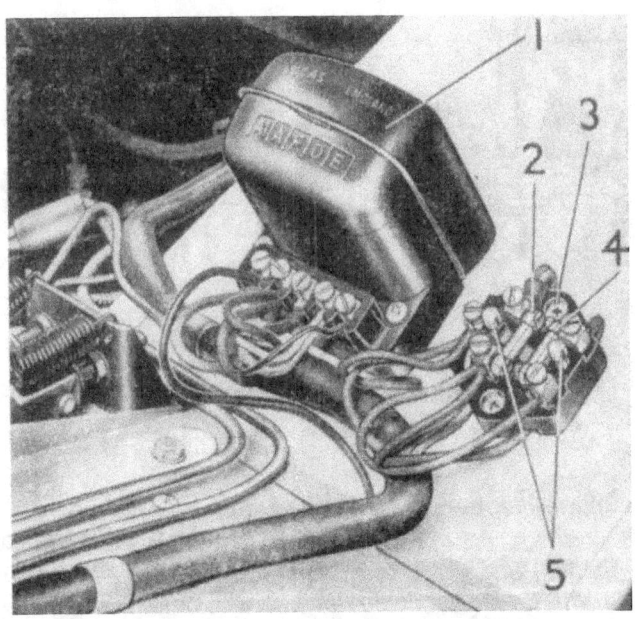

1. *Control box.*
2. *Auxiliary ignition fuse* (35 **amps.**)
3. *Fuse unit.*
4. *Auxiliary fuse* (50 *amps.*)
5. *Spare fuses.*

The fuse unit which is located on the right-hand side of the engine compartment, is an open insulated moulding carrying two single-pole 35-amp. cartridge-type fuses which are held in spring clips between the grub-screw-type terminal blocks. Two spare fuses are carried in recesses in the fuse unit box and are positioned by retaining springs. The fuse which bridges the terminal blocks (A1—A2) is to protect general auxiliary circuits, e.g. the horn which is independent of the ignition switch. The other fuse, bridging terminal blocks (A3—A4) is to protect the ignition and auxiliary circuits, e.g. the fuel gauge, windscreen wiper motor and flasher indicators which only operate when the ignition is switched on.

THE FLASHER UNIT

The Lucas flasher unit is situated in the engine compartment on the right-hand side, and is operated by a switch centrally mounted on the facia panel, a warning light being provided on the right side of the facia.

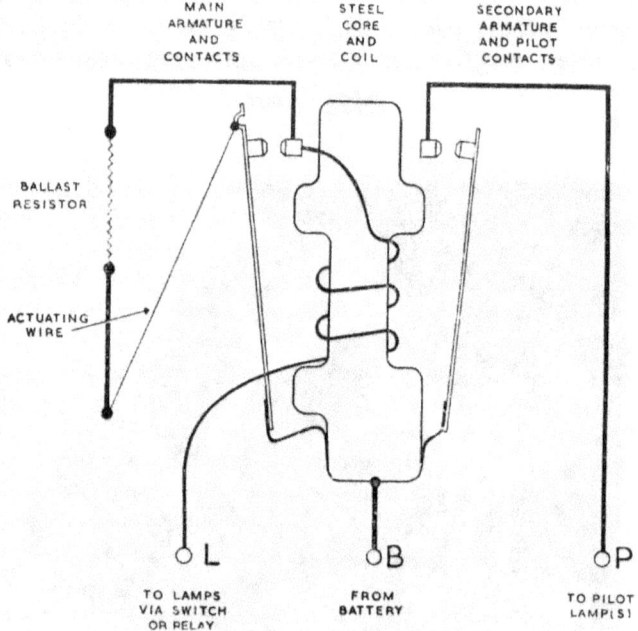

The unit is contained in a small cylindrical metal container, one end of which is rolled over on to an insulated plate carrying the mechanism and three terminals. The unit depends for its operation on the linear expansion of a length of wire which becomes heated by an electric current flowing through it. This actuating wire controls the movement of a spring loaded armature attached to a central steel core and carrying a moving contact — the sequence of operation being as follows:

When the direction-indicator switch is turned either to the left or right, current flows through the actuating wire, ballast resistor and coil wound on the central core and hence to earth via the flasher lamp filaments. This current is limited by the ballast resistor to a valve which will ensure that the flasher lamp filaments do not light at this stage. The actuating wire grows in length under the heating influence of the current and allows the armature to move inwards to its alternative position, thereby closing a pair of contacts in the supply circuit to the flasher lamps, and at the same time, short circuiting the actuating wire. The increased electro-magnetic attraction of the armature to the core, due to the full lamp current now flowing through the coils, serves to hold the closed contacts firmly together. At the same time a secondary spring loaded armature is attracted to the core and closes a pilot warning lamp circuit so that now both flasher lamps and warning lamp are illuminated.

Since, however, heating current no longer flows through the short-circuited actuating wire, the latter cools and consequently contracts in length. The main armature is therefore pulled away from the core, the contacts opened and the light signals extinguished. The consequent reduction of electro-magnetism in the core allows the secondary armature to return to its original position and so extinguish the pilot warning light. The above sequence of operations continues to be repeated until the indicator switch is returned to the off position. A symbolic representation of the flasher unit is shown in Fig. M. 20.

Functions of Warning Lamp

The warning lamp not only serves to indicate that the flasher unit is functioning correctly but also gives a warning of any bulb failure occurring in the external direction-indicator lamps — since a reduction in bulb current flowing through the coil reduces the electro-magnetic effect acting on the secondary armature and so prevents closure of the pilot light contacts.

Checking Faulty Operation

In the event of trouble occurring with a flashing light direction-indicator system, the following procedure should be followed:
(1) Check the bulbs for broken filaments.
(2) Refer to the vehicle wiring diagram and check all flasher circuit connections.
(3) Switch on the ignition.
(4) Check with the voltmeter that the flasher unit terminal 'B' is a battery voltage with respect to earth.
(5) Connect together flasher unit terminals 'B' (or 'X') and 'L' and operate the direction-indicator switch. If the flasher lamps now light, the flasher unit is defective and must be replaced.

Maintenance

Flasher units cannot be dismantled for subsequent reassembly. A defective unit must therefore be replaced, care being taken to connect as the original.

Replacement of Flasher Unit

When replacing a flasher unit or installing a flashing light system, it is advisable to test the circuits before connections to flasher terminals are made. When testing join the cables normally connected to those terminals (green, green with brown, and light green) together and operate the direction indicator switch. In the event of a wrong connection having been made, the ignition auxiliaries fuse will blow but no damage will be done to the flasher unit.

WINDSHIELD WIPERS

Maintenance

(1) Inspection should be made of the rubber wiping elements which after long service become worn and should be renewed.

(2) The rubber grommet or washer around the wheel box spindle should be lubricated with a few drops of glycerine.

(3) De-natured alcohol should be used to remove oil, tar spots and other stains from the glass. It has been founded that the use of some silicone and wax-based polishes for this purpose can be detrimental to the rubber wiping elements.

(4) The gearbox and cable rack are packed with grease during manufacture and need no further lubrication.

Checking Switching Mechanism

If the wiper fails to park or parks unsatisfactorily, the limit switch in the gearbox cover should be checked. Unless the limit switch is correctly set, it is possible for the wiper motor to overrun the open circuit position and continue to draw current.

Resetting the Limit Switch

Slacken the four screws securing the gearbox cover and observe the projection near the rim of the limit switch. Position the projection in line with the groove in the gearbox cover. Turn the limit switch 25° in an anti-clockwise direction and tighten the four securing screws. If the wiping blades are required to park on the opposition of the screen, the limit switch should be turned back 180° in a clockwise direction.

Checking Current Consumption

If the wiper fails to operate, or operates unsatisfactorily, switch on the wiper and note the current being supplied to the motor. The normal running current should be 2.3 to 3.1 amps. Use a 0 to 15 amp. moving coil ammeter connected in the wiper circuit, then proceed as follows:

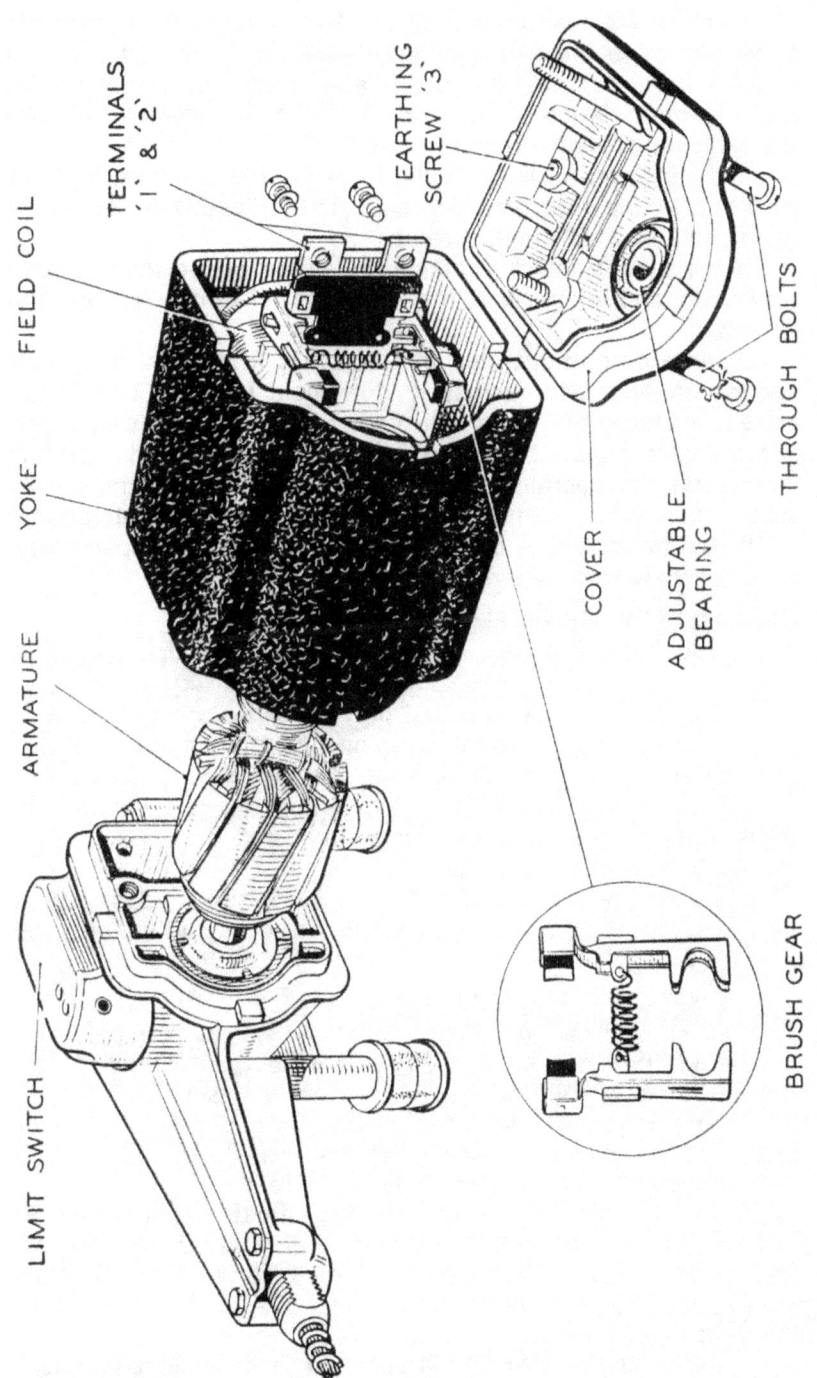

Wiper Takes No Current

Examine the fuse protecting the wiper circuit. If the fuse has blown, examine the wiring of the motor circuit and of all other circuits protected by that fuse. Replace any cables which are badly worn or chafed, if necessary fitting protective sleeving over the cables to prevent a recurrence of the fault.

If the external wiring is found to be in order, replace the fuse with one of the recommended size. Then proceed as for wiper taking an abnormally high current.

If the fuse is intact, examine the wiring of the motor circuit for breaks and ensure that the wiper control switch is operating correctly.

When a current-operated thermostat is fitted, test it by connecting an ohmmeter across its terminals in place of the two cables. If closed circuit is indicated, the thermostat is in order, and the cables must be refitted. An open circuit means that the thermostat has operated but not reset. Check the thermostat by substitution. Adjustment of the thermostat must not be attempted.

If the thermostat is in order, proceed as for the wiper taking an abnormally high current.

Wiper Takes Abnormally Low Current

Check that the battery is fully charged. The performance of the motor is dependent on the condition of the battery.

Remove the commutator end bracket and examine the brush gear, ensuring that it bears firmly on the commutator. The tension spring must be renewed if the brushes do not bear firmly on the commutator. Brush levers must move freely on the pivots. If these levers are stiff they should be freed by working them backwards and forwards by hand.

Examine the commutator and, if necessary, clean with a fuel-moistened cloth. A suspected armature should be checked by substitution.

Wiper Takes Abnormally High Current

If an abnormally high current is shown on the ammeter, this may be due to excessive load on the driving shaft. The stall current of the motor cold is 14 amp., and hot is 8 amp.

If there is no obvious reason for this, such as a sticking wiper blade, a check should be made at the gearbox.

Remove the gearbox cover and examine the gear assembly, checking that a blow on the gearbox end bracket has not reduced the armature end float. The armature end float adjusting screw must be set to give an armature end play of 0.008 in. (.20 mm.) to 0.012 in. (.30 mm.).

Sluggish operation with excessive current consumption may be caused through frictional losses in badly positioned or defective connecting tubes.

Pieces of carbon short-circuiting adjacent segments of the

commutator will also cause excessive current consumption. The resistance between adjacent commutator segments should be 0.34 to 0.41 ohms. Cleaning the commutator and brushgear removes this fault. When dismantling, check the internal wiring of the motor for evidence of short-circuiting due to chafed or charred insulation. Slip a new piece of sleeving over any charred connections, and arrange them so that they do not rub against sharp edges.

While the motor is dismantled check the valve of the field resistance. If it is found to be lower than 12.8 to 14 ohms, a short-circuit in the windings is indicated and a new field coil must be fitted. Other evidence of a short-circuit will be given by charred leads from the field coil.

To Remove the Rack and Motor Unit

Release the wiping arms from the spindles, disconnect the union on the Bundy tube at the gearbox, and remove the nuts from the motor mounting bolts. Withdraw the motor and cable rack clear of the Bundy tube.

To Dismantle the Motor

(1) Withdraw the four screws securing the gearbox cover and remove the cover.
(2) Withdraw the terminal screws and through bolts at the commutator end bracket.
(3) Remove the commutator end bracket clear of the yoke.
(4) The brush gear can be removed by lifting it clear of the commutator and withdrawing it as a unit. Care should be taken at this point to note the particular side occupied by each brush so that each may be replaced in its original setting on the commutator.
(5) Access to the armature and field coils can be gained by withdrawing the yoke.
(6) If it is necessary to remove the field coil, unscrew the two screws securing the pole piece to the yoke. These screws should be marked so that they can be returned to their original holes.
(7) Press out the pole pieces complete with field coil, marking the pole piece so that it can be replaced in its correct position inside the yoke. The pole piece can now be pressed out of the field coil.

To Dismantle the Gearbox Unit

Remove the circlip and washer from the crosshead connecting link pin and lift off the crosshead and cable rack assembly. Then remove the circlip and washer from the final gear shaft located underneath the gearbox unit. Remove any burr from the circlip groove before lifting out the final gear. The armature and worm drive can now be withdrawn from the gearbox. All gear teeth should be examined for signs of damage or wear.

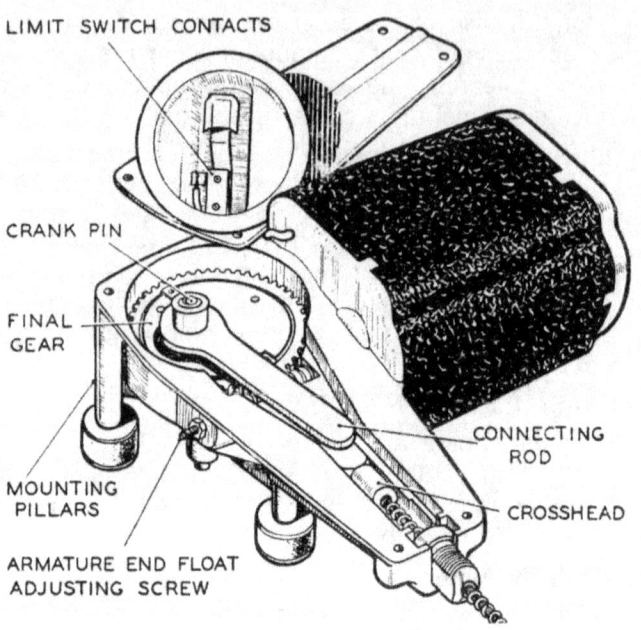

Reassembly

Reassembly is a reversal of the above procedures. When reassembling, the following components should be lubricated, using the lubricants recommended:

    (1) **Armature bearings.** These should be lubricated with S.A.E. 20 engine oil — the self-aligning bearing being immersed in this for 24 hours before assembly.

    (2) **Armature shaft (commutator end).** Apply S.A.E. 20 engine oil sparingly.

    (3) **Felt lubricator in gearbox.** Apply S.A.E. 20 engine oil carefully.

    (4) **Worm wheel bearings, crosshead, guide channel, connecting rod, crank pin, eccentric coupling assembly, worm and final gear shaft.** Grease liberally as for front hubs.

    (5) **Cable rack and wheelboxes.** Grease liberally as for front hubs.

Testing

Switch on the ignition and the wiper control. The two wiper areas should be approximately symmetrical on the windshield.

Fitting a Blade to a Wiper Arm

Pull wiper arm away from the windshield and insert the curved 'wrist' of the arm into slotted spring fastening of the blade. Swivel the two components into engagement.

Fitting a Wiper Arm to Driving Spindle

(1) First ensure that the wiper spindles are in the correct parking position by switching on the ignition and turning the wiper control on and then off.
(2) To fit the arms, press the headpieces on to the spindles at the correct parking angle until the retaining clip is heard to snap over the end of the spindle drum.
(3) Switch off the wiper control. The arms should come to rest in the correct parking position.

Adjusting

Correct operation can be obtained by adjusting the position of the arms relative to the spindles. If necessary the position of the arms may be adjusted by removing and re-engaging them with the splined driving spindles, the angular pitch of the splines being 5°.

Do not attempt to turn the arms whilst in position, but press back the retaining clip in the headpieces and withdraw the arms from the driving spindles. Refit in the desired position. The above adjustment may affect the self-parking position. If so, it may be corrected by adjustment of the limit switch position, as described above.

If the arms and blades are required to come to rest on the opposite side, the limit switch should be turned through 180°. It should be noted that the switch cover is designed for turning through a sector only and not through 360°. This feature prevents unnecessary twisting of the external flexible connections.

HEADLAMPS

Home and U.S.A. types

Headlamps fitted to vehicles operating on the Home or U.S.A. markets are of the sealed-beam type and are serviced as complete units only.

European type

Headlamps fitted to vehicles exported to Europe are of the double-filament bulb type.

Removing the light unit (Home and U.S.A. types)

The lamp rims are fitted without rubber dust excluders and rim retaining screws. Insert a screwdriver between the bottom of the rim and the lamp body and prise off the lamp rim. Remove the inner rim securing screws and lift away the sealed beam assembly after disconnecting the three-pin socket.

Removing the light unit (European type)

To remove the light unit for bulb replacement unscrew the retaining screw at the bottom of the plated lamp rim and lift the rim away from the dust-excluding rubber.

Remove the dust-excluding rubber, which will reveal the three spring-loaded screws. Press the light unit inwards against the tension of the springs and turn it in an anti-clockwise direction until the heads of the screws can pass through the enlarged ends of the keyhole slots in the lamp rim.

This will enable the light unit to be withdrawn sufficiently to give attention to the wiring and bulbs.

Bulb replacement (European type)

The headlamps fitted to left-hand-drive cars for use in European countries are fitted with special front lenses giving an asymmetrical light beam to the right-hand side.

The bulb is released from the reflector by withdrawing the three-pin socket and pinching the two ends of the wire retaining clip to clear the bulb flange. When replacing the bulb make certain that the rectangular pip on the bulb flange engages the slot in the reflector seating.

Replace the spring clip with its coils resting in the base of the bulb flange and engaging the two retaining lugs on the reflector seating.

Refitting the light unit (Home and U.S.A.)

Refitting is reverse of the removal procedure.

NOTE: When refitting a headlamp rim make certain it is placed over the retaining lip at the top of the lamp body and held firmly in this position while pressure is applied to the bottom of the rim to snap it into position.

Refitting the light unit (European type)

Position the light unit so that the heads of the adjusting screws coincide with the enlarged ends of the attachment slots. Push the light unit towards the wing to compress the springs and turn the unit to the right as far as it will go — that is, approximately ½ in. (13 mm.).

Replace the dust-excluding rubber on the light rim with its flanged face forward and refit the plated rim.

Beam-setting (European type)

The lamps should be set so that the main driving beams are parallel with the road surface or in accordance with local regulations.

If adjustment is required this is achieved by removing the plated rim and dust-excluding rubber. Vertical adjustment can then be made by turning the screw at the top of the lamp in the necessary direction. Horizontal adjustment can be effected by using the adjustment screws on each side of the light unit.

Certain countries have lighting regulations to which the foregoing arrangements do not conform, and cars exported to such countries have suitably modified lighting equipment.

Beam-setting (Home and U.S.A. type)

The lamps should be set in the dip position, and should be adjusted to comply with the regulations in the country or state in which the vehicle is operating.

If adjustment is required, this is achieved by removing the headlamp rim. Vertical adjustment can then be made by turning the screw at the top of the lamp in the necessary direction. Horizontal adjustment can be effected by using the adjustment screw on the right-hand side of the lamp.

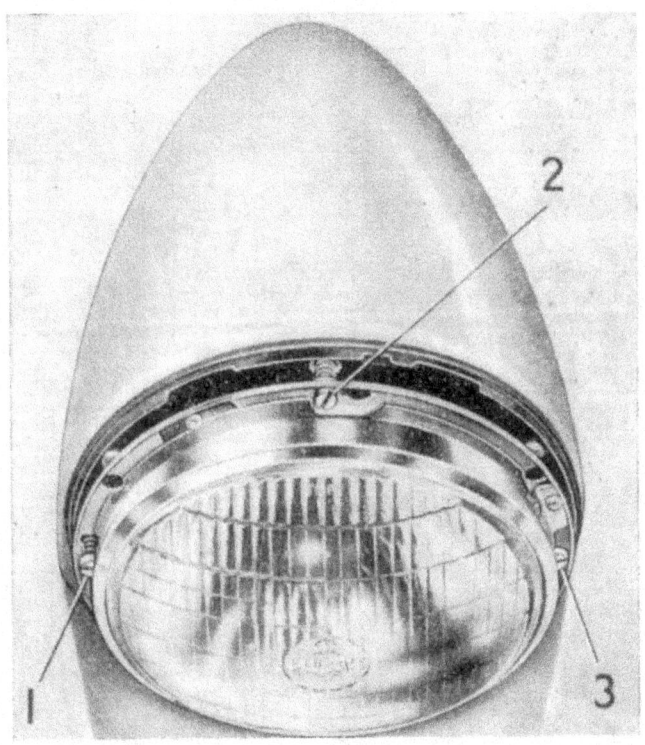

1. *Horizontal adjustment screw.*   2. *Vertical adjustment screw.*
3. *Horizontal adjustment screw.*

REPLACEMENT BULBS

	Volts	Watts	B.M.C. Part No.
Headlamp—United Kingdom only	12·8	60/45	13H496
Headlamp (L.H.D.)—except U.S.A. and Europe	12	42/36	3H1893
Headlamp (L.H.D.)—Europe except France	12	45/40	13H138
Headlamp—France only	12	45/40	13H139
Headlamp—Sweden only	12	45/40	13H138
Sidelamp	12	4	1D9081
Sidelamp, direction indicator—North America and Italy	12	6/21	1F9026
Direction indicator—front	12	21	1F9012
Direction indicator—rear	12	21	1F9012
Tail and stop lamp	12	6/21	1F9026
Number-plate illumination lamp	12	6	2H4817
Panel and warning lights	12	2·2	2H4732

FAULT DIAGNOSIS

Symptom	No.	Possible Fault
(a) Battery discharged	1 2 3 4 5	Terminals loose or dirty Lighting circuit shorted Generator not charging Regulator unit not operating properly Battery internally defective
(b) Insufficient current flow to battery	1 2	Loose or corroded terminal connections Generator belt slipping
(c) Battery fails to retain charge	1 2 3 4	Electrolyte levels low Battery plates badly sulphated Electrolyte leakage due to cracked cell or sealing compound Plate separators not effective
(d) Battery overcharged	1	Voltage regulator out of adjustment
(e) Generator not charging properly or inoperative	1 2 3 4 5 6 7 8 9 10 11	Driving belt slipping or broken Regulator unit not operating properly Badly worn bearings or pole pieces loose Short between commutator bars Armature worn or shaft bent Commutator out of round Insulation high between commutator bars Commutator greasy, glazed or burned Brush springs weak or broken Brushes sticking Field coils shorted, open or burned

Symptom	No.	Possible Fault
(f) Starter motor lacks power or fails to turn the engine	1 2 3 4 5 6 7 8	Battery in need of attention Loose or broken connection in starter circuit Starter motor pinion jammed in mesh with flywheel gear Starter switch faulty Brushes worn, sticking or not bedded Engine abnormally stiff Commutator dirty or worn Starter shaft bent
(g) Starter motor operates but does not turn the engine	1 2	Pinion sticking on the screwed sleeve Broken pinion or flywheel gear teeth
(h) Noise from starter pinion when engine is running	1	Restraining spring weak or broken
(j) Starter motor inoperative	1 2 3 4	Battery needs attention Loose or broken connection in starter circuit or switch Armature faulty Field coils earthed
(k) Starter motor rough or noisy engagement	1 2 3	Starter motor loose on mounting bolts Damaged pinion and/or flywheel gear teeth Main spring broken
(l) Lamps inoperative	1 2 3 4	Battery discharged Lamp bulbs burned out Loose or broken connections Lighting switch faulty
(m) Lamps operate when switched on but gradually fade out	1	Battery discharged
(n) Lamps give insufficient illumination	1 2 3 4	Battery in low state of charge Headlamps out of alignment Bulbs discoloured through use Reflector surface deteriorated

Symptom	No.	Possible Fault
(o) Lamps erratic	1 2 3	Lights switch contacts faulty Battery to earth connections faulty Lamp earth faulty
(p) Flashing indicator warning lamp or direction indicator lamp inoperative	1	Check the bulbs and renew if necessary Also see 'The Flasher Unit'
(q) Horn inoperative	1 2 3	Fuse blown Faulty connection Horn faulty internally
(r) Horn operates continuously	1 2	Horn-push stuck or earthed Horn cable (brown with black) to horn-push earthed
(s) Horn note unsatisfactory	1 2	Loose cable connection Horn out of adjustment
(t) Wiper motor inoperative or takes no current	1 2 3 4 5	Fuse blown Battery needs attention Loose or broken connection in the motor circuit Armature faulty Field coils earthed
(u) Wiper motor takes abnormally low current	1 2 3 4	Battery needs attention Armature faulty Commutator dirty Brushes worn or not bedded
(v) Wiper motor sluggish and takes abnormally high current	1 2 3 4	Armature faulty Armature bearings out of alignment Commutator dirty or short-circuited Wheelbox spindle binding or bent
(w) Wiper motor operates but does not drive the wiper arms	1 2 3	Wheelbox gear and spindle worn Driving cable rack faulty Gearbox components worn
(x) Fuel gauge fails to register	1 2 3	Gauge supply interrupted Gauge case not earthed Cable between gauge and tank unit earthed
(y) Fuel gauge registers full	1	Cable between gauge and tank unit broken or disconnected

ENGINE

The engines fitted to Sprite, Sprite Mk. II and MG Midget are of the same basic construction, differing only in compression ratio, carburetors and minor refinements from the earliest to the latest. The four cylinder, overhead valve powerplant is a sturdy unit capable of withstanding much abuse if properly maintained. Its performance can also be increased by a wide margin over "stock" and still remain reliable. Racing Sprites which regularly take the measure of Alfa Romeos and other cars of considerably displacement (particularly on the West Coast) are mobile proof of the inherent possibilities. Formula Juniors using the 948 cc block and components have also given a good account of themselves.

However, the fact that these engines can be thrashed under competition circumstances does not mean that they can be consistently overrevved in stock form or that they can be considered unbreakable. The red line on the tachometer face is put there by a manufacturer who wants to have happy customers. Observe it. A well-tuned and maintained Sprite or Midget is a satisfying car to drive. If you want more power, follow the tips under 'Increasing Power and Performance', don't try to extract it from a poorly prepared stock engine or one which has not been properly kept in condition.

The average owner may never want to go past merely keeping his car clean and in perfect adjustment. On the other hand, he may find the time when some more major repair is either necessary or desirable and want to perform the chore himself. The following instructions, which are compatible in every detail with factory recommendations through shop manuals, can be followed with good results by the semi-experienced or experienced home mechanic. Many operations can be performed with the engine in place in the chassis, but if lifting tackle is available, most of them become far easier. So, to begin, we will outline the steps involved in removing the entire assembly from the car.

REMOVING ENGINE WITHOUT GEARBOX

(1) Detach the earth lead from the battery.
(2) Detach the bonnet from the bonnet hinges.
(3) Remove the radiator.
(4) Disconnect the heater inlet and outlet hoses at the heater unit (if applicable).
(5) Detach the choke cable and its outer casing at the carburetors.
(6) Detach the throttle cable at the carburetors throttle lever.
(7) Unscrew the oil pressure gauge pipe at its terminal in the cylinder block.
(8) Unscrew the reduction drive (if fitted) complete with

tachometer cable from the rear end of the generator.
(9) Release the generator, coil and distributor low tension cables.
(10) Release the high tension cables from their connections at the coil and spark plugs.
(11) Remove the distributor as detailed in the Ignition Section.
(12) Remove the starter as described in the Electrical System.
(13) Disconnect the petrol (gasoline) inlet pipe at the fuel pump union.
(14) Release the clamp attaching the exhaust manifold to the down pipe.
(15) Attach lifting tackle as illustrated.

(16) Place a suitable jack beneath the vehicle to support the gearbox and unscrew the nuts, bolts and setpins securing the gearbox bell housing to the engine backplate.
Note: The bottom right-hand nut and bolt also secures the engine earthing wire.
(17) Remove the four nuts and spring washers securing the engine front mounting bracket to the chassis frame.
(18) Ascertain that the engine mounting bracket is clear of its mounting studs by jacking the gearbox and at the same time lifting the engine.
(19) Hoist and pull the engine forward to disengage the gearbox first motion shaft splines and lift clear of the vehicle.

Note: Replacing the engine is the reverse of the procedure 'To Remove'.

REMOVING ENGINE WITH GEARBOX

(1) Perform the operations (1) to (14) as detailed previously and then proceed as follows:

(2) Within the car remove the four self tapping screws securing the gear lever aperture cover to the gearbox surround and withdraw the cover.

(3) Unscrew and remove the anti-rattle plunger, spring and cap (accessible within the car).

(4) Unscrew the three setscrews attaching the change speed lever retaining plate and remove the change speed lever.

(5) Peel back the carpet surrounding the gearbox cover to expose the two 5/16 in. gearbox rear mounting setpins, and unscrew the setpins. (See Gearbox chapter for illustration.)

(6) Working beneath the vehicle unscrew the speedometer drive cable at its union with the gearbox rear extension.

(7) Detach the slave cylinder from the gearbox bell housing by unscrewing its two mounting setpins and withdrawing the push rod from the rear of the cylinder.

(8) Disconnect the propeller shaft from the rear axle. This operation is performed by removal of the four self-locking nuts.

(9) Unscrew the remaining two gearbox rear mounting setpins.

(10) By means of lifting tackle, support the engine.

(11) Remove the four nuts and spring washers securing the engine front mounting bracket to the chassis frame.

(12) Hoist the engine, gearbox and propeller shaft, and at the same time pull the whole assembly forward clear of the vehicle.

ENGINE LUBRICATION

The oil supply is carried in the sump below the cylinder block, and the filler cap is fitted to the valve rocker cover. The dipstick is on the right-hand side of the engine and is marked to indicate the 'FULL' level.

The eccentric vane non-draining-type oil pump is mounted on the rear end of the crankcase and is driven by the camshaft.

The sump on new and reconditioned engines must be drained and filled with new oil after the first 500 miles (800 km.). The hexagon-headed sump drain plug is at the rear on the right-hand side.

The sump should be allowed to drain for at least ten minutes before the drain plug is replaced. The oil will flow more readily if it is drained while the engine is hot. When the sump has been drained, approximately 6 pints (7.2 U.S. pints, 3.41 litres) of oil are required to fill it. The capacity of the filter is approximately 1 pint (1.2 U.S. pints, 0.57 litres). giving a total of 7 pints (8.4 U.S. pints, 3.98 litres). Do not forget to replace the sump drain plug.

Never use petrol or kerosene for flushing purposes. Such cleaning mediums are never completely dispersed from the engine lubricating system, and will remain to contaminate any fresh oil. This may cause premature bearing failure.

Every 6,000 miles (9600 km.), a new oil filter element must be fitted after the filter bowl has been carefully cleaned in petrol.

When refilling the sump do not pour the oil in too quickly, as it may overflow from the filler orifice and mislead the operator as to the quantity of lubricant in the engine.

Before testing the level of the oil, ensure that the vehicle is as near level as possible. Always wipe the dipstick clean with a non-fluffy cloth before taking the reading. It must be remembered that time must be allowed for new oil to reach the sump before reading the dipstick.

Oil Pressure

The normal operating pressure is 60 lb./sq. in. (4.2 kg/cm^2).

The oil gauge is combined with the thermometer on the instrument panel.

A minimum pressure of 15 lb./sq. in. (1.05 kg/cm^2) should be registered when the engine is idling. **If no pressure is registered by the gauge stop the engine at once and investigate the cause.**

Note: The automatic release valve in the lubrication system deals with any excessive oil pressure when starting from cold.

Check for Low Pressure

Check the level of the oil in the sump by means of the dipstick and top up if necessary. Ascertain that the gauze strainer in the sump is clean and not choked with sludge, also that there is no leakage at the strainer union on the suction side of the sump.

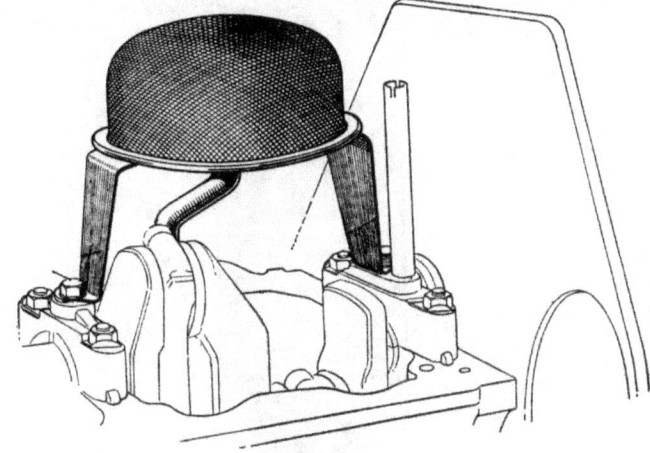

If the engine bearings are worn the oil pressure will be reduced. A complete bearing overhaul and the fitting of replacement parts is the only remedy, necessitating the removal of the engine from the vehicle.

OIL FILTER

The external oil filter is of the full flow type, thus ensuring that all oil in the lubrication system passes through the filter before reaching the bearings.

The element of the filter is of star formation in which a special quality felt, selected for its filtering properties, is used.

Oil is passed to the filter from the pump at a pressure controlled at 60 lb./sq. in. by the engine oil release valve. This pressure will, of course, be somewhat higher until the oil reaches a working temperature. Some pressure is lost in passing the oil through the filter element, this will only be a pound or two per square inch with a new element, but will increase as the element becomes progressively contaminated by foreign matter removed from the oil.

Should the filter become completely choked due to neglect, a balance valve is provided to ensure that oil will still reach the bearings. This valve, set to open at pressure difference of 15-20 lb./sq. in., is non-adjustable and is located in the filter head casting. When the valve is opened, unfiltered oil can by-pass the filter element and reach the bearings.

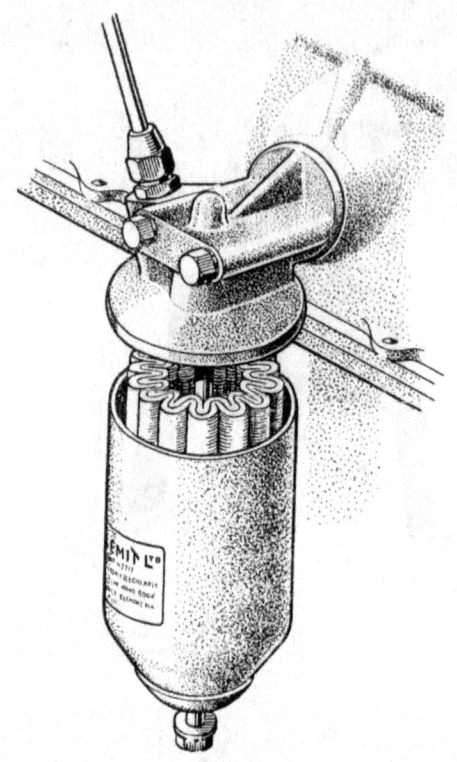

To renew the filter element proceed as follows:
(1) Stop the engine, extract the centre fixing bolt, remove container and drain.
(2) Withdraw the contaminated element and carefully cleanse the container of all foreign matter that has been trapped.
(3) After ensuring that no fibres from the cleansing operation **have been left in the container,** put in a new element. Care must be taken to ensure that the washers below the element inside the bowl are fitted correctly. The small felt washer must be positioned between the element pressure plate and the metal washer above the pressure spring. It is essential for correct oil filtration that the felt washer should be in good condition and be a snug fit on the centre-securing bolt. Hold centre bolt firm, prime the filter, and refit to head casting, tightening the centre fixing bolt sufficiently to make an oil-tight joint and then top up the engine with oil.

It is highly recommended that the filter container should not be disturbed other than for cleaning or fitting a new element; to do so invites the hazard of added contamination from accumulated dirt on the outside of the filter entering the container and thus being carried into the bearings on **restarting the engine.**

SUMP AND GAUZE STRAINER

Removing

(1) Drain off the oil into a suitable container and then extract the setscrews and washers, thus enabling the sump to be removed.
(2) Detach the oil suction pipe at its connection with the crankcase.
(3) Unscrew the two setpins securing the strainer support bracket to the main bearing caps.
(4) The strainer and support bracket may now be removed from the engine.
(5) Swill the strainer in petrol or paraffin and thoroughly dry with a non-fluffy rag.
(6) Inspect the sump joint washers and renew if necessary.

Refitting

(1) Install the strainer and its securing bracket into position, ascertaining that the oil suction pipe is located in its connection to the crankcase.
(2) Tighten the suction pipe connection.
(3) Clean out the sump by washing it in paraffin. Take care to remove any traces of the paraffin before refitting the sump to the engine.
  Pay particular attention to the sump and crankcase joint faces, and remove any remainder of old jointing material. Examine the joint washers and renew if necessary. The old joint washers may be used again if they are sound, but it is advisable to fit new ones.
(4) Smear the faces of the joints with grease and fit the joint washers. Lift the sump into position and insert the setscrews into the flange tightening them up evenly.

OIL PUMP

To Remove

(1) The detachment of the oil pump first entails the removal of the engine from the car.
(2) Remove both flywheel and engine backplate. To gain access to the oil pump.
(3) Tap back the locking washers and remove the three ¼ in. setscrews.
(4) Withdraw the pump noting the position of the slot in the driving shaft in order to assist replacement. If the paper joint washer is damaged in any way it must be renewed.

Dismantling

(1) Remove the oil pump cover after unscrewing its two securing setpins.
(2) The oil pump cover, the outer rotor and the combined oil pump shaft and inner rotor are all now removable.

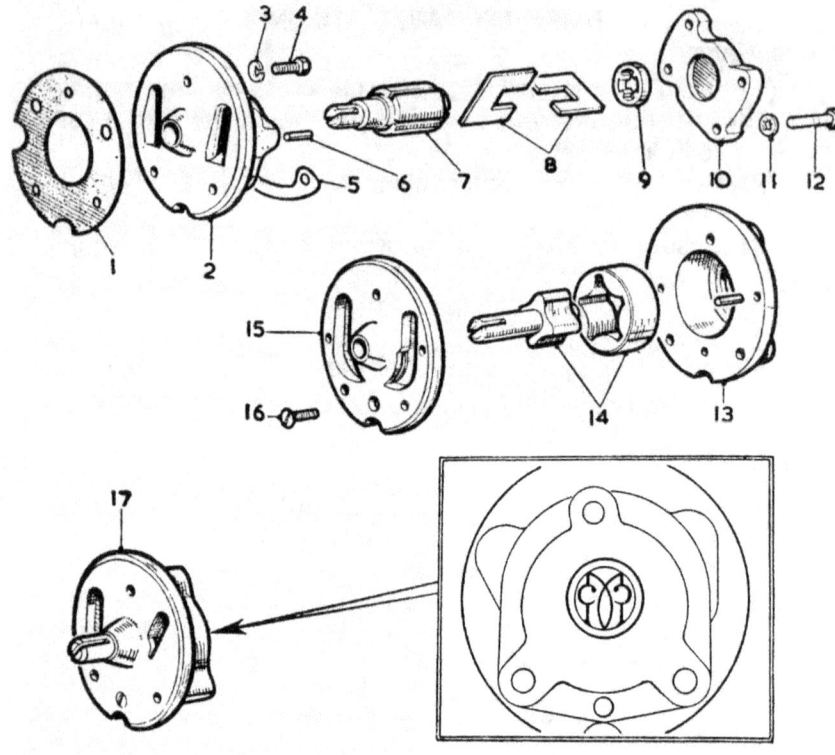

The three types of oil pump which may be fitted

Burman
1. Joint washer.
2. Pump body.
3. Washer.
4. Set screw.
5. Lock plate.
6. Dowel.
7. Rotor.
8. Vane.
9. Sleeve.
10. Body cover.
11. Shakeproof washer.
12. Screw—cover to body.

Hobourn-Eaton
13. Body.
14. Shaft and rotor.
15. Cover.
16. Screw—cover to body.

Centrifugal Manufacturing Co.
17. Pump (serviced as assembly only).

Replacing

The replacement of the oil pump is a reversal of the removal procedure; however, the operator must pay particular attention when positioning the paper joint washer to ensure that the intake and delivery ports are not obstructed.

RELIEF VALVE

The oil relief valve is situated at the rear right-hand side of the cylinder block, alongside the distributor. It is non-adjustable and is held in position by a compressed coil spring. This compression is maintained by two fibre washers and a domed screw plug.

The function of the valve is to provide an extra return passage for the oil should the pressure become excessive.

A pre-determined spring rating allows a release pressure of 60 lb./sq. in., and this can be checked by measuring the length of the spring, the correct figure being 2⅞ in. Fit a new spring if the tension has been lost.

ADJUSTING VALVE CLEARANCE

Lift off the valve cover after removing the two cap nuts.

Between the rocker arm and the valve stem there must be a clearance of .012 in. (.305) for both inlet and exhaust, clearance being set with the engine hot.

(1) If adjustment is necessary slacken off the locknut while pressure is applied, with a screwdriver, to the adjusting screw.

(2) Insert a .012 in. feeler gauge between the valve stem and rocker arm and raise or lower the adjusting screw

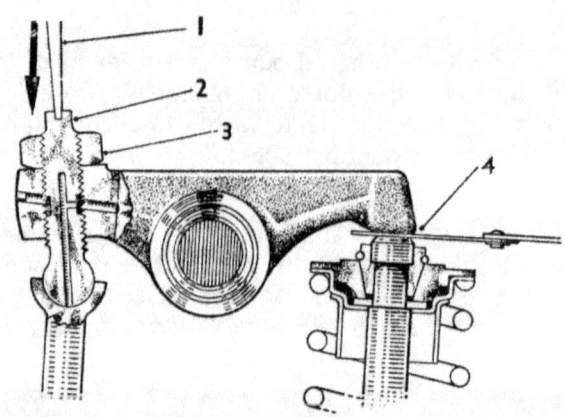

1. Screwdriver 2. Adjusting screw 3. Locknut 4. Feeler gauge (.012")

until the correct clearance is achieved.
(3) Tighten the locknut but re-check the clearance in case the adjustment has been disturbed during the locking process.
(4) When replacing the valve cover, take care that the joint washer (using a new one if necessary) is properly seated to ensure an oil tight joint.

VALVE ROCKER SHAFT

Of hollow construction, the valve rocker shaft is mounted on the cylinder head and secured by means of four pedestal brackets.

It is supplied with oil through a drilling in the foremost pedestal bracket for lubrication to each rocker bearing.

The shaft is plugged at each end, one of the plugs being screwed in order that the shaft may be cleaned internally.

ROCKER SHAFT ASSEMBLY

Removal

(1) Drain the cooling system.
(2) Unscrew the two nuts securing the rocker cover to the cylinder head, taking care not to damage the cork gasket, and remove the rocker cover.
(3) Unscrew the eight rocker shaft bracket fixing nuts and the five external cylinder head securing nuts gradually, a turn at a time, in the order shown, until all load has been released.
Note: The special locking plate mounted on each rocker bracket.
(4) Completely unscrew the eight rocker shaft bracket nuts and remove the rocker assembly, complete with brackets and rockers.

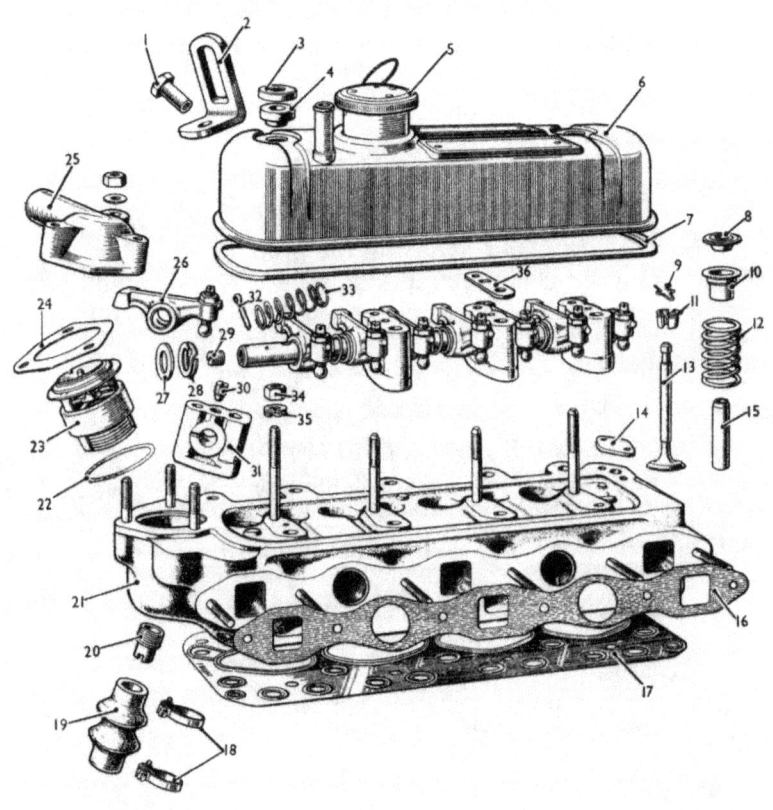

1 Valve rocker cover cap nut   2 Engine sling bracket
3 Cup washer   4 Rubber bush   5 Oil filler cap
6 Valve rocker cover   7 Rocker cover joint washer   8 Valve spring cap
9 Valve cotter circlip   10 Valve oil seal retainer
11 Valve cotters   12 Valve spring   13 Valve   14 Cover plate   15 Valve guide
16 Joint washer   17 Gasket
18 Hose clips   19 Bypass hose   20 Bypass tube   21 Cylinder head
22 Thermostat joint washer   23 Thermostat
24 Water outlet elbow joint washer   25 Water outlet elbow   26 Rocker
27 Plain washer   28 Spring washer
29 Rocker shaft plug   30 Locating grub screw   31 Rocker shaft pedestal
32 Splitpin   33 Rocker spacing spring
34 Rocker bracket nut   35 Rocker bracket washer   36 Rocker bracket plate

Dismantling

(1) Remove the grub screw which locates the rocker shaft to the front rocker mounting bracket.
(2) Remove the split pins from each end of the rocker shaft to release thrust washers and double coil springs.
(3) Withdraw rocker, rocker shaft brackets, thrust washers and springs, retaining them in their original order for reassembly.

Reassembly

When reassembling the rocker gear, commence with the front mounting bracket, securing it with the grub screw. Follow up with the remaining brackets and springs. The screwed in end plug of the rocker shaft should be positioned towards the front of the engine.

All springs, remaining brackets, rockers and locking plates are interchangeable.

PUSH ROD REMOVAL

If the valve rocker assembly has already been removed all that remains is for the push rods to be lifted out. They may on the other hand be taken out without detaching the rocker assembly as described below:

(1) Remove the valve rocker cover as described in section above and slacken the valve adjustment screw to its full extent.
(2) With the aid of a screwdriver supported under the rocker shaft, depress the valve and slide the rocker sideways free of the push rod.
(3) Withdraw the push rod.
(4) In the case of the rocker at each end, it is necessary to take out the split pins at the end of the shaft.
(5) The above sequence should be reversed when replacing push rods and rockers.

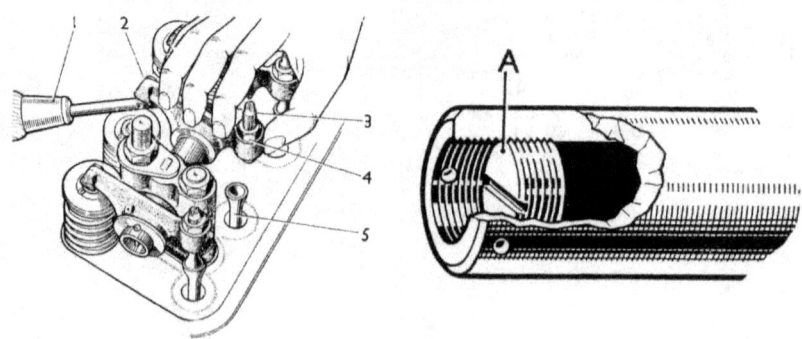

1. *Screwdriver.*
2. *Valve rocker.*
3. *Adjusting screw.*
4. *Locknut.*
5. *Push rod.*

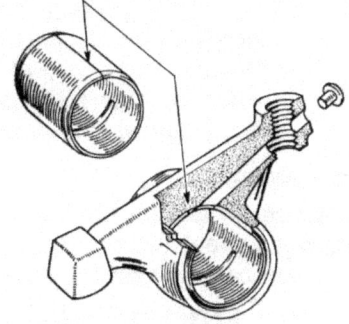

The pressed-steel type of valve rocker, which must not be rebushed

When rebushing the forged-type rocker make certain that the joint in the bush is in the position indicated

FORGED TYPE ROCKER ARM

(1) While the rocker gear is detached from the head, check for play between the rocker shaft and the rocker arm bushes. If this is excessive new bushes should be fitted. To do this dismantle the rocker assembly as described above.

(2) The bush is best removed by using a drift and anvil (Service Tool 18G 226 with 18G 226A). The anvil is recessed to retain the rocker in position while the bush is gently knocked out by the drift. File and drill out the rivet in the rocker arm oilway.

(3) The flange of the drift is also recessed to prevent the new split bush from opening when being driven into position with the joint immediately above the rocker arm oilway.

(4) Drill an oilway through the bush from the top of the rocker using a No. H.7 .0785 in. diameter drill. A second oilway must be drilled through the bush via the rocker arm using a No. 43 drill .089 in. diameter.

(5) Plug the oilway in the rocker arm with a rivet and weld its head to the rocker boss. Reamer the internal diameter of the bush to suit the shaft.

PRESSED TYPE ROCKER ARM

The pressed steel type of rocker arm is not capable of being re-bushed. If excessive clearance is present a new rocker assembly must be fitted.

TAPPETS

Removal

(1) Remove the pushrods after detaching the valve rocker assembly.

(2) Release the engine side covers by withdrawing their securing setscrews and fibre washers. The front cover is removed together with its vent pipe.

(3) Lift out the tappets, keeping them in their same respective locations. Inspect the tappet cam contacting surfaces for wear. New tappets should be fitted by selective assembly so that they just fall into their guides under their own weight when lubricated.

Replacement

Assembly is a reversal of the above procedure, but care should be taken to see that the tappet cover joints are oil-tight and that the rockers are adjusted to give the correct valve clearance.

RENEWING VALVE SPRING IN POSITION

(1) In an emergency a new valve spring can be fitted without lifting the cylinder head, but it is advisable first to bring the piston to top dead centre, to ensure that the valve cannot fall into the cylinder during the process.

(2) Remove the spark plug, and by means of a length of copper tubing or similar tool inserted through the plug hole, the valve can be held on its seat while the spring is compressed. The valve rocker shaft can be used as a fulcrum point by an operator using two screwdrivers to bear on the valve spring cap each side of the valve stem, while the cotters are removed.

INLET MANIFOLD

Removal and Replacement

(1) Detach the air cleaners from the carburetors by unscrewing the four setpins and releasing the breather pipe attached to the rear air cleaner.

(2) Disconnect the carburetors.

(3) Disconnect the exhaust down pipe by releasing its securing clip.

(4) Disconnect the throttle and choke linkages to the carburetors, together with the vacuum control pipe and petrol feed pipe.

(5) Unscrew and remove the six nuts and washers which secure the exhaust and inlet manifolds to the cylinder head. Four of these nuts bear on special clamping washers. The remaining two secure the end flanges of the exhaust manifold.

(6) The inlet and exhaust manifolds can now be drawn off their studs and lifted clear of the engine.

(7) The inlet and exhaust manifolds are separated by withdrawing the four connecting setscrews, noting the respective positions of the special hot spot and joint washer (gasket).

(8) Reassembly is the reverse of the above procedure; always use a new gasket for the manifolds to ensure a gas-tight joint.

CYLINDER HEAD

Removing

(1) Drain all water from the cooling system, if the water contains anti-freeze mixture, it should be run into a clean container and used again.
(2) Detach the top water hose from cylinder head.
(3) Disconnect the high tension wires from the spark plugs.
(4) Detach the inlet and exhaust manifolds, complete.
(5) Remove rocker cover and breather pipe.
(6) Release the vacuum advance pipe clip from its securing point on the cylinder head. Also slacken the retaining clip and detach the heater inlet hose, if fitted.
(7) Remove the rocker assembly.
(8) Withdraw the push rods, keeping them in order of removal taking care not to pull the tappets out of their guides in the block.
(9) Remove the five external cylinder head nuts together with their flat washers and lift off the cylinder head.
(10) If removal of the cylinder head presents difficulty, rotate the engine by means of a wrench applied to the crankshaft pulley nut, then the head should lift off.

Replacing

(1) Replace the cylinder head joint washer with the side marked 'Top' uppermost, it is not necessary to use jointing compound or grease for the gasket.
(2) Having slipped the gasket over the studs, next lower the cylinder head into position and position the cylinder head stud nut washers. Ensure that the vacuum advance pipe clip is replaced in its original position on the cylinder head.
(3) Insert the push rods, ensuring that the ball ends are correctly located in the tappets.
(4) Replace the rocker gear.
(5) Fit the nuts finger tight and then tighten them a turn at a time, in the order given in the illustration, to the recommended torque wrench readings (see 'General Data.')

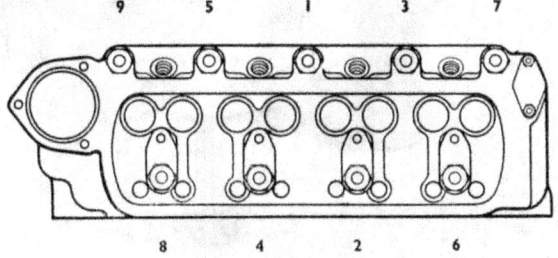

This figure illustrates the order of tightening cylinder head nuts.

(6) Reset the valve clearance, and replace the rocker cover using a new joint washer if the old one is damaged in any way.
(7) Replace the inlet and exhaust manifold assemblies and Connect up the fuel line, throttle and choke controls and heater outlet pipe, if fitted. Tighten the manifold nuts evenly ensuring that a good joint is made.
(8) Reconnect heater inlet pipe, water hose from the thermostat housing to the radiator, and breather pipe.
(9) Refill the cooling system, replace the spark plugs and their washers, and the high tension wires to their respective plugs.
(10) Check the valve clearance again after the vehicle has run about 100 miles (160 km.) as the valves have a tendency to bed down. At the same time it is advisable to test the cylinder head nuts for tightness. Tightening the cylinder head nuts may affect valve clearances, although not usually enough to justify resetting.

REMOVING AND REFITTING VALVES

With the cylinder head removed, a valve lifting tool can be used to compress the springs (such as the one illustrated). Take away the circlip, split cotters, and valve stem cap, so releasing the spring and shroud and allowing **the valve** to be removed.

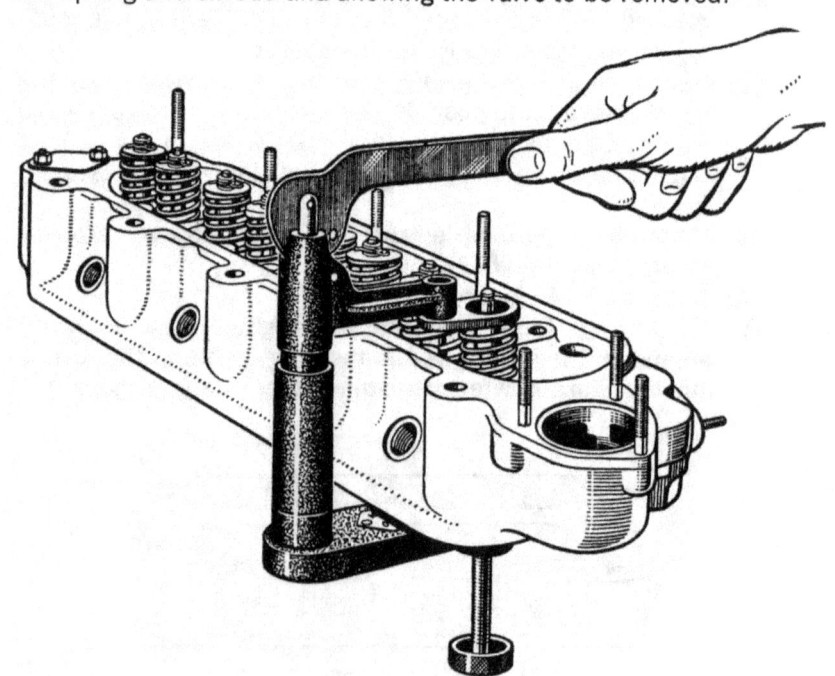

Using Service Tool 18G 45 to compress a valve spring.

(1) When removing the valves, place them in a rack, thus enabling them to be paired up with their correct cylinders.
(2) Clean the carbon from the top and bottom of the valve heads, as well as any deposit that may have accumulated on the stems. The valve heads should, if necessary, be refaced at an angle of 45° for both exhaust and inlet valves. If the valve seats show signs of excessive pitting it is advisable to reface these also.
(3) The valves are made without any indentures or slots in the head, this necessitates the use of a rubber suction valve grinding tool.
(4) Reassembly is a reversal of the operations for removal.

MODIFIED VALVE SHROUDS AND OIL SEALS

From Engine No. 9C/U/H 1397 valve packing rings (Part No. 2A879) of circular cross-section are fitted in place of the valve oil seals previously used. The oil seal retainer has been deleted from the valve guide shroud. The part number of the shroud without the oil seal retainer is 2A545. This modification involves changes in the inlet and exhaust valves and the valve spring caps.

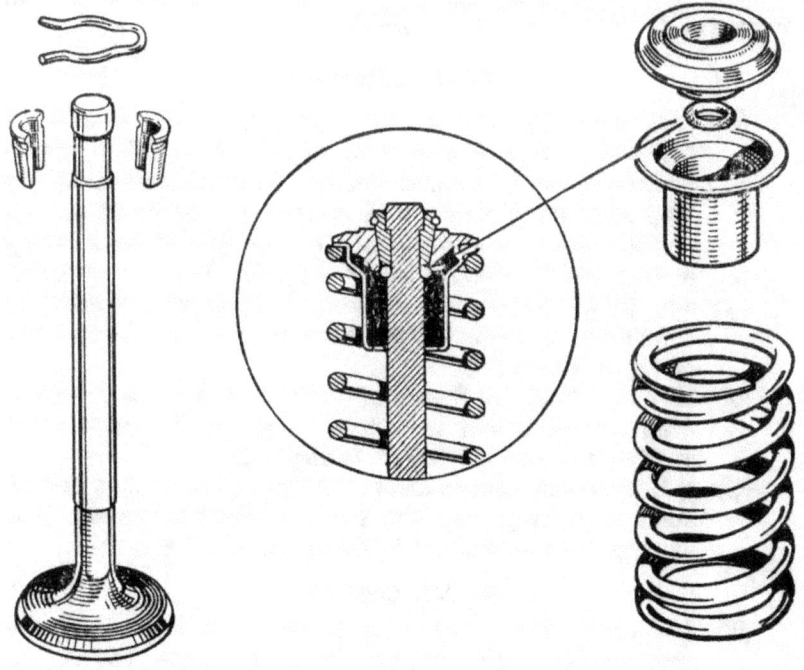

Parts of the valve assembly, showing the valve, cotters, circlip, spring, shroud, packing ring, and spring cap. The inset shows the valve packing ring fitted correctly at the bottom of the cotter groove below the cotters.

If it is desired to fit the new valve packing rings on earlier engines the modified shrouds (Part No. 2A545), valves (Part Nos. 2A877 [inlet] and 2A878 [exhaust]), and valve springs caps (Part No. 2A880) must be used.

Removal

Remove the valve circlip. Compress the valve spring, using Service Tool 18G 45, and remove the two valve cotters. Release the valve spring and remove the compressor, valve spring cap, shroud, and spring.

Remove the valve packing ring from the cotter groove and withdraw the valve from its guide.

Replacement

Place each valve into its guide and fit the springs, shrouds, and caps. Compress the valve spring and push a new synthetic rubber packing ring over the tip of the valve stem down to the bottom of the cotter groove. Refit the two valve cotters and remove the compressor. Replace the valve circlip.

NOTE: Do not fit old valve packing rings, or oil sealing may suffer. The rings are fitted more easily if they have been soaked in clean engine oil for a short period before use.

VALVE GRINDING

(1) For valve grinding a little grinding paste should be smeared evenly on the valve face, and the valve rotated backwards and forwards against its seat, advancing it a step at short intervals until a clean and unpitted seating is obtained. The cutting action is facilitated by allowing a light spring situated under the valve head, to periodically lift the valve from its seat. This allows the grinding compound to re-penetrate between the two faces after being squeezed out.

(2) On completion, all traces of compound must be removed from the valve and seat. It is essential that each valve is ground-in and refitted to its own seat.

(3) It is also desirable to clean the valve guides; this can be done by dipping the valve stem in petrol or solvent, and moving it up and down in the guide until it is free.

VALVE GUIDES

(1) The valve guides are of a one-piece design. They are pressed into the cylinder head to allow 19/32 in. (15.0812 mm.) of the guide to protrude above the machined face when fitted.

(2) To position each valve spring on the cylinder head, a stepped pressed steel seating collar is fitted over the part of the guide protruding from the cylinder head.

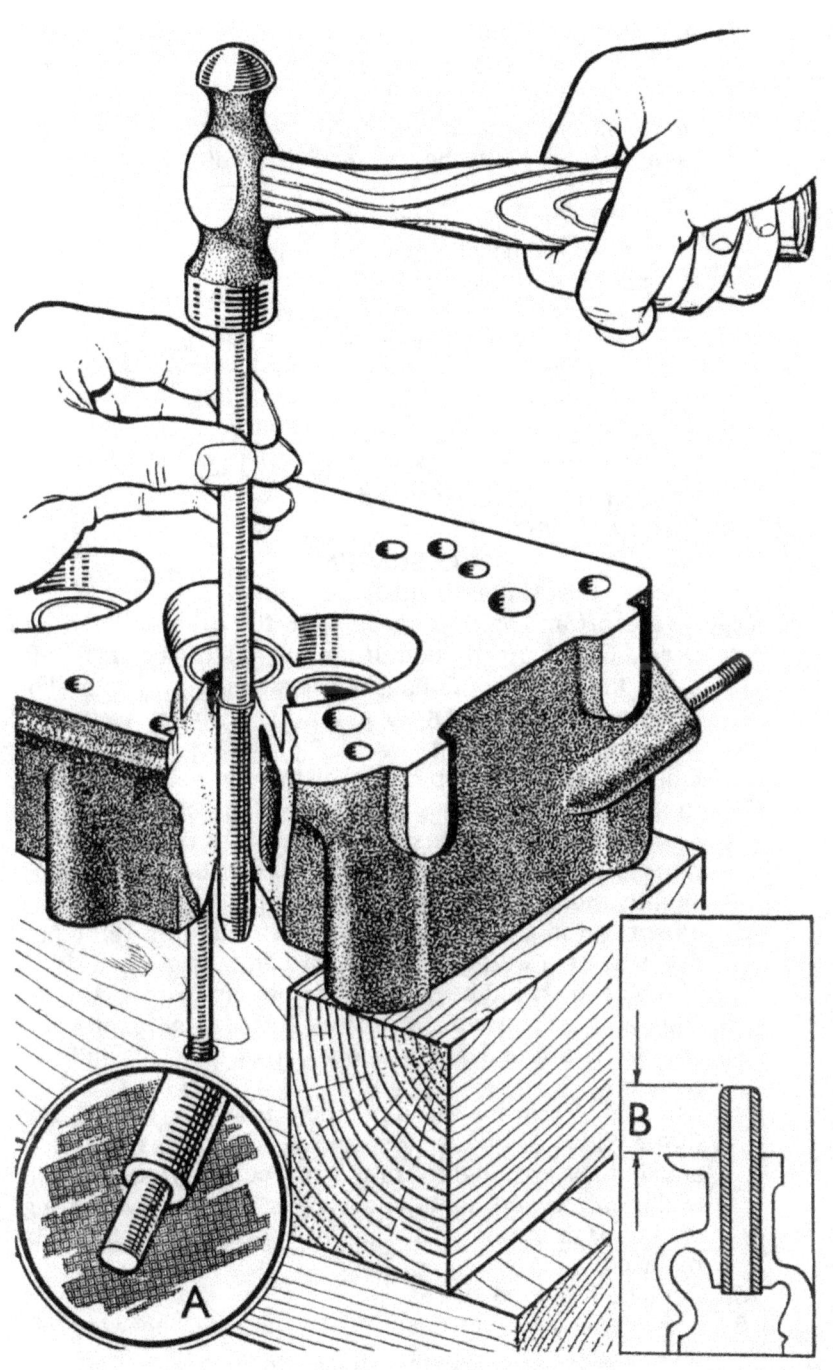

The inset 'A' shows the form of the tool.
B. The valve guide should be $\frac{11}{32}$ in. above the cylinder head.

(3) Valve guides should be tested for wear whenever valves are removed, and if excessive side play is present, a close check should be made of the valve stem and the guide. In the event of wear being noticeable, the defective components should be renewed. If a valve is at fault the wear will be evident on the stem. It should be borne in mind that the valve stem and guide should be a running fit to avoid the possibility of an air leak.

(4) If renewal is necessary due to wear, the valve guide may be driven out after removal of the valve.

(5) The drift is stepped in order to ensure location and to obviate it slipping off the guide and damaging the port. Knock out the guide in the direction shown.

(6) A new guide should be driven into position in the same direction, that is, inserting it from the top of the cylinder head and knocked downwards.

(7) The final position of the guide is shown.

DECARBONISING

(1) Remove the cylinder head as described.

(2) Scrape off all carbon deposit from the cylinder head and ports. Clean the carbon from the piston crowns, care being taken not to damage the pistons, and not to allow dirt or carbon deposit to enter the cylinder barrels or push rod compartment.

When cleaning the top of the pistons do not scrape right to the edge as a little carbon left on the chamfer assists in keeping down oil consumption; with the pistons cleaned right to the edge of new pistons, oil consumption is often slightly though temporarily increased.

(3) Blow out the oil passages and wash out the water passages using a water hose. The gasket contacting surfaces of the head should be checked for flatness with a straight-edge and the surfaces examined for scores. If the cylinder head is found to be badly out of true it should be renewed.

(4) Remove all carbon accumulation from the valves and thoroughly clean them. Inspect the valve bases and seats and if they are slightly pitted or rough, grind them in. If the valves and seats show signs of excessive pitting, or the faces are not flat, the valves and seats should be replaced.

(5) Examine the valve guides.

(6) Broken or weak valve springs should be renewed. The other valve springs should be tested and the results compared with the specifications. (see 'General Data.')

(7) Clean the rocker shaft gear and blow out the oil passages.

(8) Inspect the rocker shaft, rockers and bushes for wear.

(9) Reassemble and install the cylinder head assembly.

Note: The following operations should be carried out with the engine removed, although in some cases it is possible to perform them with the engine in position.

Before removing or replacing any component it is important to ensure that all surrounding surfaces are perfectly clean, to prevent the entry of foreign matter into the engine. It is also important to note that fluffy rags should never be used, as there is danger of causing obstruction to small oilways.

CONNECTING RODS AND BEARINGS

Removal

(1) Remove the cylinder head assembly.
(2) Drain and remove the sump.
(3) Unlock and remove the nuts securing the caps and bearings to the connecting rods. Remove the caps and bearings.
(4) Withdraw the pistons and connecting rods upwards through the cylinder bores.
(5) It may be necessary to remove the carbon or ridge from the top of the bores prior to pushing the pistons upwards, to avoid piston-ring fracture.
(6) Remove the pistons from the connecting rods by unscrewing the clamp bolt from the small end of the connecting rod and pushing the gudgeon pin out.
(7) Ensure that each connecting rod, cap and bearing is marked with the cylinder number from which it was removed.
(8) The big ends are offset, and rods in numbers 1 and 3 cylinders are offset towards the front, with 2 and 3 cylinders offset towards the rear.

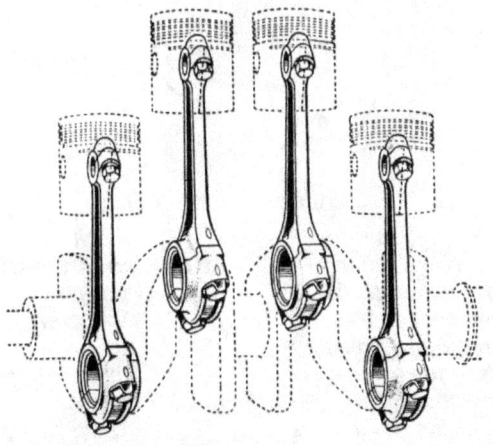

Showing the positions of the offsets and the correct method of assembly.

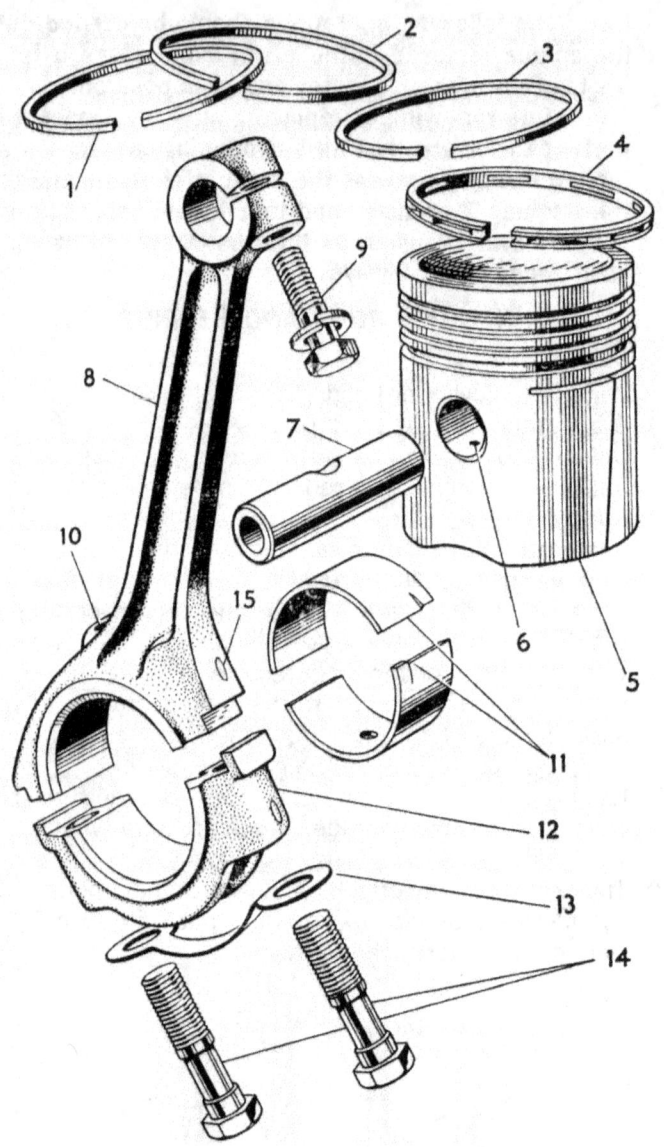

1. Piston ring, parallel.
2. Piston ring, taper.
3. Piston ring, taper.
4. Piston ring, scraper.
5. Piston.
6. Gudgeon pin lubricating hole.
7. Gudgeon pin.
8. Connecting rod, less cap.
9. Clamping screw and washer.
10. Cylinder wall lubricating jet.
11. Connecting rod bearings.
12. Connecting rod cap.
13. Lockwasher.
14. Setscrews.
15. Mark on rod and cap.

(9) The alignment of the connecting rods should be checked on an alignment fixture. On no account must the rods or caps be filed.
(10) Examine the bearing shells for wear and pits. Renew the bearing shell if necessary. Bearings are pre-finished with the correct diametral clearance and do not require bedding in.
(11) Check the crankpins with a micrometer if they are worn oval or are scored, the crankshaft will have to be removed for regrinding.

Replacing

Before installing the connecting rods and bearings it is assumed that the pistons and rings have been serviced.

The pistons and connecting rods must be fitted in the same cylinder bores and the same way round as when removed.

(1) Assemble the piston and the connecting rod to the gudgeon pin, so that the split in the piston skirt is adjacent to the split in the top of the connecting rod.
(2) Refit the piston rings very carefully, make quite sure that the pistons and bores are perfectly clean and smear the bores with clean engine oil.
(3) Use a piston ring clamp, when replacing the pistons from the top of the bore, and make sure that the split in the piston faces the camshaft.
(4) Clean the crankpins and both sides of the shell bearings, locate the feathered ends in the connecting rod and its cap, and smear the crankpins with engine oil.
(5) Before fitting the cap, check that the number stamped on the rod is the same as that on the cap. Note that the recess in the cap and rod must be on the same side. Tighten and lock the nuts. Turn the crankshaft after fitting each rod, to ensure that the bearing is not binding on the crankpin. Also check the side clearance of each rod, as given under 'General Data'.
(6) Refit the cylinder head assembly.
(7) Refit the sump and refill with recommended grade of oil.

PISTONS, RINGS AND GUDGEON PINS

Removal

The split-skirt pistons are of aluminium alloy material. Four rings are fitted above the gudgeon pin, the bottom ring being of the oil-control type. The pistons are fastened to the connecting rods by gudgeon pins which are clamped rigidly in the small ends of the connecting rods. Bushings are not needed in the gudgeon pin bosses of the pistons because the aluminium alloy material serves as a suitable bearing for the gudgeon pins, the bearing surfaces of which are lubricated by means of splash through the

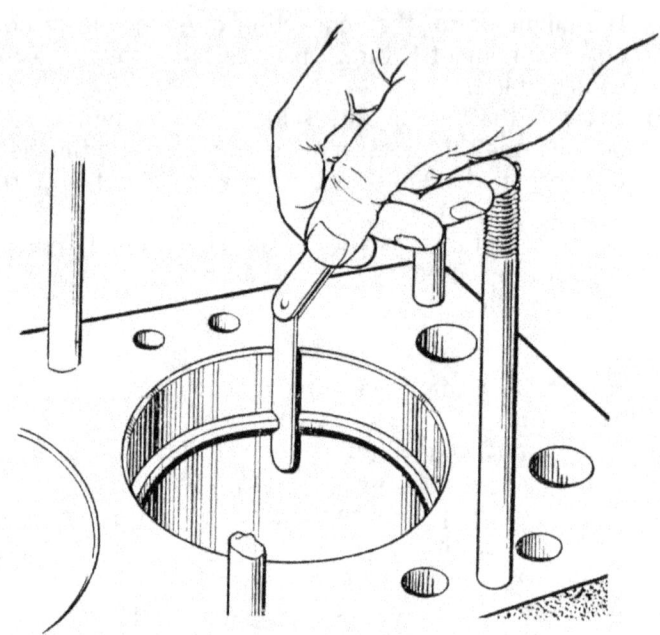

Measuring the piston ring gap.

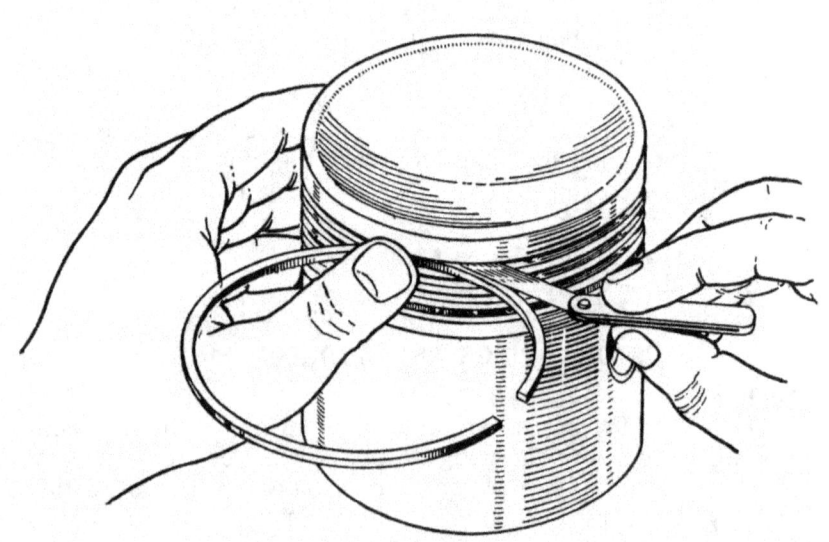

*Checking the **piston** ring groove clearance.*

two holes drilled in each boss.

To view and overhaul

(1) Remove the rings over the tops of the pistons.

(2) Scrape all accumulation of carbon off the piston heads and, using a piston ring groove-cleaning tool or an old ring section, carefully scrape all carbon out of the ring grooves of the pistons. Clean the carbon out of the oil holes in the piston ring grooves.

(3) Thoroughly clean all the dismantled components in solvent.

(4) Examine all parts for wear and damage, renew if necessary.

(5) If cylinder reconditioning is required, determine the amount of material to be removed (refer to "Piston Sizes and Cylinder Bores" concerning oversize pistons available).

(6) When fitting new or oversize pistons and rings to reconditioned cylinder bores, the clearances should be controlled within the limits given under 'General Data'.

Selective assembly is necessary, and for this purpose pistons are stamped with distinguishing symbols of grade and oversize.

(7) Piston rings should have a gap clearance (see 'General Data') when installed in the cylinder bores. If new rings are being installed, each ring should be checked in the cylinder bore to determine whether its gap clearance is within the range specified. To do this, use the bottom of a piston to insert the ring part way into the bore. The ring will be squared up in the bore to measure the gap clearance as shown. To check the ring clearance in the piston grooves, install the rings on the pistons and determine the clearances with a feeler gauge. If the piston ring grooves are worn excessively, as indicated when comparing the actual clearances with those given under 'General Data', renew the rings and pistons.

(8) Gudgeon pins should be a hand-push fit in the pistons. The fit can be checked after the rod has been assembled by holding the piston with the connecting rod in an approximately horizontal position. The weight of the large end of the connecting rod should be just in sufficient to turn the gudgeon pin in the piston. On no account must gudgeon pin piston bosses be reamed out as oversize gudgeon pins are not supplied or permitted.

Replacement

See preceding section.

PISTON SIZES AND CYLINDER BORES

In production pistons are fitted by selective assembly, and to facilitate this the pistons are stamped with identification figures on their crowns.

The number enclosed in a diamond, e.g. a piston stamped with a figure 2, is for a bore bearing a similar stamp.

In addition to the standard pistons there is a range of four oversize pistons available for service purposes. Oversize pistons are marked with the actual oversize dimensions enclosed in an ellipse. A piston stamped .020 is suitable only for a bore .020 in. (.508 mm.) larger than the standard bore, and similarly, pistons with other markings are suitable only for the oversize bore indicated.

The piston markings indicate the actual bore size to which they must be fitted, the requisite running clearance being allowed for in the machining.

After reboring an engine, or whenever fitting pistons differing in size from those removed during dismantling, ensure that the size of the piston fitted is stamped clearly on the top of the cylinder block alongside the appropriate cylinder bore.

Pistons are supplied in the sizes indicated in the following table.

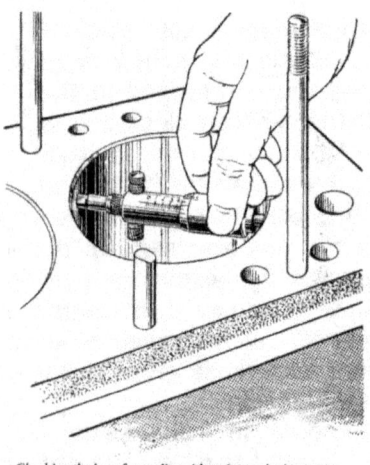

Checking the bore for ovality with an internal micrometer.

Piston marking	Suitable bore size	Metric equivalent
STANDARD	2·4778 in. to 2·4781 in.	62·935 mm. to 62·940 mm.
OVERSIZE		
+·010 in. (·254 mm.)	2·4878 in. to 2·4881 in.	63·189 mm. to 63·194 mm.
+·020 in. (·508 mm.)	2·4978 in. to 2·4981 in.	63·443 mm. to 63·448 mm.
+·030 in. (·762 mm.)	2·5078 in. to 2·5081 in.	63·697 mm. to 63·702 mm.
+·040 in. (1·016 mm.)	2·5178 in. to 2·5181 in.	63·951 mm. to 63·956 mm.

TIMING COVER

Removal and Replacement

(1) Drain the cooling system.
(2) Remove the radiator.
(3) Slacken the generator attachment bolts and remove the belt.
(4) Bend back the tab on the crankshaft pulley nut locking washer. Unscrew the nut.
(5) Pull off the crankshaft pulley.

(6) The timing cover is secured by four large setpins and six small ones. Each setpin has a shakeproof washer and a plain washer. Unscrew all ten setpins with their washers and remove the timing cover.

(7) Take care not to damage the timing cover gasket. If it is damaged, clean the face of the cover flange and the engine front mounting plate and fit a new gasket when reassembling.

(8) The felt washer situated in the timing cover should also be renewed if necessary.

*** It should be noted that the oil thrower, which is located behind the crankshaft pulley, is fitted with its concave side facing forward.

(9) When the special aligning tool (Service Tool 18G 138) is not available the crankshaft pulley should be assembled to the cover before the cover is refitted to the engine. This will ensure that the timing cover and oil seal are concentric with the crankshaft. Lubricate the hub of the pulley and, with a rotating movement to avoid damage to the oil seal, insert it in the cover. Push the pulley and timing cover on to the crankshaft, lining up the pulley bore keyway with the Woodruff key fitted to the crankshaft. Replace the cover set screws and tighten them up evenly.

(10) Reassembly is now a reversal of the removal procedure.

TIMING CHAIN AND SPROCKETS

Removal

(1) Remove the timing cover and oil thrower as described in the previous Section.

(2) Unlock and remove the camshaft chain wheel nut and remove the nut and lockwasher. Note that the locating tag on the lockwasher fits into the keyway of the camshaft chain wheel.

(3) Remove the camshaft and crankshaft chain wheels, together with the timing chain, by easing each wheel forward a fraction at a time with suitable small lever. Note the packing washers immediately behind the crankshaft gear wheel.

Replacement

(1) Unless new camshaft or crankshaft components have been fitted, replace the same number of packing washers behind the crankshaft gear wheel. If adjustment is necessary, however, it is required to determine the thickness of packing washers. This is achieved by placing a straight-edge across the sides of the camshaft wheel teeth and measure with a feeler gauge the gap between the straight-edge and the crankshaft gear.

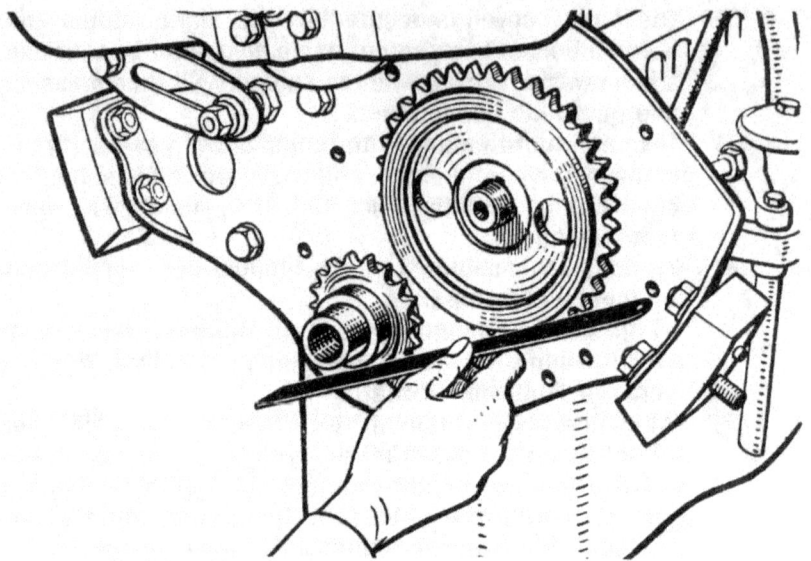

(2) Set the crankshaft with its keyway at T.D.C. and the camshaft with its keyway approximately at the one o'clock position when seen from the front.
(3) Assemble the gears into the timing chain with the two marks on the gear wheels opposite each other.
(4) Keeping the gears in this position, engage the crankshaft gear keyway with the key on the crankshaft and rotate the camshaft until the camshaft gear keyway and key are aligned.
(5) Push the gears onto the shafts and secure the camshaft gear with the lockwasher and nut.
(6) Replace the oil slinger, concave side forward, and the remaining components.

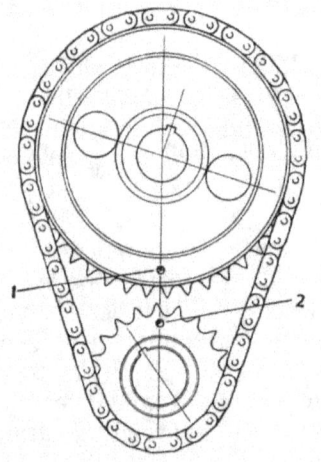
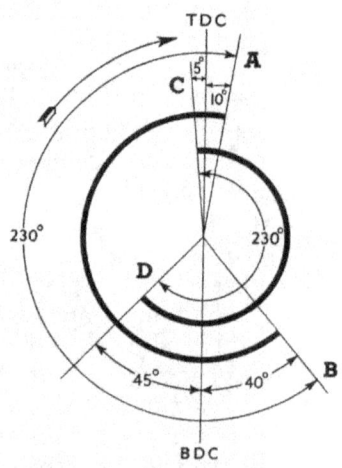

VALVE TIMING

Set clearance on No. 1 cylinder inlet valve to .019" (.021" on Mk II or Midget) with the engine cold. Then turn the crankshaft until the valve is about to open. The indicator groove in the flange of the crankshaft pulley should then be opposite the center pointer (on the indicator bracket below) which indicates 5° before top dead center (BTDC) of No. 1 and No. 4 pistons.

NOTE: It is not possible to check the valve timing accurately with normal (running) valve clearances. Set as above, then do not fail to reset the gap between rocker and pushrod to .013" (.33 mm) cold in order to assure a running clearance of .012" (.30 mm) hot.

CAMSHAFT AND BEARINGS

Removal
(1) Drain the sump and release it from the engine. Remove the rocker assembly.
(2) Remove the push rods and take out the tappets.
(3) Remove the timing cover, timing chain tensioner, chain and gears.
(4) Detach the oil pump.
(5) Remove the distributor and spindle drive. Do not slacken the clamping plate bolt or the ignition timing setting will be lost.
(6) Take out the two setscrews which secure the camshaft locating plate to the cylinder block.
(7) Withdraw the camshaft forward, rotating it slowly to assist the withdrawal.
(8) Inspect the camshaft bearing journals and cams for signs of scoring. If the journals are not within the required diameter limits (see under 'General Data'), the camshaft should be renewed.
(9) Examine the camshaft front bearing for scores, pits or evidence of failure. If the bearing has to be renewed it will necessitate the removal of the engine back plate as described under 'Flywheel & Engine Rear Plate'.
The old bearing can then be withdrawn and a new one installed, using Service Tool 18G 124A with 18G 124K. Oil holes must be lined up carefully and the front bearing reamed in line to give .001 to .002 in. (.025 to .051 mm.) clearance, using Service Tool 18G 123 with 18G 123AH. The centre and rear camshaft bearings are cast in the block and are therefore non-renewable.
(10) Inspect the tappet cam contacting surfaces for wear. New tappets should be installed wherever evidence of unusual wear is found.
(11) The installation of the camshaft and tappets is a reversal

of the procedure '**Removal**'. Lubricate the camshaft journals with engine oil.

FLYWHEEL AND ENGINE REAR PLATE

To Remove

The flywheel complete with starter ring is secured to the flange on the rear of the crankshaft by four set bolts, which are locked in position by two lockplates. The engine rear plate is secured to the crankcase by set bolts and lockwashers. To remove the flywheel and rear plate, after the engine is removed from the vehicle, proceed as follows:

(1) Remove the gearbox from the engine (See Gearbox chapter).
(2) Remove the clutch (See Clutch chapter).
(3) Knock back the tabs of the lockplates, unscrew the bolts and withdraw the flywheel.
(4) Unscrew the set bolts and withdraw the engine rear plate.
(5) Examine the flywheel teeth and friction face for excessive wear. If the teeth on the starter ring are damaged or badly worn, a replacement flywheel and ring should be fitted.
(6) Examine the engine rear plate for distortion and damage and clean the joint faces of the plate and crankcase and check for scores.

To Install

(1) Refit the engine rear plate to the crankcase, using a new joint washer. Tighten the securing bolts evenly and firmly with a torque wrench to 22 lb. ft. (3.042 kg. m.).
(2) Place the flywheel over the flange and flange bolts of the crankshaft so that the timing mark '¼' is at T.D.C. when the first throw of the crankshaft is at T.D.C. The joint faces should be perfectly clean. Fit the lockplates and nuts on the bolts and tighten them in diagonal sequence with a torque wrench to 40 lb. ft. (55 kg. m.).

CRANKSHAFT AND MAIN BEARINGS

To Remove

The forged-steel crankshaft is statically and dynamically balanced and is supported in the crankcase by three renewable main bearings of the sintered copper and lead steel-backed type. Crankshaft end float is controlled by thrust washers fitted on both sides of the centre main bearing.

(1) Remove the engine from the vehicle and place it upside-down in a dismantling fixture.
(2) Remove the sump and oil strainer.
(3) Remove the timing chain.
(4) Remove the flywheel and engine rear plate.

(5) Check the crankshaft end float to determine whether the renewal of the thrust washers is necessary. (See General Data.)

(6) Remove the connecting rod bearing caps and inserts, keeping the inserts with their respective caps for correct replacement, and release the connecting rods from the crankshaft. Remove the spark plugs from the cylinder head to facilitate the turning of the crankshaft.

(7) Withdraw the main bearing caps complete. Caps and both insert halves should be kept together. Remove the screwed plug from the rear bearing cap oil return pipe and withdraw the pipe. Note that each main bearing is stamped with a common number, which is also stamped on the centre web of the crankcase near the main bearing. The bottom halves of the two thrust washers will be removed with the centre main bearing cap.

(8) Remove the crankshaft, the two remaining halves of the thrust washers and the top half-inserts of the main bearings from the crankcase.

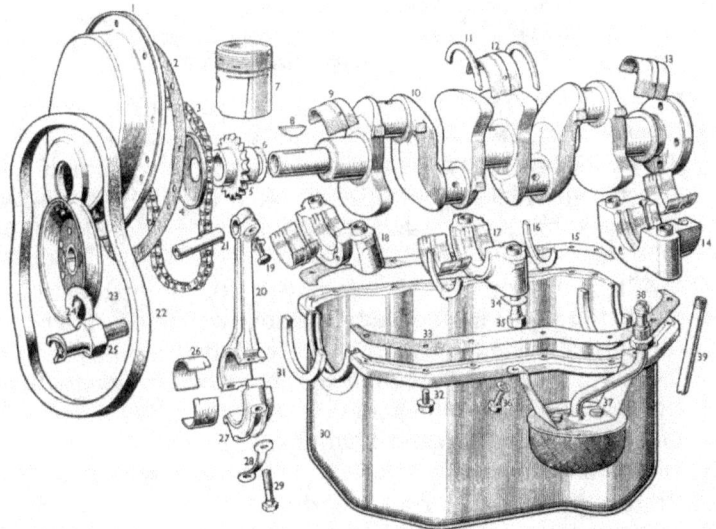

The crankshaft and sump assembly.

1. Engine front cover.
2. Joint washer for cover.
3. Timing chain.
4. Crankshaft oil thrower.
5. Crankshaft gear.
6. Packing washers.
7. Piston.
8. Woodruff key.
9. Front main half bearing.
10. Crankshaft.
11. Thrust washer, upper.
12. Centre main half bearing.
13. Rear main half bearing.
14. Rear main bearing cap and dowels.
15. Oil sump joint washer, right.
16. Thrust washer, lower.
17. Centre main bearing cap and dowels.
18. Front main bearing cap and dowels.
19. Clamping screw and washer for (20).
20. Connecting rod, less cap.
21. Gudgeon pin.
22. Vee-belt for fan and pulley.
23. Crankshaft pulley.
24. Lockwasher.
25. Starting nut.
26. Connecting rod half bearing.
27. Connecting rod cap.
28. Lockwasher.
29. Setscrew for connecting rod.
30. Oil sump.
31. Cork sealing washer.
32. Set screw and captive washer.
33. Oil sump joint washer, left.
34. Main bearing cap lockwasher.
35. Setscrew for main bearing cap.
36. Setscrew and shakeproof washer for strainer bracket.
37. Oil strainer.
38. Suction pipe.
39. Drain pipe for rear main bearing cap

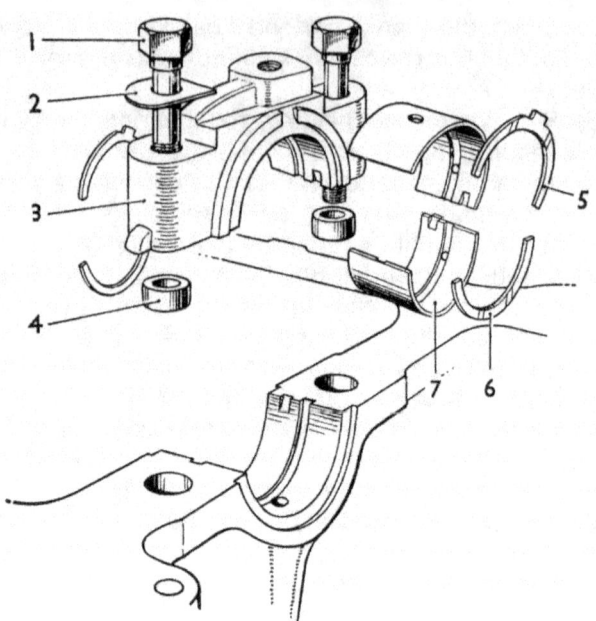

1. *Main bearing setscrews.*
2. *Lockwasher.*
3. *Main bearing cap.*
4. *Dowels.*
5. *Thrust washer, lower.*
6. *Thrust washer, upper.*
7. *Main bearing shell.*

(9) Inspect the crankcase main journals and crankpins for wear, scores, scratches and ovality. If necessary the crankshaft may be re-ground to the minimum limits shown under 'General Data'. Main bearings for re-ground crankshafts are available in sizes shown under 'General Data'.

(10) Clean the crankshaft thoroughly, ensuring that the connecting oilways between the journals and crankpins are perfectly clear. They can be cleaned out by applying a pressure gun containing fuel or solvent. When clean, inject a thin oil in the same manner.

(11) Thoroughly clean the bearings, caps and housings above the crankshaft.

(12) Examine the bearing inserts for wear and pitting, and look for evidence of breaking away or picking-up. Renew if necessary.

(13) Bearings are pre-finished with the correct diametral clearance, and do not require bedding in. New bearings should be marked to match up with the marking on the cap, and **on no account should they be filed to take up wear or to reduce running clearance.**

(14) Check the thrust washers for wear on their bearing surfaces, and renew if necessary to obtain the correct end float.

To Install

The installation of the crankshaft and main bearings is a reversal of the procedure **'To Remove'**, noting the following points:
(1) Ensure that the thrust washers are replaced the correct way round, the oil grooves should face outwards, and locate the bottom half tab in the slot in the bearing cap.
(2) The bearing inserts are notched to fit the recesses machined to the housing and cap.
(3) Remember to fit the packing washers behind the crankshaft timing chain wheel.
(4) Lubricate the bearings freely with engine oil.
(5) The rear main bearing cap horizontal joint surfaces should be thoroughly cleaned and lightly covered with WEL-SEAL (manufactured by Messrs. Wellworthy Ltd.) sealing compound before the cap is fitted to the cylinder block. This ensures a perfect oil seal when the cap is bolted down to the block.
(6) Tighten the main bearing nuts, see 'General Data' for torque wrench settings.

CYLINDER BLOCK

To Remove and Dismantle
(1) Remove and dismantle the engine.
(2) Remove all studs, unions and screwed plugs, etc., if necessary.
(3) If an expansion plug has blown, or leaks, remove the plug by drilling a hole in its centre and lever it out with a screwdriver or other suitable tool.

To View and Overhaul
(1) Scrape as much sediment as possible from the water passages and thoroughly wash out with a water hose.
(2) Clean all gasket surfaces.
(3) Inspect for cracks and scores on gasket surfaces.
(4) It may be advisable to remove the ridge above the ring travel at the top of the cylinder bores before checking the fit of the pistons.
(5) Wipe the cylinder bores clean and examine them for scores, out-of-round and taper. If the cylinders are found to be out-of-round or excessively tapered when measured with a dial test indicator, they should be reconditioned.
(6) If cylinder reconditioning is required, determine accurately the amount of material to be removed (refer to 'General Data' concerning oversize pistons available).
(7) Make sure that all traces of abrasives are cleaned from all parts of the cylinder block after the cylinder reconditioning operation is completed.
(8) Check the camshaft bearings.

To Reassemble and Install

(1) Install all studs, unions and screwed plugs, etc.
(2) When installing new expansion plugs, coat the edge of the plug with a sealing compound and insert the plug with the 'bulge' on the outside. A carefully aimed blow at the centre of the plug with a small hammer direct or with a blunt punch will expand the plug sufficiently to make a watertight joint. If too heavy a blow is used, the plug will be useless and must be replaced by another new one.
(3) Reassemble, install and test the engine.

FAULT DIAGNOSIS

Symptom	No.	Possible Fault
(a) Will Not Start	1	Defective coil
	2	Faulty condenser
	3	Dirty, pitted, or incorrectly set contact breaker points
	4	Ignition wires loose or leaking
	5	Water on spark plugs leads
	6	Corrosion of terminals or discharged battery
	7	Faulty starter
	8	Wrongly connected plug leads
	9	Vapour lock in fuel line
	10	Defective fuel pump
	11	Over-choking
	12	Under-choking
	13	Choked petrol filter or jets
	14	Valves leaking
	15	Sticking valves
	16	Valve timing incorrect
	17	Ignition timing incorrect
(b) Engine Stalls	1	In (a), check 1, 2, 3, 4, 10, 11, 12, 13, 14 and 15 Plugs defective or incorrect gap
	2	Retarded ignition
	3	Mixture too weak
	4	Water in fuel system
	5	Petrol tank breather choked
	6	Incorrect valve clearance
(c) Poor Idling	1	In (b), check 1 and 6 Air leak at manifold joints
	2	Incorrect slow running adjustment
	3	Air leak in carburetter(s)
	4	Slow running jet choked
	5	Over-rich mixture
	6	Worn piston rings
	7	Worn valve stems or guides
	8	Weak exhaust valve springs

Symptom	No.	Possible Fault
(d) Misfiring	1	In (a), check 1, 2, 3, 4, 5, 8, 10, 13, 14, 15, 16 and 17 In (b), check 1, 2, 3 and 6 Weak or broken valve springs
(e) Overheating		See Chapter on Cooling System
(f) Low Compression	1 2	In (a), check 14 and 15 In (c), check 6 and 7 In (d), check 1 Worn piston ring grooves Scored or worn cylinder bores
(g) Lack of Power	1 2 3	In (a), check 3, 10, 11, 13, 14, 15 and 16 In (b), check 1, 2, 3 and 6 In (c), check 6 and 7 In (d), check 1 Check (e) and (f) Leaking joint washers Fouled sparking plugs Automatic advance not functioning
(h) Burnt Valves or Seats	1	In (a), check 14 and 15 In (b), check 6 In (d), check 1 Check (e) Excessive carbon around valve seat and head
(j) Sticking Valves	1 2 3	In (d), check 1 Bent valve stem Scored valve stem or guide Incorrect valve clearance
(k) Excessive Cylinder Wear	1 2 3 4 5 6	Check 11 in (a) Check (e) Lack of oil Dirty oil Dirty air cleaner Gummed up or broken piston rings Badly fitting piston rings Misalignment of conrods
(l) Excessive Oil Consumption	1 2 3 4 5 6	In (c), check 6 and 7 Check (k) Ring gap too wide Oil return holes in piston choked with carbon Scored cylinders Oil level too high External oil leaks Ineffective valve oil seal

Symptom	No.	Possible Fault
(m) Crankshaft and Connecting Rod Bearing Failure	1 2 3 4 5	In (k), check 1 Restricted oilways Worn journals on crankpins Loose bearing caps Extremely low oil pressure Bent connecting rod
(n) Internal Water Leakage		See Chapter on Cooling System
(o) Poor Circulation		See Chapter on Cooling System
(p) Corrosion		See Chapter on Cooling System
(q) High Fuel Consumption		See Chapter on Fuel System
(r) Engine Vibration	1 2 3 4 5	Loose generator bolts Fan blades out of balance Exhaust pipe mountings too tight

COOLING SYSTEM

The circulation of the cooling water is effected by a centrifugal pump mounted in front of the cylinder block and driven by a belt from the crankshaft pulley. A thermostat is fitted in the water outlet pipe at the front end of the engine.

When filling or topping-up the radiator, do so when the engine is cold, and if possible use rainwater or clean soft water. Fill up to the filler plug orifice.

The capacity of the system is 10 pints (5.68 litres, 12 U.S. pints.)

ADJUSTMENTS IN VEHICLE

Overheating may be caused by a slack fan belt, excessive carbon deposit in the cylinders, running with the ignition too far retarded, improper carburetor adjustment, a partially choked radiator causing failure of the water to circulate, or loss of water due to leakage or evaporation.

The belt should be just sufficiently tight to prevent slip yet it should be possible to move it laterally about 1 in. (2.54 cms.). To make an adjustment slacken the 3 bolts which hold the generator in position, then raise or lower the generator until the desired tension of the belt is obtained. Securely lock the generator in position again when the adjustment has been made.

RADIATOR

To Remove

(1) Drain the cooling system.
(2) Slacken the hose clip, on the upper water hose, at the thermostat housing and with the aid of a screwdriver ease the pipe off the housing extension.
(3) Take off the radiator bottom hose by releasing the clips on the water pump and water outlet pipe if a heater is fitted.
(4) Remove the four nuts (two on each side) which secure the radiator to the mounting flanges and remove the radiator.

(5) Inspect the radiator core for damage and test it for water leaks. Solder at the points where leakage occurs or renew the core if necessary.
(6) Inspect the drain tap for leaks and renew it if necessary.
(7) Test the filler cap.
(8) Inspect the hose connections for deterioration and renew them if necessary.

To Replace

Installation is a reversal of the procedure 'To remove.'

THERMOSTAT

To Remove

(1) Drain the cooling system.
(2) Disconnect the outlet hose from the outlet elbow.
(3) Remove the three nuts and spring washers from the thermostat cover and lift the cover off its studs.
(4) Remove the paper joint washer and lift out the thermostat.
(5) Test the thermostat opening temperature by immersing it in water at a temperature between 154° and 167°F. (68° and 75°C.). If the thermostat valve does not start to open, or the valve sticks in the fully open position, the thermostat should be renewed. No attempt should be made to repair the thermostat.
(6) Clean the joint faces at the outlet elbow and at the housing in the cylinder head.

To Replace

The installation of the thermostat is a reversal of the procedure 'to remove'. Fit a new paper joint washer between the cover and the cylinder head. In an emergency the engine can be run with the thermostat removed.

TEMPERATURE GAUGE

A temperature gauge unit, consisting of a thermal element and dial indicator is fitted to the vehicle. The thermal element is held in the radiator header tank by a gland nut. The dial indicator is situated in the instrument panel and is connected to the element by a capilliary tube filled with mercury.

Damage to any of the above mentioned parts will necessitate the renewal of the complete temperature gauge unit.

The combined water temperature and oil pressure gauges are of integral construction, and should one of these instruments fail, both will have to be renewed.

FAN AND PUMP ASSEMBLY

To Remove

(1) Remove the radiator.
(2) Remove the generator.

(3) Remove the pump unit from the cylinder block by removing the four securing bolts and spring washers and disconnecting the lower hose, bypass hose, and interior heater hose if any.

(4) Remove the fan blades if necessary by withdrawing the four set screws from the pulley.

To Replace

The installation of the fan and pump assembly is a reversal of the procedure 'To remove'. Particular note should be made of the following:

(1) Fit a new joint washer between the pump body and the cylinder block.

(2) Inspect the fan belt for uneven wear or frayed fabric, and renew the belt if required.

(3) Remove the water pump oiling plug (A) on the water pump casing and add a small quantity of S.A.E. 140 oil. The oiling of the pump must be done sparingly, otherwise oil will flow past the bearings on to the face of the carbon sealing ring and impairing its efficiency.

(4) Check to see that the bearings run freely without excessive end play by spinning the fan.

(5) Adjust the fan belt tension.

DRAINING AND FLUSHING THE SYSTEM

To Drain the System

When the vehicle is to be stored the entire cooling system

should be drained to protect against corrosion, and in certain instances, freezing. To drain the system proceed as follows:
  (1) With the vehicle standing on level ground, remove the radiator filler cap.
  Caution — As the system is pressurised, do not remove the radiator filler cap while the engine is running and always wait until the water has cooled.
  If it is necessary to remove the filler cap while the engine is hot it is essential to remove it gradually and the filler neck is provided with a shaped cam to enable this to be done.
  Unscrew the cap slowly until the retaining tongues are felt to engage the small lobes at end of the filler neck cam, and wait until the pressure in the radiator is fully released before finally removing the cap.
  (2) Open the cylinder block and radiator drain taps. If the system contains anti-freeze mixture it should be drained into clean containers, strained and preserved for re-use.
  (3) To prevent the possibility of operating the vehicle with the system drained make sure that a suitable notice is placed on the vehicle or other precautions taken.

To Flush the System

Because there are impurities in the water in certain localities, deposits are left in the system. These deposits tend to clog the system and so impair cooling efficiency. It is therefore desirable to flush the radiator and water passages every 12,000 miles (19200 km.).
  (1) Remove the filler cap and drain tap and allow the system to be thoroughly cleansed by flushing clean water through the filler orifice.
  (2) Remove the radiator from the vehicle turn it upside down and reverse flush by feeding clean water through the elbow on the bottom tank and allowing waste water to escape through the filler orifice.
  (3) Remove and clean the thermostat.

FROST PRECAUTIONS

Care should be taken to see that the water is drained off completely, for in case of freezing it will do harm by expansion taking place and fracture of the cylinder block may result. There are two drain taps, one of them on to the rear of the engine on the left hand side, and the other at the base of the radiator. Both taps must be opened to drain the system and the vehicle must be on level ground while draining. Freezing may occur first at the bottom of the radiator or in the lower hose connection. Ice in the hose will stop water circulation and may cause boiling.

A muff can be used to advantage but care must be taken not **to run with the muff fully closed, or boiling will result.**

It must be noted that in the case of a car fitted with a heater no provision is made for draining the heater unit. Draining the radiator and cylinder block is not, therefore, a sufficient safeguard against freezing, an anti-freeze mixture must be used.

When frost is expected or when the vehicle is to be used in very low temperatures, make sure that the strength of the solution is, in fact, up to the strength recommended by the manufacturers, for conditions likely to be encountered.

The strength of the solution must be maintained by topping-up with anti-freeze solution as necessary. Excessive topping-up with water will reduce the degree of protection afforded.

If the cooling system has to be emptied run the mixture into a clean container and use it again.

HEATER UNIT

Description

The Smith's heating and ventilating system is designed to provide heated fresh air to the car interior at floor level and to the windscreen for demisting and defrosting.

Air for the heater is drawn from a forward-facing intake via an auxiliary blower which should only be needed at speeds below about 25 m.p.h. A shut-off valve is incorporated in the heater intake to prevent fumes from entering the car in traffic. The valve must always be open when heating is required. A water tap is fitted at the rear end of the engine. In summer conditions this tap may be shut off and the system may then be used for cool air ventilation.

Controls

The heating and ventilating system is operated by a single control located on the fascia panel. This control takes the form of a knob marked 'Air — Push and Turn'. For heating and demisting, push in the air control knob. The blower may be switched on if required by turning the knob in a clockwise direction. The knob MUST be pushed in before the blower can be switched on. Two doors located forward at either side of the gearbox tunnel control distribution of air between screen and car interior. For heating, open the doors. For defrosting (i.e., boosting flow of hot air to screen) close the doors.

Heater Removal

(1) Drain the cooling system.
(2) Disconnect the butterfly valve control wire situated at the right-hand side of the heater unit.
(3) Detach the heater inlet and outlet pipes at their heater connections.
(4) Remove the four setpins securing the heater unit to the engine bulkhead.

(5) Withdraw the heater and at the same time slip it off the air intake pipe.

Heater Replacement

Installation of the heater unit is a reversal of the removal procedure.

MODIFIED ENGINE DRAIN TAP

From Engine No. 9C/U/H 6359 a cylinder block drain tap (Part No. 3H576) of improved design is fitted. This tap is introduced to overcome any difficulty of operation and has a plain British Standard Pipe thread in place of the taper thread previously used. A fibre washer must, therefore, be fitted between the cylinder block and the tap.

The new tap is interchangeable with that previously used.

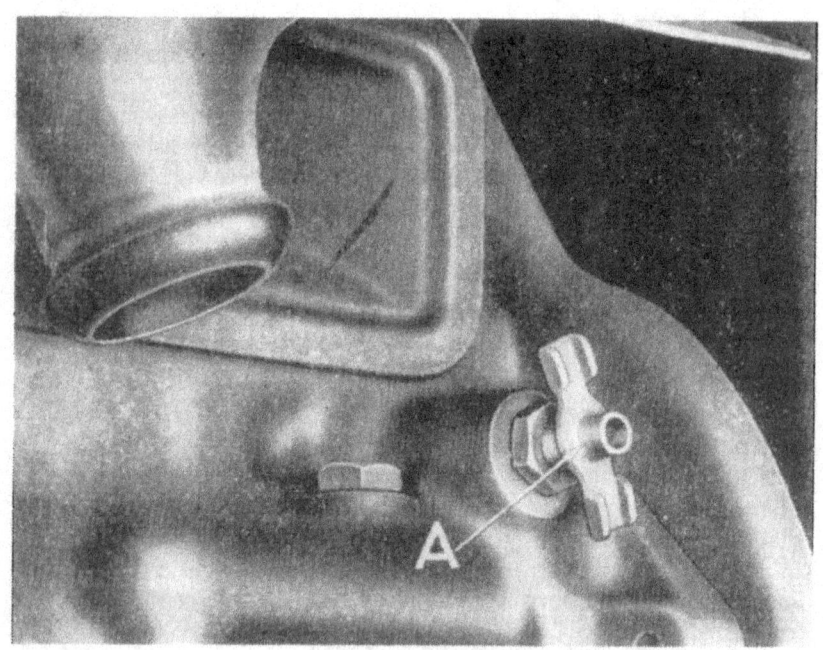

CLUTCH

The clutch is a Borg & Beck single dry-plate-type operated hydraulically. A steel cover bolted to the flywheel encloses the driven plate, the pressure plate, the pressure springs, and the release levers. The driven plate, to which the friction linings are riveted, incorporates springs assembled around the hub to absorb power shocks and torsional vibration. The pressure springs force the pressure plate against the friction linings, gripping the driven plate between the pressure plate and the engine flywheel. When the clutch pedal is depressed, the release bearing is moved forward against the release plate which bears against the three levers. Each release lever is pivoted on a floating pin, which remains stationary in the lever and rolls across a short flat portion of the enlarged hole in the eyebolt. The outer ends of the eyebolts extend through holes in the clutch cover and are fitted with adjusting nuts, by means of which each lever is located and locked in position. The outer or shorter ends of the release levers engage the pressure plate lugs by means of struts which provide knife-edge contact between the outer ends of the levers and the pressure plate lugs, so eliminating friction at this point. Pressure applied by the release bearing causes the pressure plate to be pulled away from the driven plate, compressing the pressure springs which are assembled between the pressure plate and the clutch cover. As the friction linings wear, the pressure plate moves closer to the flywheel face and the outer or shorter ends of the release levers follow. This causes the inner or longer ends of the levers to travel farther towards the gearbox and decreases the clearance between the release lever plate and the release bearing. This is automatically compensated unless the master cylinder has been disturbed.

A free movement of 5/32 in. must be maintained at the clutch pedal pad. This clearance is adjusted by means of the hexagon on the master cylinder push rod.

CLUTCH PEDAL

To Remove

The removal of the clutch and brake pedal assembly is detailed below.

(1) Working under the bonnet (hood) disconnect the clutch and brake pedal levers from the master cylinder push-rods by removing the spring clips and withdrawing the clevis pins.

(2) Within the car remove the nut and spring washer and withdraw the fulcrum pin, noting that a distance piece separates the two pedals.

(3) Remove the pedals downwards.

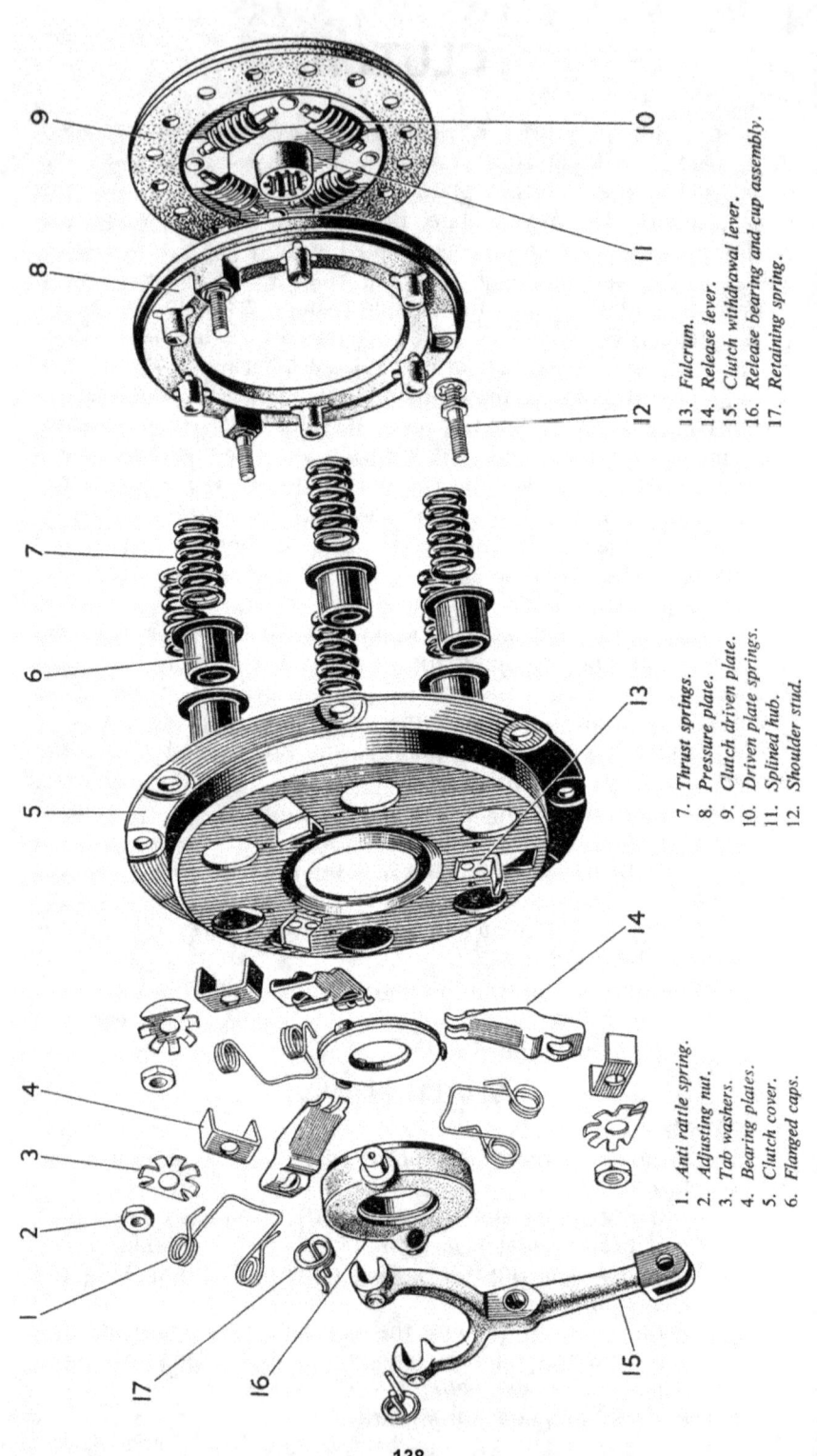

It is possible, to remove the pedals combined with the clutch and brake master cylinder unit, and this operation is described in both clutch and brake master cylinder sections of this handbook.

MASTER CYLINDER

The master cylinder caters for operation of both brake and clutch. It has two bores which are side by side and, except for the fact that one has no check valve, each bore accommodates normal master cylinder parts. The bore with the check valve serves the brakes, the other serves the clutch slave cylinder.

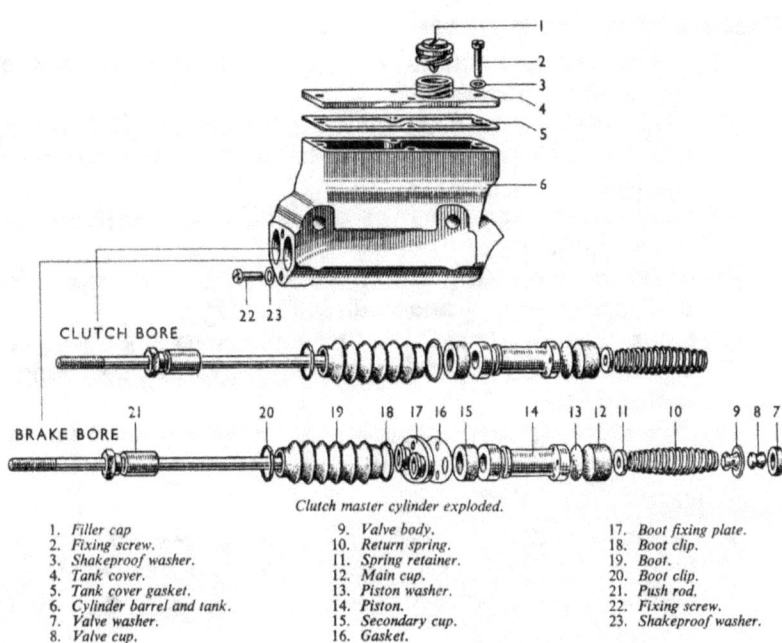

Clutch master cylinder exploded.

1. Filler cap
2. Fixing screw.
3. Shakeproof washer.
4. Tank cover.
5. Tank cover gasket.
6. Cylinder barrel and tank.
7. Valve washer.
8. Valve cup.
9. Valve body.
10. Return spring.
11. Spring retainer.
12. Main cup.
13. Piston washer.
14. Piston.
15. Secondary cup.
16. Gasket.
17. Boot fixing plate.
18. Boot clip.
19. Boot.
20. Boot clip.
21. Push rod.
22. Fixing screw.
23. Shakeproof washer.

Removal

The following removal procedure involves the withdrawal of the master cylinder unit complete with clutch and brake pedals, as it is not necessary to disconnect the pedals for normal master cylinder maintenance.

Note: Before disconnecting the master cylinder ascertain, for assembly purposes, which bore is communicated with the clutch slave cylinder.

(1) Remove the heater blower unit by first releasing the wire (green and brown) and the earth wire (white) and then unscrewing the two setpins securing the heater blower bracket to the bulkhead.

(2) Unscrew the ten setpins securing the master cylinder mounting plate to the engine bulkhead.

(3) Disconnect the two hydraulic lines at their unions with

the rear of the master cylinder unit.

(4) Withdraw the master cylinder unit upwards and at the same time manipulate the clutch and brake pedals through the aperture in the bulkhead.

(5) Disconnect each pedal from their master cylinder push-rods by removing the spring clips and withdrawing the clevis pins.

(6) The master cylinder unit is attached to its mounting plate by two bolts, nuts and washers, and when these are unscrewed and withdrawn the master cylinder unit is free to be disconnected.

Dismantling the Clutch Cylinder

(1) Unscrew the set screws securing the boot fixing plate to the master cylinder body.

(2) Detach the fixing plate from the master cylinder leaving the boots and push rods attached to the clutch and brake pedals.

(3) Unscrew the common filler cap and drain the fluid into a clean container.

(4) Withdraw the piston, piston washer (13), main cup (12), spring retainer (11) and return spring (10).

(5) Using only the fingers to prevent damage, remove the secondary cup (15) by stretching it over the end flange of the piston.

(6) Examine all parts, especially the washers, for wear or distortion, and replace with new parts where necessary.

Assembling the Clutch Cylinder

(1) Fit the secondary cup (15) on the piston (14), so that the lip of the cup faces the piston head and gently work the cup round the groove with the fingers to ensure that it is properly seated.

(2) Assemble the retainer (11) on the smaller end of the return spring and insert the assembly into the cylinder.

(3) Install the main cup (12) into the cylinder, lip foremost, taking care not to damage or turn back the lip of the cup.

(4) Follow up with the piston washer, pay particular attention to the illustration showing method of assembly.

(5) Press the piston (14) into the cylinder taking care not to damage or turn back the lip of the secondary cup (15).

(6) Insert the push rod in the piston and maneuver the boot fixing plate into position. Secure the plate by its two set screws and then ascertain that the rubber boots are seating correctly. The vent holes in each boot should be at the bottom where the cylinder is mounted on the vehicle.

If the boots are damaged or perished, new ones should be fitted.

(7) Fill the reservoir with clean Lockheed brake fluid and test the clutch cylinder by pushing the piston inwards and allowing it to return unassisted. After a few applications, fluid should flow from the outlet connection in the cylinder barrel.

Replacement

The installation of the master cylinder unit is the reversal of the removal procedure.

If no further maintenance of the clutch is necessary, remember to bleed the system.

SLAVE CYLINDER

The cylinder is bolted to the underside of the clutch housing and comprises a piston, rubber cup, cup filler, return spring, push rod and bleeder screw. Fluid from the master cylinder is delivered via a metal pipe.

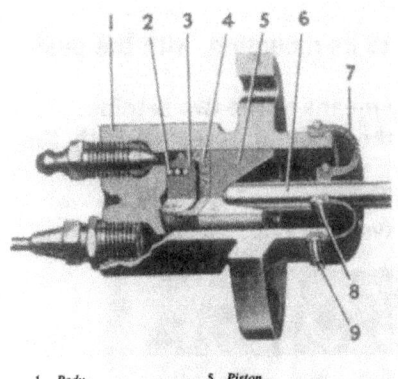

1. Body.
2. Spring.
3. Cup filler.
4. Cup.
5. Piston.
6. Push rod.
7. Boot.
8. Boot clip (small).
9. Boot clip (large).

Gearbox drain plug (1). Slave cylinder setpins (2).

To Remove

(1) Place a receptacle to catch the fluid and remove the flexible hose from the slave cylinder.
(2) Remove the split pin and clevis pin from the clutch withdrawal lever jaw end, thus freeing the slave cylinder push rod.
(3) Unscrew the two setpins securing the slave cylinder to the clutch housing.

To Dismantle

(1) Remove all dirt from the exterior of the cylinder.
(2) Remove the large boot clip (9) and if an air line is available — apply a **low** pressure to the fluid connection to expel the internal parts.
(3) **Clean** the slave cylinder components, **using only hydraulic fluid or alcohol.** The main casting may be cleaned with

any of the normal cleaning fluids, but all traces of the cleaning fluid must be dried out.

(4) Dry off and examine all rubber components and renew them if they are swollen, distorted or split. If there is any doubt as to their condition they must be renewed.

(5) Inspect the piston and cylinder bore for wear and scores, and renew them as necessary.

Assembling the Slave Cylinder

(1) Fit the spring (2) in the cup filler (3) and insert the parts, spring innermost, into the bore of the body (1).

(2) Follow up with the cup (4), lip leading, ensuring that the lip is not turned back or bucked.

(3) Insert the piston (5), flat face innermost, and then fit the circlip.

(4) If a new boot is being used, stretch the small end on to the push-rod and secure with the small boot clip.

To Replace

(1) Offer up the slave cylinder to its mounting, with the push-rod entering the bore.

(2) Secure the slave cylinder by means of the two setpins.

(3) Stretch the large end of the boot and secure with the boot clip (9).

(4) Screw in the hydraulic pipe union.

(5) Bleed the clutch hydraulic system.

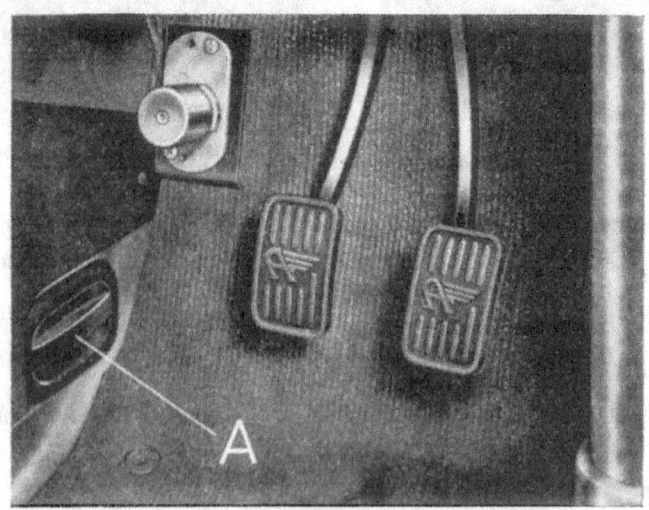

Depicting the position of the plug which must be removed in order to gain access to the slave cylinder bleed nipple.

BLEEDING THE CLUTCH SYSTEM

(1) Fill the master cylinder reservoir with brake fluid and keep at least a quarter full throughout the operation,

otherwise air will be drawn in, necessitating a fresh start.

(2) Attach a rubber tube to the bleeder screw on the slave cylinder, allowing the free end to be submerged in a little brake fluid in a clean glass jar.

(3) Slacken the bleeder screw and depress the clutch pedal slowly; tighten the screw before the pedal reaches the end of its stroke and allow the pedal to return unassisted.

(4) Repeat (3) until air bubbles cease to appear from the end of the tube in the jar.

REMOVAL

To remove the clutch assembly, it is necessary to remove the engine (without gearbox) as outlined in the Engine chapter, at which point the clutch cover screws can be unscrewed. Release these screws a turn at a time and work diagonally, to equalize pressure and avoid warpage, until spring pressure is relieved and the cover can be removed. A faulty clutch, with broken or weak springs, etc. should be replaced in toto. Exchange units are available at BMC dealers and parts suppliers.

FAULT DIAGNOSIS

Symptom	No.	Possible Fault
(a) Drag or Spin	1	Oil or grease on driven plate linings
	2	Bent engine backplate
	3	Misalignment between engine and first motion shaft
	4	Leaking operating cylinder, pipe line or air in system
	5	Driven plate hub binding on first motion shaft splines
	6	First motion shaft binding on its spigot bush
	7	Distorted clutch plate
	8	Warped or damaged pressure plate or clutch cover
	9	Broken clutch plate linings
	10	Dirt or foreign matter in clutch
	11	Air in clutch hydraulic system
	12	Bad external leak between the clutch master cylinder and slave cylinder
(b) Fierceness or Snatch		Check 1, 2 and 3 in (a)
	1	Check 4 in (a)
	2	Worn clutch linings
(c) Slip		Check 1, 2 and 3 in (a)
		Check 1 in (b)
	1	Weak thrust springs
	2	Weak anti-rattle springs
	3	Seized piston in clutch slave cylinder
(d) Judder		Check 1, 2 and 3 in (a)
	1	Pressure plate out of parallel with flywheel face
	2	Friction facing contact area not evenly distributed
	3	Bent first motion shaft
	4	Buckled driven plate
	5	Faulty engine or gearbox rubber mountings
	6	Worn shackles
	7	Weak rear springs
	8	Propeller shaft bolts loose
	9	Loose rear spring clips
(e) Rattle		Check 3 in (d)
	1	Damaged driven plate, i.e. broken springs, etc.
	2	Worn parts of release mechanism
	3	Excessive transmission backlash
	4	Wear in transmission bearings
	5	Release bearing loose on fork
(f) Tick or Knock	1	Worn first motion shaft bush
	2	Badly worn centre plate hub splines
	3	Out of line thrust plate
	4	Faulty bendix drive on starter
	5	Loose flywheel

GEARBOX

The gearbox has four forward speeds and one reverse, and synchromesh is incorporated on second, third and top gears.

Top gear is a direct drive; third and second are in constant mesh; first and reverse are obtained by sliding spur pinions.

LUBRICATION

Every 1,000 miles (1600 km.)

Check the oil level and top up if necessary. To gain access remove the rubber plug on the left side of the gearbox covering. The filler plug is then accessible. Remove the plug and fill up to the bottom of the threads. This gives the correct level.

Every 6,000 miles (9600 km.)

Drain after a run when the oil is warm, and refill with new oil. Capacity 2 1/3 imp. pints (1.33 litres, 2.8 U.S. pints).

REMOVAL AND REPLACEMENT

The engine and gearbox may be removed from the vehicle as a complete unit as described earlier. Whereupon the gearbox and engine are separated. The alternative method of gearbox removal is first to remove the engine and then withdraw the gearbox in the following manner:

(1) Remove the four self tapping screws from the change-speed-lever cover, and withdraw the cover off the lever.
(2) Remove the anti-rattle plunger, spring and cap from the side of the change-speed-lever turret.
(3) Unscrew the three change-speed-lever cover setpins and remove the lever.
(4) Peel back the carpet surrounding the gearbox cover to expose the gearbox rear mounting setpins. The location of the setpins is shown. Unscrew both setpins.

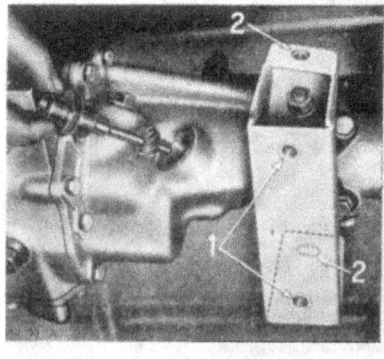

1. Location of the ⅜ in. AF rear mounting setpins.
2. Location of the 5/16 in. AF rear mounting setpins.

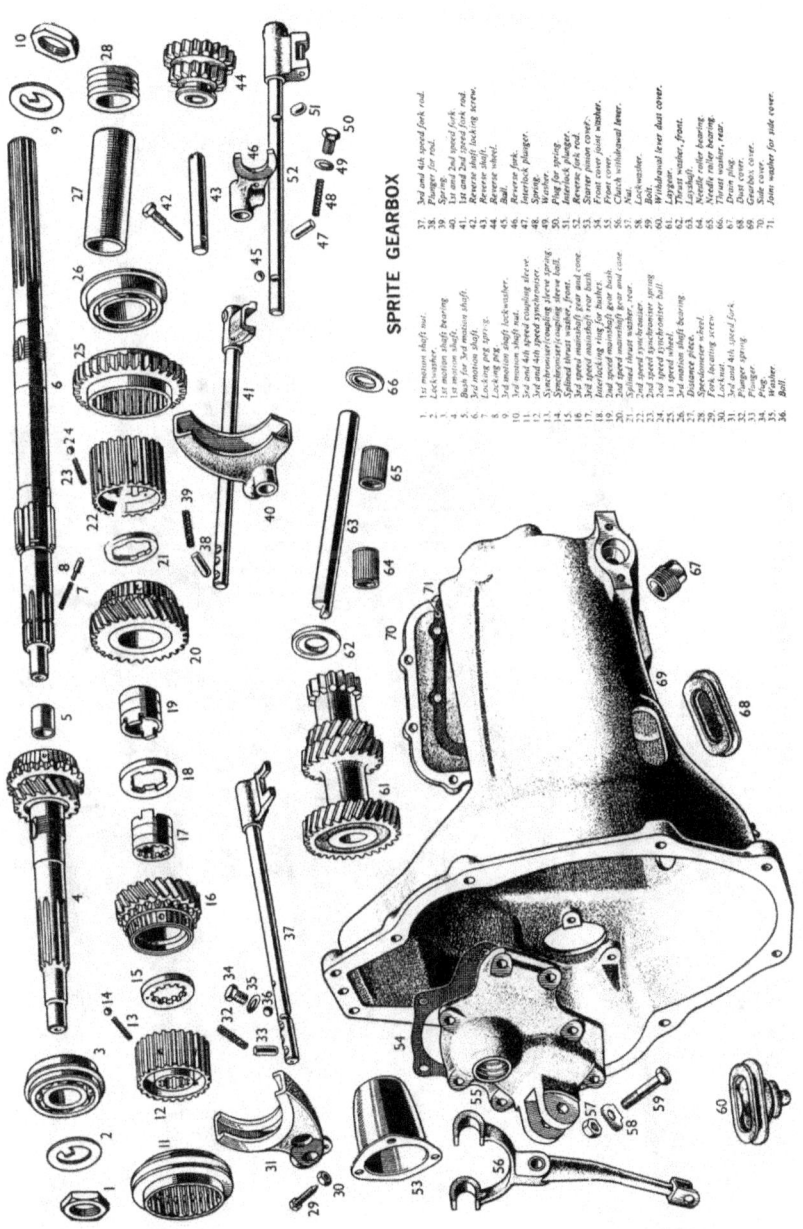

SPRITE GEARBOX

1. 1st motion shaft nut.
2. Lockwasher.
3. 1st motion shaft bearing.
4. 1st motion shaft.
5. Bush for 3rd motion shaft.
6. 3rd motion shaft.
7. Locking peg spring.
8. Locking peg.
9. 3rd motion shaft lockwasher.
10. 3rd motion shaft nut.
11. 3rd and 4th speed coupling sleeve.
12. 3rd and 4th speed synchromesh.
13. Synchroniser/coupling sleeve spring.
14. Splined thrust washer, front.
15. 3rd speed mainshaft gear and cone.
16. 3rd speed mainshaft rear bush.
17. Interlocking ring for bushes.
18. 2nd speed mainshaft gear and cone.
19. 2nd speed mainshaft gear bush.
20. 2nd speed synchromesh spring.
21. Splined thrust washer, rear.
22. 1st speed wheel.
23. 1st speed synchroniser.
24. 1st and 2nd speed synchroniser spring.
25. 1st and 2nd speed synchroniser ball.
26. Distance piece.
27. 3rd motion shaft bearing.
28. Speedometer wheel.
29. Fork locating screw.
30. Lockwasher.
31. 3rd and 4th speed fork.
32. Plunger spring.
33. Plunger.
34. Washer.
35. Ball.
37. 3rd and 4th speed fork rod.
38. Plunger for rod.
39. Spring.
40. 1st and 2nd speed fork rod.
41. 1st and 2nd speed fork.
42. Reverse shaft locking screw.
43. Reverse shaft.
44. Reverse wheel.
45. Ball.
46. Reverse fork.
47. Interlock plunger.
48. Spring.
49. Washer.
50. Plug for spring.
51. Interlock plunger.
52. Reverse fork rod.
53. Starter pinion cover.
54. Front cover (cover washer).
55. Front cover.
56. Clutch withdrawal lever.
57. Nut.
58. Lockwasher.
59. Bolt.
60. Withdrawal lever dust cover.
61. Laygear.
62. Thrust washer, front.
63. Layshaft.
64. Needle roller bearing.
65. Needle roller bearing.
66. Thrust washer, rear.
67. Drain plug.
68. Dust cover.
69. Gearbox cover.
70. Side cover.
71. Joint washer for side cover.

MK. II AND MIDGET GEARBOX

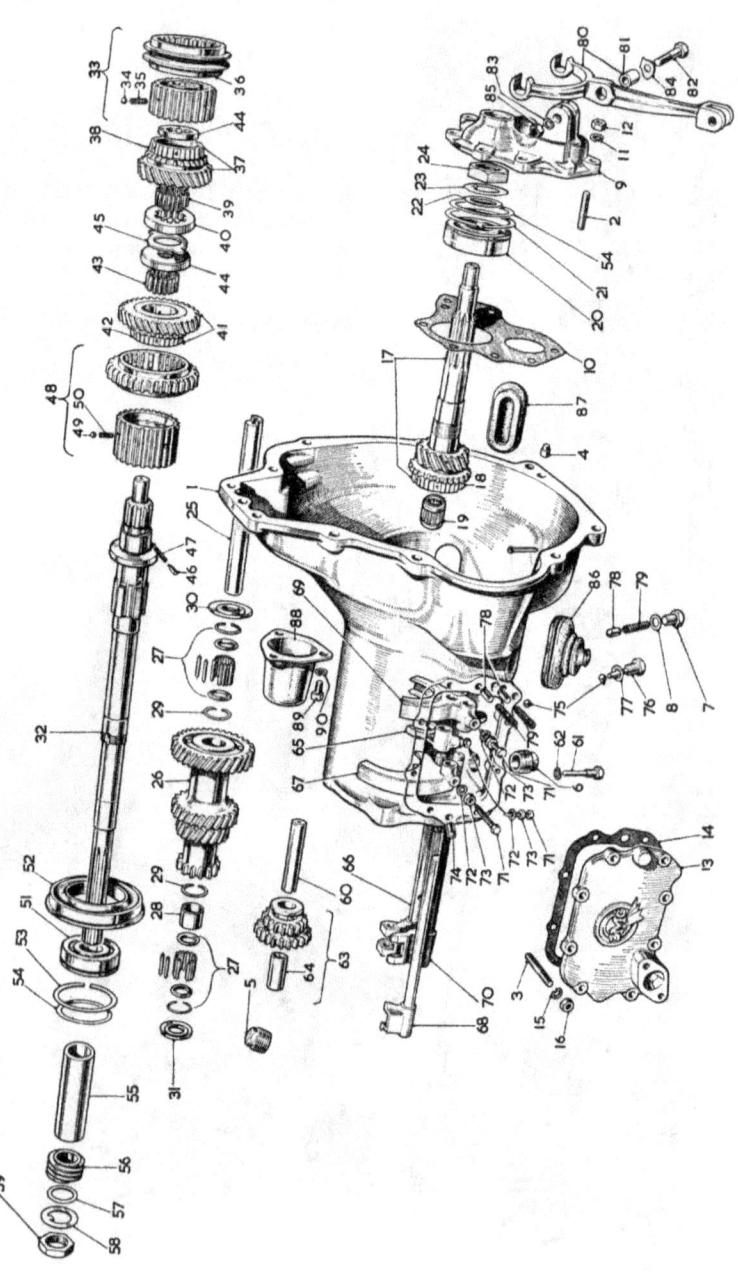

146

KEY TO THE GEARBOX COMPONENTS

No.	Description	No.	Description	No.	Description
1.	Case assembly.	31.	Thrust washer (rear).	61.	Screw.
2.	Stud for front cover.	32.	Third motion shaft.	62.	Spring washer.
3.	Stud for side cover.	33.	Third and fourth speed synchronizer.	63.	Reverse wheel with bush.
4.	Dowel.	34.	Ball.	64.	Bush.
5.	Filler plug.	35.	Spring.	65.	Reverse fork.
6.	Drain plug.	36.	Sleeve.	66.	Reverse fork rod.
7.	Plug for reverse plunger spring.	37.	Third speed gear with cone.	67.	First and second speed fork.
8.	Washer.	38.	Synchronizing cone.	68.	First and second speed fork rod.
9.	Front cover.	39.	Needle roller.	69.	Third and fourth speed fork.
10.	Front cover joint.	40.	Third speed gear locking collar.	70.	Third and fourth speed fork rod.
11.	Spring washer.	41.	Second speed gear with cone.	71.	Fork locating screw.
12.	Nut.	42.	Synchronizing cone.	72.	Shakeproof washer.
13.	Side cover.	43.	Needle roller.	73.	Nut.
14.	Joint for side cover.	44.	Second speed locking collar.	74.	Interlock plunger.
15.	Spring washer.	45.	Collars.	75.	Interlock ball.
16.	Nut.	46.	Peg for locking collar.	76.	Plug.
17.	First motion shaft with cone.	47.	Spring for peg.	77.	Washer.
18.	Synchronizing cone.	48.	First speed gear assembly.	78.	Plunger for fork rod.
19.	Needle-roller bearing.	49.	Ball.	79.	Spring.
20.	First motion shaft journal ball bearing.	50.	Spring for ball.	80.	Clutch withdrawal lever with bush.
21.	Spring ring.	51.	Third motion shaft journal ball bearing.	81.	Bush.
22.	Washer.	52.	Bearing housing.	82.	Bolt.
23.	Lock washer.	53.	Spring ring.	83.	Spring washer.
24.	Nut.	54.	Bearing packing washer.	84.	Locking washer.
25.	Layshaft.	55.	Third motion shaft distance piece.	85.	Nut.
26.	Laygear.	56.	Speedometer gear.	86.	Dust cover.
27.	Needle-roller bearing with spring ring.	57.	Plain washer.	87.	Dust cover for bell housing.
28.	Distance piece.	58.	Locking washer.	88.	Starter pinion cover.
29.	Spring ring.	59.	Third motion shaft nut.	89.	Screw.
30.	Thrust washer (front).	60.	Reverse shaft.	90.	Washer.

(5) Working beneath the vehicle, unscrew the speedometer drive cable at its union with the gearbox rear extension.
(6) Detach the clutch slave cylinder from the clutch bell-housing by unscrewing its two mounting setpins and withdrawing the push rod from the rear of the cylinder.
(7) Disconnect the propeller shaft from the rear axle by unscrewing the four self locking nuts.
(8) Unscrew the remaining two gearbox rear mounting setpins.
(9) Lift the gearbox together with the propeller shaft clear of the vehicle as shown.

Reassembly is a reversal of the above procedure. The propeller shaft **must** be connected to the rear end of the gearbox before the gearbox is replaced in the vehicle.

DISMANTLING

(1) Unscrew the filler plug. Drain the oil by removing the plug from the bottom of the gearbox.
(2) Unscrew the speedometer pinion sleeve from the left side of the gearbox rear cover, remove the fibre washer and withdraw the speedometer pinion.
(3) Remove the eight nuts securing the remote control housing and lift the housing off the rear cover.
(4) Unscrew the nine set screws and spring washers securing the rear cover to the gearbox.

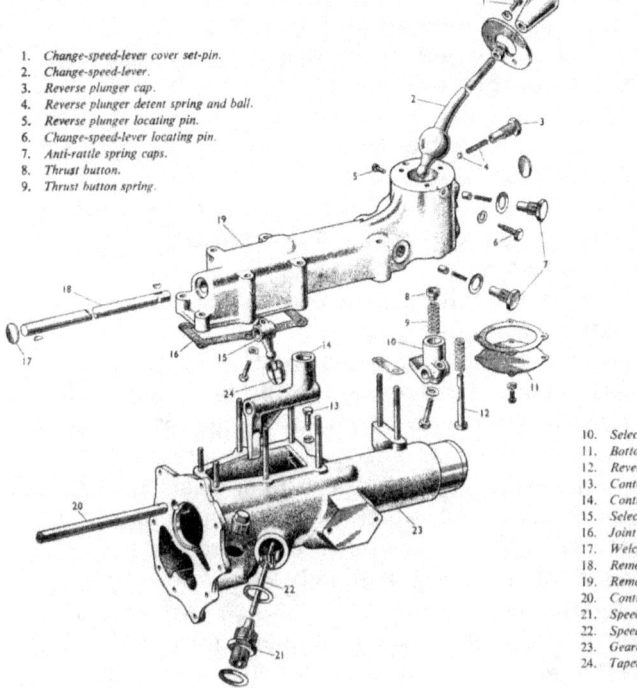

1. Change-speed-lever cover set-pin.
2. Change-speed-lever.
3. Reverse plunger cap.
4. Reverse plunger detent spring and ball.
5. Reverse plunger locating pin.
6. Change-speed-lever locating pin.
7. Anti-rattle spring caps.
8. Thrust button.
9. Thrust button spring.
10. Selector lever rear.
11. Bottom cover.
12. Reverse selector plunger.
13. Control shaft locating screw.
14. Control lever.
15. Selector lever front.
16. Joint washer.
17. Welch plug.
18. Remote control shaft.
19. Remote control housing.
20. Control shaft.
21. Speedometer pinion sleeve.
22. Speedometer pinion.
23. Gearbox rear cover.
24. Tapered bush.

(5) Pull the rear cover back slightly and turn it in an anti-clockwise direction as viewed from the rear, to enable the control lever to clear the fork rod ends, and then remove the rear cover from the gearbox.

(6) Remove the control shaft locating screw, and screw it into the tapped front end of the control shaft. Slight pressure on the screw will facilitate the removal of the control shaft, which is a push fit in the rear cover. The control lever will slip off the end of the shaft as the shaft is removed.

(7) The two halves of the control lever bush can be lifted out after removal of the circlip. From Gearbox No. 14495, a one-piece Nylon bush, which is interchangeable, is used and the circlip is deleted.

(8) Unscrew the four set screws securing the bottom cover to the change-speed-lever tower. Retain the paper joint washer if undamaged.

(9) Unscrew and remove the change-speed-lever locating peg and the two anti-rattle springs. The latter are removed by unscrewing the two caps and then tilting the remote control housing so that the springs and plungers drop out.

(10) Unscrew the three set pins securing the change-speed-lever cover to the top of the change-speed-lever tower

and remove the lever care being taken to retain the thrust button, and thrust button spring.
(11) Release the set screws in the front and rear selector levers, remove the welch plugs at either ends of the remote control housing, and using a suitable drift tap out the remote control shaft. The front and rear selector levers can then be removed.
(12) To remove the reverse selector plunger first unscrew the reverse plunger cap and remove the detent spring and ball, then remove the locating pin.
(13) Remove the clutch release bearing by levering out the two retaining springs.
(14) To remove the clutch withdrawal lever bend back the locking washer and remove the nut and washer. The bolt may then be unscrewed. Do not attempt to knock the bolt out, as it is threaded into the support bracket. To unscrew the bolt remove the rubber dust cover from the hole opposite that which the clutch withdrawal lever passes, and pass a suitable tool through the hole. On lefthand drive cars the clutch withdrawal lever passes through the hole on the left hand side of the bell-housing.
(15) Remove the seven nuts and washers from the front cover, situated within the clutch bell-housing. The front cover may then be withdrawn by gripping the clutch withdrawal lever brackets with the finger and thumb and pulling. Remove the paper joints and packing shim.
(16) Release the eight screws set in the side cover. Remove the side cover and joint washer. Remove the two springs from the front edge of the side cover joining face. Turn the gearbox on its side so that the two plungers fall out of the holes from which the springs were removed.
(17) Remove the two plugs situated near the clutch bell-housing on the side cover side of the gearbox casing. They each have a fibre washer and the lower of the two plugs covers the reverse plunger and spring, which may be removed by tilting the gearbox on its side. The other plug which has a long shank blocks the hole through which the interlock ball between the 1st and 2nd, and 3rd and 4th selector rods is inserted.
(18) Select neutral by aligning the slots in the rear ends of the selector rods. Working on the gearbox, with the side cover facing upwards, unlock and remove the reverse fork locating screw, lock nut and shakeproof washer through the drain plug hole. Similarly remove the locating screw lock nut and shakeproof washer from the 1st and 2nd, and 3rd and 4th speed forks.
(19) Tap the 3rd and 4th speed selector rod from the front end, and draw it out through the back of the gearbox.

Similarly remove the 1st and 2nd speed selector rod (nearest side cover) and then the reverse selector rod. As the selector rods are being drawn out care must be taken to remove the two interlock balls from the front end of gearbox casing. Also the double ended interlock plunger should be removed from the back end of the gearbox casing. The three selector forks may now be lifted out of the gearbox.

(20) Tap the layshaft out of the front of the gearbox with a bronze drift. On removing the drift the laygear cluster and thrust washers will drop into the bottom of the gearbox.

(21) Draw the main shaft assembly rearwards out of the gearbox case.

(22) Insert a long soft metal drift through the main shaft opening in the rear of the casing and drive the first motion shaft forwards out of the gearbox. The laygear cluster and thrust washers may now be removed.

(23) Remove the reverse shaft locking screw. Place a screwdriver on the slotted end of the reverse shaft and push it into the gearbox with a turning motion. The reverse shaft and gear may now be removed.

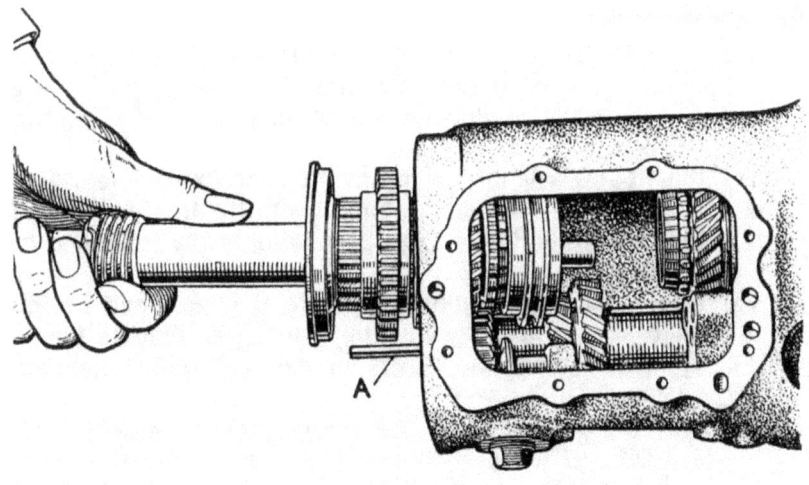

Drawing out the third motion shaft assembly after lowering the laygear on to the dummy layshaft 'A.'

EXAMINATION FOR WEAR

Bearings

The first and third motion shaft bearings become worn after a considerable length of service and should be renewed if there are signs of looseness between the inner and outer races.

Third Motion Shaft Spigot Bush

The bush is fitted to give a clearance of .002 to .003-in. to (.0508 to .0762 mm.) with the 3rd motion shaft. Any appreciable wear above this figure, necessitates examination of the bush and shaft and renewal where necessary.

Main Gear Bushes

The 2nd and 3rd speed main shaft gear bushes have an extremely low tolerance of .00025 to .0015-in. (.0064 to .0381 mm.) with the shaft. They should be replaced if any appreciable wear occurs between these bushes and the 3rd motion shaft.

Laygear Thrust Washers

These washers are designed to permit a laygear end float of .001 to .003-in. (.0254 to .0762 mm.). If the end float exceeds this amount, the thrust washers must be renewed. The smaller thrust washer, at the rear, is made in varying thicknesses to allow correct end float to be obtained.

Gear Synchronizing Cones

These cones are 'shrunk on' to the second, third and fourth speed gears and are normally supplied as a complete unit for spares purposes.

Gearbox Reassembly

(1) Reassembly the reverse gear on its shaft in the gearbox. Align the hole in the shaft with the hole in the casing and lock the shaft with the locking screw and spring washer.

(2) Put the laygear in position in the gearbox complete with its thrust washers, supporting it with the thin part of the dummy layshaft, the thick part being at the front end of the gearbox.

(3) Insert the third motion shaft into the back end of the gearbox and drift the bearing housing so that its flange is flush against the recess in the rear of the gearbox casing.

(4) Turn the gearbox casing to ensure that the laygear teeth are clear of the first motion shaft bearing housing. Now drift the first motion shaft into position from the front end (Service Tool 18G 4) ensuring that the spring ring registers properly in the recess in the gearbox casing.

(5) By drawing the dummy layshaft rearwards slightly lift the laygears into mesh. Smear the layshaft with oil and follow the dummy.
When the layshaft is being pushed into position maintain contact between it and the dummy layshaft or one of the thrust washers will slip out of position. With the side cover end uppermost, the half-mooned end in the front

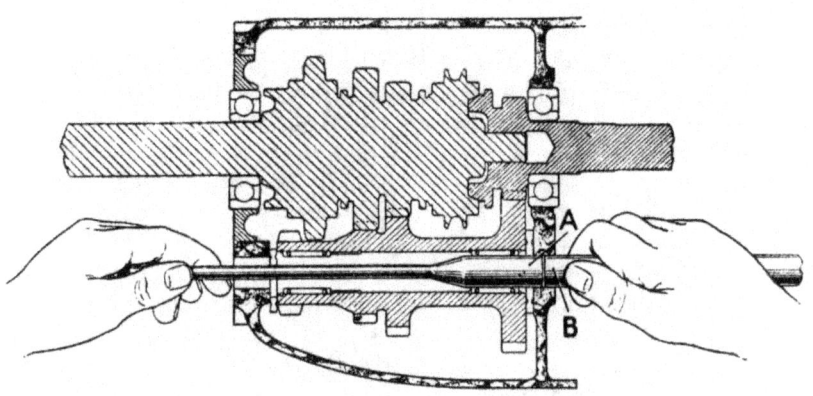

Dummy layshaft Service Tool 18G 471

of the layshaft should be in the U-position with its diameter horizontal.

(6) Place the reverse fork in position with its tapped hole towards the drain plug hole.
Fit the 1st and 2nd speed fork over the first speed wheel, and the 3rd and 4th speed fork over the 3rd and 4th speed coupling sleeve.

(7) With the side cover facing upwards push the reverse fork rod through the lowest hole in the rear of the gearbox casing, through the reverse fork, and through the clearance hole in the 3rd and 4th speed fork. Align the hole in the rod with the tapped hole in the fork, screw in the locking screw and lock it up with the shakeproof washer and nut.

(8) Drop the double ended plunger through the hole in the middle of the side cover rear face on the gearbox casing.

(9) Push the first and second fork rod through the uppermost selector rod hole in the rear of the gearbox casing, through its fork and into the front of the casing. As before, but through the side cover end of the casing, insert the locating screw and lock it in position.

(10) The third and fourth speed fork rod goes through the hole in the rear of the casing between the other two rods, through the fork and into the front of the gearbox casing. Push it through till it just enters the hole in the front of the gearbox casing.
Drop a ball down the hole in the edge of the side cover on the drain plug side of the casing and see that it goes between the reverse and third and fourth fork rods. This can be done by looking from the clutch housing end. Place a rod down the same hole and push hard against the ball to centralize the slot in the selector rod. If this is not done the third and fourth fork rod will be damaged

in trying to force it into position.

Turn the gearbox so that the drain plug is towards the top and drop a ball in the upper hole (in line with the drain plug hole) and see that it goes between the first and second, and third and fourth fork rods. As before guide a rod up the hole and push hard against the ball to centralize the slot in the rod. Push the third and fourth fork rod home and lock it in position.

Do not knock the selector rods in with a hammer. If any obstruction is felt when pushing the rods through the front of the gearbox casing, it is an indication that the balls are not seating correctly in their slots. Centralize the slots in the rod as previously described, so that the balls do not stand proud of their holes. It will be found that they can now be pushed home quite easily, by hand.

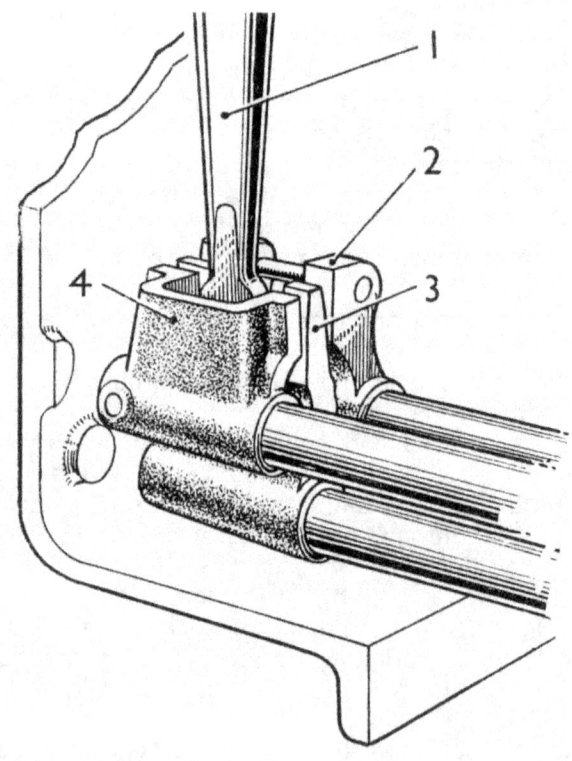

1. Change speed lever.
2. Reverse rod.
3. Third and fourth speed rod.
4. First and second speed rod.

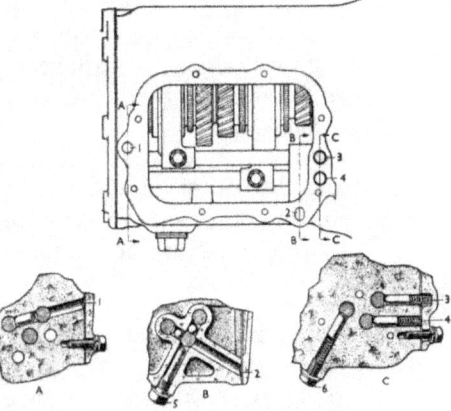

1. Hole for interlock plunger between reverse and 1st and 2nd speed fork rods.
2. Hole for ball between reverse and 3rd and 4th speed fork rods.
3. Hole for 1st and 2nd speed fork rod plunger.
4. Hole for 3rd and 4th speed fork rod plunger.
5. Plug for 1st and 2nd, and 3rd and 4th speed ball hole.
6. Plug for reverse plunger hole.

A, B and C are scrap views of sections AA, BB and CC respectively, looking in the direction of the arrows.

(11) Put the reverse plunger (rounded end first) in the lower hole on the drain plug side, followed by a spring, and fill the hole with its plug and fibre washer. The upper hole is blocked with a long shanked aluminum plug and fibre washer. The two remaining plungers go into the two holes in the front edge of the side cover face of the gearbox casing. Drop one into each hole, rounded end first and follow each plunger with a spring.

(12) Locate the side cover and paper joint washer on the studs, and screw on the eight nuts and spring washers and tighten up evenly by diagonal selection.

(13) Position the front cover joint washer; put the packing shims in the front cover holding it in position with grease; locate the front cover on the studs and secure it with the seven nuts and spring washers.
Although a .006-in. (.1524 mm.) shim is usually found to be sufficient, use the following method to shim the front and rear covers. Measure the depth of the cover recess and the amount by which the bearing outer race protrudes from the casing, tighten the cover with only the paper joint washer in position to allow it to be compressed. Take off the cover and remove the paper joint washer and measure its thickness. Add the thickness of the joint washer to the depth of the cover recess and subtract the amount by which the bearing protrudes from the casing. The result gives the thickness of shims to be used. Use the least possible number of shims to arrive at the correct thickness. Shims are available in various thicknesses.

(14) Hold the clutch withdrawal lever in position and screw in the pivot bolt.
Place the lockwasher on the bolt and tighten the withdrawal lever from the side opposite the steering. The leg

of the clutch withdrawal lever bracket on the steering side of the car is threaded. Screw the bolt through the leg and tighten it sufficiently to take out all play. Lock it in position with the nut and spring washer, and turn the lockwasher over.

Fit the rubber dust cover over the withdrawal lever and plug the other hole with a flat rubber grommet.

(15) Reassembly of the rear cover is affected by reversing the procedure described under "Dismantling" Nos. 5 to 15.

Rear Cover

(16) Position the paper joint washer, place a .006-in. (.1524 mm.) shim in the rear cover bearing recess and fit the rear cover. Shims are also available in thicknesses of .004-in. (.1016 mm.) and .010-in. (.254 mm.) Tighten the rear cover (evenly by diametrical selection) with the nine long setpins and spring washers. Correct shimming is done in exactly the same way as for the front cover.

(17) Flush the gearbox with flushing oil and replace the drain plug.

FAULT DIAGNOSIS

Symptom	No.	Possible Fault
(a) Jumping out of Gear	1	Broken change speed fork rod spring
	2	Excessively worn fork rod groove
	3	Worn coupling dogs
	4	Fork rod securing screw loose
(b) Noisy Gearbox	1	Insufficient oil in gearbox
	2	Excessive end play in laygear
	3	Damaged or worn bearings
	4	Damaged or worn teeth
(c) Difficulty in Engaging Gear	1	Incorrect clutch pedal adjustment
(d) Oil Leaks	1	Damaged joint washers
	2	Damaged or worn oil seals
	3	Front, rear or side covers loose or damaged

DRIVESHAFT

The drive shaft and universal joints are of Hardy Spicer manufacture.

The fore and aft movement of the rear axle and other components is allowed for by a sliding spline between the shaft and gearbox unit. Each universal joint consists of a center spider, four needle roller bearings and two yokes.

LUBRICATION

An oil nipple is fitted to each center spider for lubricating the bearings. Always use oil and never grease. The central oil chamber is connected to the four oil reservoirs and to the needle roller bearing assemblies.

The needle roller bearings are filled with oil on assembly. Oil from the gearbox lubricates the sliding splined joint between the drive shaft and the gearbox. Before refitting the shaft to the gearbox smear the splines with oil.

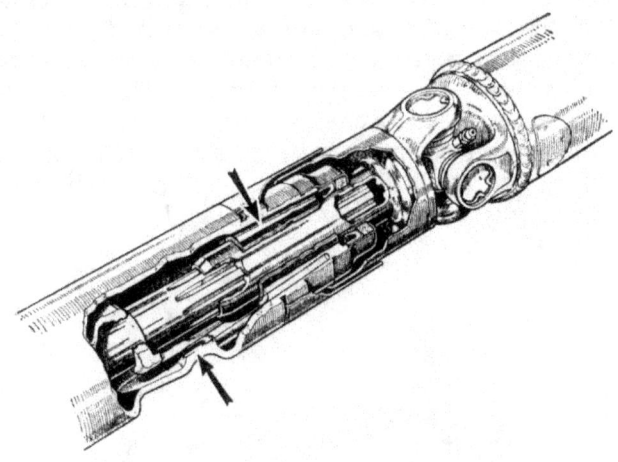

The propeller shaft sliding joint, showing the oilways which conduct oil from the gearbox

Tests for Wear
  (1) Wear on the thrust faces is located by testing the lift in the joint, either by hand or by using a length of wood suitably supported.
  (2) Any circumferential movement of the shaft relative to the flange yokes, indicates wear in the needle roller bearings or the sliding spline.

Removal and Replacement

Although the shaft can be removed separately by withdrawing it rearwards from the car, replacement presents some difficulty. It is therefore advisable to remove and replace it together with the engine and gearbox.

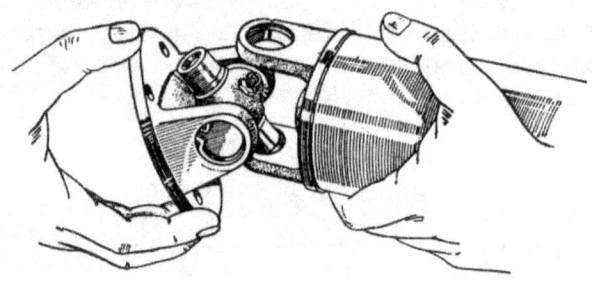

Separating the joint

Dismantling

The following directions apply to both universal joints except for the fact that the front joint can be separated from the shaft, whereas the rear joint has one yoke permanently fixed to the tube.
 (1) Clean away the enamel from all the snap rings and bearing faces, to ensure easy extraction of the bearings.
 (2) Remove the snap rings by pressing their ends together and prise out with a screwdriver. If the ring does not come out, tap the bearing face lightly to relieve the pressure against the ring.

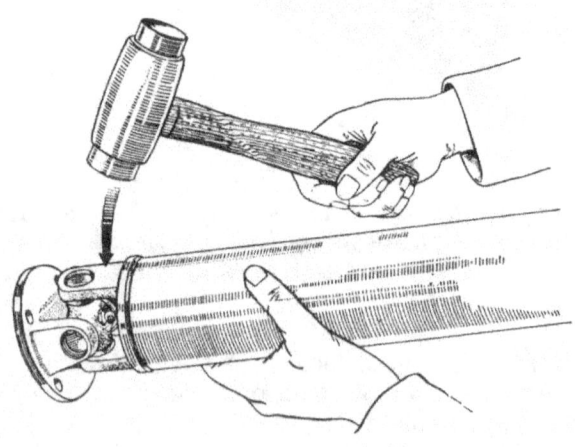

Tapping the joint to extract the bearing

(3) Hold the splined end of the shaft in one hand and tap the radius of the yoke with a lead or copper hammer, when the bearing will begin to emerge. If difficulty is experienced, use a small bar to tap the bearings from the inside, taking care not to damage the race itself. Turn the yoke over and extract the bearing with the fingers being careful not to lose any of the needles.
(4) Repeat this operation for the other bearing, and the splined yoke can be removed from the spider.
(5) Using a support and directions as above remove the spider from the other yoke.

Examination and Checking for Wear

When the drive shaft has been in use for a long time, the parts most likely to show signs of wear are the bearing races and the spider journals.

The complete assembly should be renewed if looseness of stress marks are observed, as no oversize journals or bearings are provided.

It is essential that bearing races are a light drive fit in the yoke trunnions. Any ovality in the trunnion bearing holes, indicates the fitting of new yokes.

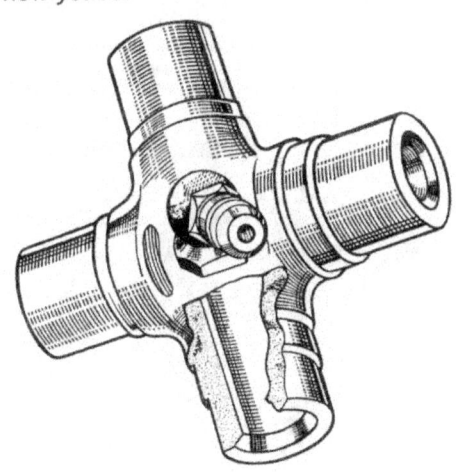

Showing the oil channels in the spider

Reassembly

(1) See that the drilled holes in the journals of the universal joints are cleaned out and filled with oil.
(2) Assemble the needle rollers in the bearing races and fill with oil. Should difficulty be experienced in assembly, smear the walls of the races with vaseline to retain the needle rollers in place.
(3) Insert the spider in the flange yoke.

(4) Using a soft-nosed drift about 1/32-in. (.794 mm.) smaller in diameter than the hole in the yoke, tap the bearing in position. It is essential that the bearing races are a light drive in the yoke trunnion.
(5) Repeat this operation for the other bearings. The spider journal shoulder should be coated with shellac prior to fitting the retainers to ensure a good seal.
(6) If the joint appears to bind, tap lightly with a wooden mallet which will relieve any pressure of the bearings on the end of the journals. It is advisable to renew cork washers and washer retainers on spider journals, using a tubular drift.

FAULT DIAGNOSIS

Symptom	No.	Possible Fault
(a) Vibration	1	Shaft bent or misaligned
	2	Worn universal joint bearings or spider bearing journal
	3	Sliding joint splines badly worn
	4	Loose flange bolts

REAR AXLE

LUBRICATION

For the lubrication of the hypoid axle use lubricants only from approved sources. Do not, under any circumstances mix various brands of hypoid lubricant. If there is any doubt as to the oil previously used, drain and flush the axle with a little new hypoid oil before finally filling up. Do not use paraffin as a flushing medium. On a new car the oil should be drained and the axle refilled at 500 miles (800 km.) **and subsequently every 6,000 miles (9600 km.), failure to do this will eventually lead to axle break-down.**

The filler plug is situated on the rear side of the axle, and the drain plug in the bottom of the banjo casing.

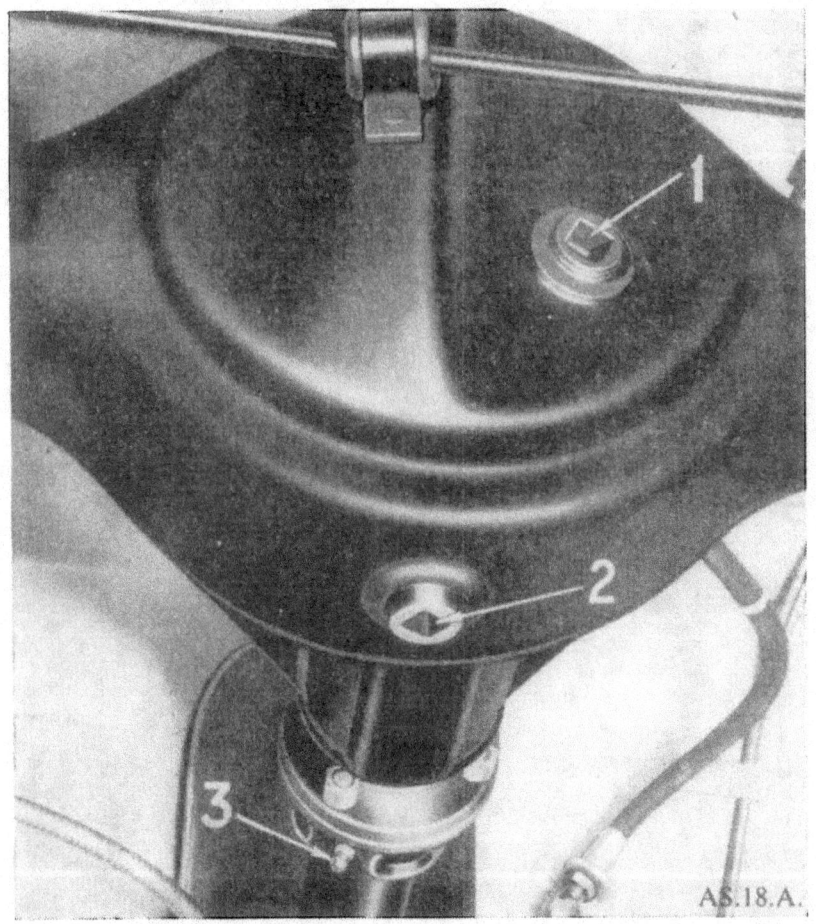

1. *Filler plug.*   2. *Drain plug.*   3. *Propeller shaft universal nipple.*

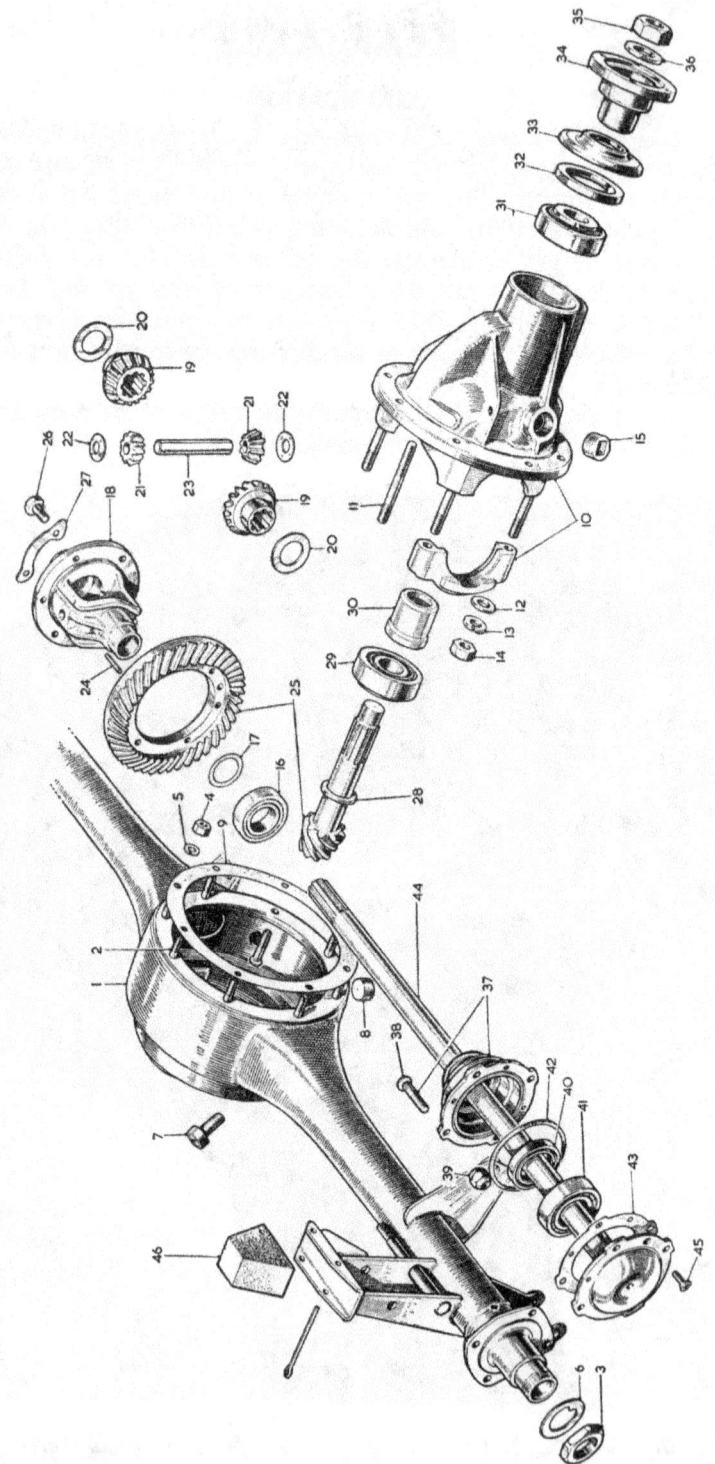

THE REAR AXLE COMPONENTS

KEY TO THE REAR AXLE COMPONENTS

No.	Description	No.	Description	No.	Description
1.	Case assembly.	17.	Bearing packing washer.	32.	Oil seal.
2.	Gear carrier stud.	18.	Differential cage.	33.	Dust cover.
3.	Bearing retaining nut.	19.	Differential wheel.	34.	Universal joint flange.
4.	Gear carrier to axle case nut.	20.	Thrust washer.	35.	Pinion nut.
5.	Spring washer.	21.	Differential pinion.	36.	Spring washer.
6.	Washer.	22.	Thrust washer.	37.	Hub assembly.
7.	Breather assembly.	23.	Pinion pin.	38.	Wheel stud.
8.	Drain plug.	24.	Pinion peg.	39.	Nut.
9.	Gear carrier joint.	25.	Crown wheel and pinion.	40.	Oil seal.
10.	Carrier assembly.	26.	Bolt.	41.	Hub bearing.
11.	Bearing cap stud.	27.	Lock washer.	42.	Oil seal ring.
12.	Plain washer.	28.	Pinion thrust washer.	43.	Hub shaft joint.
13.	Spring washer.	29.	Inner pinion bearing.	44.	Axle shaft.
14.	Nut.	30.	Bearing spacer.	45.	Screw.
15.	Filler plug.	31.	Pinion outer bearing.	46.	Bump rubber.
16.	Differential bearing.				

AXLE UNIT

To Remove and Replace

(1) Raise up the vehicle by placing a jack under the differential housing. Place supports under the rear spring body anchorage.
(2) The down pipe, muffler and exhaust pipe should be withdrawn from the car.
(3) Keeping the jack in position release the check strap by unscrewing the nut and bolt at its body connection.
(4) Release the shock absorber arm from its connecting linkage.
(5) Disconnect the suspension upper link from the rear axle bracket by unscrewing the nut and bolt and tapping the bolt from its housing.
(6) Disconnect the handbrake cable at the cable adjustment.
(7) Working from under the car, unscrew the four self-locking nuts and remove the bolts (U.N.F.) securing the drive shaft flange to the axle pinion flange.

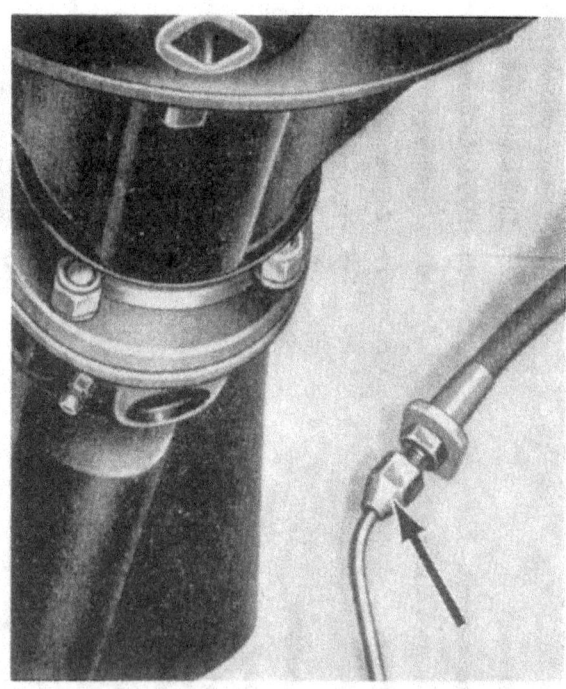

(8) Disconnect the hydraulic brake pipe at the main union just forward of the differential housing.
(9) After ascertaining that the weight of the axle is fully on the jack, unscrew and remove the shackle pins.
(10) Lower the axle and withdraw it from the car.

The replacement of the rear axle is a reversal of the removal procedure with attention to the following:

If, for any reason, it has been necessary to remove the suspension upper link and at the same time the rear axle has been withdrawn from the car, do not tighten the shackle pins until the upper link is mounted in position.

AXLE SHAFTS

To Remove and Replace

(1) Loosen the wheel nuts of the wheel concerned before jacking up the car.
(2) Remove the wheels after further unscrewing the wheel nuts.
(3) Take out the drum locating screw, using a screwdriver.
(4) The drum can be tapped off the hub and brake linings, provided the handbrake is released and the brake shoes are not adjusted so closely as to bind on the drum.

Should the brake linings hold the drum when the handbrake is released, it will be found necessary to slacken the brake shoe adjuster a few notches.

(5) Remove the axle shaft retaining screw and draw out the axle shaft by gripping the flange outside the hub. It should slide easily but if it is tight on the studs it may need gently prising with a screwdriver inserted between the flange and the hub. Should the paper washer be damaged it must be renewed when reassembling.
(6) Replacement is a reversal of the above operations.

HUBS

To Remove and Replace

(1) Remove the drum and axle shaft as described above.
(2) Knock back the tab of the locking washer and unscrew the nut with Service Tool 18G 152 (Puller).
(3) Tilt the lock washer to disengage the key from the slot in the threaded portion of the axle casing; remove the washer.
(4) The hub can then be withdrawn with a suitable extractor such as Service Tool 18G 146.

The bearing and oil seal will be withdrawn with the hub.

Hub Assembly

The hub bearing is non-adjustable and is replaceable in one operation, by pressing it into place.

It is essential when fitting the differential shaft that the paper joint washer between its flange and the hub is compressed before the abutment shoulder of the shaft pulls up against the bearing races. If, in an emergency, a paper joint washer is hand made, ensure that it is about .010 in. (.254 mm.) thick. An oil leak

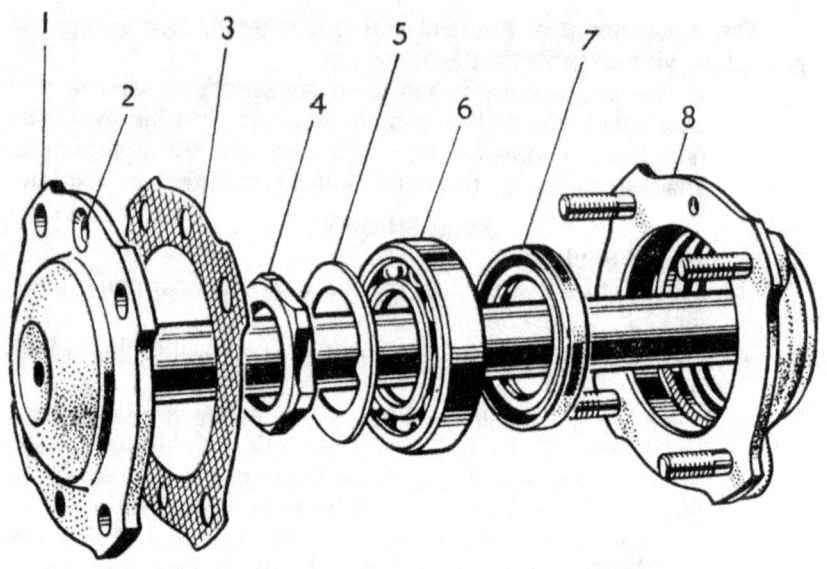

1. *Differential shaft flange.*
2. *Fixing screw countersunk hole.*
3. *Joint washer.*
4. *Hub securing nut.*
5. *Lockwasher.*
6. *Hub bearing.*
7. *Oil seal.*
8. *Hub casing.*

will invariably result if this washer is too thin.

If the oil seal has been removed, it must be drifted into position with Tool 18G 134 and adaptor 18G 134Q (lip towards the bearing) before the bearing is inserted.

The hub is then drifted on to the axle casing with Service Tool 18G 134 and adaptor 18G 134Q followed by a new lockwasher, whose peg must register in its location, and nut.

When the nut has been tightened, bend the lockwasher against one of its flats so locking it.

Assemble the axle shaft, brake drum and wheel as previously described.

During reassembly the hubs should be packed with fresh grease although they receive some lubricant from the axle during normal running.

SUSPENSION

REAR SUSPENSION

Rear suspension on the Sprite, Mk II and Midget is conventional by quarter elliptic springs, damped by Armstrong double acting shock absorbers. The stock spring consists of 15 leaves, of which 5 are 5/32" thick and 10 are ⅛" thick. The optional heavy duty springs have 10 leaves, all 3/16" thick and a higher rate of 118 lb./in. (compared to 97 lb./in.).

The rear axle is of a non-independent, "solid" type wherein axle haves are carried in a housing which accepts both torque and driving forces. The particular bearing arrangement in the outboard hubs causes this to be called a "¾ floating" axle. The final drive gears are of the hypoid type.

1. *Spring securing set bolts.* 2. *Shock absorber nuts.*
3. *'U' bolt nuts.*

REAR SPRING REMOVAL

To remove a rear spring proceed as detailed under 'Axle Unit'.

The spring can now be removed simply by extracting the two set bolts which pass upwards at the forward end of the spring into caged nuts on the upper leaf. The 'U' bolt must also be removed when the spring can be pulled out of its mounting.

Removing Rear Shock Absorbers

Remove the nut and spring washer that secures the shock absorber lever to the link arm between lever and axle. Withdraw the two fixing bolts from the shock absorber body and body frame, then remove the shock absorber, threading the lever over the link arm bolt.

Refitting Rear Shock Absorbers

Shock absorbers may be replaced by simply reversing the removal procedure. However, when handling shock absorbers that have been removed from their mountings, it is important to keep the assemblies upright as far as possible, otherwise air may enter the working chamber and cause erratic resistance.

The rubber bushes integral with both ends of the shock absorber to axle connecting links cannot be renewed. When these bushes are worn renew the arm.

INDEPENDENT FRONT SUSPENSION

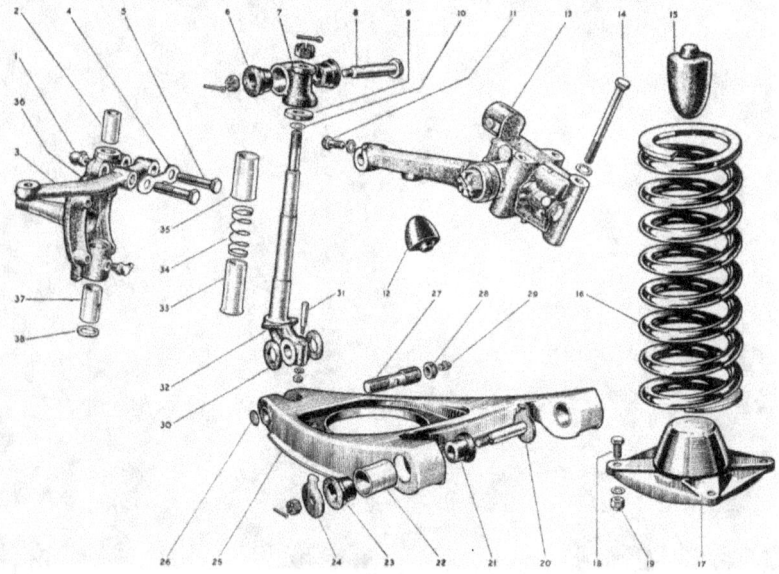

1. Lubricator.
2. Swivel axle bush (top).
3. Steering side tube arm.
4. Lockwasher.
5. Setscrew.
6. Trunnion bush (bearing).
7. Trunnion link.
8. Trunnion fulcrum pin.
9. Oilite thrust washer.
10. Adjustment washer (shim).
11. Clamp bolt.
12. Rebound buffer.
13. Shock absorber.
14. Setscrews.
15. Rebound rubber bumper.
16. Coil spring.
17. Spring seat.
18. Bolts.
19. Simmonds nut.
20. Fulcrum pin.
21. Rubber bush (bearings).
22. Lower link bush (inner).
23. Rubber bush (bearing).
24. Special washer.
25. Lower link.
26. Welch plug.
27. Fulcrum pin (outer).
28. Screwed plug.
29. Lubricator.
30. Cork rings.
31. Cotter.
32. Swivel axle pin.
33. Dust excluder (bottom).
34. Spring.
35. Dust excluder (top).
36. Swivel axle.
37. Swivel axle bush (bottom).
38. Cork sealing ring.

The independent suspension is of the 'wishbone' type. It consists of a single armed Armstrong double-acting shock absorber, bolted to its support bracket, at its upper end. The single arm is towards the front of the car and is secured to the king pin trunnion link by a fulcrum pin and metalastik rubber bushes. The bottom end of the king pin is secured to the outer end of the lower links by a fulcrum which is cottered in position.

The inner arms of the lower links are fixed to brackets by metalastik rubber bushes and fulcrum pins.

A rebound buffer is fitted to the bottom of the coil spring top bracket and a smaller rebound buffer under the shock absorber arm.

A spring seat is secured to the lower links by four bolts, flat washers and self-locking nuts, thus keeping the spring compressed.

AS.4.A.

1. *Swivel adjuster.*
2. *Swivel axle pin top bush.*
3. *Swivel axle pin bottom bush.*
4. *Tie rod end.*
5. *Lower link outer bushes.*

Checking for wear

The following tests should be made to check for wear in various components of the suspension unit.

(1) Wear of the king pin, its bushes, or both, may be checked by jacking up the car until the front wheels are clear of the ground. Grip two parts wheels are clear of the ground. Grip two parts of the tire diametrically opposite in a vertical plane and endeavor to rock the wheel in that plane. If any movement is felt at the wheel, the pin, its bushes, or both are worn.

(2) Vertical or horizontal movement of the shock absorber cross shaft relative to its body, denotes wear in the shock absorber bearings, and can only be remedied by fitting a new shock absorber. These bearings are best checked with the suspension dismantled, when with some freedom of movement it is possible to move the shock absorber arm which is attached to the cross shaft.

(3) The metalastik fulcrum pin bushes slowly deteriorate due to wear and weather conditions. They must therefore be renewed if softening of the rubber or side movement is evident.

(4) The threaded bushes of the screwed trunnion fulcrum pin in the lower links may develop excessive play due to wear. Dismantle the assembly, check and renew as necessary. The threaded bushes are not renewable by themselves, but only by changing the lower links.

LOWER LINK MOUNTINGS

On later chassis, from Car No. 11126, the lower link inner fulcrum pins are secured by Nyloc (self-locking) nuts which replace the castellated nuts and split pins formerly used. In the event of the lower links being removed from the frame, **NEW** Nyloc nuts must be used to secure the inner fulcrum pins upon re-assembly.

CASTOR AND CAMBER ANGLES AND KING PIN INCLINATION
Description

The castor, angle camber angles and king pin inclination are three design settings of the front suspension assembly. They have a very important bearing on the steering and general riding of the car. Each of these settings is determined by machining and assembly of the component parts during manufacture.

Should the car suffer damage to the suspension affecting these settings, the various angles must be verified to ensure whether replacements are necessary.

Camber Angle

This is the outward tilt of the wheel and a rough check can

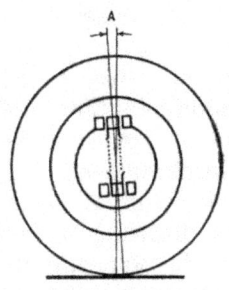
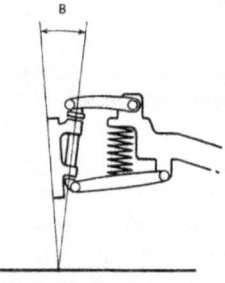
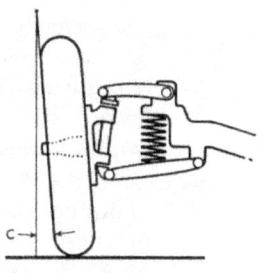

A. *Castor angle*—3°.   B. *Swivel pin inclination*—6¼°.   C. *Camber angle* 1°.

be made by measuring the distance from the outside wall of the tire immediately below the hub to a plumb line hanging from the outside wall to the tire above the hub. The distance must be the same on both wheels. Before making this test it is very important to ensure that the tires are in a uniform condition and at the same pressure. Also that the car is unladen and on level ground.

Damage to the upper and lower wishbone arms may well affect the camber angle.

Castor Angle

This is the tilt of the king pin when viewed from the side of the car. This also is only likely to be affected by damage to the upper and lower wishbone arms.

King Pin Inclination

This is the tilt of the swivel pin when viewed from the front of the car and is again only likely to be affected by damage to the wishbone arms.

FRONT HUBS

To Check Wear

The inner and outer ball bearings of the front hub are non-adjustable, the amount of thrust on the bearings being determined by a collapsible distance piece. Wear in the bearings can be checked by jacking up the front of the car until the wheel on the hub in question is off the ground. Remove the wheel cap and hub cap, and rock the wheel in a horizontal plane. Movement between the wheel and hub as one unit and the swivel axle nut at the center of the hub indicates wear in the hub bearings. A very positive movement indicates bearing renewal.

To Remove and Dismantle

(1) Jack up the car, remove the wheel cap and wheel. Release the screw in the counter-sunk hole and draw off the brake drum.

(2) Wipe away any excess grease, extract the split pin and release the castellated nut and washer. Employ extractor

18G 146 (puller) to draw the complete hub assembly off the swivel axle.

(3) Should the inner bearing remain on the swivel axle it should be carefully extracted. It is usually only the inner race of the inner bearing that is left behind and removal will be found easier if the backplate is first removed.

(4) With the hub removed, the outer bearing and collapsible distance piece can be taken out by inserting a drift through the inner bearing and carefully knocking the bearing clear of the hub. Similarly the inner bearing and oil seal can be detached by drifting them off from the other side of the hub.

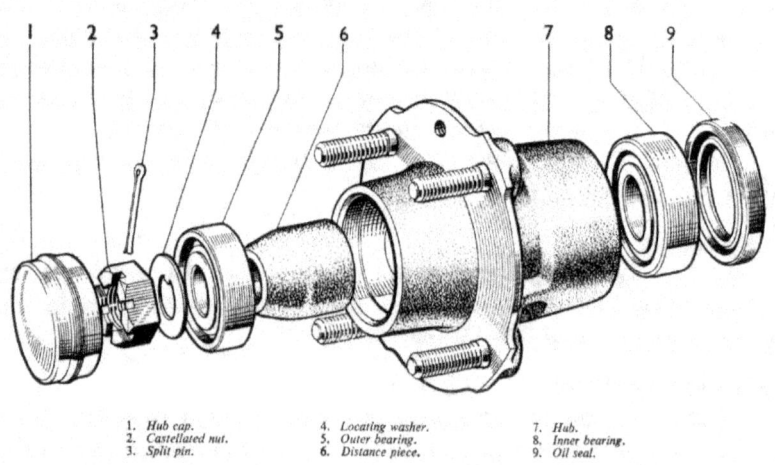

1. Hub cap.
2. Castellated nut.
3. Split pin.
4. Locating washer.
5. Outer bearing.
6. Distance piece.
7. Hub.
8. Inner bearing.
9. Oil seal.

To Assemble and Replace

(1) Press or drift in the outer bearing with the side marked 'thrust' towards the center of the hub.

(2) Turn the hub over, pack it with recommended grease and place the collapsible distance piece in position with its domed end towards the outer bearing.

(3) As before press or drift in the inner bearing with side marked 'thrust' towards the distance piece. Then press in the oil seal with its lipped end towards the inner bearing. The oil seal should be renewed if damaged in any way.

(4) Replace the hub on the swivel axle; place the drift over the outer bearing so that the pressure is evenly distributed over the face of the bearing. Drift the hub into position until the inner race bears against the shoulder of the swivel axle. A good way of knowing when the hub is home is by listening for the change in tone when knocking the hub on. It is a good policy to place a pilot

cap over the threaded end of the swivel axle to protect the thread and also to prevent the outer bearing inner race from striking the shoulder at the end of the threads.

(5) Place the pegged washer on the swivel axle so that its peg locates in the slot. Screw the castellated nut up to the flat washer.

(6) Put the brake drum on and tighten its securing screw in the countersunk hole. Tighten a pair of wheel nuts on diametrically opposite studs and see that the brake drum is quite free of the brake shoes.

(7) Tighten the castellated nut to a torque wrench reading of 50 to 55 lbs. ft. (6.913 to 7.604 kg.m.). Rock the drum to check that play in the bearings has been taken out, and rotate it to ensure that the hub is correctly preloaded. Line up the nearest slot in the nut with the hole in the swivel pin, insert the split pin and lock the nut.

(8) Charge the hub with grease, drift on the hub cap and wipe off any grease that exudes through the little hole at its center.

Replace the wheel, wheel nuts, lower the car, tighten the wheel nuts, and position the wheel cap.

SHOCK ABSORBERS

The shock absorbers are of the hydraulic double acting piston type. All the working parts are submerged in oil. They are carefully set before dispatch and cannot be adjusted without special equipment. Any attempt to dismantle them will seriously affect their operation and performance. Should adjustment or repair be necessary, they must be returned to their makers.

The maintenance of the hydraulic shock absorbers should include a periodical examination of their anchorages to the body fame. The fixing bolts must be tightened as necessary (25 to 30 lb./ft.).

The cheese-headed screws securing the cover-plates must be kept fully tightened to prevent leakage of the fluid.

When checking the fluid level every 6,000 miles (9600 km.) all road dirt must be carefully cleared away from the vicinity of the filler plugs before the plugs are removed. This is most important as it is absolutely vital that no dirt or foreign matter should enter the operating chamber.

The correct fluid level is just below the filler plug threads.

The use of Armstrong Super (thin) Shock Absorber Oil is recommended. When this is not available any good quality mineral oil to Specification S.A.E. 20/20 W is acceptable. This alternative is not suitable for low temperature operation and is deficient in various other ways.

To Remove Front Shocks

Jack up the car and place stands under the body in safe

positions. Remove the road wheel and place a jack beneath the outer end of the lower wishbone arm and raise it until the damper arm is clear of its rebound rubber.

Remove the shock absorber arm clamp bolt and its shakeproof washer. Withdraw the split pin and release the castellated nut on the fulcrum pin. Withdraw the fulcrum pin and retrieve the trunnion link rubber bushes.

Once the three securing bolts and their shakeproof washers have been removed the shock absorber may be taken from the car.

NOTE: The jack must be left in position under the suspension wishbone while the top link remains disconnected in order to keep the coil spring securely in position and to avoid straining the steering connections.

To Replace

Replacement is a reversal of the above procedure, but attention must be given to the following points:

(1) The shock absorber mounting bolts should not be tightened beyond a torque wrench loading of 30 lb. ft. Overtightening beyond this point will be detrimental to the performance of the shock absorber.

(2) Before fitting the upper trunnion fulcrum pin, work the shock absorber arm three or four times through its full travel to expel any air which may have found its way into the operating chamber.

(3) The metalastic fulcrum pin bushes must be renewed if softening of the rubber or side movement is evident.

FAULT DIAGNOSIS

Symptom	No.	Possible Fault
(a) Wheel Wobble	1 2 3 4 5 6 7	Unbalanced wheels and tires Slack steering connections Incorrect steering geometry Excessive play in steering gear Broken or weak front springs Worn hub bearings Loose or broken shackles
(b) Wander	1 2 3 4	Check 2, 3 and 4 in (a) Front suspension and rear axle mounting points out of alignment Uneven tire pressures Uneven tire wear Weak shock absorbers or springs
(c) Heavy Steering	1 2 3 4 5 6	Check 3 in (a) Excessively low tire pressures Insufficient lubricant in steering rack "Dry" steering connections Out of track Incorrectly adjusted steering gear Misaligned steering column

STEERING

The steering gear is of the rack and pinion type and is secured above the front frame cross member immediately behind the radiator. Tie-rods, operating the swivel arms, are attached to each end of the steering rack by ball joints enclosed in rubber gaiters.

The steering column engages the splined end of a helical-toothed pinion to which it is secured by a clamp bolt.

End play of the pinion is eliminated by adjustment of the shims fitted beneath the pinion tail end bearing. A damper pad inserted in the steering rack controls the backlash between the pinion and the rack.

MAINTENANCE

Provision has been made to replenish the rack housing with hypoid oil every 12,000 miles (19200 km.). The oil nipple is situated on the left side (right side for L.H.D. vehicles) of the rack housing and is positioned to enable the lubricant to be injected from above. Avoid over-filling the rack housing and keep the clips on the rubber gaiters fully tightened to prevent the oil escaping.

Apply the lubricating gun to the nipple on each tie-rod ball joint every 1,000 miles (1600 km.).

ADJUSTMENTS

The following adjustments maintain the performance of the steering at its maximum, and consists of aligning the front wheels and taking up backlash in the steering gear. Proceed as detailed below:

(1) Front wheel alignment is governed by four factors — camber, castor, swivel pin inclination and wheel toe-in. The correct camber and swivel pin angles are built into the front suspension and will change only if the suspension is distorted by accidental damage. It is most important that the front wheels should toe-in 1/16 in. (1.58 mm.) to 1/8 in. (3 mm.) and this is governed by the length of the tie-rods. Adjustments are provided so that the tie-rods may be lengthened or shortened to maintain the correct alignment.

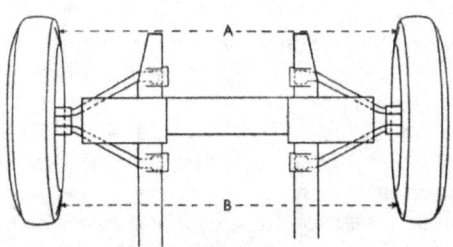

The toe-in must be adjusted so that 'A' is 1/16" to 1/8" less than 'B.'

Should adjustment be necessary, slacken the locknut of each tie-rod ball joint and the clips securing the rubber gaiters to the tie-rods, then rotate each tie-rod equally in the necessary direction. Both tie-rods have right-hand threads and should be rotated with a wrench applied to the flats provided.

When making adjustments remember that they are double, that is to say, adjustments of the rim in one direction makes a similar increase of the opposite portion of the rim in the other direction.

When adjustment are completed make sure to re-tighten the locknuts and rubber gaiter clips and particularly that the bottom surfaces of the ball joints are in the correct plane.

When the track is correctly adjusted and the wheels are in the straight-ahead position the tie-rods should be adjusted to equal lengths. This can be checked by measuring the distance from the flats to the ball joint locknuts.

When adjusting the track the following precautions should be observed:

(a) The car should have come to rest from a forward movement. This ensures, as far as possible, that the wheels are in their natural running position.

(b) It is preferable for alignment to be checked with the car laden and the tires inflated to the standard pressure of 18 lb./sq. in. (1.27 kg./cm^2).

(c) With conventional base-bar type alignment gauges measurements in front of and behind the wheel centers should be taken at the same points on the tires or rim flanges. This is achieved by marking the tires where the first reading is taken and moving the car forwards approximately half a road wheel revolution before taking the second reading at the same points. With an optical gauge two or three readings should be taken with the car moved forwards to different positions — 180° road wheel turn for two readings and 120° for three readings. The average figure should then be calculated.

Wheels and tires vary laterally within their manufacturing tolerances, or as the result of service, and alignment figures obtained without moving the car are unreliable.

(2) Adjustment is provided between the rack damper cap and the rack body. This is to eliminate back-lash between the pinion and the rack.

To adjust the damper cap proceed as follows:

(a) Disconnect the tie-rods from their respective swivel arms in order to free the gear of all loads.

(b) Unscrew the steering column clamp bolt and withdraw the column from the pinion shaft splines.
(c) Unscrew the damper cap and remove its shims and plunger spring. Position the plunger in the cap and replace the cap. Then screw down the cap until it is just possible to rotate the pinion shaft by drawing the rack through its housing.
(d) A feeler gauge is then used to measure the clearance between the hexagon of the damper cap and its seating in the rack housing. To this figure must be added a clearance of .002 to .005 in. (.05 to .127 mm.) to arrive at the correct thickness of shims which must be placed beneath the damper cap. The shims are available in thicknesses of .003 and .010 in. (.076 and 0.254 mm.).
(e) Remove the damper cap and plunger, Insert the spring beneath the plunger and replace and tighten the assembly with the requisite number of shims fitted as defined in the previous paragraph.
(f) Refit both steering column and swivel arms to the steering rack assembly.

BRAKES

The brakes on all four wheels are hydraulically operated by foot pedal application, directly coupled to a master cylinder in which the hydraulic pressure of the brake operating fluid is orginated. A supply tank cast integrally with the master cylinder provides a reservoir by which the fluid is replenished, and a pipe line consisting of tube, flexible hose and unions, interconnect the master cylinder and the wheel cylinders.

The pressure generated in the master cylinder by application with the foot pedal is transmitted with equal and undiminished force to all wheel cylinders simultaneously. This moves the pistons outwards, which in turn expand the brake shoes thus producing automatic equalization, and efficiency in direct proportion to the effort applied at the pedal.

When the pedal is released the brake shoe springs return the shoes which then return the wheel cylinder pistons, and therefore the fluid back into the lines and master cylinder.

An independent mechanical linkage actuated by a handbrake, mounted alongside the drive shaft tunnel, operates the rear wheels by mechanical expanders attached to the rear wheel cylinder bodies.

The front brakes are of the two leading shoe types with sliding shoes which ensure automatic centralization of the brake shoe in operation.

The rear brakes are also fitted with sliding shoes, and incorporate the handbrake mechanism.

Front Brakes

The front brakes are operated by two wheel cylinders situated diametrically opposite each other on the inside of the backplate and interconnected by a bridge pipe on the outside.

Each cylinder operates one shoe only. A single piston in each cylinder acts on the leading tip of its respective shoe, while the trailing tip of the shoe finds a floating anchor by utilizing the closed end of the actuating cylinder of the other shoe as its abutment. Between the piston the leading tip of each shoe is a 'Micram' adjuster which is located in a slot in the shoe.

Each wheel cylinder consists of a casting containing a piston fitted with a cover and backed by a rubber cup. The space in front of the rubber cup is partially occupied by a cup filler which is loaded by a spring.

The brake shoes are held in position by two return springs.

The bleed screw is incorporated in the farthest brake cylinder from the master cylinder, being on a banjo connection at the back of the backplate. When the bleed screw is turned in an anti-clockwise direction a steel valve ball is released from its seat and hydraulic fluid escapes.

Rear Brakes

The rear brake shoes are not fixed but are allowed to slide and centralize with the same effect as in the front brakes. They are hydraulically operated by a single acting wheel cylinder. The cylinder which is fitted in a slot in the rear backplate is free to slide in the slot between the tips of the brake shoes (which are of the leading and trailing type). The cylinder has a single piston operating on the tip of the leading shoe and this shoe butts against the fixed anchor block on the backplate, the web of the shoe being free to slide in a slot in the block. The trailing shoe is located in a similar way between the anchor block and the closed end of the hydraulic cylinder, and is free to slide and therefore self-centering, this shoe is operated by movement of the cylinder assembly as a result of the reaction of the leading shoe against the brake drum.

A 'Micram' adjuster is located in a slot in the tip of the leading shoe.

The wheel cylinder contains two pistons, the inner being hydraulically operated while the outer is manually operated by the handbrake lever. The inner piston is backed by a rubber cup and the space in front of the cup partially occupied by a cup filler which is loaded by a spring. When operated hydraulically, the inner piston butts against the outer piston leaving the handbrake lever undisturbed, and applies a thrust to the tip of the leading shoe through the dustcover, 'Micram' adjuster and mask. When operated manually, an inwards movement of the handbrake lever brings the heel of the lever into contact with the outer piston, thrusting it outwards against the leading shoe without disturbing the inner piston. A rubber boot is fitted to exclude foreign matter.

The brake shoes are held in position by two return springs.

Note: When refitting brake shoes the springs must lie between the brake shoes and the backplate, this also applies to the front brake shoes.

The rear brake shoes are located relative to the backplate by two steady springs.

FRONT BRAKE ASSEMBLIES

To Remove

(1) Disconnect the hydraulic pipe from the master cylinder at the backplate.

(2) Remove the front brake backplate from the front suspension.

To Dismantle

(1) Pull one of the brake shoes against the load of the return springs, away from the abutment on the closed end of the adjacent cylinder and slide the 'Micram' mask off the piston cover of the operating cylinder; on releasing the tension of the return springs the opposite brake shoe will fall away.

(2) Disconnect the bridge pipe between the two brake cylinders complete with the banjo adaptors.

(3) Unscrew the nuts and withdraw the brake cylinders from the backplate.

(4) To dismantle a brake cylinder withdraw the piston complete with the piston cover from the cylinder and apply a gentle air pressure to the fluid connection to blow out the rubber cup, and cup filler.

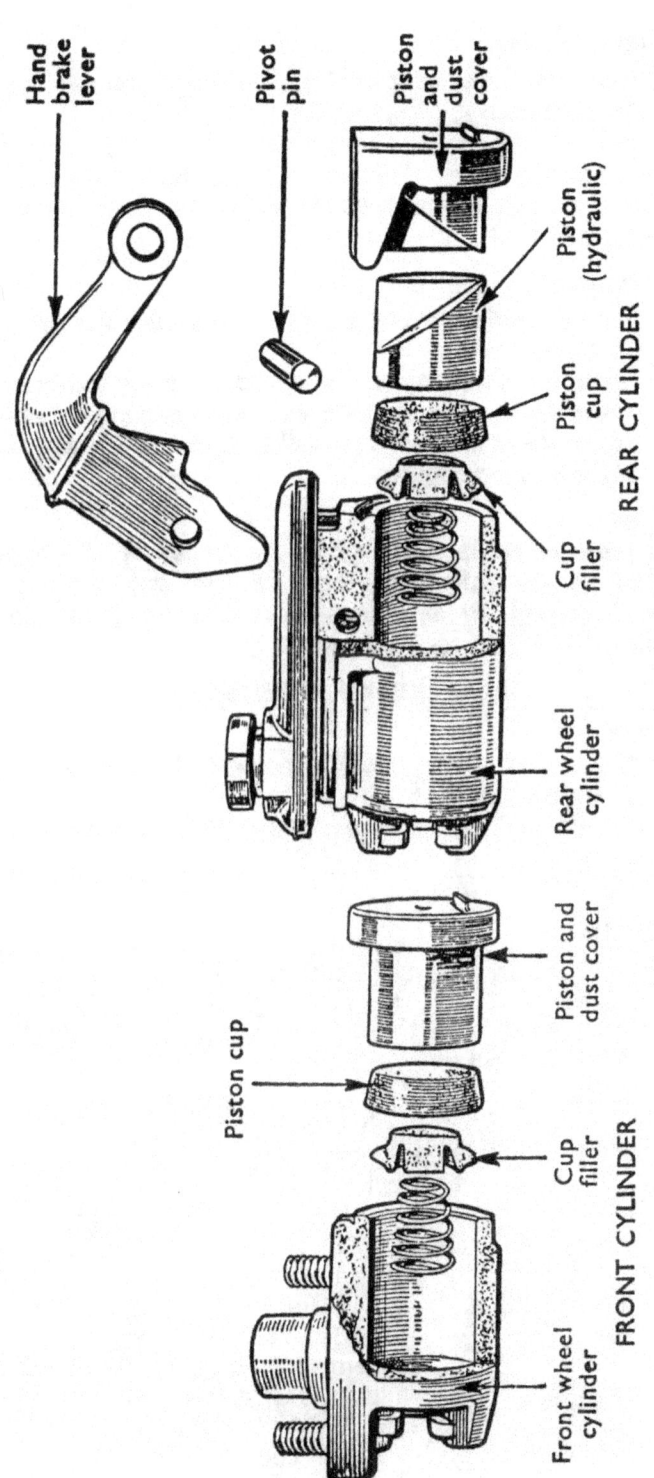

Components of the front and rear wheel cylinders.

Examination for Wear

Examine the rubber cups for wear perishing and swelling, and renew where necessary.

Any rust on the cylinder bore or piston must be removed or this will eventually cause a seizure of the piston. If the cup filler is fractured it must be renewed. Clean all the components with Lockheed brake fluid.

To Reassemble

(1) Fit the smaller end of the coil spring over the projection in the cup filler.

(2) Place the assembly in the cylinder, spring foremost, followed by the cup, lip foremost, and the piston. Take care not to damage or turn back the lip of the cup when entering the cylinder bore.

To Replace

The replacement is a reversal of the procedure. 'To Remove'.

Before replacing the brake shoes examine them for excessive wearing or glazing. Brake linings may be removed, or complete exchange brake shoes are available.

REAR BRAKE ASSEMBLIES

To Remove

(1) Disconnect the hydraulic pipe from the master cylinder at the backplate.

(2) Disconnect the rod from the hand brake lever at the backplate.

(3) Remove the rear brake backplate from the back axle.

To Dismantle

(1) Pull the trailing shoe against the load of the return springs and away from its abutment at either end. On releasing the tension of the return springs the leading shoe will fall away. Collect the 'Micram' adjuster and mask.

(2) Unscrew the banjo bolt securing the banjo adaptor to the wheel cylinder and remove the rubber boot.

(3) Remove the wheel cylinder piston, swing the handbrake lever until the shoulder is clear of the backplate and slide the cylinder casting forward. Pivot the cylinder about its forward end and withdraw the rear end from the slot in the backplate, a rearward movement of the cylinder will now bring its forward end clear of the backplate.

(4) Withdraw the piston complete with cover from the cylinder. Remove the handbrake pivot pin and lever. Apply a gentle air pressure to the fluid connection and blow out the hydraulic piston, rubber cup, and cup filler.

To Reassemble

(1) Fit the spring in the cup filler and insert the parts, spring leading, into the bore followed by the rubber cup, lip foremost, taking care not to damage or turn back the lip of the cup.

(2) Insert the hydraulic piston ensuring that the slot in the piston coincides with the lever slot in the cylinder casting.

(3) Place the handbrake lever in position and fit the pivot pin. Insert the handbrake piston complete with dust cover, ensuring that the lever is engaged in the slot in the piston.

(4) Offer up the wheel cylinder to the backplate with the handbrake lever through the slot, and the piston pointing in the direction of forward rotation of the wheel. Engage the forward end of the cylinder in the slot and slide it well forward, taking care to position the lever so that its shoulder clears the backplate. Engage the rear end of the cylinder in the slot and slide it back to hold it in position.

(5) Fit the rubber boot. Mount the banjo connection on the cylinder and, using a new copper washer fit the banjo bolt.

(6) Assemble the brake shoes, ensuring that the 'Micram' adjuster is in the slot in the leading shoe with the mask in position, and that the return springs lie between the brake shoes and the backplate. It should be noted that the unlined end of the leading shoe is to be nearest to the brake cylinder, whilst the unlined end of the trailing shoe is to be nearest the abutment block.

(7) Reassemble the backplate to the back axle. Ensure that all the adjustment is backed-off, fit the brake drum and the road wheel, connect the handbrake pull-rod and hydraulic line, 'bleed' and adjust the brakes.

BRAKE PEDAL

To Remove

(1) Working under the hood disconnect the pedal from the master cylinder by removing the clevis pin anchoring the master cylinder push-rod to the brake pedal.

(2) Working within the car unscrew the nut securing the brake and clutch pedal shaft, and withdraw the shaft to release the brake and clutch pedals and their distance piece.

(3) Withdraw the brake pedal downwards out of the car.

(4) Inspect the lever bush for wear and renew if necessary.

MASTER CYLINDER

Description

The master cylinder caters for operation of both brake and clutch. It has two bores which are side by side and, except for

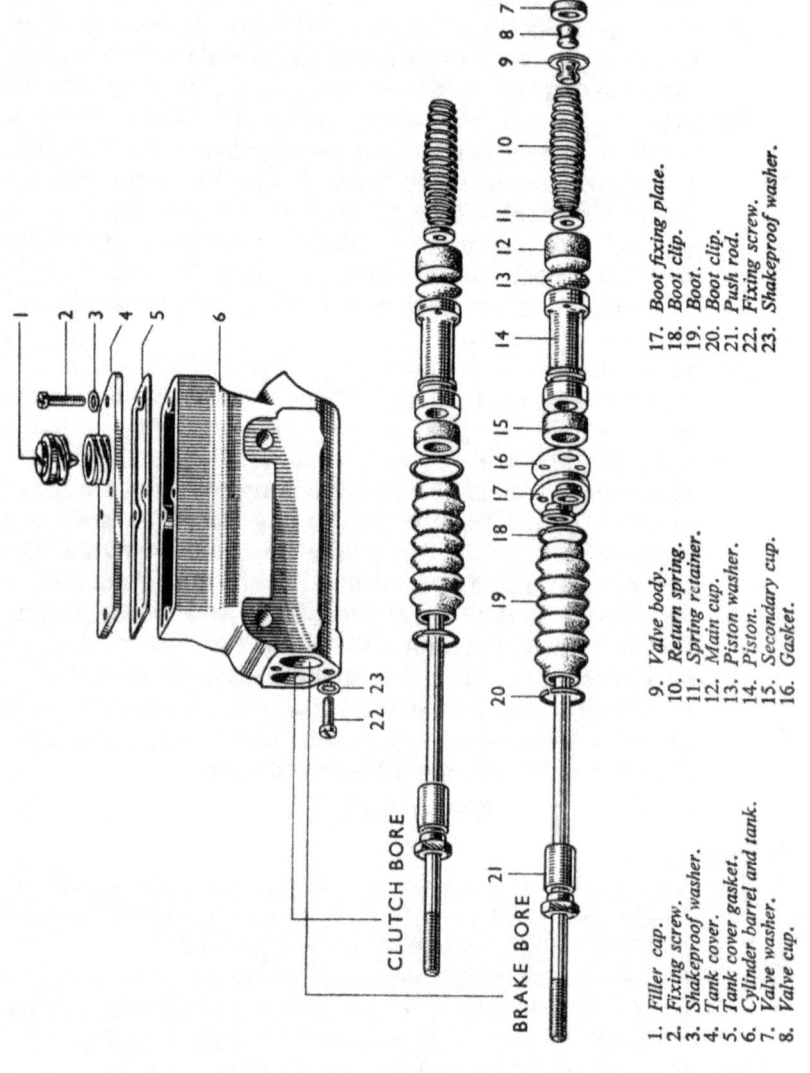

1. Filler cap.
2. Fixing screw.
3. Shakeproof washer.
4. Tank cover.
5. Tank cover gasket.
6. Cylinder barrel and tank.
7. Valve washer.
8. Valve cup.
9. Valve body.
10. Return spring.
11. Spring retainer.
12. Main cup.
13. Piston washer.
14. Piston.
15. Secondary cup.
16. Gasket.
17. Boot fixing plate.
18. Boot clip.
19. Boot.
20. Boot clip.
21. Push rod.
22. Fixing screw.
23. Shakeproof washer.

the fact that one has no check valve, each bore accommodates normal master cylinder parts. The bore with the check valve serves the brakes, the other serves the clutch slave cylinder.

Dismantling the Brake Cylinder

(1) Unscrew the set screws securing the boot fixing plate to the master cylinder body.
(2) Detach the fixing plate from the master cylinder leaving the boots and push rods attached to the clutch and brake pedals.
(3) Unscrew the common filler cap and drain the fluid into a clean container.
(4) Withdraw the piston (14), piston washer (13), main cup (12) and return spring (10), valve body (9) complete with rubber cup (8) and rubber washer (7).
(5) Using only the fingers to prevent damage, remove the secondary cup (15) by stretching it over the end flange of the piston.
(6) Examine all parts, especially the washers, for wear or distortion, and replace with new parts where necessary.

Assembling the Brake Cylinder

(1) Fit the secondary cup (15) on the piston (14), so that the lip of the cup faces the piston head and gently work the cup round the groove with the fingers to ensure that it is properly seated.
(2) Place the rubber washer (7) in position in the bottom of the cylinder bore. Fit the rubber cup (8) in the valve body (9) and assemble the body on the larger end of the return spring (10).
(3) Assemble the retainer (11) on the smaller end of the return spring and insert the assembly into the cylinder.
(4) Install the main cup (12) into the cylinder, lip foremost, taking care not to damage or turn back the lip of the cup.
(5) Follow up with the piston washer. Pay particular attention to the illustration showing method of assembly.
(6) Press the piston (14) into the cylinder taking care not to damage or turn back the lip of the secondary cup (15).
(7) Insert the push rod in the piston and maneuver the boot fixing plate into position. Secure the plate by its two set screws and then ascertain that the rubber boots are seating correctly. The vent hole in each boot should be at the bottom where the cylinder is mounted on the vehicle.
   If the boots are damaged or perished, new ones should be fitted.
(8) Fill the reservoir with clean Lockheed brake fluid and test the brake cylinder by pushing the piston inwards and allowing it to return unassisted. After a few applications, fluid should flow from the outlet connection.

Replacement

The installation of the master cylinder is the reversal of the removal procedure.

If no further maintenance of the brake is necessary remember to bleed the system.

HANDBRAKE

The handbrake operates on the rear wheels only and is applied by a pull-up type of lever situated on the side of the drive shaft tunnel. The Bowden cable from the control is attached to the compensator mounted on the rear axle. From compensator to the brake levers are transverse rods which are non-adjustable.

The handbrake linkage is set when leaving the works and should not require any attention. Only when a complete overhaul is necessary should the handbrake linkage require re-setting.

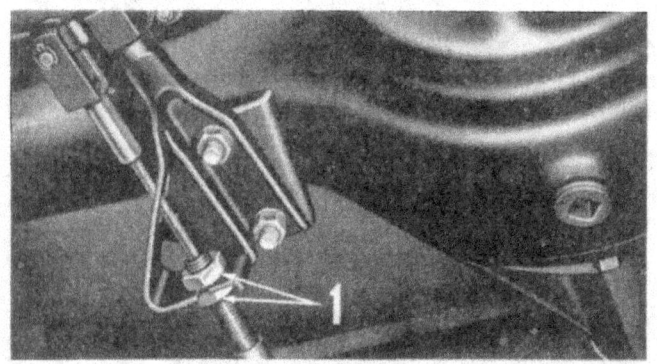

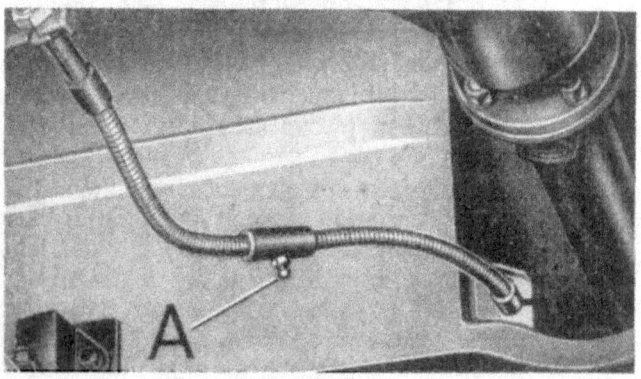

To adjust the handbrake, the rear shoes should be locked to the drums, the handbrake control just slightly applied, and the cable slackness just removed, by means of adjusting the sleeve nut at the rear of the Bowden cable.

The handbrake mechanism is lubricated by two grease nipples, one on the compensating mechanism and the other on the Bowden cable.

MAINTENANCE

Replenishment of Hydraulic Fluid

Inspect the reserve tank at regular intervals and ascertain that the fluid level is up to the bottom of the filler plug threads.

Great care should be exercised when adding brake fluid, to prevent dirt or foreign matter entering the system.

Important: Serious consequences may result from the use of incorrect fluids, and **Lockheed Genuine Brake Fluid** or a fluid conforming to specification S.A.E. 70 R.1. must be used. This fluid has been specially prepared and is unaffected by high temeprature or freezing.

Bleeding the Hydraulic System

Bleeding is necessary any time a portion of the hydraulic system has been disconnected, or if the level of the brake fluid has been allowed to fall so low that air has entered the master cylinder.

With all the hydraulic connections secure and the reserve tank topped up with the fluid, remove the rubber cap from the rear bleed nipple which is farthest away from the master cylinder and fit the bleed tube over the bleed nipple, immersing the free end of the tube in a clean jar containing a little brake fluid.

Unscrew the bleed nipple about three-quarters of a turn and then operate the brake pedal with a slow full stroke until the fluid entering the jar is completely free of air bubbles. Then, during a down stroke of the brake pedal, tighten the bleed screw sufficiently to seat the ball, remove bleed tube and replace the bleed nipple dust cap. **Under no circumstances must excessive force be used when tightening the bleed screws.**

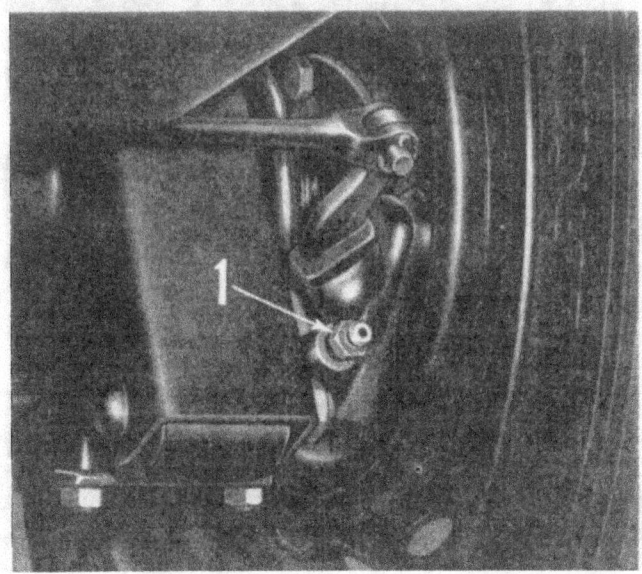

This process must now be repeated for each bleed screw at each of the three remaining backplates, finishing at the wheel nearest the master cylinder. Always keep a careful check on the supply tank during bleeding, since it is most important that a full level is maintained. Should air reach the master cylinder from the supply tank, the whole of the bleeding operation must be repeated.

After bleeding, top up the supply tank to its correct level.

Never use fluid that has just been bled from a brake system for topping up the supply tank, as this brake fluid may be to some extent aerated. Such fluid must be allowed to stand for at **least** twenty-four hours before it is used again. This will allow the air bubbles in the fluid time to disperse.

Great cleanliness is essential when dealing with any part of the hydraulic system, and especially so where the brake fluid is concerned. Dirty fluid must never be added to the system.

Note: It is advisable to turn all the brake shoe adjusters to their full 'off' position before bleeding. After bleeding adjust brakes as described below.

Adjusting the Brake Shoes

The brakes are adjusted for lining wear, **only** at the brakes themselves, and on no account should any alteration be made to the handbrake cable for this purpose.

Front Brakes

A separate 'Micram' adjuster is provided for each shoe. Jack up the car until the wheel concerned is clear of the ground. Remove the wheel disc, and rubber dust plug from the adjusting hole.

Rotate the wheel until the adjusting hole comes opposite one of the adjusters (located at 8 and 2 o'clock). Using a screwdriver turn the adjuster in a clockwise direction until the brake shoe is in contact with the brake drum, then turn the adjuster back one notch, this should provide correct clearance between the shoe and the drum. If closer adjustment is required spin the drum and apply the brakes hard, this will correctly position the shoe after which a further adjustment check should be made. Repeat these operations on the second adjuster. Adjust the other wheel cylinders in similar manner.

Rear Brakes

Place chocks under one of the front wheels and release the handbrake. Proceed as for the front brake adjustment but noting that there is only one wheel adjuster to adjust each rear wheel, and that it may be necessary to back off two notches to provide adequate clearance for the two shoes.

FAULT DIAGNOSIS

Symptom	No.	Possible Fault
(a) Spongy Pedal (loss of fluid pressure)	1 2 3 4 5	Leak in system Master cylinder plunger worn Wheel cylinder leaking Air in system Lining not "down" on shoe
(b) Excessive Pedal Depression	1 2 3	In (a) check 1 and 4 Excessive lining wear Extremely low brake fluid level Too much pedal free movement
(c) Brakes Grab or Pull to Side	1 2 3 4 5 6 7 8 9 10	Brake backplate loose on axle Scored, cracked or distorted drum High spots on drum Incorrect shoe adjustment Oily or wet linings Rear axle or front suspension anchorage loose Worn or loose rear spring anchorage Worn steering connections Different grade or types of lining fitted Uneven tyre pressures

Symptom	No.	Possible Fault
(d) Dragging Brakes	1 2 3 4 5 6 7	In (c), check 3 Wheel cylinder piston seized Weak or broken brake shoe return springs Master cylinder by-pass port restricted Too little pedal free movement Handbrake mechanism seized Supply tank overfilled Filler cap air vent choked
(e) Springy Pedal	1 2 3	Lining not 'bedded-in' Brake drums weak or cracked Master cylinder fixing loose
(f) Brakes Inefficient	1	In (c), check 4 In (d), check 7 Incorrect type of linings fitted

WHEELS & TIRES

Even tire wear is promoted by changing the positions of the tires on the car at intervals of about 3,000 miles (4800 km.). The spare should be brought into use with the others.

Attention should be paid to the following points with a view to obtaining the maximum mileage from the tire equipment of the vehicle.

Test the pressures daily by means of a suitable gauge and restore any air lost. It is not sufficient to make a visual inspection of the tire for correct inflation. Inflate the spare to the correct front wheel pressure.

Keep the treads free from grit and stones and carry out any necessary repairs. Clean the wheel rims and keep them free from rust. Paint the wheels if necessary.

Keep the clutch and brakes adjusted correctly and in good order. Fierceness or uneven action in either of these units has a destructive effect upon the tires.

Misalignment is a very costly error. Suspect it if rapid wear of the front tires is noticed and correct the fault at once. See 'Suspension' for details on front wheel alignment.

Should the tires get oily, petrol (gasoline) should be applied sparingly and wiped off at once.

Avoid under- and over-inflation.

Avoid causes of severe impact.

Have any damage repaired immediately.

To Repair Simple Tire Penetrations

Normally a tubeless tire will not leak as the result of penetration by a nail or other normal puncturing objects provided that it is left in the tire, but repair should be effected at the earliest convenient time.

In the case of a nail penetrating the tire, a repair can be carried out externally without removing the tire from the rim, providing the special repair kit is available. If the hole fails to seal, mark the spot and extract the nail, taking note of the direction of penetration. If the tire is leaking and the puncturing object

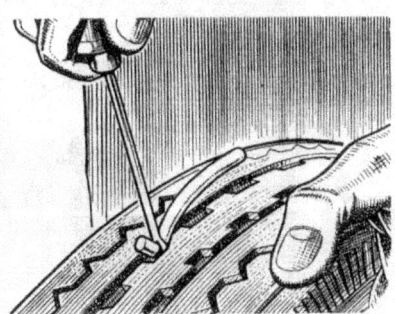

cannot be located by sight, immerse the wheel and tire in water. Repair as follows:

(1) Insert the needle of the repair kit through the hole in the tire in the same direction as the penetration to free it from road grit. Dip the needle into the rubber solution and re-insert it through the hole, repeating this operation until the hole is well lubricated with the solution.

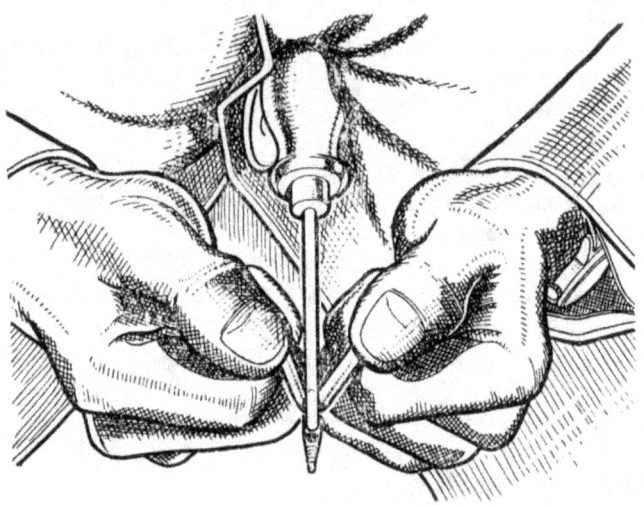

(2) Select a repair plug of about twice the diameter of the puncturing object, stretch and roll it into the eye of the needle, about ¼ in. (6 mm.) from its end. Dip the plug into the rubber solution and insert the needle through the hole in the tire so that the end of the rubber plug passes through the hole into the interior. Withdraw the needle, leaving the plug in the tire, and cut off the plug about 1/8 in. (3 mm.) from the surface of the tread.

(3) Inflate the tire.

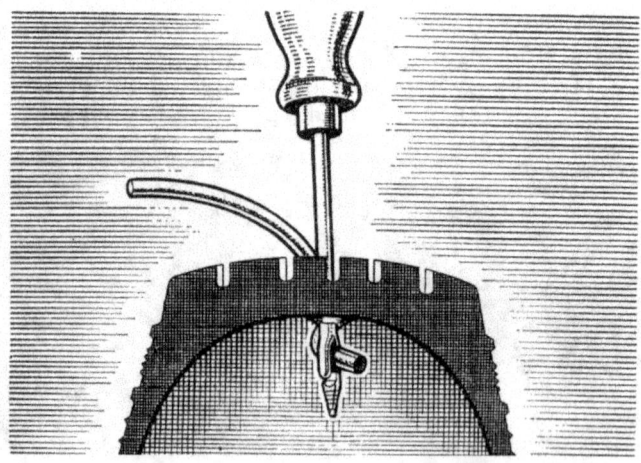

To Dismantle
(1) Lay the wheel on the ground, with the valve uppermost. Deflate by removing the valve cap and interior.
(2) Using tire levers, which must be in good condition, separate the beads from the rim flange until both beads are in the base of the rim. As inextensible wires are incorporated in the edges of the tires, no attempt should be made to stretch the edges over the rim as the beads must in **NO WAY BE DAMAGED**. Keep the levers moistened with water.
(3) With the bead of the tire held in the base of the rim at a point diametrically opposite the valve, insert a lever close to the valve and carefully lift the tire over the rim. Using two levers at intervals of about 6 in. (15 cm.) apart, continue to lift the bead over the rim until this bead is entirely free.
(4) Stand the tire and wheel upright, keeping the bead in the base of the rim. Lever the bead over the rim flange, and at the same time push the wheel away from the tire with the other hand to completely remove the tire off the wheel.

To Repair Penetrations
Severe penetrations which are outside the scope of the small repair kit can be repaired in a similar manner to conventional covers which will necessitate the removal of the tire (see above).
Repair as follows:
(1) Inspect for damage and remove any puncturing objects.
(2) Clean the area around the hole on the inside of the tire, roughen with a scratchbrush and apply a rubber solution to the surface to receive an ordinary tube patch such as the Dunlop "Vulcafix" patch, or preferably use an uncured rubber patch and vulcanise it in position.
(3) In the event of more serious damage, the tubeless tire can undergo a major vulcanized repair in the same way as a normal tire. The tubeless tire can also be re-treaded.

FACTORS AFFECTING TIRE LIFE AND PERFORMANCE
Inflation Pressures

All other conditions being favorable there is an average loss of 13% tread mileage for every 10% reduction in inflation pressure below the recommended figure.

A tire is designed so that there is a minimum pattern shuffle on the road surface and a suitable distribution of load over the contact area when deflection is correct.

Moderate underinflation causes an increased rate of tread wear although the tire's appearance may remain normal. Severe and persistent underinflation produces unmistakable evidence on the tread, see photo. It also causes structural failure due to excessive friction and temperature within the casing.

Pressures which are higher than those recommended for the car reduce comfort. They may also reduce tread life due to a concentration of the load and wear on a smaller area of tread, aggravated by increased wheel bounce on uneven road surfaces. Excessive pressures overstrain the casing cords, in addition to causing rapid wear, and the tires are more susceptible to impact fractures and cuts.

Effect of Temperature

Air expands with heating and pressures increase as the tires warm up. Pressures increase more in hot weather than in cold weather and as a result of high speed. These factors are taken into account when designing the tire and in preparing Load Pressure schedules.

Pressures in warm tires should not be reduced to standard pressure for cold tires. "Bleeding" the tires increases their deflections and causes their temperatures to climb still higher. The tires will also be underinflated when they have cooled.

Speed

High speed is expensive and the rate of tread wear may be twice as fast at 50 m.p.h. as at 30 m.p.h.

High speed involves:
(1) Increased tire temperatures due to more deflections per minute and a faster rate of deflection and recovery. The resistance of the tread to abrasion decreases with increase of temperature.
(2) Fierce acceleration and braking.
(3) More distortion and slip when negotiating bends and corners.
(4) More "thrash" and "scuffing" from road surface irregularities.

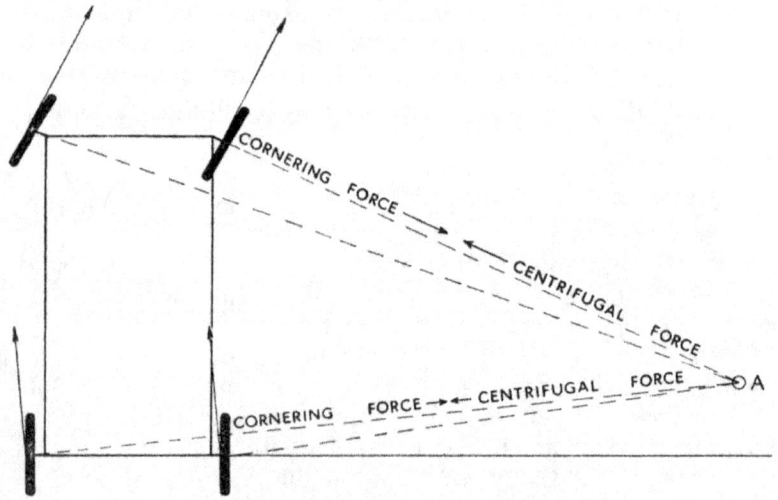

Braking

"Driving on the brakes" increases the rate of tire wear, apart from being generally undesirable. It is not necessary for wheels to be locked for an abnormal amount of tread rubber to be worn away.

Other braking factors not directly connected with the method of driving can affect wear, for instance correct balance and lining clearances, and freedom from binding, are very important. Braking may vary between one wheel position and another due to oil or foreign matter on the shoes even when the brake mechanism is free and correctly balanced.

Brakes should be relined and drums reconditioned in complete sets. Tire wear may be affected if shoes are relined with non-standard material having suitable characteristics or dimensions, especially if the linings differ between one wheel position and another in such a way as to upset the brake balance. Front tires, and particularly near front tires, are very sensitive to any condition which adds to the severity of front braking in relation to the rear.

"Picking-up" of shoe lining leading edges can cause grab and reduce tire life. Local "pulling-up" or flats on the tread pattern can often be traced to brake drum eccentricity. The braking varies during each wheel revolution as the minor and major axis of the eccentric drum pass alternately over the shoes. Drums should be free from excessive scoring and be true when mounted on their hubs with the road wheels attached.

Climatic Conditions

The fate of tread wear during a reasonably dry and warm summer can be twice as great as during an average winter.

Water is a rubber lubricant and tread abrasion is much less on wet roads than on dry roads. In addition resistance of the tread to abrasion decreases with increase in temperature.

When a tire is new its thickness and pattern depth are at their greatest. It follows that heat generation and pattern distortion due to flexing, cornering, driving and braking are greater than when the tire is part worn.

Higher tread mileages will usually be obtained if new tires are fitted in the autumn or winter rather than in the spring or summer. This practice also tends to reduce the risk of road delays because tires are more easily cut and penetrated when they are wet than when they are dry. It is, therefore, advantageous to have maximum tread thickness during wet seasons of the year.

Bends and corners are severe on tires because a car can be steered only by misaligning its wheels relative to the direction of the car. This condition applies to the rear as well as the front tires. The resulting slip and distortion increase the rate of wear according to speed, load, road camber and other factors.

The effect of hills, causing increased driving and braking

torques with which the tires must cope, needs no elaboration.

Wheel Alignment and Road Camber

It is very important that correct wheel alignment should be maintained. Misalignment causes tread to be scrubbed off laterally because the natural direction of the wheel differs from that of the car.

An upstanding fin on the edge of each pattern rib is a sure sign of misalignment and it is possible to determine from the position of the "fins" whether the wheels are toed in or toed out. Fins on the inside edges of the pattern ribs — nearest to the car — and particularly on the off-side tire, indicate toe-out.

With minor misalignment the evidence is less noticeable and the sharp pattern edges may be caused by road camber even when wheel alignment is correct. In such cases it is better to make sure by checking with an alignment gauge.

Road camber affects the direction of the car by imposing a side thrust and if left to follow its natural course the car will drift to the near side. This is instinctively corrected by steering towards the road center. As a result the car runs crab-wise.

The near front tire sometimes persists in wearing faster and more unevenly than the other tires even when the mechanical condition of the car and tire maintenance are satisfactory. The more severe the average road camber the more marked will this tendency be. This is an additional reason for the regular interchange of tires.

WHEEL BALANCE

Static Balance

In the interests of smooth riding, precise steering and the avoidance of high speed "tramp" or "wheel hop," all tires are balance checked to predetermined limits.

To ensure the best degree of balance the covers are marked with white spots on one bead and these indicate the lightest part of the cover. The white balance spots near the bead should be at the valve position.

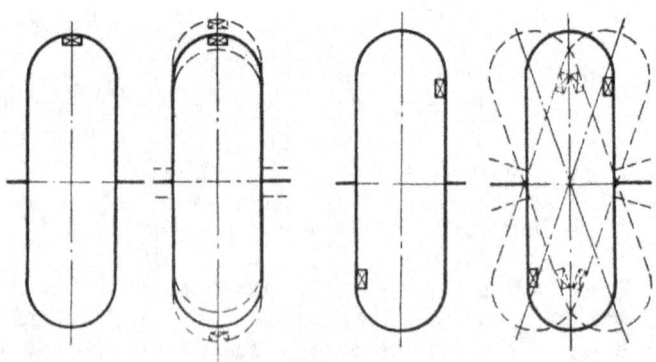

Some tires are slightly outside standard balance limits and are corrected before issue by attaching special loaded patches to the inside of the covers at the crown. These patches contain no fabric, they do not affect the local stiffness of the tire and should not be mistaken for repair patches — they are embossed "Balance Adjustment Rubber".

The original degree of balance is not necessarily maintained and it may be affected by uneven tread wear, by cover and tube repairs, by tire removal and refitting or by wheel damage and eccentricity. The car may also become more sensitive to unbalance due to normal wear of moving parts.

Should roughness or high speed steering troubles develop, and mechanical investigation fails to disclose a possible cause, wheel and tire balance should be suspected.

Dynamic Balance

Static unbalance, as its name implies, can be measured when the assembly is stationary. There is, however, another form known as dynamic unbalance which can be detected only when the assembly is revolving.

There may be no heavy spot — that is, there may be no natural tendency for the assembly to rotate about its center due to gravity — but the weight may be unevenly distributed each side of the center line.

Laterally eccentric wheels give the same effect. During rotation the offset weight distribution sets up a rotating couple which tends to steer the wheel to right and left alternately.

Dynamic unbalance of tire and wheel assemblies can be measured on balancing machine and suitable corrections made when a car shows sensitivity to this form of unbalance. Where it is clear that a damaged wheel is the primary cause of severe unbalance it is advisable for the wheel to be replaced.

Changing Position of Tires

Reference has already been made to irregular tread wear which is confined almost entirely to front tires and there may be different rates of wear between one tire and another.

It is, therefore, recommended that front tires be interchanged with rear tires at least every 3,000 miles. Diagonal interchanging between near-side front and off-side rear and between off-side front and near-side rear provides the most satisfactory first change because it reverses the direction of rotation.

Subsequent interchanging of front and rear tires should be as indicated by appearance.

Car Jack

A Smith's "Steadylift" jack is supplied with the car, which can be operated from either side, thus enabling either right or left side to be raised completely.

Before jacking up the car first apply the handbrake and if necessary (car on a gradient) chock one of the wheels on the opposite side to that requiring attention. Insert the jack lug into the socket provided under the car.

Ensure that the lug is fully engaged in the socket and that the base has a firm footing on the ground, before commencing to wind the screw clockwise with the aid of the ratchet wrench.

Immediately the car is felt to lift, recheck that the lug is correctly located within its socket.

Naturally, to lower the car the jack screw must be turned in an anti-clockwise direction.

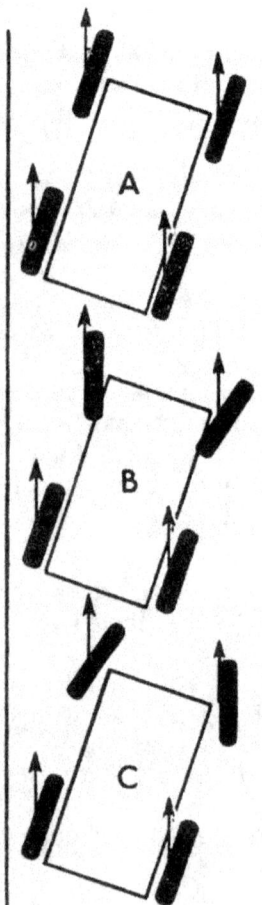

A. WHEELS PARALLEL IN MOTION; TYRE WEAR EQUAL.

B. WHEELS TOED-OUT IN MOTION; RIGHT FRONT TYRE WEARS FASTER.

C. WHEELS TOED-IN IN MOTION; LEFT FRONT TYRE WEARS FASTER.

SECTION II

1098 c.c. Engined Cars

1962-1966

This added section to the original handbook covers servicing of models produced since 1962. The pages up to this added section still apply to 1962 and prior models.

Floyd Clymer — Publisher

Beginning with engine serial No. 10CG/Da/H 101 and thereafter, larger engines have been used and a number of chassis revisions have also been made. Those changes in maintenance and repair procedures which apply are set forth in the following pages. If a part or method is not described herein, the techniques and components which apply to the 948cc powered models remain the same. See page 4 for model identification.

PERFORMANCE MAINTENANCE

Compression Ratios 8.8:1, 8.9:1, and 9:1

The high-compression engine is a highly developed unit, and it is esential that you should know something about it if you are to maintain it at the peak of its mechanical efficiency. With an engine having a very high compression ratio, the range of fuels, spark plugs, and ignition setings are very narrow and it is essential that the mixture should always be correct, and particularly never overweak at maximum power or load.

High-compression engines are very sensitive to variations in spark advance (over-advance) and to fuel/air ratio (mixture). Variations in these settings will increase the combustion temperature, and if the variation is excessive pre-ignition will cause high schock waves, resulting in damage to the engine. The engine should be decarbonized at regular intervals as excessive deposits of ash from the combustion of lubricating oil and fuel can cause pre-ignition difficulties.

Choice Of Fuel

Compression ratios of 8.9:1 and 9:1: The octane number of a motor fuel is an indication given by the fuel technicians of its knock resistance. High octane fuels have been produced to improve the efficiency of engines by allowing them to operate on high compression ratios, resulting in better fuel economy and greater power. Owing to the high compression ratio of this engine, fuels with an octane rating below 98 are NOT suitable; should it be necessary to use a fuel with a lower octane number, the car must be used very carefully until the correct fuel can be obtained.

It is necessary to use Super grade fuels in the 100-octane range unless Premium fuels of minimum 98-octane Research are available.

Compression ratio 8.8:1: Fuels with an octane rating below 94 are NOT suitable. Premium grade fuels with octane ratings of 97 to 99 must be used when optimum performance is required.

Spark Plugs

The correct grade of spark plug for use under normal driving conditions is the Champion N5. Plugs of a lower heat range (hotter running) should not be used, otherwise pre-ignition will occur, with consequent rise in combustion temperature and resulting engine damage. For competition work or hard driving where high output is consistently sustained, use the Champion N3 spark plug. This is a cooler-running plug and will ensure lower combustion temperatures and an increased safety margin. Accumulated deposits of carbon, leaking or cracked plug insulators, and thin electrodes are all causes of pre-ignition. The plugs should therefore be examined, cleaned, and adjusted at the specified intervals and defective plugs replaced. New plugs should be fitted at regular intervals.

Ignition Setting

It is of the utmost importance that the correct setting always be maintained. Any variation in the contact breaker gap will be sure to affect the ignition setting. Be sure the distributor points are adjusted and checked as specified in the IGNITION chapters of this book. After adjusting the contact breaker gap to the correct setting (see GENERAL DATA for the particular engine) it is advisable to check the ignition timing, and to correct if necessary.

An accurate static check can be carried out using a very simple electrical method. To do this, connect a 12-volt light bulb between the low-tension terminal on the side of the distributor and a good grounding point on the engine. With the ignition switched on and the spark plugs removed, turn the chankshaft until the crankshaft pulley T.D.C. pointer is exactly at the correct number of degrees (see GENERAL DATA). If the ignition timing is correct the lamp will light at exactly this point. Any discrepancy in the ignition setting can be rectified by turning the vernier adjustng nut on the distributor until the test lamp lights at exactly the correct setting.

If pinging should occur due to the use of a fuel of a lower range than is recommended, retarding the ignition 2 to 3° can be tolerated. Under no circumstances should the ignition be advanced beyond the correct setting.

IGNITION

TO TEST IN THE VEHICLE

If the ignition system fails, or misfiring occurs, first make sure that the trouble is not due to defects in the engine, carburetter or fuel supply. Faults should be diagnosed by applying the following tests:

(1) **High-tension circuit:** Start engine and run at a fairly fast idling speed. Short-circuit each plug in turn by pulling the insulator sleeve up the cable and place a hammerhead or the blade of an insulated screwdriver between the terminal and the cylinder head. No difference in engine performance will be noticed when short-circuiting the DEFECTIVE plug. Short-circuiting the other cylinders will make uneven running more pronounced.

(2) Now that the faulty plug and cylinder have been located, stop the engine and remove the cable from the spark plug terminal. Restart the engine, then hold the end of the cable about 3/16 in. (4.8 mm.) from the cylinder head. If the spark is strong and regular, the fault probably lies in the plug. Remove the plug, clean it, and adjust the gap within the limits .024 to .026 in. (.62 to .66 mm.), or alternatively fit a new plug (properly gapped).

(3) If there is no spark or it is weak and irregular examine the cable from the spark plug to the distributor. Replace the cable if the insulation is cracked or damaged. Even if the cable is replaced, check the distributor cap. Wipe it inside and out with a clean, dry cloth, see that the carbon brush moves freely in its holder, and examine the cap closely for signs of breakdown. A cap may become tracked: that is, a conducting path may have formed between two or more of the electrodes or between one of the electrodes and some part of the distributor in contact with the cap. This will be shown by a thin black line, in which case the cap must be replaced.

(4) **Low-tension circuit.** Should the above tests fail to correct the problem or the low-tension circuit must be tested, begin by checking that the contact breaker points are properly adjusted (see ADJUSTMENTS IN THE VEHICLE), that the contact points are opening and closing correctly, and that the clearance between them is correct when they are fully opened. Reset spark plug gap if necessary (see GENERAL DATA).

(5) Disconnect the cable at the contact breaker terminal of the coil and at the low tension terminal of the distributor, then connect a test light between these two terminals. If it lights when the contacts close and ex-

tinguishes when the contacts open, the low-tension circuit is operable. If the light does not glow, the contacts are dirty or there is a broken or loose connection in the low-tension wiring.

(6) To trace a fault in the low-tension circuit, switch on the ignition and turn the crankshaft until the contact breaker points have fully opened. Refer to the wiring diagram, and, with the aid of a 0 to 20 volt voltmeter, check the circuit as follows:

(a) **Cable (brown) — Battery to regulator terminal A**
Connect a voltmeter between the regulator terminal A and ground. No reading indicates a damaged cable or loose connections.

(b) **Regulator**
Connect a voltmeter between the regulator auxiliary terminal and ground. No reading indicates a broken or loose connection.

(c) **Cable (brown with blue lead) — Regulator auxiliary terminal to terminal on ignition switch**
Connect a voltmeter between the ignition switch terminal and ground. No reading indicates a damaged cable or loose connections.

(d) **Ignition switch**
Connect a voltmeter between the other ignition switch terminal and ground. No reading indicates a fault in the ignition switch.

(e) **Cable (white lead) — Ignition switch to fusebox terminal A3**
Connect the voltmeter between the fusebox terminal A3 and ground. No reading indicates a faulty cable or loose connections.

(f) **Cable (white lead) — Fusebox terminal A3 to ignition coil terminal SW**
Connect a voltmeter between the ignition coil terminal SW and ground. No reading indicates a faulty cable or loose connections.

(g) **Ignition coil**
Disconnect the cable from the CB terminal of the ignition coil and connect a voltmeter between this terminal and ground. No reading indicates a fault in the primary winding of the coil and a replacement coil must be fitted. If the reading is correct, reconnect the cable to the coil terminal.

(h) **Cable (white black lead) — Ignition coil to distributor**
Disconnect the cable from the low-tension terminal on the distributor and connect the voltmeter between the end of this cable and ground. No reading indicates a damaged cable or loose connections.

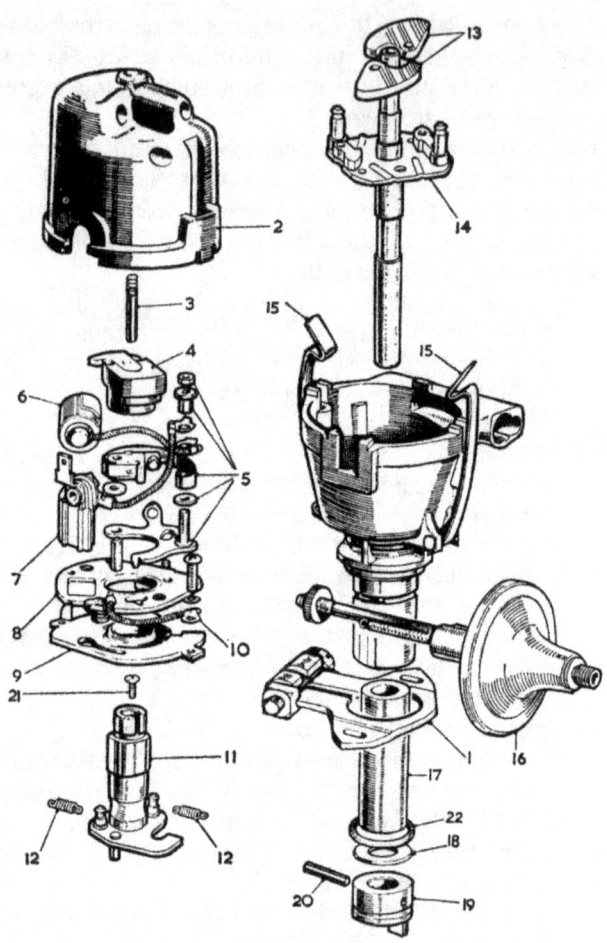

The components of the distributor

1. Clamping plate.
2. Moulded cap.
3. Brush and spring.
4. Rotor arm.
5. Contacts (set).
6. Capacitor.
7. Terminal and lead (low-tension).
8. Moving contact breaker plate.
9. Contact breaker base plate.
10. Earth lead.
11. Cam.
12. Automatic advance springs.
13. Weight assembly.
14. Shaft and action plate.
15. Cap-retaining clips.
16. Vacuum unit.
17. Bush.
18. Thrust washer.
19. Driving dog.
20. Parallel pin.
21. Cam screw.
22. 'O' ring oil seal.

Distributor

(i) **Contact breaker and capacitor (condenser)**
Connect the voltmeter across the contact breaker points. No reading indicates a faulty capacitor.

(7) If, after carrying out the foregoing tests, the fault has not been located, remove the high-tension cable from the terminal of the distributor. Switch on the ignition and crank the engine until the contacts close. Flick the contact breaker lever open while the high-tension cable from the ignition coil is held about 3/16 in. (5mm.) away from the cylinder block. If the ignition equipment is in order a strong spark should be obtained. If no spark is given, it indicates a faulty ignition coil.

DISTRIBUTOR

Lubrication
(1) **Cam bearing:** Pull up squarely on the distributor rotor to remove, then add a few drops of oil to the cam bearing. **Note:** Do not remove the screw which is exposed, since there is a clearance between the screw and the inner face of the spindle for the oil to pass.
(2) **Cam:** Lightly smear a very small amount of grease on the cam; If this is not available, use clean engine oil.
(3) **Automatic timing control:** Carefully add a few drops of oil through the hole in the contact breaker through which the cam passes. **Note:** Do not allow the oil to get on or near the contacts and do not over-oil.

FUEL SYSTEM

CARBURETTERS

Slow-running Adjustment and Syncronization

When the engine is fully run in the slow running may require adjustment. This must only be carried out after the engine has reached its operating temperature.

Since the needle size is determined during engine development, tuning of the carburetters is confined to correct idling setting. Loosen the actuating arms on the throttle spindle interconnection. Close both throttles fully by unscrewing the throttle adjusting bolts, then open each throttle by screwing down each idling adjustment screw one turn.

Remove the pistons and suction chambers and disconnect the choke control cable. Screw the jet adjusting nuts until each

THE CARBURETTER COMPONENTS

206

KEY TO THE CARBURETTER COMPONENTS

No.	Description
1.	Carburetter body (left).
2.	Carburetter body (right).
3.	Piston lifting pin.
4.	Spring.
5.	Circlip.
6.	Piston chamber assembly.
7.	Screw.
8.	Cap and damper assembly.
9.	Fibre washer.
10.	Piston spring.
11.	Screw.
12.	Jet assembly (left carburetter).
13.	Jet assembly (right carburetter).
14.	Bearing.
15.	Washer.
16.	Screw.
17.	Spring.
18.	Screw.
19.	Needle.
20.	Float-chamber.
21.	Support washer.
22.	Rubber grommet (left carburetter).
23.	Rubber grommet (right carburetter).
24.	Washer (rubber).
25.	Washer (steel).
26.	Bolt.
27.	Float assembly.
28.	Lever pin.
29.	Float-chamber lid (left carburetter).
30.	Float-chamber lid (right carburetter).
31.	Washer.
32.	Needle and seat assembly.
33.	Screw.
34.	Spring washer.
35.	Baffle plate.
36.	Throttle spindle.
37.	Throttle disc.
38.	Screw.
39.	Throttle return lever (left carburetter).
40.	Throttle return lever (right carburetter).
41.	Lost motion lever.
42.	Nut.
43.	Tab washer.
44.	Throttle screw stop.
45.	Spring.
46.	Pick-up lever (left carburetter).
47.	Pick-up lever (right carburetter).
48.	Link (left carburetter).
49.	Link (right carburetter).
50.	Washer.
51.	Screw.
52.	Bush.
53.	Cam lever (left carburetter).
54.	Cam lever (right carburetter).
55.	Pick-up lever spring (left carburetter).
56.	Pick-up lever spring (right carburetter).
57.	Cam lever spring (left carburetter).
58.	Cam lever spring (right carburetter).
59.	Bolt.
60.	Tube.
61.	Spring washer.
62.	Distance piece.
63.	Jet rod.
64.	Lever and pin assembly (left carburetter).
65.	Lever and pin assembly (right carburetter).
66.	Bolt.
67.	Washer.
68.	Nut.

jet is flush with the bridge of its carburetter (or as close as possible). Be sure both jets are in the same relative position to the bridge of their respective carburetters. Replace the pistons and vacuum chamber assemblies and check that the pistons fall freely into the bridge of the carburetters (by means of the piston lifting pins). Turn down the jet adjusting nut two complete turns (12 flats).

Restart the engine, then adjust the throttle adjusting screws to give the desired idling speed by moving each throttle adjusting screw an equal amount. By listening to the hiss in the intakes, adjust the throttle adjusting screws until the intensity of the hiss is similar on both intakes. This will synchronize the throttles.

When this is satisfactory, the mixture should be adjusted by screwing each jet adjusting nut up or down the same amount until the fastest idling speed is obtained consistent with even firing. During this adjustment it is necessary that the jets are pressed upwards to ensure that they are in contact with the adjusting nuts.

As the mixture is adjusted the engine will probably run faster, and it may therefore be necessary to unscrew the throttle adjusting screws a bit, each by the same amount, to reduce the speed.

Now check the mixture strength by lifting the piston of the front carburetter about 1/32 in. (1 mm.) when:
  (1) If the engine speed increases, this indicates that the mixture strength of the front carburetter is too rich.
  (2) If the engine speed immediately decreases, this indicates that the mixture strength of the front carburetter is too weak.
  (3) If the engine speed momentarily increases very slightly, then the mixture strength of the front carburetter is correct.

Repeat this operation at the rear carburetter, and after adjustment re-check the front carburetter, since both carburetters are interdependent. When the mixture is correct the exhaust note should be regular and even. If it is irregular, with a splashy type of misfire and colorless exhaust, the mixture is too weak. If there is a regular or rythmical type of misfire in the exhaust beat, together with a blackish exhaust, then the mixture is too rich.

Throttle Linkage

The throttle on each carburetter is operated by a lever and pin, with the pin working in a forked lever attached to the throttle spindle. A clearance between the pin and fork must be maintained when the throttle is closed and the engine is at rest to prevent any load from the accelerator linkage and return springs being transferred to the throttle butterfly and spindle.

To set this clearance: With the throttle shaft levers free on the throttle shaft, put a .012 in. (.3 mm.) feeler between the

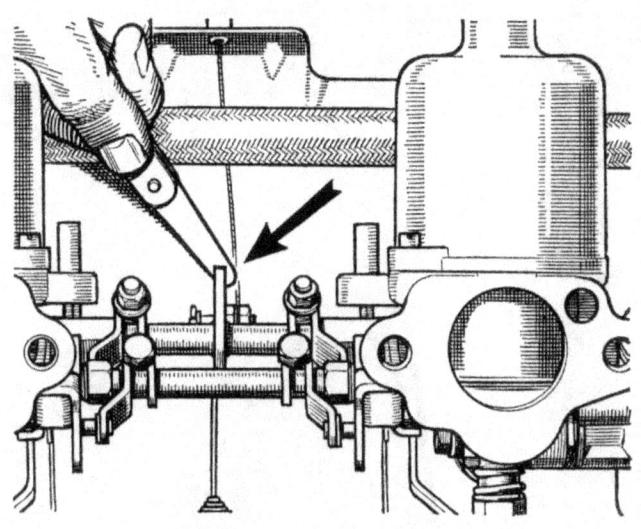

The feeler between the throttle shaft stop and the carburetter heat shield

Throttle linkage

throttle shaft stop at the top and the carburetter heat shield. Move the throttle shaft lever downwards until the lever pin rests lightly on the lower arm of the fork in the carburetter throttle lever. Tighten the clamp bolt of the throttle shaft lever at this position. When both carburetters have been dealt with, remove the feeler. The pins on the throttle shaft levers should then have clearance in the forks.

Reconnect the choke cable, ensuring that the jet heads return against the lower face of the jet adjusting nuts when the choke control is pushed in fully. Pull out the mixture control knob on the dash panel until the linkage is about to move the carburetter jets (a minimum of 1/4 in. or 6 mm.) and adjust the fast idle adjusting screws to give an engine speed of about 1,000 RPM when hot.

Float Chambers

The position of the hinged lever in the float-chamber must be such that the level of the float (and therefore the height of the fuel at the jet) is correct.

This is checked by inserting a round bar between the hinged lever and the machined lip of the float-chamber lid. The end of the lever should just rest on the bar (see illustration) when the needle is on its seating. If this is not so, the lever should be reset at the point where the end meets the shank. Do not bend the shank, which must be perfectly flat and at right angles to the needle when it is on its seating.

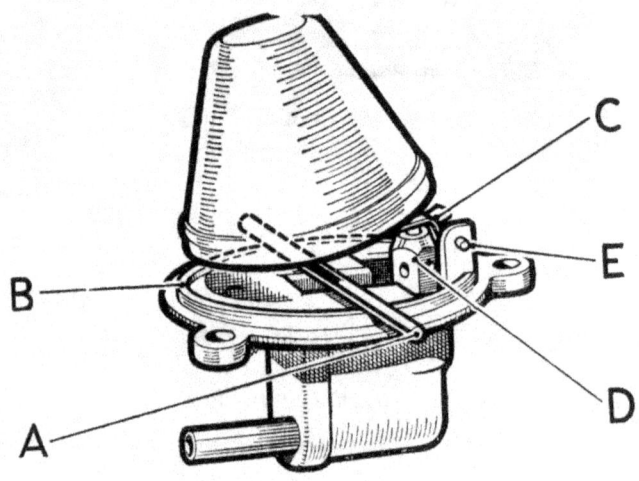

The method of checking the correct adjustment of the float lever (later cars)

A. $\tfrac{1}{8}$ to $\tfrac{3}{16}$ in. (3·18 to 4·76 mm.).
B. Machined lip.
C. Angle of float lever.
D. Float needle and seat assembly.
E. Lever hinge pin.

Float adjustment

ELECTRICAL SYSTEM

GENERATOR ASSEMBLY

To Remove
(1) Disconnect the two leads to the generator.
(2) Slacken all four attachment bolts and pivot the generator towards the cylinder block to enable the fan belt to be removed from the generator pulley.
(3) The generator can then be removed by withdrawing the two upper and one lower attachment bolts.

To Dismantle
(1) Remove the securing nut and take off the drive pulley.
(2) Remove the Woodruff key from the commutator shaft.
(3) Unscrew and remove the two through-bolts and take off the commutator end bracket. The driving end bracket, together with the armature and its ball bearing, can now be lifted out of its yoke.
(4) Unless the ball bearing is damaged or requires attention it need not be removed from the armature. Should it be necessary to remove the bearing, the armature must be separated from the end bracket by means of a hand press.

Inspection and Overhaul

Brushes: Lift the brushes up into the brush boxes and secure them in position by positioning the brush spring at the side of the brush. Fit the commutator end bracket over the commutator and release the brushes. Hold back each of the brush springs and move the brush by pulling gently on its flexible connector. If the movement is sluggish, remove the brush from its holder and ease the sides by lightly polishing it on a smooth file. Always refit the brushes in their original positions. If the brushes are badly worn, new brushes must be fitted and bedded to the commutator. The minimum permissible length of brush is 11/32 in. (8.8 mm.) (C39 type), 1/4 in. (6 mm.) (C40/1 type).

Test the brush spring tension, using a spring scale. The tension of the springs when new is 18 to 26 ozs. (510 to 737 grs.) (C39 type), 22 to 25 ozs. (624 to 709 grs.) (C40/1 type). In service it is permissible for this value to fall to 15 ozs. (425 grs.) before performance may be affected. Fit new springs if the tension is low.

Commutator: Service as previously described, except for the folowing additional information:

Some commutators fitted to the C40/1 generators are of the moulded type and may be re-skimmed to a minimum diameter of 1.45 in. (36.8 mm.). The undercut must conform to the following dimensions:

Width .... .040 in. (1.016 mm.)
Depth .... .020 in. (.508 mm.)

It is important that the sides of the undercut clear the moulded material by a minimum of .015 in. (381 mm.).

Armature: The testing of the armature winding requires the use of a voltage drop-test and growler. If these are not available the armature should be checked by substitution. No attempt should be made to machine the armature core or to true a distorted armature shaft.

LOCATION AND REMEDY OF FAULTS

Although every precaution is taken to eliminate possible causes of trouble, failure may occasionally develop through lack of attention to the equipment or damage to the wiring. The following pages set out the recommended procedure for a systematic examination to locate and remedy the causes of some of the more usual faults encountered.

The sources of trouble are by no means always obvious, and in some cases a considerable amount of deduction from the symptoms is needed before the cause is disclosed. For instance, the engine might not respond to the starter switch; a hasty inference would be that the starter motor is at fault. However, as the motor is dependent on the battery, it may be that the battery is exhausted.

This in turn may be due to the generator failing to charge the battery, and the final cause of the trouble may be, perhaps, a loose connection in some part of the charging circuit. If, after carrying out an examination, the cause of the trouble is not found, the equipment should be checked.

Charging Circuit

(1) **Battery in a low state of charge:** This condition will be shown by lack of power when starting, poor illumination from the lights, and the hydrometer readings below 1.200. It may be due to the generator not charging or giving low or intermittent output. The ignition warning light will not go out if the generator fails to charge, or will flicker on and off in the event of intermittent output.

(2) Examine the charging and field circuit wiring, tighten any loose connections, or renew any broken cables. Pay particular attention to the battery connections.

(3) Examine the generator driving belt; take up any looseness by swinging the generator outwards on its mounting after loosening the attachment bolts.

(4) Check the regulator setting, and adjust if necessary.

(5) If, after carrying out the above, the trouble is still not cured, examine the equipment.

(1) **Battery overcharged:** This will be indicated by burnt-out bulbs, very frequent need for topping up the battery, and

high hydrometer readings.
(2) Check the charge reading with an ammeter when the car is running. It should be of the order of only 3 to 4 amps.
(3) If the ammeter reading is in excess of this value it is advisable to check the regulator setting, and adjust if necessary.

Starter Motor

(1) **Starter motor lacks power or fails to turn engine:** See if the engine can be turned over by hand. If not, the cause of the stiffness in the engine must be located and remedied.
(2) If the engine can be turned over by hand, first check that the trouble is not due to a discharged battery.
(3) Examine the connection to the battery, starter, and starter switch, making sure that they are tight and that the cables connecting these units are not damaged.
(4) It is also possible that the starter pinion may have jammed in mesh with the flywheel, although this is by no means a common occurrence. To disengage the pinion rotate the squared end of the starter shaft by means of a wrench.

(1) **Starter operates but does not crank the engine:** This fault will occur if the pinion of the starter drive is not allowed to move along the screwed sleeve into engagement with the flywheel due to having dirt collected on the screwed sleeve.
(2) Remove the starter and clean the sleeve carefully with solvent.
(3) Replace the starter and test.

(1) **Starter pinion will not disengage from the flywheel when engine is running:** Stop the engine and see if the starter pinion is jammed in mesh with the flywheel.
(2) To release, rotate the squared end of the starter shaft with a wrench.
(3) If the pinion persists in sticking in mesh, examine the equipment. Serious damage may result to the starter if it is driven by the flywheel.

Lighting Circuits

(1) **Lights give insufficient illumination:** Test the state of the battery charge, recharging it if necessary from an independent electrical supply.
(2) Check the setting of the lights.
(3) If the bulbs are discolored as the result of long service they should be renewed.

(1) **Lamps light when switched on but gradually fade out:** See (1) above.
(2) Brilliance varies with speed of car. See (1) above.
(3) Examine the battery connections, making sure that they are tight and renew any faulty cables.

THE FLASHER UNIT

Checking Faulty Operation

In the event of trouble occurring with a flashing light direction-indicator system, the following procedure should be followed:
(1) Check the bulbs for broken filaments.
(2) Refer to the vehicle wiring diagram and check all flasher circuit connections.
(3) Check the appropriate fuse.
(4) Switch on the ignition.
(5) Check, using a voltmeter between the flasher unit terminal 'B' (or '+') and ground, that battery voltage is present.
(6) Connect together flasher unit terminals 'B' (or '+') and 'L' and operate the direction indicator switch. If the flasher lamps now light, the flasher unit is defective and must be renewed.

WINDSHIELD WIPERS

Removing the motor, gearbox, and wheelboxes

The motor and gearbox is located beneath the passenger's side of the fascia panel and is mounted on a bracket secured to the bulkhead panel by three set screws and nuts.

The cable rack connected to the cross-head in the gearbox passes through outer casings which connect the gearbox to the first wheelbox and the first wheelbox to the second wheelbox.
(1) Remove the fascia panel.
(2) Disconnect the wiper arms, the electrical connections from the motor, and the outer cable from the gearbox housing.
(3) Remove the three nuts securing the motor to the bulkhead panel and withdraw the motor, then the cable rack.
(4) Loosen the cover screws in each wheelbox and remove the cable rack outer casings.
(5) Remove the nut, front bush, and washer from the front of each wheelbox and remove the wheelbox together with the rear bush and spindle tube from beneath the fascia panel.
(6) To replace, reverse the removal process. Be sure that the wheelboxes are correctly lined up and that the cable rack engages the gear and spindle assemblies.

THE WINDSHIELD WIPER COMPONENTS

No.	Description
1.	Windshield wiper motor.
2.	Brush gear.
3.	Brush.
4.	Armature.
5.	Field coil.
6.	Fixing parts.
7.	Parking switch.
8.	Gear and shaft.
10.	Motor to wheelbox outer casing.
11.	Wheelbox to wheelbox outer casing.
12.	Wheelbox extension outer casing.
13.	Cross-head and rack assembly.
14.	Grommet.
15.	Wheelbox.
16.	Spindle and gear.
17.	Wiper arm.
18.	Wiper blade.
19.	Rubber tube spindle.
20.	Front bush.
21.	Rear bush.
22.	Rubber washer.
23.	Nut.
24.	Cover screw.

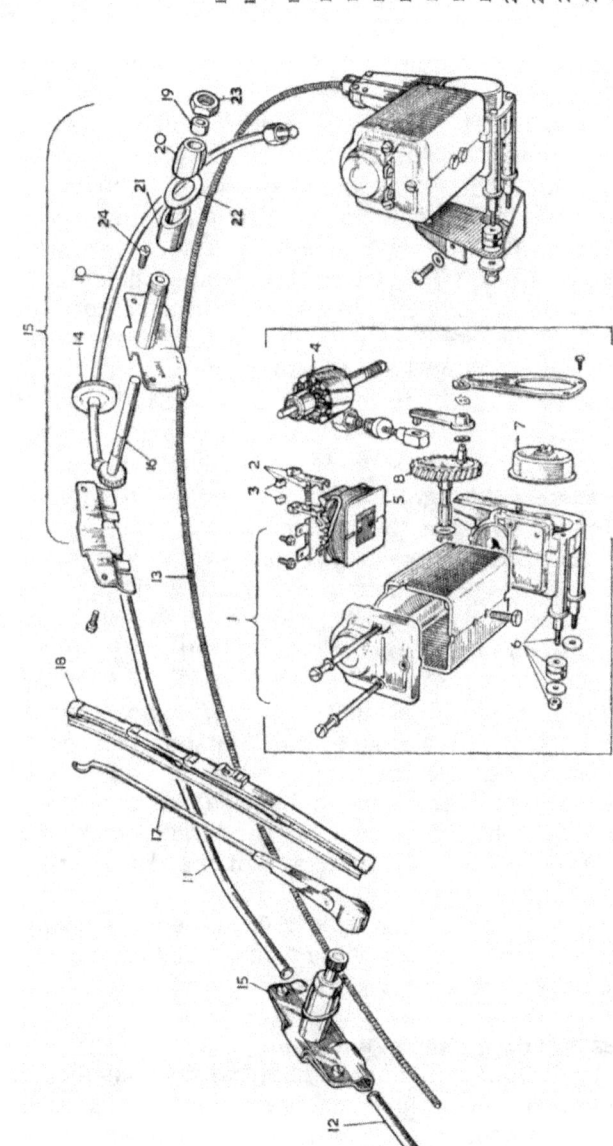

HEADLIGHTS
U.K. and North American Types

Headlights fitted to vehicles operating in the United Kingdom or in North America are of the sealed-beam type and the light units are serviced as complete assemblies only.

Removing the light unit (U.K. type): The lamp rims are fitted with rubber dust excluders and rim retaining screws. Release the retaining screw at the bottom of the rim and the lamp body and lift away the lamp rim. Remove the inner rim securing screws and lift away the sealed beam assembly after disconnecting the three-pin socket.

Replacing the light unit (U.K. type): Refit the three-pin plug to the rear of the light unit. Place the light in the back-shell, being sure that the registers moulded in the rear edge of the light unit engage in the slots in the back-shell. Replace the light unit rim and refit the securing screws. Fit the rear top edge of the lamp rim over the two raised sections of the back-shell, press downwards and inwards and refit the retaining screw.

Beam-setting (U.K. type): The lamps should be set so that the main driving beams are parallel with the road surface or in accordance with local regulations. If adjustment is required, this is achieved by removing the headlight rim. Vertical adjustment can then be made by turning the screw at the top of the lamp in the necessary direction. Horizontal adjustment can be effected by using the adjustment screw on the right-hand side of the light.

Removing the light unit (North American type): Remove the retaining screw from the bottom face of the lamp rim, lift the bottom of the rim forwards and upwards and detach the rim. Loosen the three Phillips screws securing the light unit retaining rim and turn the rim anti-clockwise to remove, supporting the light unit lens at the same time. Pull off the three-pin plug from the rear of the light unit.

Replacing the light unit (North American type): Refit the three-pin plug to the rear of the light unit. Place the light unit in the back-shell, being sure that the registers moulded on the rear edge of the unit engage in the slots in the back shell. Replace the light unit rim so that the large diameters of the three slotted holes pass over the heads of the three retaining screws, press the rim firmly inwards and rotate the rim clockwise to the full extent of the sloted holes. Retighten the securing screws. Fit the rear top edge of the lamp rim over the two raised sections of the back-shell, press downwards and inwards and refit the retaining screw.

Beam-setting (North American type): The lamps should be set in the low-beam position, and should be adjusted to comply with regulations in the country or state in which the vehicle is operating. If adjustment is necessary, this is achieved by removing the headlamp rim. Vertical adjustment can then be made by turning the screw at the top of the lamp in the necessary direction. Horizontal adjustment can be effected by using the adjustment screw on the right-hand side of the light.

PILOT AND FLASHING DIRECTION INDICATOR LAMPS

Remove the two securing screws and lift away the plated rim and glass. An amber cover is fitted over the direction indicator bulb when the vehicle is operating in countries where the lighting regulations require amber flashing indicators. Replacement is the reversal of the removal procedure.

PANEL AND WARNING LAMPS

Access to the warning lamps for the ignition and headlight beam is effected from under the fascia by withdrawing the push-in-type holders from the rear of the fascia panel. See accompanying list for replacement bulbs.

Replacement bulbs

	Volts	Watts	B.M.C. Part No.
Headlamps—L.H.D. except North America and Europe	12	50/40	BFS 415
Headlamps—Europe except France	12	45/40	BFS 410
Headlamps—France only	12	45/40	BFS 411
Sidelamps	12	6	BFS 989
Sidelamps, direction indicator lamps—North America and Italy	12	6/21	BFS 380
Direction indicator lamps (front)	12	21	BFS 382
Direction indicator lamps (rear)	12	21	BFS 382
Tail and stop lamps	12	6/21	BFS 380
Number-plate illumination lamp	12	6	BFS 989
Panel and warning lights	12	2·2	BFS 987

LICENSE-PLATE ILLUMINATION LIGHT

The license-plate is illuminated by a separate lamp with twin bulbs. The cover is removed by unscrewing the single attachment screw, which enables it to be withdrawn, giving easy access to the bulbs.

TAIL, STOP AND DIRECTION INDICATOR LAMPS

The tail light bulbs are of the double-filament type, the second filament giving a marked increase in brilliance when the brakes are applied. Access to the bulbs is gained by extracting the securing screws from the outer face of the lamp lens to release the lens. The tail and stop light bulbs must be fitted one way only; offset retaining pegs ensure that they are replaced correctly.

The tail light body can be removed when the lens is taken off and the three screws located in the body are withdawn. When refitting the glass to the body make certain that it is seating correctly over the sealing rubber.

HORN AND HORN-BUTTON

Removing and Replacing the Horn

Remove the horn bracket-to-body securing nuts, spring washers, and set screws, then disconnect the horn leads and remove the horn assembly. To replace, reverse the removal procedure.

Maintenance

If the horn fails to operate, or operates unsatisfactorily, first carry out the following external checks:

(1) Examine the cables of the horn circuit, renewing any that are badly worn or chafed. Be sure that all connections are clean and tight and that the connecting nipples are firmly soldered to the cables.

(2) Check that the bolts securing the horn brackets are tight and that the horn body does not contact any fixtures.

(3) Check the current consumption, which should be 3 to $3\frac{1}{2}$ amps. when the horn is operating correctly.

(4) After making a thorough external check remove the horn cover and examine the cable connections inside the horn. Examine the contact breaker contacts. If they are burnt or blackened clean them with a fine file, then wipe with a solvent-moistened cloth.

Removing the Horn-Button

When removing the horn-button it is a simple operation of levering the complete assembly out of the steering-wheel with a screwdriver. Take care not to damage the bakelite surround.

Replacing the Horn-Button

When replacing be sure that the brass contact strip is in line with the live contact in the steering wheel assembly.

SWITCHES

Note: In all cases when removing switches the battery terminals should be disconnected.

Lighting, Direction Indicator, and Windshield Wiper

Removal: In all cases disconnect the Lucas connectors, unscrew the fixing nut, and remove the switch assembly complete with its D-shaped locking washer.

Replacement: To replace, reverse the removal procedure.

Ignition

Removal: Disconnect the Lucas connectors, unscrew the fixing nut, and remove the switch assembly complete with its D-shaped locking washer.

Dismantling: To remove the locking barrel from the switch body insert the key and turn the switch to the IGNITION ON position to align the barrel-retaining plunger with the small hole in the switch body. Using an awl, depress the plunger and withdraw the barrel complete with key.

Reassembling and replacement: Reverse the dismantling and removal procedure.

Starter
Removing: Disconnect the battery leads from the switch terminals. Remove the switch-operating cable by loosening the lock screw on the connecting sleeve of the switch and withdraw the switch assembly from its mounting bracket.

Replacement: To replace, reverse the removal procedure.

Dimmer Switch
Removal: Remove the dimmer switch-to-bracket securing screws and withdraw the switch assembly. Disconnect the cables from the switch connectors and remove the switch assembly. Service switch as a complete unit.

Replacement: To replace, reverse the removal procedure.

Panel
Removal: Remove the securing screws and withdraw the switch assembly. Disconnect the cables from the switch connectors and remove the switch assembly.

Replacement: To replace, reverse the removal procedure.

ENGINE

Oil Pressure
The normal operating pressure is 30 to 60 psi (2.1 to 4.22 kg. per cm.^{2}) The oil gauge is combined with the thermometer on the instrument panel.

A minimum pressure of 10 to 25 psi (.7 to 1.7 kg. per cm.^{2}) should be registered when the engine is idling. **If no pressure is registered by the gauge, stop the engine at once and investigate the cause.**

OIL PUMP

Removal
- (1) The engine must be removed from the car before the oil pump can be removed.
- (2) Remove the flywheel, clutch assembly, and engine back plate as detailed in the previous ENGINE chapter.
- (3) Unscrew the oil pump retaining screws and withdraw the pump.

(4) To replace, reverse the removal procedure, using a new paper joint washer. Position washer so as not to obstruct ports.

Servicing

Note: Three types of oil pumps may be fitted. The concentric type is serviced as a unit. The other types are generally replaced as an assembly by the concentric type. Take care that the correct length bolts are purchased with the replacement unit. See the previous ENGINE chapter for oil pump illustration (except Burman).

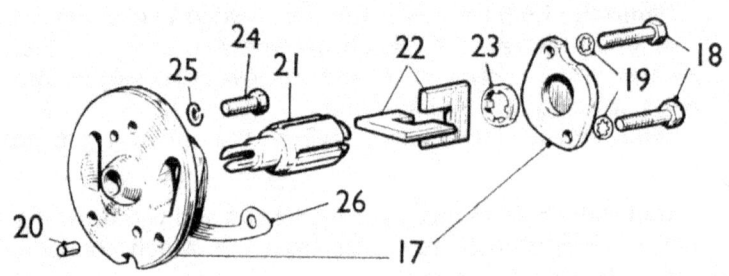

17. Body and cover assembly.
18. Screw.
19. Shakeproof washer.
20. Dowel.
21. Rotor.
22. Vane.
23. Sleeve.
24. Pump to crankcase screw.
25. Spring washer.

Burman oil pump

INLET AND EXHAUST MANIFOLD

Removal and Replacement

Follow steps (1) through (6) on this subject in the previous ENGINE chapter, then add the following steps:

(7) Remove the water pipe brackets from the induction manifold (if a heater is fitted).

(8) **To replace:** Reverse the order above, first thoroughly cleaning the joint faces and fitting a new gasket. Be sure to place the perforated metal face of the gasket towards the manifold.

CYLINDER HEAD

Removal
(1) Drain all water from the cooling system. If the coolant contains anti-freeze, it can be saved in a clean container for reuse. Be sure to drain both the radiator and engine block (tap or plug at rear left-hand side).
(2) Disconnect the negative clip from the battery.
(3) Loosen the retaining clip on the hose connecting the radiator to the thermostat housing, then pull the hose clear of the housing.
(4) Remove rocker cover retaining screws and rubber cups, then remove the cover.
(5) Remove the high-tension cables from the spark plugs and remove the spark plugs, taking care not to damage the porcelain insulators.
(6) Remove the suction pipe clip from its fixture on the hot water control valve. Release the heater hose retaining clip and detach the inlet hose (if applicable).
(7) Loosen the top clip on the water by-pass hose.
(8) Remove the rocker assembly as described in the previous ENGINE chapter, being sure to slacken the external cylinder head holding nuts at the same time (see illustration for order of loosening).
(9) Withdraw the push-rods, being sure to keep them in order of removal.
(10) To remove the cylinder head, place a block of wood against the side of the cylinder head and tap the block with a hammer. This should break the cylinder head joint. Then lift the head squarely to prevent the studs binding in their holes.

Replacement
Note: Be sure the cylinder head and block are clean. It is not necessary to use jointing compound or grease for the gasket.
(1) Slip the gasket over the studs, noting the TOP and FRONT markings.
(2) Lower the cylinder head into position and fit the five cylinder head securing nuts, then finger-tighten.
(3) Insert the push-rods, being sure to replace them in their original locations, and being sure that the ball ends are in the tappets.
(4) Replace the rocker assembly and securing nuts and fit the nuts finger-tight.
(5) Tighten all the nuts gradually, a turn at a time. **Note:** See the illustration in the previous ENGINE chapter for order of tightening. See the appropriate engine in GENERAL DATA for torque specifications.
(6) Check the valve clearance as described elsewhere in the

ENGINE chapter. Final adjustment is made after running the engine.
(7) Replace the inlet and exhaust manifold. Be sure to place the perforated metal face of the gasket toward the manifold.
(8) Attach the heater hose to the heater inlet pipe (if applicable).
(9) Replace the carburetters and air cleaners as described in the previous ENGINE chapter.
(10) Connect the negative cable to the battery terminal.
(11) Close the water drain taps and refill the system.
(12) Check, adjust, and replace the spark plugs, and then clip on the high-tension leads.
(13) Turn the engine over to check for leaks in the fuel systems.
(14) Start the engine and run it until the normal operating temperature is reached. Placing the valve cover (with cork gasket properly in place) over the rockers will prevent oil spattering. Remove the cover and check the valve clearances.
(15) Replace the valve cover with the gasket in position, then secure it by its nuts, washers, and rubber cups.
(16) Check the valve clearance again after the vehicle has run about 100 miles (160 km.) as the valves have a tendency to bed down. At the same time it is advisable to test the cylinder head nuts for tightness. Tightening the cylinder head nuts may affect valve clearances, although not usually enough to justify resetting.

REMOVING AND REFITTING VALVES

With the cylinder head removed, a valve lifting tool can be used to compress the springs (such as the one illustrated in the previous ENGINE chapter). If possible, stamp the valves with a number before removing, starting with No. 1 at the front of the engine. Otherwise, keep the valves in order on a rack.

(1) Remove the cotter clip, compress the valve springs and remove the split cotters.
(2) Release the valve spring slowly and remove the compressing tool.
(3) Keep valves and springs in their relative positions when removed from the cylinder head. Note that the exhaust valve heads are concave and are smaller than the inlet valves.
(4) **Refitting:** Replace each valve in its respective guide and fit the spring locating cup, springs and the retaining cap.
(5) Use the compressing tool to compress the springs and fit a NEW sealing rubber to the valve stem, push the seal against the bottom shoulder of the cotter recess, and refit the cotters.

(6) Be sure that the rubber seal is not pushed out of the cotter recess onto the larger diameter of the stem, then release the compressing tool.

(7) Replace the split cotter retaining clip.

VALVE GRINDING

Clean the carbon from the top and bottom of the valve heads, as well as any deposit that may have accumulated on the stems. Examine each valve CRITICALLY for warpage and pitting, placing it in its seat to determine fit. If there is the least doubt as to its condition, it is best to have the valve refaced on a valve grinder or replaced before trying to lap it into position.

The valve heads are refaced at an angle of 45° for both exhaust and inlet valves. If the valve seats show signs of excessive pitting it is advisable to reface these also. If possible, stamp any new valves with the port numbers to which they are fitted.

(1) For valve grinding a little fine- or medium-grade carborundum paste should be smeared evenly on the valve face.

Note: Avoid using too much paste and keep it in the region of the valve face only.

(2) The cutting action is facilitated by allowing a light spring, placed under the valve head, to periodically lift the valve from its seat.

(3) Using a rubber suction valve grinding tool, lap the valve to its own seat with a semi-rotary motion. Occasionally allow the valve to rise by the pressure of the light coil spring. This allows the grinding compound to re-penetrate between the two faces after being squeezed out.

(4) The grinding is completed when a dull, even, mat surface free from blemish is produced on the valve seat and valve face. Be sure each valve is ground-in and refitted to its own seat.

(5) To clean, use a solvent-soaked rag to clean the valve head, stem and seat. All traces of grinding paste must be removed.

(6) It is also desirable to clean the valve guides; this can be done by dipping the valve stem in solvent and moving it up and down in the guide until it is free.

(7) Finally, thoroughly clean all parts with compressed air.

CONNECTING RODS AND BEARINGS

Note: To assist correct assembly, note the markings on the tops of the pistons (which should face the front of the engine) and the bosses on the connecting rods and caps (which should face the camshaft). To mark, it is suggested that one prick punch mark should be put on No. One Cylinder piston, connecting rod, and rod cap, and two prick punch marks should be put on No.

Two Cylinder parts, and so forth.

Removal
    (1)   Remove the cylinder head assembly.
    (2)   Drain and remove the sump.
    (3)   Unlock and remove the nuts securing the caps and bear-

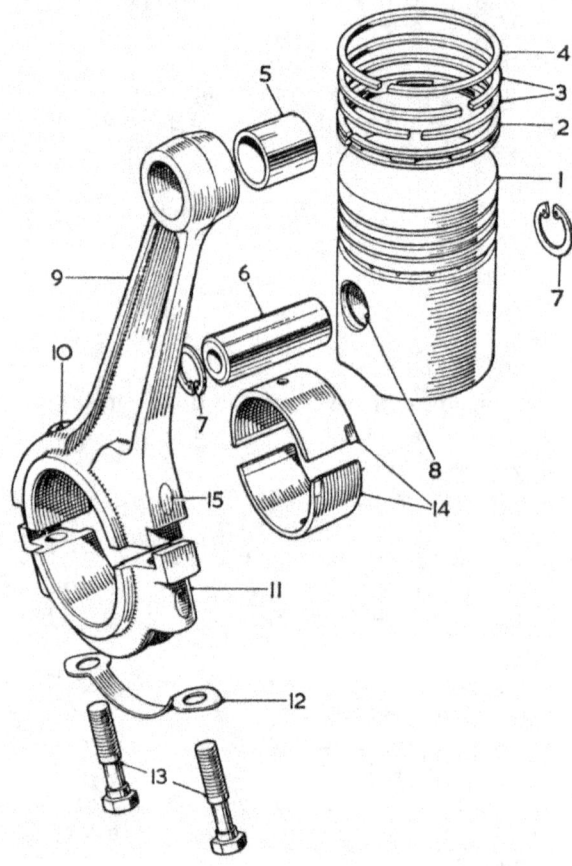

1. Piston.
2. Piston ring—scraper.
3. Piston rings—taper.
4. Piston ring—parallel.
5. Small-end bush.
6. Gudgeon pin.
7. Circlip.
8. Gudgeon pin lubricating hole.
9. Connecting rod.
10. Cylinder wall lubricating jet.
11. Connecting rod cap.
12. Lock washer.
13. Bolts.
14. Connecting rod bearings.
15. Connecting rod and cap marking.

Piston and connecting rod

ings to the connecting rods. Remove the caps and bearings.

Note: Keep all caps, bearings, connecting rods, gudgeon (wrist) pins and pistons in order for replacement in their original bores.

(4) If necessary, remove the carbon or ridge from the top of the bores prior to pushing the pistons upwards to avoid piston ring fracture.
(5) Withdraw the pistons and connecting rods upwards through the cylinder bores.
(6) Remove the pistons from the connecting rods by removing the two circlips locating each pin, then press out the floating gudgeon pins.
(7) Ensure that each connecting rod, cap and bearing is marked with the cylinder number from which it was removed.
(8) Note that the big ends are offset, with rods in numbers 1 and 3 cylinder offset towards the front, and 2 and 4 offset towards the rear (see illustration in previous ENGINE chapter).
(9) The alignment of the connecting rods should be checked on an alignment fixture. Never adjust alignment by filing caps or rods.
(10) Examine the bearing shells (in their caps) for wear and pits. Renew each bearing shell if necessary. Bearings are pre-finished with the correct diametral clearance, and do not require bedding in. Mark new bearings to match up with the markings on the caps, and NEVER file the caps to take up wear or to reduce running clearance.
(11) Check the crankpins with a micrometer. If they are worn oval or are scored, the crankshaft will have to be removed for grinding.

Reassembly

Regard the Note under REPLACEMENT (below) as the components are being assembled.

(1) Holding the piston and connecting rod together, push the gudgeon pin into position with the hand. **Note:** use light engine oil to lubricate gudgeon pin and do not heat parts.
(2) Secure each pin with the two circlips. Be sure clips are maintaining tension and the connecting rod moves freely.

Replacement

Note: Before installing the connecting rods and bearings it is assumed that the pistons and rings have been serviced. Be sure the same pistons and connecting rods are going into the same bores they came from. Be sure the marking on the piston faces the front of the engine, and the markings on the connecting rod

and the cap bosses face the camshaft.
(1) Refit the piston rings very carefully, being sure the ring gaps are staggered at 90° to each other.
(2) Be sure the pistons and bores are perfectly clean and the bore is completely coated with clean engine oil.
(3) Use a piston ring clamp when replacing the pistons from the top of the bore.
(4) Clean the crankpins and both sides of the shell bearings, locate the feathered ends in the connecting rod and its cap, and smear the crankpins with engine oil.
(5) Before fitting the cap, check that the number stamped on the rod is the same as that on the cap. Note that the recess in the cap and rod must be on the same side. Tighten and lock the nuts. Turn the crankshaft after fitting each rod, to ensure that the bearing is not binding on the crankpin. Also check the side clearance of each rod, as given under GENERAL DATA. **Note:** The top and bottom halves of new bearings are interchangeable, each being drilled for cylinder wall lubrication.
(6) Refit the cylinder head assembly.
(7) Refit the sump and refill with recommended grade of oil.

PISTON RINGS AND GUDGEON PINS
(later type)

Use the same procedure for the later type as used for the early type except for the following item. A different oil control ring (Duaflex 61) was fitted on later engines, and the following points should be carefully noted:
(1) Gap the rails and side spring to the dimension given in GENERAL DATA.
(2) The lugs of the expander must be butted together (but not crossed), and inserted into one of the holes in the scraper ring groove on the non-thrust side of the piston.
(3) Stagger the gaps of the twin rails and side spring on the non-thrust side of the piston.
(4) Be sure that the ends of the rings are fully home in the groove when compressing the rings prior to refitting the pistons.
(5) Be sure that all glaze has been removed from the cylinder bores before refitting the pistons.

PISTON SIZES AND CYLINDER BORES

In production pistons are fitted by selective assembly, and to facilitate this the pistons are stamped with identification figures on their crowns.

The number enclosed in a diamond, e.g. a piston stamped with a figure 2, is for a bore bearing a similar stamp.

In addition to the standard pistons there is a range of two oversize pistons available for service purposes. Oversize pistons are marked with the actual oversize dimensions enclosed in an

Piston and bore sizing

Piston marking	Suitable bore size	Metric equivalent
STANDARD	2·5424 to 2·5447 in.	64·576 to 64·635 mm.
OVERSIZE +·010 in. (·254 mm.)	2·5524 to 2·5547 in.	64·830 to 64·889 mm.
+·020 in. (·508 mm.)	2·5624 to 2·5647 in.	65·084 to 65·143 mm.

ellipse. A piston stamped .020 is suitable only for a bore .020 in. (.508 mm.) larger than the standard bore.

The piston markings indicate the actual bore size to which they must be fitted, the requisite running clearance being allowed for in the machining.

After reboring an engine, or whenever fitting pistons differing in size from those removed during dismantling, ensure that the size of the piston fitted is stamped clearly on the top of the cylinder block alongside the appropriate cylinder bore.

Pistons are supplied in the sizes indicated in the following table.

TIMING COVER

Removal and Replacement

(1) Drain the cooling system.
(2) Remove the radiator.
(3) Slacken the generator attachment bolts and remove the belt.
(4) Bend back the tab on the crankshaft pulley nut locking washer. Unscrew the nut.
(5) Pull off the crankshaft pulley.
(6) The timing cover is secured by both large and small setscrews, each with a plain washer and a lock washer. Unscrew all setscrews and remove the cover.
(7) The oil seal in the cover must be renewed if it shows signs of damage. Use Service Tool 18G 134 together with adapter 18G 134 BD. A new cover gasket should also be fitted.
(8) Be sure the oil thrower behind the crankshaft pulley is fitted with the face marked 'F' away from the engine.

(9) Fill the annular groove between the lips of the oil seal with grease, then use Service Tool 18G 1044 to centralize the oil seal of the crankshaft.

(10) **Note:** If the engine has the early felt type oil seal, replace the cover with a cover incorporating a rubber type seal (Part. No. 12A 1419), and the matching oil slinger (Part No. 12A 1148). **Both parts must be used together.** If possible, use Service Tool 18G 138 to centralize the rubber seal on the crankshaft, **or use the following procedure:**

(11) When the special aligning tool (Service Tool 18G 138) is not available the crankshaft pulley should be assembled to the cover before the cover is refitted to the engine. This will ensure that the timing cover and oil seal are concentric with the crankshaft. Lubricate the hub of the pulley and, with a rotating movement to avoid damage to the oil seal, insert it in the cover. Push the pulley and timing cover on to the crankshaft, lining up the pulley bore keyway with the Woodruff key fitted to the crankshaft. Replace the cover set screws and tighten them up evenly.

(12) Reassembly is now a reversal of the removal procedure.

VALVE TIMING

Set clearance on No. 1 cylinder inlet valve to .021 in. (.74 mm.) with the engine cold, then turn the crankshaft until the valve is about to open. The indicator groove in the flange of the crankshaft pulley should then be opposite the center pointer (on the indicator bracket below) which indicates 5° before top dead center (BTDC) of No. 1 and No. 4 pistons.

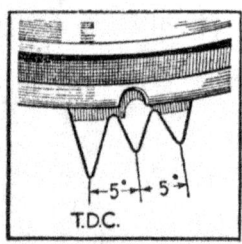

Note: It is not possible to check the valve timing accurately with normal (running) valve clearances. Set as above, then do not fail to reset the gap between rocker and pushrod to .012 in. (.30 mm.) with the engine cold.

CAMSHAFT AND BEARINGS

Camshaft Removal and Replacement

Follow steps (1) through (8) on this subject in the previous ENGINE chapter, then add the following steps:

(9) Examine the three camshaft bearings (liners) for scores, pits or evidence of failure, then check the clearances (see GENERAL DATA).
(10) If examination proves that new bearings are needed, they are removed and replaced with steel-backed white-metal bearings using a special camshaft liner removing and replacing tool. These new bearings must then be reamed to give the correct running clearance.
(11) Inspect the tappet cam contacting surfaces for wear. New tappets should be installed wherever evidence of unusual wear is found.
(12) The instalation of the camshaft and tappets is a reversal of the removal procedure. Lubricate the camshaft journals with engine oil.

Fitting Flywheel Starter Ring
(1) Remove old starter ring from the flywheel flange by splitting the ring gear with a cold chisel, being careful not to damage the flywheel.
(2) Remove any burrs and thoroughly clean the bore of the new ring and its mating surface on the flywheel.
(3) The new ring must be heated to a temperature of 300° to 400° C. (572 to 752° F.), indicated by a light-blue surface color, for it to fit. **Note:** Do not exceed this temperature, or the temper of the teeth will be affected. Use a thermostatically controlled furnace if possible.
(4) Place the heated ring on the flywheel with the ring teeth lead towards the flywheel register. Press or tap the ring lightly until it is fitted against its register. The heating should expand it sufficiently to fit quite easily.
(5) Allow the assembly to cool naturally since this will make the 'shrink fit' permanent, needing no further treatment.

ENGINE MOUNTINGS
Removal
(1) Either support the engine with lifting equipment or work with the engine removed.
(2) Remove both the left- and right-hand mounting rubber securing nuts and mounting rubber bracket-to-body securing set bolts.
(3) Unscrew the exhaust down pipe manifold clamp and remove the front down pipe strap from the support bracket.
(4) If engine is in place, lift it aproximately ¾ in. (19 mm.) to ensure the fan assembly will not strike the radiator fan cowling.
(5) Using the lifting equipment, swing the engine to the left as far as possible, then remove the right-hand rubber mounting together with its body bracket.

(6) Remove the left-hand front rubber mounting and bracket assembly.

Reassembly
(1) Position the right-hand front rubber mounting and bracket first.
(2) Position the left-hand front rubber mounting and bracket.
(3) Reverse removal procedure, replacing set bolts and nuts lastly.

CRANKCASE EMISSION CONTROL

General Description

This system consists of a diaphragm control valve connected by hoses between the inlet manifold and the engine crankcase. The crankcase outlet connection has an oil separator to prevent oil being pulled over with the vapors leaving the crankcase. A filtered, restricted orifice (9/64 in. diameter) in the oil filler cap provides a supply of fresh air into the crankcase as vapors are withdrawn by inlet manifold vacuum. The control valve diaphragm varies the opening to the inlet manifold according to the vacuum or pressure existing in the crankcase. With a decrease in crankcase vacuum or when the crankcase obtains a positive pressure the diaphragm opens the valve allowing the crankcase vapors to be drawn into the inlet manifold. During conditions of high crankcase vacuum, i.e. low engine speeds, the diaphragm closes the valve and restricts the flow into the inlet manifold, thus preventing a leaning-off of the air/fuel mixture to the cylinders.

Oil Filler Cap

An air filter is incorporated in the oil filler cap. The cap and filter are exchanged only as complete assembly. Replace every 12,000 miles or 12 months.

Breather Control Valve
(1) **Testing procedure:** After warming engine to normal operating temperature, run it at idling speed.
(2) If the engine speed rises by approximately 200 RPM as the oil filler cap is removed, the valve is functioning correctly.
(3) If there is no audible change in engine speed as the oil filler cap is removed, the valve needs servicing.
(4) **Servicing procedure:** Disconnect the hoses and renew the valve assembly, or clean, starting by removing the spring clip, then disassembling the valve.

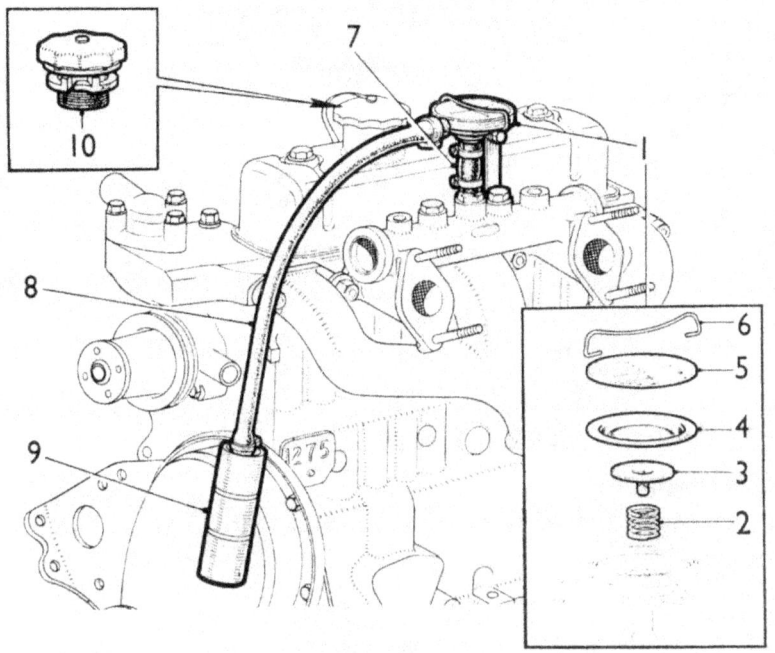

1. Emission control valve.
2. Valve spring.
3. Metering valve.
4. Diaphragm.
5. Cover plate.
6. Spring clip.
7. Manifold connection.
8. Breather hose.
9. Oil separator.
10. Filtered filler cap.

Crankcase emission control

(5) Use solvent to clean all metal parts. If there are hardened deposits, immerse parts in boiling water before applying solvent. **Note:** Do not use any abrasives.

(6) Use detergent or methylated spirits to clean the diaphragm.

(7) Replace any parts that are worn or damaged.

(8) Assemble the valve, making sure the metering needle is in the cruciform guides and the diaphragm is seated correctly.

COOLING SYSTEM

RADIATOR

To Remove
(1) Drain the cooling system.
(2) Release the hose clip on the thermostat housing and remove the hose from the housing extension.
(3) Remove the radiator bottom hose by releasing the clips on the bottom radiator connection.
(4) Remove the fresh air induction pipe from its connection on the front cowling.
(5) Remove the temperature gauge thermal element from the right-hand side of the radiator.
(6) Remove the bolts which secure the radiator to the support brackets and remove the radiator.

To Replace
To replace, reverse the removal procedure.

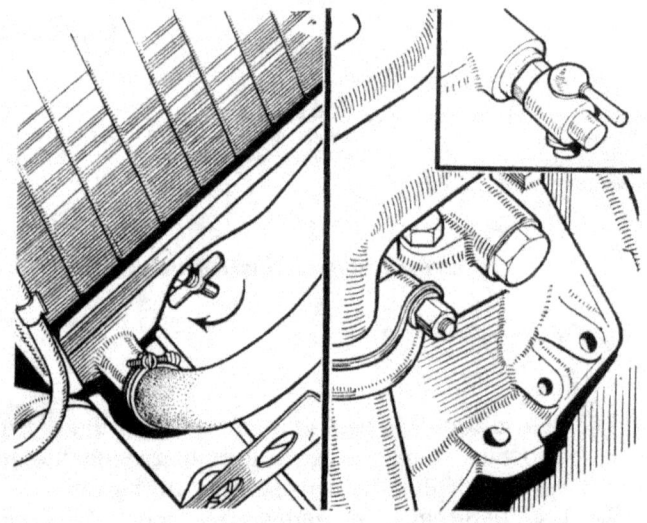

(*Left*) Access to the radiator drain tap is gained from beneath the front of the car. Turn in the direction of the arrow to open the tap
(*Right*) The drain tap or plug (*later models*) for the cylinder block is located on the right-hand side of the block at the rear.

Cooling system drains

RADIATOR FILLER CAP

The cooling system is under 7 pound psi (49 kg. per cm.^{2}) pressure while the engine is hot, and the radiator filler cap must be removed very carefully or left in position until the water has cooled.

THERMOSTAT

To Remove
   (1) Drain the cooling system.
   (2) Disconnect the outlet hose from the outlet elbow.
   (3) Remove the securing nuts and spring washers from the thermostat cover and lift the cover away from its studs.
   (4) Remove the paper joint washer and lift out the thermostat.
   (5) Examine the thermostat for damage and check that the valve is in the closed position. If the thermostat is damaged or the valve is in the open position, renew the thermostat.
   (6) To test the thermostat, immerse it in water heated to the temperature marked on the thermostat. The valve will open if the thermostat is functioning correctly. If the valve fails to open renew the thermostat.

To Replace
Installation of the thermostat assembly is the reverse of the removal procedure. Fit a new paper joint washer if the existing one is damaged.

FAN AND PUMP ASSEMBLY

The water pump is of the centrifugal impeller type mounted on a common spindle with the fan and operating in a cast-iron housing mounted on the front of the cylinder block. Water-sealing is effected by a spring-loaded carbon washer bearing upon a seating in the impeller housing. It is necessary to dismantle the pump and fan assembly to obtain access to the sealing gland.

To Remove
   (1) Drain the water from the cooling system and remove the radiator.
   (2) Remove the hose from the water pipe inlet connection and loosen the top clip of the thermostat by-pass hose, the generator mounting bolts, and the adjusting screw.
   (3) Withdraw the set screws securing the fan blades to the water pump hub and withdraw the blades, belt and pulley.
   (4) Unscrew the set screws securing the pump to the cylinder block and remove the pump complete with the by-pass hose.

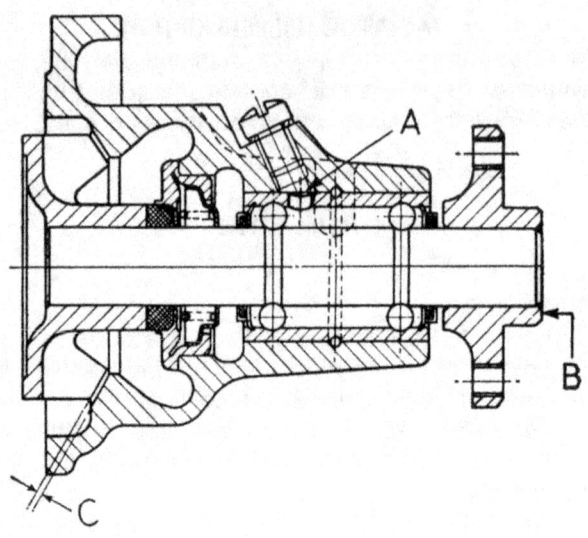

A section through the water pump showing the location of the components. When assembled, the hole (A) in the bearing must coincide with the lubricating hole in the water pump and the face of the hub (B) must be flush with the end of the spindle. (C) is a clearance of ·020 to ·030 in. (·508 t ·762 mm.)

Water pump components

To Dismantle
(1) Pull out the bearing locating wire through the holes in the top of the pump body.
(2) Gently tap the spindle rearwards to release the combined spindle and bearing assembly together with the seat and vane.
(3) Withdraw the vane from the spindle with a suitable extractor and remove the pump seal assembly.
(4) If the bearing show signs of wear or damage, replace it with a new bearing and spindle assembly: bearings alone are not serviced.
(5) Renew the seal assembly if wear or damage is apparent or if the pump is leaking.

Reassembly

To reassemble, reverse the dismantling procedure. Be sure that the hole in the bearing is lined up with the lubricating hole in the pump body before pressing the bearing and spindle into position. Should the interference fit of the fan hub have been impaired when the hub was withdrawn from the spindle, a new hub must be fitted.

Replacement

To replace, reverse the removal procedure. The bypass hose, unless virtually new, should be replaced with Part No. 12A 1093. DO NOT use heater hose. Also inspect the bypass hose adapter (Part No. 2A 243) in both the head and the water pump and replace if necessary. See preceding COOLING SYSTEM chapter for additional notes.

CLUTCH

WARNING: All B.M.C. cars use NATURAL RUBBER COMPONENTS in their clutch systems, NOT neoprene rubber components as do American makes. Therefore, it is extremely important that Castrol Girling Amber or Crimson Brake Fluid or BRITISH Lockheed Disc Brake Fluid be used in these systems, since they are the only brake fluids compatible with the natural rubber parts. Some American brake fluids are only suitable for all-neoprene rubber parts, and will cause natural rubber parts to swell and deteriorate, leading to eventual rupture.

Clutch Adjustment

The correct amount of free movement between the master cylinder push-rod and piston is set at the factory and should never need correction. Should the adjustment have been disturbed, reset the effective length of the rod connecting the piston to the pedal until the pedal pad can be depressed about 5/32 in. (4mm.) before the piston begins to move. The clearance can be felt if the pedal is depressed by hand. It is very important that the push-rod should have a minimum free movement of 1/32 in. (.8 mm.) before the piston starts to move.

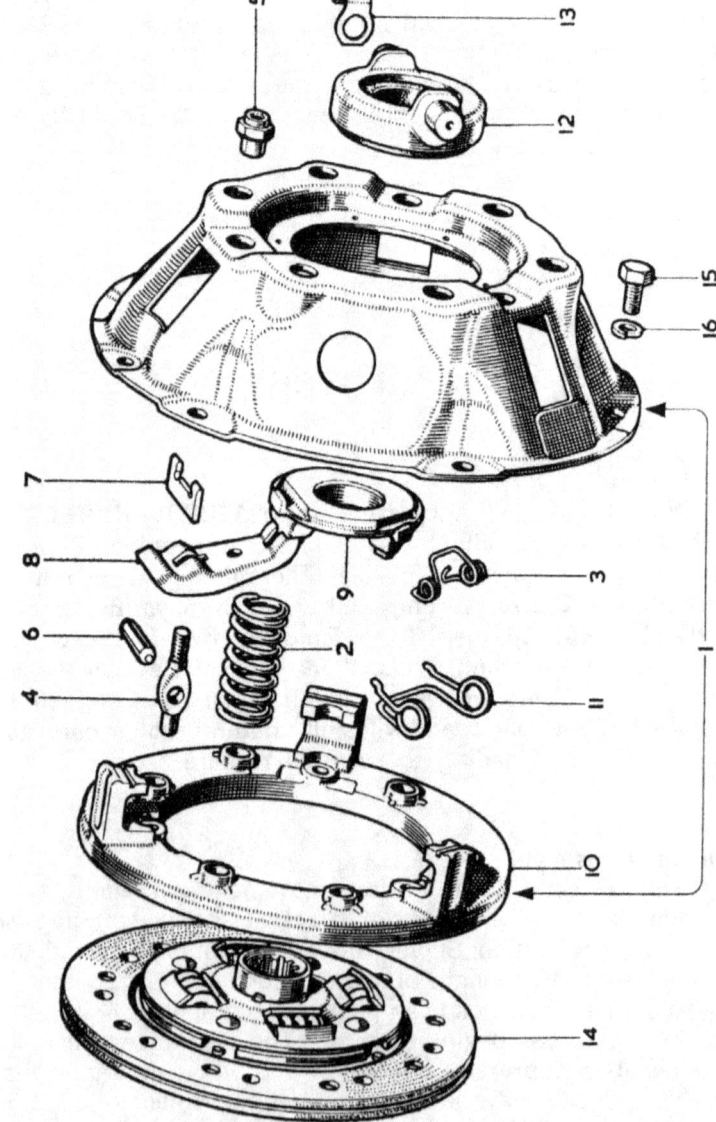

Clutch components (later cars)

No.	Description
1.	Clutch assembly.
2.	Thrust spring.
3.	Release lever retainer.
4.	Eyebolt.
5.	Eyebolt nut.
6.	Release lever pin
7.	Strut.
8.	Release lever.
9.	Bearing thrust plate.
10.	Pressure plate.
11.	Anti-rattle spring.
12.	Release bearing.
13.	Retainer.
14.	Driven plate assembly.
15.	Clutch to flywheel screw.
16.	Spring washer.

GEARBOX

THIRD MOTION SHAFT (Early Cars)

Dismantling
(1) Remove the 3rd and 4th speed synchronizer assemblies. Depress the spring-loaded plunger which locks the front splined ring at the end of the third motion shaft. Turn the ring so that one of the splines covers the plunger. A peg spanner is useful for turning the splined ring. Slide the splined ring and third speed gear off the end of the shaft and remove the plunger and spring. The third speed gear has needle-roller bearings.
end of the shaft and remove the plunger and spring. The third sped gear has needle-roller bearings.
(2) At the end of the shaft knock back the locking washer and unscrew the securing nut. The lock washer, washer, speedometer wheel, and distance piece may now be removed. Draw the ball journal bearing off the end of the shaft with its housing, then drift the bearing out of the housing. Draw the first speed gear and synchronizer asembly off the shaft.
(3) Depress the spring-loaded plunger which locks the rear splined ring at the end of the third motion shaft. Turn the ring so that one of its splines covers the plunger and slide the splined ring off the shaft. Remove the plunger and spring and lift the two halves of the

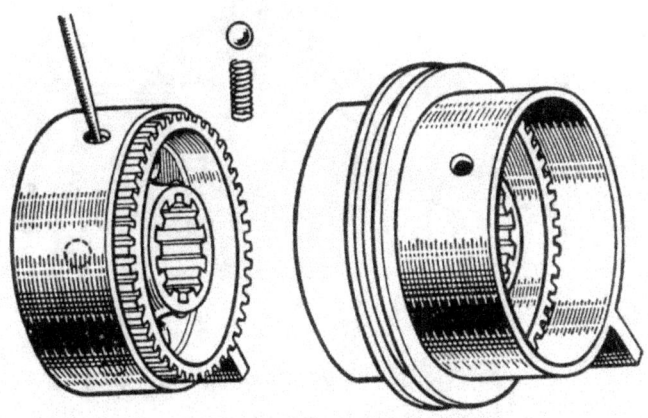

Using Service tool 18G 144 to assemble the spring-loaded balls to a coupling sleeve and synchronizer

Synchromesh assembly ring use

washer for the splined ring off the shaft. Slide the second speed gear off the shaft, taking care to retain the needle rollers.

Reassembly
(1) The third motion shaft ball journal bearing outer race is grooved to take a spring ring. This spring ring registers in a recess in the bearing housing. Press the bearing into the flanged end of the housing so that the spring ring end of the bearing is trailing. Assembly the needle rollers on the shaft and fit the second speed gear.
(2) Place the two halves of the washer for the splined ring on the shaft behind the second speed gear. Be sure that the two halves of the washer are assembled with the locking pegs registered in the correct position in the splined ring. Assemble the spring and plunger in the hole in the shaft and refit the splined ring.
(3) Slide the first speed gear and synchronizer assembly onto the shaft with the protruding end of the synchronizer towards the bearing. Press the bearing and its housing onto the shaft so that the flange of the bearing housing

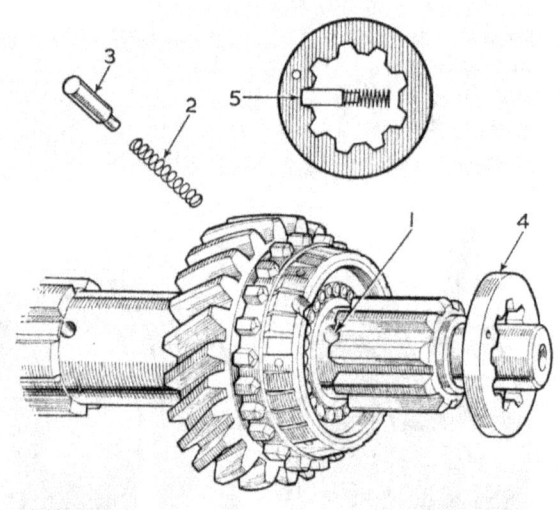

Securing the third motion shaft gears

1. Hole in shaft for locking plunger.   3. Locking plunger
2. Spring.   4 Locking washer.
5. Locking washer with plunger engaged.

Gear assembly

(when fitted) is towards the rear of the shaft. Refit the distance piece, speedometer drive, plain washer, lock washer, and locknut in position.

(4) From the opposite end of the shaft assemble the needle-roller bearing and refit the third speed gear assembly. Place the spring and plunger in the hole in the shaft and refit the splined ring. Slide the third and fourth speed synchronizer onto the shaft with the boss on the synchronizer hub, away from the splined ring.

FIRST MOTION SHAFT

Dismantling

(1) Unlock and remove the securing nut and withdraw the lock washer and packing shim.
(2) Press the bearing from the shaft and remove the circlip from the bearing.

Reassembly

Reverse the dismantling procedure, being sure that the inner tag of the lock washer, which engages the keyway in the shaft, is turned away from the bearing.

LAYGEAR ASSEMBLY

Dismantling and Reassembly

Needle-roller bearings are fitted in each end of the laygear. The needles are held in position in their races (one at each end)

The first and second speed gear assembly, showing the gear and hub correctly assembled (later cars). The plunger is shown at (1)

Gear and hub assembly

by spring rings. Current needle rollers (Part No. 88G 396) are now of the caged type, and the outer retaining circlip is no longer needed. When installing a new laygear, use 2 spring rings (Part No. 22G 278) ONLY (one at each end), on the inside to position the rollers, and the distance piece (Part No. 22G 277). These rollers are free-floating and no spring ring is used on the outer end.

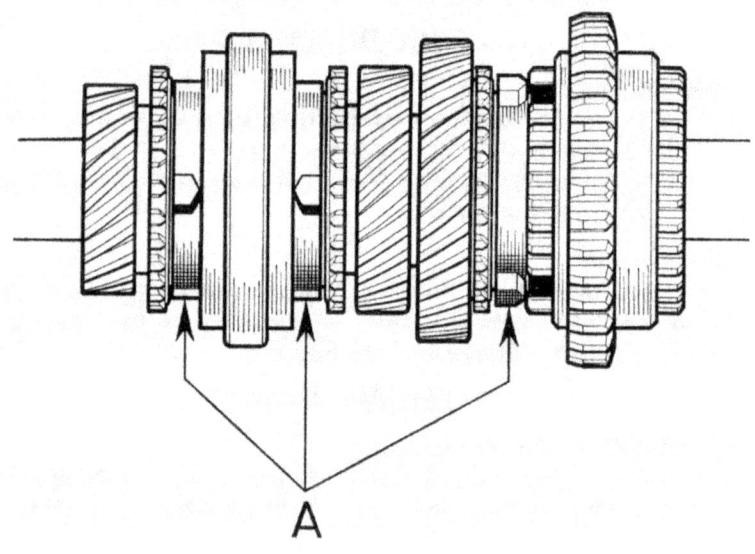

The mainshaft, showing (A) the baulk rings (later cars)

Baulk Ring Use

THIRD MOTION SHAFT (Later Cars)

Dismantling and Reassembly

The dismantling and reassembly sequences are the same as outlined earlier in this chapter except that the second and third/top gear synchronizers are fitted with baulk rings (see illustrations).

Note: Should the first and second speed gear assembly have been dismantled, the correct position of the gear on the hub when reassembling is most important. Should the gear be incorrectly assembled on the hub, selection of first gear will be impossible.

Note: When reassembling the gear to the hub be sure that the plunger in the hub aligns with the cut-away tooth in the gear assembly (see illustration).

DRIVE SHAFT

Reassembly (early style)
(1) See that the drilled holes in the journals of the universal joints are cleaned out and filled with oil.
(2) Assemble the needle rollers in the bearing races and fill with oil. Should difficulty be experienced in assembly, smear the walls of the races with vaseline to retain the needle rollers in place.
(3) It is advisable to renew, if necessary, the cork washer and the washer retainers on the spider journals.
(4) Continue assembling in the reverse of the dismantling procedure.

Refitting
(1) When refitting the drive shaft a second mechanic is required.
(2) With the aid of a screwdriver about 8 in. (20 cm.) long inserted through the front universal joint lubricating hole in the drive shaft tunnel, lift the shaft and guide it onto the splines of the third motion shaft and into the gearbox rear extension.

DRIVE SHAFT (Later Cars)

Removing and Dismantling
Perform operations detailed in the previous DRIVE SHAFT chapter.

Inspection
Wash all parts thoroughly in solvent or fuel to remove old grease, then carry out the examination detailed in the previous DRIVE SHAFT chapter.

Reassembly
Carry out assembly of the journals under absolutely clean, dust-free conditions.
(1) Fill the reservoir holes in the journal spider with the recommended grease (see GENERAL DATA), taking care to exclude all air pockets. Fill each bearing assembly with grease to a depth of $\frac{1}{8}$ in. (3 mm.).
(2) Fit new seals to the spider journals and insert the spider into the flange yoke, tilting it to engage in the yoke bores.
(3) Fit a bearing assembly into the yoke bore in the bottom position then, using a soft-nosed drift slightly smaller in diameter than the hole in the yoke, tap it into the yoke

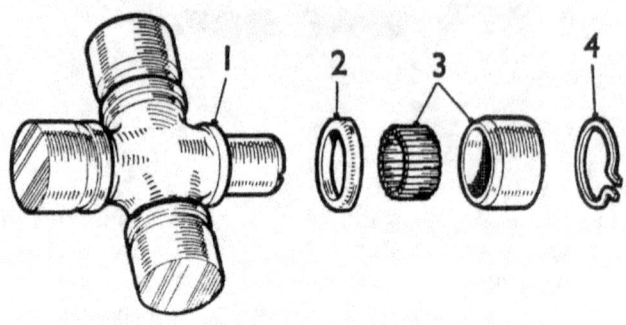

A universal joint bearing—sealed type

1. Journal spider.
2. Rubber seal.
3. Needle rollers and bearings.
4. Circlip.

Sealed universal bearing

bore until it is possible to fit the circlip. Repeat the operation for the other three bearings starting opposite the bearing first fitted.

(4) After assembly, carefully remove all surplus grease with a soft cloth. If the bearing appears to bind, tap lightly with a wooden mallet; this will relieve any pressure of the bearing on the ends of the journals.

Refitting

Perform operations detailed previously in the early style refitting section.

REAR AXLE

To Remove and Replace
 (1) Raise the vehicle by placing a jack under the differential housing and support the body. Remove the wheels.
 (2) Continue the procedure outlined in the previous REAR AXLE chapter.

AXLE SHAFTS

To Remove and Replace
(1) Raise the vehicle by placing a jack under the differential housing. Place supports under the rear springs and remove the wheels.
(2) Release the handbrake and back off the brake shoe adjusters.
(3) To remove DISC WHEELS, see previous REAR AXLE chapter.
(4) To replace, reverse the removal procedure.

Wire Wheels
(1) Remove the nuts securing the drum to the hub and tap the drums off the hubs.

39. Nut.
40. Oil seal.
41. Hub bearing.
42. Oil seal ring.
43. Hub shaft joint.

46. Bump rubber.
47. Axle shaft.
48. Hub assembly.
49. Wheel stud.
50. Hub extension.
51. Welch plug.

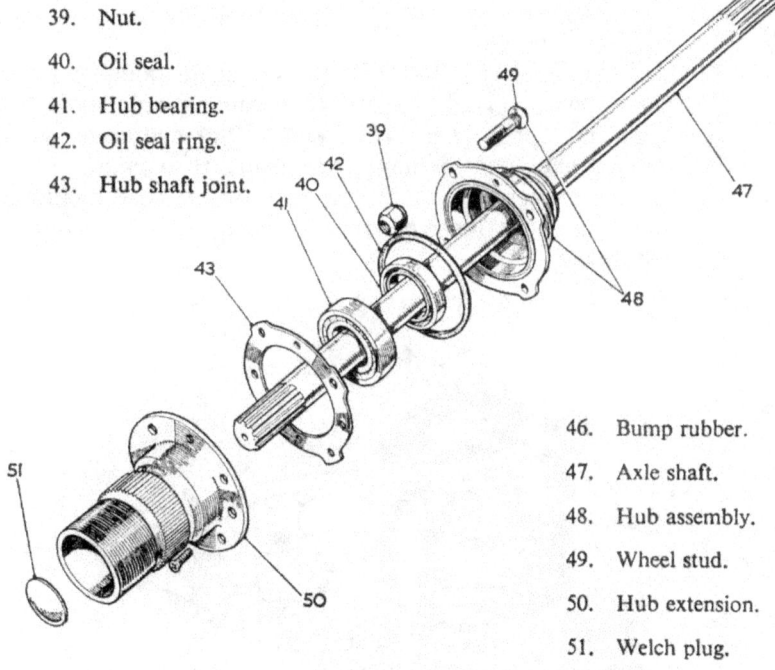

Wire wheel axle shaft

(2) Remove the retaining screws securing the hub extension flanges to the hubs.
(3) Withdraw the hub extensions and axle shafts. Should the paper washer be damaged, renew it when reassembling.

SUSPENSION

Replacing Springs (rear)
Reverse the removal procedure described in the previous SUSPENSION chapter when refitting the spring assemblies.

NOTE: Tighten the spring bolts when the normal working load has been applied to the springs.

Removing Springs (front)
(1) Place a hardwood or metal block 1¼ in. (28.57 mm.) long under the hydraulic damper arm to keep the arm off its rubber rebound buffer when the car is raised off its wheels.
(2) Remove two diametrically opposite spring seat securing nuts and bolts.
(3) Use service tool 18G 153 (or two slave bolts) to compress the spring. Remove the remaining nuts and bolts from the spring seat and release the center screw of the Service tool to allow the spring to expand.
(4) Check the spring against manufacturers' specifications. If it has sustained damage in any way it should be renewed.

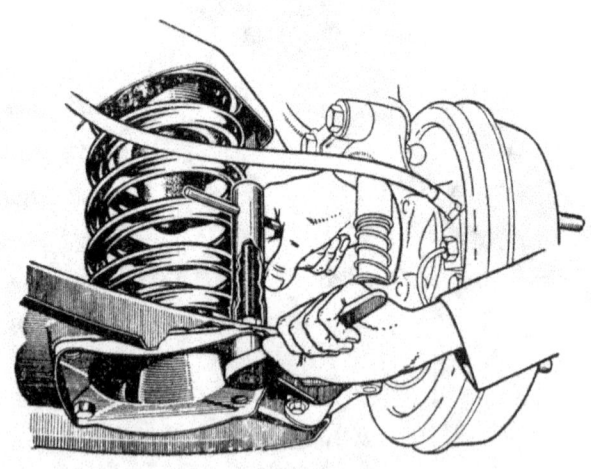

Using a pair of slave bolts to remove or replace a coil spring

Coil spring removal

Replacing

Reverse the removal procedure when refitting, giving special attention to inserting two guide rods in diametrically opposite holes to bring the spring seat and wishbone lower links into line when in the process of compressing the spring.

LUBRICATION

A grease gun filled with lubricant should be applied to each of the eight nipples and three or four strokes given at regular intervals. Nipples are provided on both lower arm joints where they meet the swivel axle housings and the two tie rod ball joints. There are two nipples on each swivel axle pin which are best lubricated when the weight of the car has been taken off the suspension with a jack or a lift. This will allow the lubricant to penetrate around the bushes more effectively.

CASTOR AND CAMBER ANGLES AND KING PIN INCLINATION

Should the car suffer damage to the suspension, the angles (as given in GENERAL DATA) must be verified with a camber, castor, and swivel pin inclination gauge and new parts fitted as required or a Service tool 18G 253 front suspension assembly fixture can be used.

FRONT HUBS

Refitting (early cars)
(1) Pack the bearings and the cavity between them with grease.
(2) Surplus grease must be removed after the hub has been fitted, to allow for expansion, and NEVER put grease into the retaining cap.
(3) Reverse the removal procedure, with special attention being given to ensure that the inner and outer bearings are drifted on with their sides marked THRUST towards the center of the hub, using Service tool 18G 134 together with adaptors 18G 134 B and 18G 134 C.
(4) Be sure that the oil seal is pressed in with its lipped end toward the inner bearing.
(5) Use Service tool 18G 7 to refit the hub assembly on the swivel axle.
(6) Fit the washer and nut, then tighten the nut to the torque wrench reading given in GENERAL DATA.

Removing (later cars)
(1) Raise the car to a workable height, lifting it under the body.
(2) Remove the road wheel and disconnect the brake calliper assembly as in the BRAKE chapter.
(3) DO NOT allow the calliper assembly to hang on the hydraulic hose, instead support it somehow.

(4) Remove the split pin and nut and pull off the hub casing and disc asembly, using Service tool 18G 304 and adaptor 18G 304 B.

Brake Disc Removal and Replacement
(1) Remove the securing set screws and remove the hub from the disc assembly.
(2) Refitting is a reversal of the removal procedure.
(3) Should the maximum run-out at the outer periphery of the braking surface exceed .006 in. (.152 mm.) after fitting, the disc must be removed and repositioned on the hub.

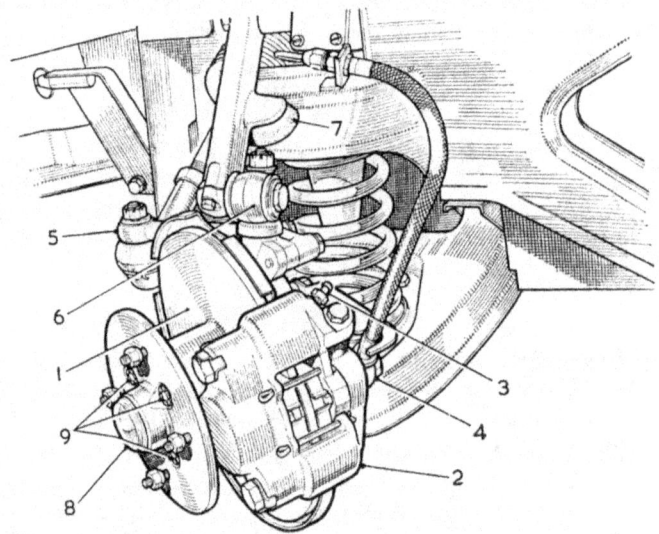

1. Brake disc.
2. Calliper assembly.
3. Bleeder screw.
4. Calliper fluid connector.
5. Steering lever.
6. Suspension trunnion link.
7. Rebound buffer.
8. Retaining cap.
9. Brake disc to hub securing bolts.

Suspension assembly (later cars)

Replacement
(1) Pack the bearings and the cavity between them with grease.
(2) Surplus grease must be removed after the hub has been fitted to allow for expansion, and never put grease into the retaining cap.
(3) To refit the hubs, reverse the removal procedure. Be sure that the bearings are fitted with their side marked THRUST adjacent to the bearing spacer.

STEERING

STEERING LOCK IGNITION SWITCH

On cars fitted with a combined ignition/starter switch and steering column lock mounted on the steering column, a sleeve integral with the inner column is slotted to permit engagement of the lock tongue; the outer column is also slotted to allow the lock tongue to pass through. A hole drilled in the upper surface of the outer column locates the steering lock bracket. The bracket is secured by two bolts each waisted below the head to permit removal of the heads by shear action during assembly.

To remove the lock, disconnect the battery and the ignition/starter switch connections, then turn the lock setting to GARAGE to unlock the steering. Free the steering-column assembly and remove the lock securing bolts with an easy-out.

BRAKES

WARNING: All B.M.C. cars use NATURAL RUBBER components in their brake systems, NOT neoprene rubber components as do American makes. Therefore, it is extremely important that Castrol Girling Amber or Crimson Brake Fluid or BRITISH Lockheed Genuine Brake Fluid be used in these systems, since they are the only brake fluids compatible with the natural rubber parts. Some American brake fluids are only suitable for all-neoprene rubber parts, and will cause natural rubber parts to swell, deteriorate, and rupture.

FRONT BRAKE ASSEMBLIES (Drum Brakes)

Removal
   (1) **Brake-shoes:** Raise the front of the car and remove the wheel.
   (2) Remove the countersunk screw (disc wheels) or nuts (wire wheels) securing the brake-drum and withdraw the drum.
   (3) Lift one brake-shoe, against the tension of the return springs, from its abutment with the closed end of one of the wheel cylinders, and slide the Micram mask off the piston cover of the other cylinder.

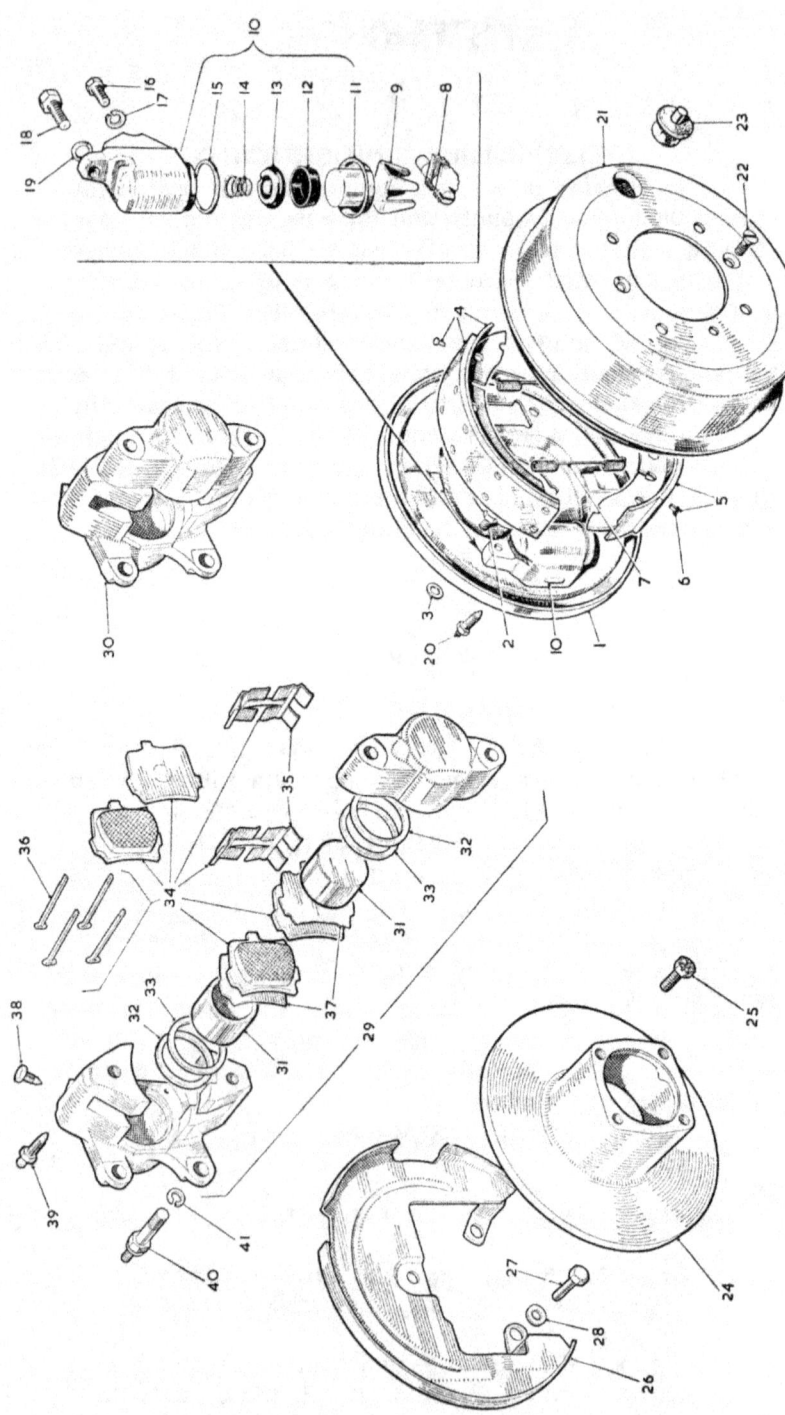

Front brake components (drum and disc brakes)

KEY TO THE FRONT BRAKE COMPONENTS

No.	Description		No.	Description	
1.	Brake-plate.		15.	Sealing ring.	
2.	Set screw.		16.	Set screw (small).	
3.	Shakeproof washer		17.	Spring washer.	
4.	Brake-shoe assembly.		18.	Set screw (large).	
5.	Liner with rivets.		19.	Spring washer.	
6.	Rivet.		20.	Bleeder screw.	
7.	Pull-off spring.	Drum type.	21.	Brake-drum.	Drum type.
8.	Micram adjuster.		22.	Set screw.	
9.	Mask.		23.	Plug.	
10.	Wheel cylinder assembly.		24.	Brake disc.	
11.	Piston with dust cover.		25.	Set screw.	Disc type.
12.	Cup.		26.	Dust cover.	
13.	Cup filler.		27.	Set screw.	
14.	Spring.		28.	Shakeproof washer.	
			29.	Calliper unit assembly—L.H.	
			30.	Calliper—L.H.	
			31.	Piston.	
			32.	Inner seal.	
			33.	Dust seal and retainer.	
			34.	Pad assembly.	Disc type.
			35.	Pad retaining spring.	
			36.	Split cotter pin.	
			37.	Pad shim.	
			38.	Plug.	
			39.	Bleed screw.	
			40.	Calliper mounting bolt.	
			41.	Spring washer.	

(4) With the return spring tension released, detach the springs and remove both shoes.
(1) **Wheel cylinders:** Perform the previous operations.
(2) Disconnect the hydraulic bridge pipe from the wheel cylinders.
(3) Remove the bolts securing the wheel cylinder to the backplate, then withdraw the cylinder from the backplate.

Disassembly
(1) **Wheel cylinders:** Withdraw the piston, complete with its cover, from the cylinder.
(2) Apply a gentle air pressure to the fluid connection to blow out the rubber cup, cup filler, and spring.
(3) Remove the sealing ring, then the bleed screw.

Inspection
(1) **Brake-shoes:** Clean the dust from the brake-shoes and linings using an air hose, then examine the linings for wear.
(2) **Wheel cylinders:** Clean the components thoroughly using Girling Amber Brake Fluid (or Lockeed Genuine Brake Fluid or alcohol) ONLY, then dry them with a clean, non-fluffy cloth.
(3) Examine the metal parts for wear and damage, inspect the rubber cup for swelling or signs of deterioration. Replace all damaged, worn or suspect parts.

Reassembly
(1) **Wheel cylinders:** Dip the components in the recommended brake fluid and assemble them wet.
(2) Fit the cup filler into the small diameter end of the spring and insert the spring, large diameter end first, into the cylinder.
(3) Fit the piston and piston cover.

Replacement
(1) **Wheel cylinders:** Reverse the removal procedure under REMOVAL — Wheel cylinders, then bleed the system and adjust the brake shoes as described under MAINTENANCE in the previous BRAKE chapter.
(2) **Brake-shoes:** Reverse the removal procedure under REMOVAL — Brake-shoes, then adjust the brake-shoes as described under MAINTENANCE in the previous BRAKE chapter.

FRONT BRAKE ASSEMBLIES (Disc Brakes)

Removal
(1) **Friction pads:** Raise the front of the car and remove the road wheel.

(2) Depress the friction pad retaining spring and remove the split pins.
(3) Remove the retaining springs.
(4) Rotate the friction pads and anti-squeak shims slightly, then lift them from the calliper.

(1) **Calliper assembly:** Perform the previous operations.
(2) Disconnect the hydraulic supply hose.
(3) Remove the nuts securing the hose retaining plate to the calliper.
(4) Remove the studs retaining the calliper to the stub axle, then withdraw the calliper.

(1) **Brake discs:** Perform all the above operations.
(2) Remove the hub cap, then withdraw the split pin locking the hub retaining nut.
(3) Remove the retaining nut and washer.
(4) Withdraw the hub complete with the brake disc from the swivel axle using tool 18G 304 with adaptors 18G 304 F (disc wheels) or tool 18G 363 (wire wheels — early cars) or 18G 1032 (wire wheels — later cars).
(5) Remove the bolts retaining the brake disc to the hub, then remove the disc.

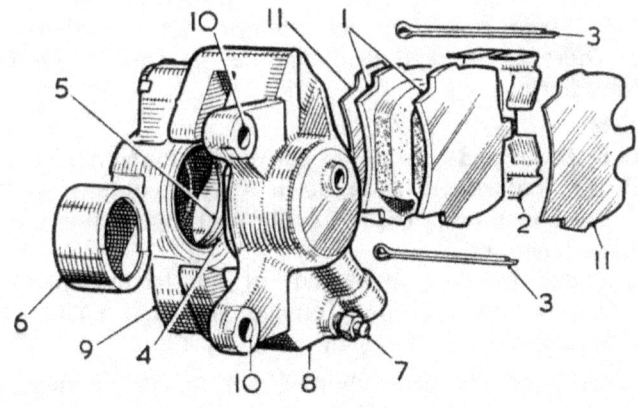

1. Friction pads.
2. Pad retaining spring.
3. Retaining pin.
4. Piston dust seal.
5. Piston fluid seal.
6. Piston.
7. Bleeder screw.
8. Calliper (mounting half).
9. Calliper (rim half).
10. Calliper mounting point.
11. Anti-squeak shims.

Front brake calliper assembly

(1) **Calliper pistons and seals:** Remove the friction pads and the calliper assembly as previously described.
(2) Clean the outside of the calliper, being sure that all dirt and cleaning fluid has been completely removed.
(3) Note the position of the relieved portion of the piston face.
(4) Reconnect the hydraulic supply hose and support the calliper to avoid strain on the hose.
(5) Use tool 18G 590 to clamp the piston in the mounting half of the calliper.
(6) Place a receptacle under the calliper and gently press the brake pedal until the piston in the rim half has emerged sufficiently for it to be removed by hand.
(7) Withdraw the piston.
(8) Gently pry the dust seal retainer from the mouth of the calliper bore, then remove the dust seal, taking care not to damage the bore of the calliper or the seal groove.
(9) Remove the fluid seal from its groove in the calliper bore, taking great care not to damage the bore of the calliper or the seal groove.
(10) Remove the clamping tool.
(11) To remove the mounting-half piston it is first necessary to refit the lip-half piston, then repeat the procedure in (5) through (9) but with the lip-half piston clamped.

NOTE: There should be no attempt made to dismantle the calliper. There is no need to dismantle the calliper for cleaning and inspection.

Inspection
(1) **Friction pads:** Examine the lining material for wear; if the material is worn down to a maximum permissible thickness of 1/16 in. (1.59 mm.) the friction pads must be renewed.
(2) Check for free movement of the friction pads in the calliper recess, then remove any high spots from the pad pressure plates by carefully filing.
(3) Examine the pad retaining springs for damage or loss of tension, renewing the springs if necessary.
(1) **Calliper assembly:** Clean any dirt or rust from the friction pad recesses. Thoroughly clean the exposed faces of the pistons or bores. Use only Girling Amber Brake Fluid or Lockheed Genuine Brake Fluid or alcohol for cleaning, but NEVER use solvents.
(2) Blow the fluid passages clear with air.

Replacement
(1) **Brake discs:** Refit the brake disc to the hub.
(2) Fit the hub assembly to the stub axle.
(3) Check the maximum run-out of the brake disc at the

periphery of the braking surface; if the run-out exceeds .006 in. (.152 mm.) the components must be examined for damage and, where necessary, replaced.

(1) **Calliper pistons and seals:** Be sure that the new fluid seal is absolutely dry, then coat it with Lockheed Disc Brake Lubricant.

(2) Ease the seal into its groove in the calliper bore, then gently work round with the fingers until it is seated correctly.

(3) Slacken the bleeder screw one complete turn.

(4) Coat the piston with Lockheed Disc Brake Lubricant, then locate the piston squarely in the mouth of the bore, with the cut-away portion of the piston face correctly positioned downwards.

(5) Press the piston into the bore until about 5/16 in. (8 mm.) of the piston is protruding from the bore. Take great care to prevent the piston from lifting during this operation.

(6) Be sure that the new dust seal is absolutely dry, then coat it with Lockheed Disc Brake Lubricant and fit the seal into its retainer.

(7) Position the seal assembly on the protruding portion of the piston with the seal innermost, being sure that the assembly is square with the piston.

(8) Use tool 18G 590 to press the piston and seal assembly home.

(9) Retighten the bleeder screw.

(10) Fit the seals and pistons into the mounting half of the calliper by the same procedure used in (1) through (9), noting that the hydraulic feed pipe must be disconnected to allow the clamping tool to be used.

(1) **Calliper assembly:** Reverse the removal procedure used under REMOVAL - Calliper assembly, noting that the brake pedal must not be depressed.

(1) **Friction Pads:** Check that the exposed surface of each piston is clean and the recesses in the calliper are free from rust and grit.

(2) Using tool 18G 590, press each piston fully back into the bore.

(3) **NOTE: During this operation, fluid displaced by the pistons will cause the fluid level in the master cylinder to rise, and it may be necessary to siphon off some of the fluid to prevent it from overflowing.**

(4) Check that the relieved face of each piston is correctly positioned downwards, then fit the friction pads.

(5) Check that the friction pads are free to move easily in the calliper recesses and fit the anti-squeak shims between the pistons and friction pad pressure plates.

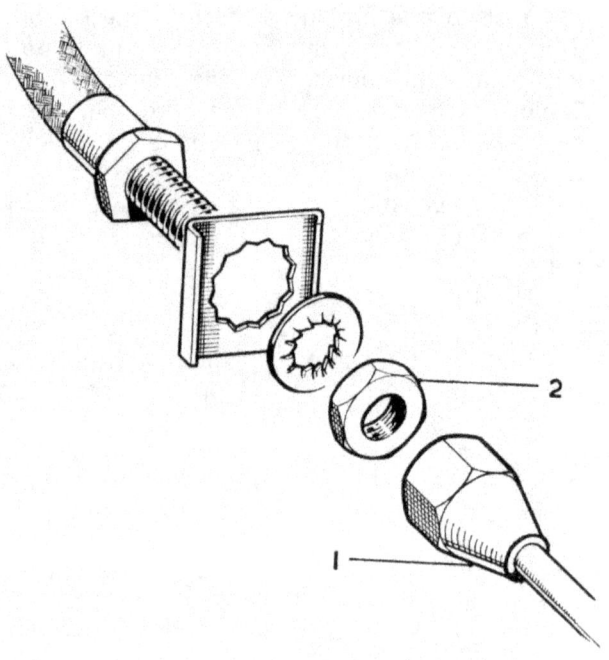

The union nut (1) is the one which must be first unscrewed to release the flexible hose from the pipeline. The attachment nut (2) can then be removed.

Flexible hose assembly

(6) Fit the pad retaining springs, press the spring down, then insert the split pins.
(7) Bleed the system as instructed under MAINTENANCE in the previous BRAKE chapter.
(8) Pump the brake pedal several times to adjust the friction pads and top up the master cylinder reservoir to a level of ¼ in. (6.5 mm.) below the bottom of the filler neck. Use Girling Amber Brake Fluid or Lockheed Genuine Brake Fluid ONLY.

REAR BRAKE ASSEMBLIES

Removal
(1) **Brake-shoes (early cars):** Block both front wheels, fully release the hand brake, and raise the rear of the car.
(2) Remove the road wheel.
(3) Back off the brake-shoe adjuster and remove the brake drum by removing the nuts securing the drum to the hub and tapping the drum off the hub.

(4) Depress each shoe steady spring and turn it, which will release it from the backplate.
(5) Pull the trailing shoe, against the tension of the return springs, away from its abutment at either end.
(6) With the return spring tension released, detach the springs and remove both shoes. The Micram adjuster will also come free when the shoes are removed.
(1) **Brake-shoes (later cars):** Perform operations (1) to (3) and (5).
(2) Remove the shoes and springs.
(1) **Wheel cylinder (early cars):** Remove the brake shoes as detailed previously.
(2) Disconnect the hydraulic feed pipe at the wheel cylinder.
(3) Disconnect the hand brake rod at the wheel cylinder lever.
(4) Remove the rubber boot.
(5) Withdraw the piston and cover from the wheel cylinder.
(6) Swing the hand brake lever until the shoulder is clear of the backplate, then slide the cylinder assembly forward.
(7) Pivot the cylinder about its forward end and withdraw the rear end from the slot in the backplate.
(8) Move the cylinder rearwards and disengage the forward end from the backplate.
(1) **Wheel cylinder (later cars):** Remove the brake-shoes as previously described.
(2) Disconnect the hydraulic feed pipe at the wheel cylinder.
(3) Disconnect the hand brake rod from the wheel cylinder lever and remove the rubber boot.
(4) Remove the bleed screw.
(5) Remove the circlip retaining the wheel cylinder to the backplate and withdraw the cylinder assembly.

Disassembly
(1) **Wheel cylinders (early cars):** Withdraw the hand brake lever pivot pin and remove the lever.
(2) Apply a gentle air pressure to the fluid connection and blow out the hydraulic piston, rubber cup, cup filler, and spring.
(3) Remove the seal from the outer piston.
(1) **Wheel cylinders (later cars):** Remove the dust seals from the ends of the cylinder.
(2) Withdraw both pistons complete with their seals.
(3) Withdraw the hand brake lever pivot pin and remove the lever.
(4) Remove the seals from the pistons.

Inspection
(1) **Brake-shoes:** Clean the dust from the brake-shoes and linings using an air blast, and examine the linings for

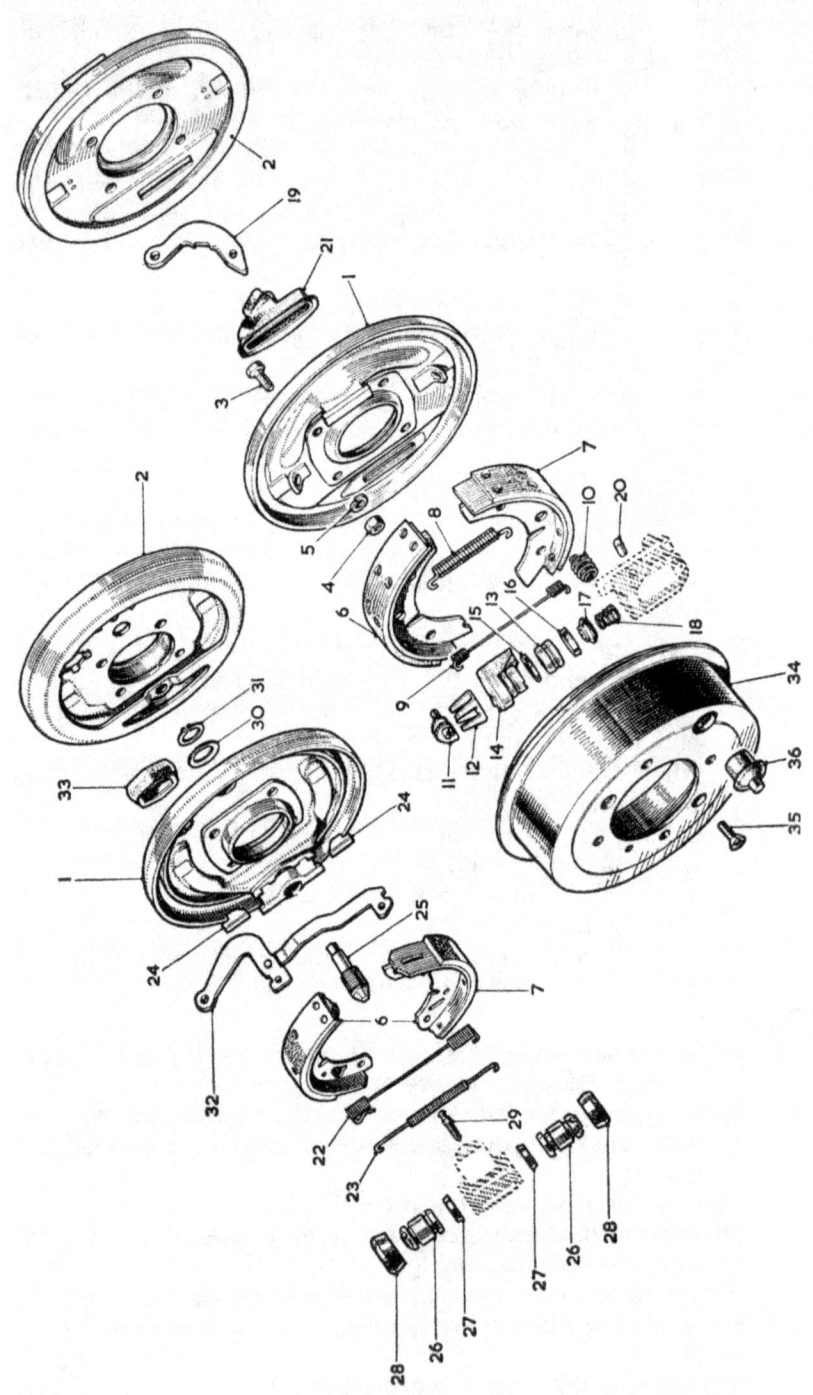

Rear brake components (early and later)

KEY TO THE REAR BRAKE COMPONENTS

No.	Description	No.	Description	No.	Description
1.	Brake-plate—R.H.	13.	Piston.	25.	Wedge.
2.	Brake-plate—L.H.	14.	Piston with dust cover.	26.	Piston.
3.	Set screw.	15.	Seal.	27.	Seal.
4.	Nut.	16.	Cup.	28.	Boot.
5.	Spring washer.	17.	Cup filler.	29.	Bleeder screw.
6.	Brake-shoe assembly.	18.	Spring.	30.	Belleville washer.
7.	Liner with rivets.	19.	Hand brake lever.	31.	Circlip.
8.	Shoe return spring (abutment end).	20.	Pivot pin.	32.	Hand brake lever.
9.	Shoe return spring (cylinder end).	21.	Boot.	33.	Boot.
10.	Steady spring.	22.	Shoe return spring (cylinder end).	34.	Brake-drum.
11.	Adjuster assembly.	23.	Shoe return spring (adjuster end).	35.	Set screw.
12.	Mask adjuster.	24.	Tappet.	36.	Plug.

wear. Replace as neeeded.
- (1) **Wheel cylinders:** Clean the components thoroughly using Girling Amber Brake Fluid or Lockheed Genuine Brake Fluid or alcohol, then dry them with a clean, non-fluffy cloth.
- (2) Examine the metal parts for wear and damage.
- (3) Inspect the rubber cup and seals for swelling or signs of deterioration.
- (4) Renew all damaged, worn, or suspect parts.

Reassembly
- (1) **Wheel cylinders (early cars):** Dip the internal components in the Girling Amber Brake Fluid or the Lockheed Genuine Brake Fluid and assemble them wet.
- (2) Fit the seals to the pistons, small diameter end of the spring into the cup filler, then insert the spring, large diameter end first, into the cylinder.
- (3) Fit the cup, lip side first, into the cylinder.
- (4) Insert the hydraulic piston, aligning the slot in the piston with the slot in the cylinder.
- (5) Fit the hand brake lever and pivot pin.
- (6) Ease the seal into its groove in the outer piston.
- (7) Fit the outer piston assembly.
- (1) **Wheel cylinders (later cars):** Dip the internal components in Girling Amber Brake Fluid or Lockeed Genuine Brake Fluid and assemble them wet.
- (2) Fit the seals to the pistons.
- (3) Insert the pistons and fit the dust covers.
- (4) Fit the hand brake lever and pivot pin.

Replacement
- (1) **Wheel cylinders (early cars):** Reverse the removal procedure under REMOVAL — Wheel cylinders (early cars).
- (2) Bleed the system and adjust the brake-shoes as described under MAINTENANCE in the previous BRAKES chapter.
- (1) **Wheel cylinders (later cars):** Reverse the removal procedure under REMOVAL — Wheel cylinders (later cars).
- (2) Be sure that the Micram adjuster is in the slot on the leading shoe with the mask in position.
- (3) The interrupted return spring must be fitted on the wheel cylinder side and both springs must lie between the brake-shoes and backplate.
- (4) The shoes must be fitted with the unlined end of the leading shoe to the whel cylinder, and the unlined end of the trailing shoe to the abutment block.
- (1) **Brake-shoes (later cars):** Reverse the removal procedure under REMOVAL — Brake shoes (later cars).
- (2) Be sure that the brake-shoes register correctly in the

slots in the wheel cylinder pistons and on the adjuster tappets.

(3) Be sure that the return springs are anchored in their correct holes in the shoe webs, with the interrupted spring fitted on the wheel cylinder side.

(4) After refitting, adjust the brake shoes as described under MAINTENANCE following in this section.

MASTER CYLINDER

Removal

(1) Disconnect the electrical connections from the heater blower unit, remove the screws securing the blower unit to the firewall, then remove the blower unit.
scribed under MAINTENANCE in the previous BRAKES

(2) Remove the screws securing the master cylinder mounting plate to the firewall.

(3) Disconnect the two hydraulic pipes from their unions on the master cylinder. Note which one of the pipes connects to the clutch slave cylinder.

(4) Withdraw the master cylinder upwards and at the same

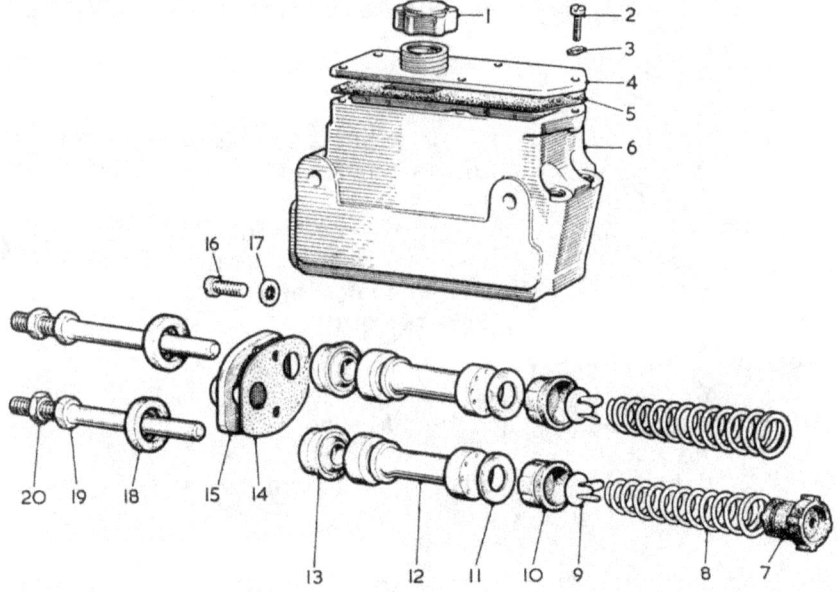

1. Filler cap.
2. Fixing screw.
3. Shakeproof washer.
4. Tank cover.
5. Tank cover gasket.
6. Cylinder barrel and tank.
7. Valve (Brake bore only).
8. Return spring.
9. Spring retainer.
10. Main cup.
11. Piston washer.
12. Piston.
13. Secondary cup.
14. Gasket.
15. Boot fixing plate.
16. Fixing washer.
17. Shakeproof washer.
18. Boot.
19. Push rod.
20. Push rod adjuster.

Master cylinder assembly

time manipulate the clutch and brake pedals through the hole in the firewall.
(5) Remove the spring clips, then withdraw the clevis pins from the push-rods to disconnect both pedals.
(6) Unscrew the bolts securing the master cylinder to the mounting plate and remove the complete unit.

Dismantling
(1) Remove the filler cap and drain the fluid.
(2) Proceed as described under MASTER CYLINDER — Dismantling the Brake Cylinder, in the previous BRAKES chapter.

Reassembly
(1) Dip all the internal components in Girling Amber Brake Fluid or Lockheed Genuine Brake Fluid and assemble them while wet.
(2) Stretch the secondary cup over the piston with the lip of the cup facing towards the head of the piston. When the cup is in its groove, work it round with the fingers to be sure that it is correctly seated.
(3) Fit the spring retainer into the small diameter end of the spring and the valve assembly into the large diameter end.
(4) Insert the assembled spring into the body, valve assembly end first.
(5) Fit the main cup, piston washer, and piston. Fit the cup by carefully entering the lip edge of the cup into the barrel first.
(6) Fit the boot fixing plate, boots, and push-rods. Each boot must be fitted with the vent hole at the bottom when the master cylinder is mounted in the car.

MAINTENANCE

Adjusting Disc Brakes
(1) Wear on the friction pads is automatically compensated during braking and therefore no manual adjustment is provided.
(2) If both friction pads are not worn the same amount change their operating positions as described previously in this section.
(3) If the friction pads are worn down to the minimum thickness of 1/16 in. (1.59 mm.) renew the pads as previously described in this section.

Adjusting Rear Brakes (later cars)
(1) Block both front wheels, fully release the hand brake, and lack up the car until the wheel is free to rotate.
(2) Turn the adjuster, located on the back of the brake backplate, in a clockwise direction until the shoes lock the

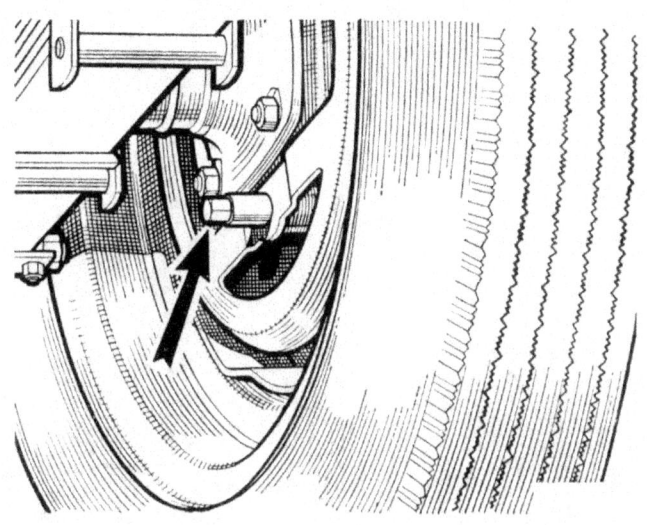

One square-headed brake adjusting bolt is provided on each rear brake-plate

Brake adjusting bolt (later cars)

      brake-drum.
- (3) Turn the adjuster back just sufficiently for the wheel to rotate without the brake-shoes rubbing.
- (4) Repeat the operations above for the other rear brake adjustment.

Adjusting Hand Brake
- (1) Adjust the rear brake-shoes as detailed in the previous BRAKES chapter under MAINTENANCE (early cars), or above in this section (later cars).
- (2) Block both front wheels and jack up the rear of the car.
- (3) Apply the hand brake so that the pawl engages with third notch on the ratchet.
- (4) Adjust the hand brake cable, with the sleeve nut (see illustration in the previous BRAKES chapter), until it is just possible to rotate each wheel by heavy hand pressure.
- (5) Both wheels must offer equal resistance in order to get full braking power.
- (6) Release the hand brake and check that both wheels rotate freely.

NOTES

SECTION III

1275 c.c. Engined Cars

1966-1971

(See 'Tuning Data' page 30)

IGNITION

Distributor
The information previously given also applies to the distributor fitted to the Sprite (Mk. IV) and the Midget (Mk. III) with the exception that there is no vacuum unit or moving contact plate fitted. The instructions for removing, dismantling, and reassembling may be followed but references to the above mentioned components should be ignored.

Ignition Adjustment
To adjust the ignition setting, slacken the distributor clamp screw and turn the distributor body clockwise to advance or counterclockwise to retard. The correct static ignition timing is given in GENERAL DATA.

FUEL SYSTEM

The fuel system is similar to that used on earlier cars, with the exception of the fuel pump, which is now an S.U. AUF 200 electrically operated diaphragm type.

FUEL PUMP

Removal and Refitting
The pump is situated beneath the luggage compartment on the right-hand side. For removal, do the following:
  (1) Disconnect the battery ground lead and detach the ground and supply leads from the terminals on the pump.
  (2) Disconnect the inlet, outlet, and vent pipe connections.
  (3) Remove the two bolts securing the pump bracket to the rear foot-well panel.
  (1) **Refitting:** Be sure that the outlet is vertically above the inlet port, i.e. the inlet and outlet nozzles are horizontal.
  (2) Be sure there is a good ground connection.

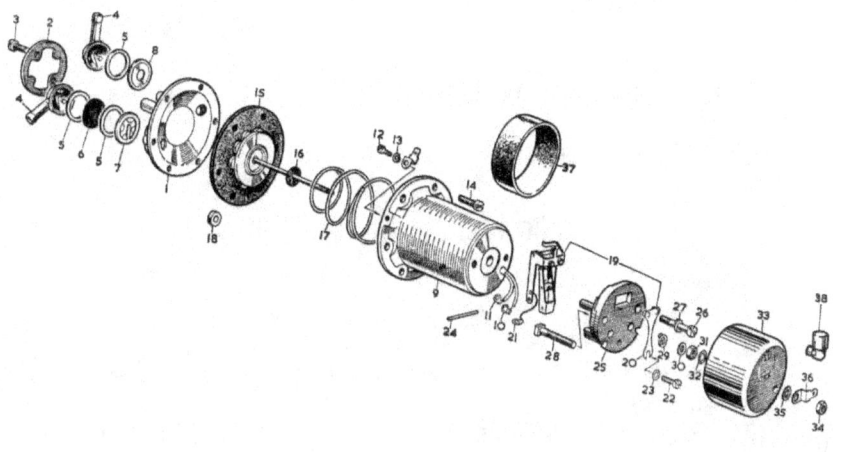

No.	Description	No.	Description	No.	Description
1.	Body.	14.	Screw—housing to body.	27.	Washer—spring.
2.	Spring clamp plate.	15.	Diaphragm assembly.	28.	Screw for terminal.
3.	Screw.	16.	Impact washer.	29.	Washer—spring.
4.	Nozzle—inlet/outlet.	17.	Spring.	30.	Washer—lead—for screw.
5.	Sealing washer.	18.	Roller.	31.	Nut for screw.
6.	Filter.	19.	Rocker and blade.	32.	Spacer—nut to cover.
7.	Valve—inlet.	20.	Blade.	33.	Cover—end.
8.	Valve—outlet.	21.	Tag—2 B.A. terminal.	34.	Nut for cover.
9.	Housing—coil.	22.	Screw for blade.	35.	Washer—shakeproof.
10.	Tag—5 B.A. terminal.	23.	Washer—dished.	36.	Connector—Lucar.
11.	Tag—2 B.A. terminal.	24.	Spindle for contact breaker.	37.	Packing sleeve.
12.	Screw—earth.	25.	Pedestal.	38.	Non-return valve.
13.	Washer—spring.	26.	Screw—pedestal to housing.		

Fuel pump components

ELECTRICAL

WARNING: Models produced since 1968 have a negative ground polarity in their electrical systems. Previously, the polarity had been positive ground.

DIRECTIONAL INDICATOR SWITCH
Removal and Replacement
(1) Disconnect the battery.
(2) Remove the set screws securing the two halves of the cover and disconnect the snap connections beneath the column.
(3) Remove the set screws securing the switch to the column and lift away the assembly.
(4) To replace, reverse the removal procedure.

HORN BUTTON
Removal and Replacement
(1) Disconnect the battery.
(2) Press the horn button and turn counterclockwise to remove.
(3) To replace, reverse the removal procedure.

IGNITION AND STARTER SWITCH
Removal and Replacement
(1) Disconnect the battery.
(2) Remove the bezel ring with service tool 18G 671.
(3) Disconnect the leads and pull the switch from the rear of the instrument panel.
(4) To replace, reverse the removal procedure.

ENGINE

Many operations can be performed with the engine in place in the chassis, but if lifting equipment is available, most of them become far easier. Thus we begin with outlining the steps involved in removing the entire assembly from the car.

Removing Engine (with gearbox)
(1) Remove the hood by removing the set screws securing each hinge to the under side of the hood, then lift the

hood, complete with hood prop, clear of the vehicle.
Note: Outline the profile of the hinge levers where they contact the mounting brackets on the hood to aid refitting.
(2) Disconnect the battery ground lead.
(3) Drain the cooling system, the engine sump and the gearbox. See appropriate sections of previous ENGINE and GEARBOX chapters for procedure.
(4) Remove the radiator.
(5) Remove the two through-bolts from both air cleaners and remove the air cleaners.
(6) Disconnect the inlet and outlet heater hoses from the heater unit (if applicable).
(7) Disconnect the fuel feed pipe from the front carburetter, then disconnect the choke cable from the mixture control lever.
(8) Release the clamp holding the exhaust pipe to the manifold and lower the pipe.
(9) Disconnect the throttle cable from the accelerator pedal cross-shaft, then pull the cable through the engine firewall.
(10) Disconnect the wiring from the generator and oil filter and the low-tension cables from the coil and distributor.
(11) Detach the high-tension cables from the spark plugs and coil and remove the distributor cap.
(12) Disconnect the cable from its connection on the starter, then disconnect the oil pressure gauge pipe from the union on the cylinder block.
(13) Remove the carpet covering the gearbox tunnel, then remove the gear lever cover screws and the cover.
(14) Unscrew the plug in the speed change tower and withdraw the damper spring and plunger.
(15) Remove the three screws holding the gear lever retaining plate and lift out the lever complete with the retaining plate.
(16) Remove the gearbox rear mounting bolts at the sides of the gearbox tunnel.
(17) Remove the bolts securing the clutch slave cylinder, then withdraw the cylinder from its push-rod.
(18) Disconect the speedometer cable from the gearbox.
(19) Remove the two gearbox mounting bolts fitted through the chassis.
(20) Remove the propeller shaft rear universal joint flange securing bolts, disconnect the propeller shaft, then withdraw it rearwards out of engagement with the gearbox shaft. **Note:** To assist correct reassembly, mark the propeller shaft rear universal joint flange and the rear axle flange.

(21) Support the engine using suitable lifting equipment, remove the three bolts securing the left-hand engine mounting to the body and the two nuts securing the right-hand engine mounting to the engine front plate.
(22) Ease the engine and gearbox assembly forward until the rear extension of the gearbox is clear of the tunnel, then tilt the assembly and lift it from the car.

Engine Replacement (With Gearbox)
(1) Lower the assembly into the car with the lifting equipment positioned at the front of the engine. Raise the rear of the engine and enter the rear gearbox extension into the tunnel.
(2) Working through the gear lever aperture in the tunnel, enter the propeller shaft coupling onto the gearbox shaft splines.
(3) Push the assembly back into its correct position and fit the two gearbox rear mounting bolts.
(4) Reverse the procedures in (1) through (15) and (17) through (21), then refill the engine and gearbox with a recommended oil. Refill the cooling system.

OIL PUMP

Removal
(1) To detach the oil pump, first remove the engine from the car.

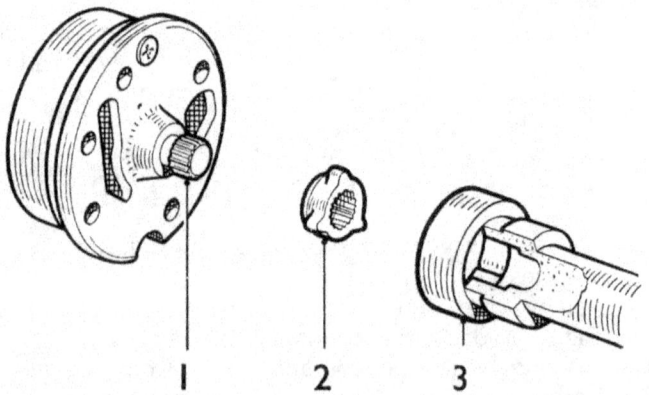

The oil pump drive, showing the correct position for the driving flange

1. Oil pump drive shaft.   2. Driving flange.
3. Camshaft.

Oil pump drive

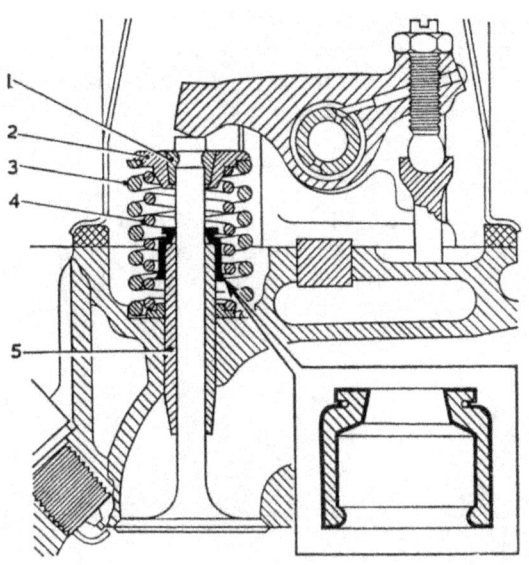

The valve components assembled. (The valve oil seal is shown inset)

1. Split cotters.   3. Outer spring.
2. Retaining cup.   4. Inner spring.
   5. Valve guide.

Valve assembly

(2) Remove the clutch assembly, flywheel, and the engine back plate as previously described.

(3) Unscrew the oil pump retaining bolts and withdraw the pump.

Dismantling and Replacing

(1) Refer to the previous ENGINE chapter (Section II) for instructions covering the Concentric or Hobourn-Eaton pumps.

(2) Refit as described, noting that the oil pump driving flange is fitted with the drive lug side towards the oil pump.

ROCKER SHAFT ASSEMBLY

Follow the instructions in Section I for removal and re-assembly, noting that the six distance pieces are fitted; one to each side of the two outer rockers, and one to the bracket side of the two middle rockers.

VALVES

Follow the instructions in Section II for removing the cylinder head and compressing and removing the valves. Then remove the valve oil seals and mark the valves for replacement in their

original positions. Replace as follows:
(1) Fit each valve into its respective guide, slide the oil seal down the valve stem and fit it over the valve guide.
(2) Fit the spring seat, springs, and spring cups.
(3) Compress the springs using tool 18G 45 (or equivalent) and fit the cotters.

VALVE SEAT INSERTS

If the valve seats cannot be restored by the recutting process as described in Section II, machine out the seatings to the dimensions given in the illustration and press special inserts into

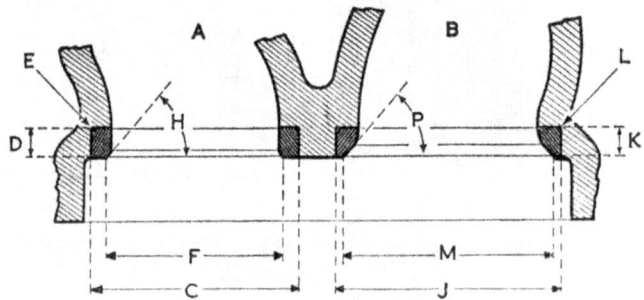

Valve seat machining dimensions

Exhaust (A)   *Inlet (B)*

C. 1·2505 to 1·2515 in.   J. 1·3805 to 1·3815 in.
(26·048 to 26·073 mm.).   (35·063 to 35·088 mm.).

D. ·186 to ·188 in.   K. ·186 to ·188 in.
(4·72 to 4·77 mm.).   (4·72 to 4·77 mm.).

E. Maximum radius   L. Maximum radius
·015 in.   ·015 in.
(·38 mm.).   (·38 mm.).

F. 1·144 to 1·164 in.   M. 1·2995 to 1·3195 in.
(29·046 to 29·554 mm.).   (32·89 to 32·38 mm.).

H. 45°.   P. 45°.

Valve seat insert dimensions

the cylnder head. Each insert must have an interference fit of .0025 to .0045 in. (.063 to .11 mm.).

After fitting, grind or machine the new seating to the dimensions given in the illustration. Normal valve-grinding may be necessary to ensure efficient valve seating.

PISTONS AND CONNECTING RODS

Gudgeon (Wrist) Pin

The gudgeon pin is a press fit to the connecting rod small-end. The interference fit of the pin in the small-end retains the gudgeon pin in its correct relative position and the piston bosses form the

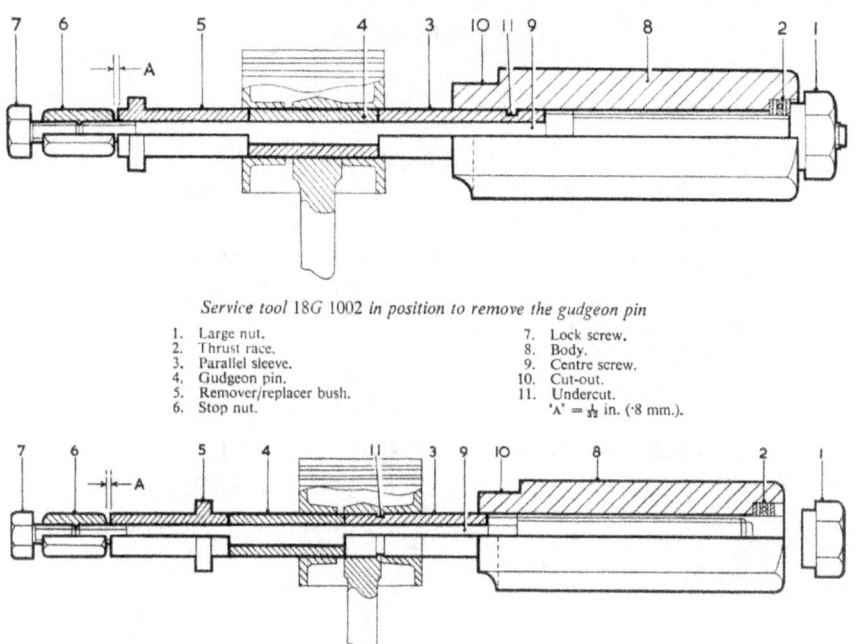

Service tool 18G 1002 *in position to remove the gudgeon pin*

1. Large nut.
2. Thrust race.
3. Parallel sleeve.
4. Gudgeon pin.
5. Remover/replacer bush.
6. Stop nut.
7. Lock screw.
8. Body.
9. Centre screw.
10. Cut-out.
11. Undercut.
'A' = $\frac{1}{32}$ in. (·8 mm.).

Service tool 18G 1002 *in position to refit the gudgeon pin*

Tool 18G 1002

pin bearing surfaces. It is therefore essential that the specified interference fit (see GENERAL DATA) be maintained. To remove the gudgeon pin Service tool 18G 1002 must be used (see illustration) to prevent crushing or distorting the piston.

PISTON SIZES AND CYLINDER BORES

In addition to the standard pistons there are also two oversize pistons available for replacement purposes.

Oversize pistons are marked with the actual oversize dimension enclosed in an ellipse, and are suitable for a bore oversize to standard by the same dimension.

The piston markings indicate the actual bore size to which they must be fitted, the requisite running clearance being allowed for in the machining.

Pistons are available in the sizes indicated in the following table.

REPLACING PISTONS AND CONNECTING RODS

Reverse the removal procedure outlined in the previous ENGINE chapter (Section II), noting the following points:

(1) Stagger the piston ring gaps at 90° to each other. See

Piston size table

Piston marking	Suitable bore size	Metric equivalent
STANDARD	2·7803 to 2·7800 in.	70·622 to 70·615 mm.
OVERSIZE +·010 in. (·254 mm.) +·020 in. (·508 mm.)	2·7903 to 2·7900 in. 2·8003 to 2·8000 in.	70·876 to 70·869 mm. 71·13 to 71·123 mm.

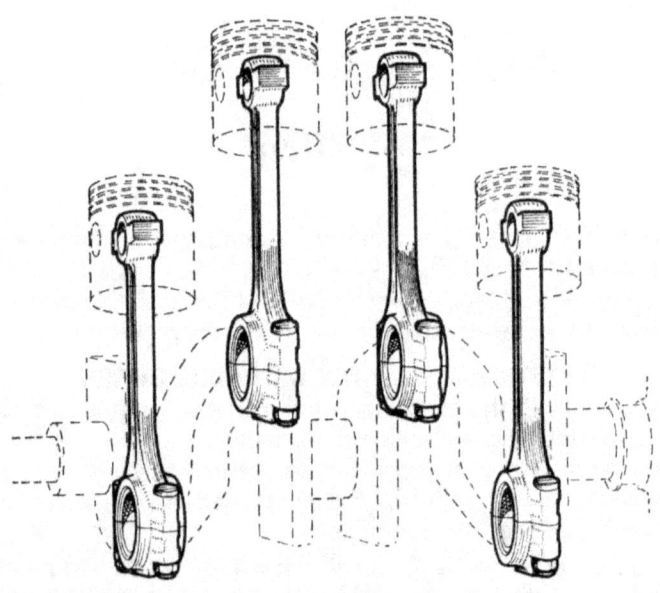

The correct assembly of the connecting rods and pistons to the crankshaft

Connecting rod replacement

OIL CONTROL PISTON RINGS for this detail.
(2) Be sure that each connecting rod and piston is refitted to its original bore, the correct way round.
(3) Check that the big-end bearings are correctly located in the connecting rods and caps.
(4) Tighten the bolts to the torque figure given in GENERAL DATA.
(5) Note that the big-end bearings are offset on the connecting rods, and the rods should be fitted so that the bearings of Nos. 1 and 3 are offset towards the rear of the engine, and the bearings of Nos. 2 and 4 are offset towards the front as shown in the illustration.

CAMSHAFT

Removal and Replacement

Perform all operations outlined in Section II to remove the camshaft up to but not including actual removal, then:
(1) Invert the engine to allow the tappets to fall clear of the camshaft.
(2) Withdraw the camshaft, rotating it slowly to assist disengagement of the distributor drive.
(3) The oil pump drive flange may come away with the camshaft as it is withdrawn, if so refit it to the oil pump drive shaft (drive lug side toward the oil pump).
(4) **Replacement:** Reverse the above removal procedure, noting the following points:
   (a) Be sure that the oil pump driving flange is correctly positioned on the pump drive shaft.
   (b) Rotate the camshaft slowly when refitting to assist engagement of the oil pump drive flange.
   (c) Fit the camshaft locating plate with its white-metal side towards the camshaft.

TAPPETS

Removal

Perform above operations to remove the camshaft, then remove the tappets from the cylinder block using a magnet or alternatively, turn the engine upright and allow the tappets to slide out under their own weight. Label the tappets to ensure correct assembly in their correct positions.

CLUTCH

WARNING: All B.M.C. cars use NATURAL RUBBER COMPONENTS in their clutch systems, NOT neoprene rubber components as do American makes. Therefore, it is extremely important that Castrol Girling Amber or Crimson Brake Fluid or BRITISH Lockheed Disc Brake Fluid be used in these systems, since they are the only brake fluids compatible with the natural rubber parts. Some American brake fluids are only suitable for all-neoprene rubber parts, and will cause natural rubber parts to swell and deteriorate, leading to eventual rupture.

Removal and Inspection
(1) Remove the clutch as described in the CLUTCH chapter of Section I, then rotate the release bearing spring retainers through 90° and withdraw the bearing from the withdrawal lever fork.
(2) Examine the clutch driven plate facings for wear and darkening. If the grain of the material cannot be clearly distinguished, renew the plate.
(3) Inspect the splines, springs and spring pockets in the driven plate for wear, and renew the plate if necessary. Excessive wear of the driven plate splines may be due to misalignment and the flywheel should be checked for true using a dial indicator. If the reading varies by more than .003 in. (.07 mm.) anywhere on the flywheel face, replace it.
(4) Examine the pressure plate and the diaphragm spring for signs of overheating; if so, renew the complete clutch cover assembly.
(5) Check the release bearing for excessive wear, and renew it if necessary.

Replacement
(1) Position the driven plate assembly on the flywheel with the long side of the hub towards the flywheel.
(2) Centralize the driven plate by inserting tool 18G 139 through the splined hub and entering the pilot end of the tool into the spigot bearing of the crankshaft.
(3) Locate the clutch cover assembly on the flywheel dowels, screw in the securing bolts, and tighten the bolts a turn at a time in diagonal sequence to the torque figure given in GENERAL DATA.
(4) Remove the clutch centralizing tool.
(5) Fit the release bearing to the withdrawal lever fork and be sure the spring retainers are correctly located.

(6) Refit the engine to the gearbox, being sure that the gearbox is supported during the refitting, to avoid strain on the first motion shaft, and distortion or displacement of the clutch components.
(7) Fit the starter motor.
(8) Refit the engine and gearbox assembly as described in Section II.

MASTER CYLINDER

Description

The clutch master cylinder fitted on the Sprite Mk. IV and the Midget Mk. III is a single unit, and is not part of the brake master cylinder as in the past. Note the warning at the beginning of this chapter before beginning inspection and reassembly.

Removal
(1) Remove the pedal box lid in the engine compartment.
(2) Disconnect the hydraulic pipe from the clutch master cylinder.
(3) Withdraw the split pin from the clevis pin connecting the push-rod to the clutch pedal and remove the clevis pin.

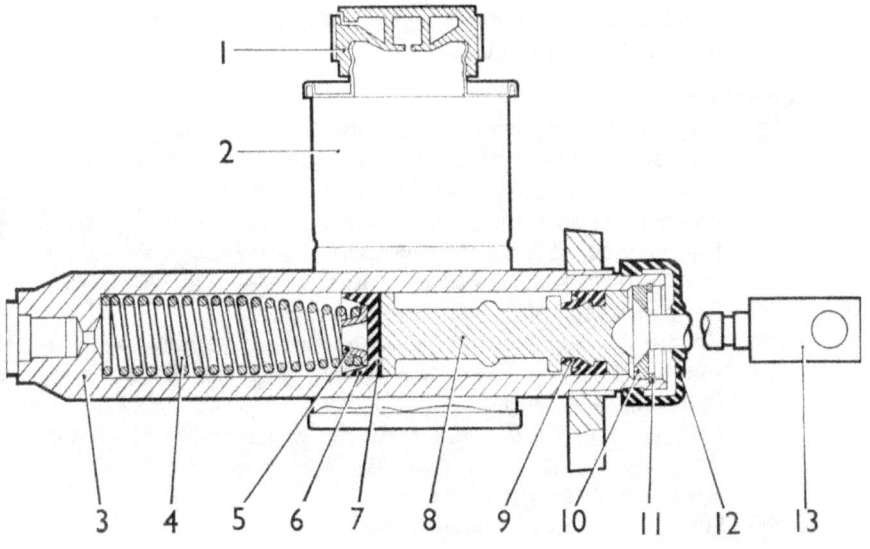

A section through the master cylinder

1. Filler cap.
2. Reservoir.
3. Body.
4. Spring.
5. Spring retainer.
6. Main cup.
7. Piston washer.
8. Piston.
9. Secondary cup.
10. Dished washer.
11. Circlips.
12. Rubber boot.
13. Push-rod.

Clutch master cylinder

(4) Unscrew the two bolts securing the master cylinder to the pedal box and remove the master cylinder.

Disassembly
(1) Remove the filler cap and drain the fluid.
(2) Detach the rubber boot from the body and slide it up the push rod.
(3) Remove the circlip retaining the push-rod, then withdraw the push-rod complete with the rubber boot and dished washer.
(4) Withdraw the piston complete with the secondary cup, the piston washer, main cup, spring retainer, and spring from the body.
(5) Remove the secondary cup from the piston by carefully stretching it over the end of the piston using only the fingers.

Inspection
(1) Clean all the parts thoroughly using Girling Amber or Crimson Brake Fluid or Lockheed Disc Brake Fluid, Series II, then dry them with a clean, non-fluffy cloth.
(2) Examine the metal parts for wear and damage, then inspect the rubber cups for swelling, deterioration, distortion, or any other signs of damage. Renew all worn, damaged or supect parts.

Reassembly
(1) Dip all the internal components in Girling Amber or Crimson Brake Fluid or Lockheed Disc Brake Fluid, Series II, and assemble the parts while wet.
(2) Stretch the secondary cup over the piston with the lip of the cup facing towards the head of the piston. When the cup is in its groove work round it gently with the fingers to ascertain that it is correctly seated.
(3) Fit the spring retainer into the small diameter end of the spring and insert the spring into the body, large diameter end first.
(4) Fit the main cup, cup washer, piston, and push-rod. When fitting the cups carefully enter the lip edge of the cups into the barrel first.
(5) Fit the circlip and rubber boot.

Replacement
(1) Reverse the removal procedure previously described, fill the master cylinder with Girling Amber or Crimson Brake Fluid or Lockheed Disc Brake Fluid, Series II, then bleed the system as described in the CLUTCH chapter in Section I.

REAR AXLE

Removal
(1) Loosen the wheel nuts on both wheels before jacking up the car.
(2) Raise the vehicle by placing a jack under the differential housing, and also support the body. Remove the wheels.
(3) Remove the down pipe, muffler, and exhaust pipe as described in the ENGINE chapter in Section I.
(4) Keeping the jack in this position, release each check strap at its axle location.
(5) Release each shock absorber arm from its connecting linkage.
(6) Disconnect the brake cable at the cable adjuster.
(7) Unscrew the nuts and remove the bolts securing the drive shaft flange to the axle pinion flange.
(8) Disconnect the hydraulic brake pipe at the main union just forward of the differential housing. Remove the U-bolt securing nuts.
(9) Making certain that the weight of the axle is fully on the jack, unscrew and remove the rear shackle pins.

Replacement
To replace, reverse the removal procedure, noting the following:
Before tightening the spring bolts it is essential that the normal working load be applied to the springs so that the flexing rubber bushes are deflected to an equal extent in both directions during service. Failure to take this precaution will inevitably lead to early deterioration of the bushes.

REAR SUSPENSION

SPRINGS

Removal
(1) Raise the vehicle by placing a jack under the differential housing and support the body. **Note:** Be sure that the weight of the axle is fully on the jack and that the springs are in the fully unloaded position.
(2) Remove the wheels.

(3) Working within the car, remove the set screws securing the front anchor bracket to the rear of the body foot-well.
(4) Working beneath the car, remove the two front bracket securing set screws.
(5) Remove the four U-bolt securing nuts and the shock-absorber anchorage plate.
(6) Remove the rear shackle nuts, pins, and plates, then lift out the spring assembly.

Replacement

(1) Remove the axle check strap to assist fitting the U-bolts.
(2) Tighten the spring bolt when the normal working load has been applied to the spring.
(3) Reverse the removal procedure previously described.

BRAKES

WARNING: All B.M.C. cars use NATURAL RUBBER component in their brake systems, NOT neoprene rubber components as do American makes. Therefore, it is extremely important that Castrol Girling Crimson or Amber Brake Fluid or BRITISH Lockheed Disc Brake Fluid be used in these systems, since these are the only brake fluids compatible with the natural rubber parts. Some American brake fluids are only suitable for all-neoprene rubber parts, and will cause natural rubber parts to swell and deteriorate, leading to eventual rupture.

MASTER CYLINDER

Description

The brake master cylinder fitted on the Sprite Mk. IV and the Midget Mk. III is a single unit, and is not part of the clutch master cylinder as in the past (see illustration).

Service Procedure

All service procedures are similar to the CLUTCH master cylinder, described previously in Section III, except for the following important details:

(1) During disassembly, withdraw the piston complete with the secondary cup, then remove the piston washer, main cup and the **spring complete with the spring retainer and valve.**

(2) During reassembly, fit the spring retainer **and the valve** to the spring, then fit the spring, **valve end first,** into the body.

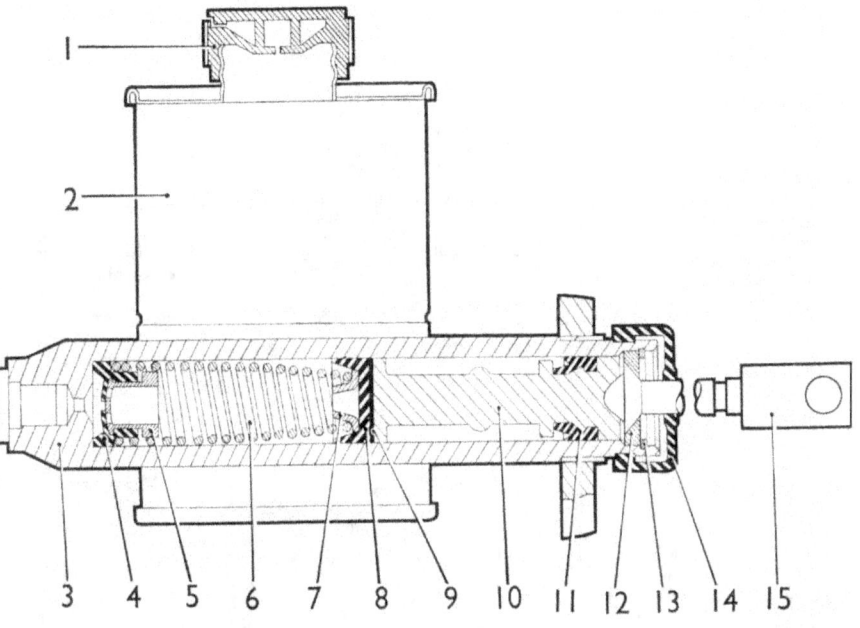

A section through the master cylinder

1. Filler cap.
2. Reservoir.
3. Body.
4. Valve.
5. Valve seat.
6. Spring.
7. Spring retainer.
8. Main cup.
9. Piston washer.
10. Piston.
11. Secondary cup.
12. Dished washer.
13. Circlip.
14. Rubber boot.
15. Push-rod.

Brake master cylinder

SERVICING

General

The efficient operation of the exhaust emission control system is dependent on the engine being in good mechanical condition and correctly tuned to the settings given in GENERAL DATA.

Tuning and test procedure for the carburetters, ignition system, and engine are given at the end of the manual. These procedures are the quickest and surest way of locating engine faults or maladjustments and are the only methods that should be used for engine tuning.

Fault diagnosis

After tuning the engine to the correct settings, check for indications of the following symptoms:

Symptoms	Causes	Cure
Backfire in exhaust system	1. Leak in exhaust system	Locate and rectify leak
	2. Leaks in hoses or connections to gulp valve or vacuum sensing pipe	Locate and rectify leak
	3. Faulty gulp valve	Test gulp valve, and renew if faulty
	4. Leak in intake system	Locate and rectify leak
	5. Faulty carburetter limit valve	Fit new throttle plate and limit valve assembly
Hesitation to accelerate after sudden throttle closure	1. Leaks in hoses or connections to gulp valve or vacuum sensing pipe	Locate and rectify leak
	2. Faulty gulp valve	Test gulp valve, and renew if faulty
	3. Leak in intake system	Locate and rectify leak
Engine surges (erratic operation at varying throttle openings)	1. Leaks in hoses or connections to gulp valve or vacuum sensing	Locate and rectify leak
	2. Faulty gulp valve	Test gulp valve, and renew if faulty
Erratic idling or stalling	1. Leaks in hoses or connections to gulp valve or vacuum sensing pipe	Locate and rectify leak
	2. Faulty gulp valve	Test gulp valve, and renew if faulty
	3. Faulty carburetter limit valve	Fit new throttle plate and valve assembly
Burned or baked hose between air pump and check valve	1. Faulty check valve	Test check valve, and renew if faulty
	2. Air pump not pumping	Test air pump, service or renew if faulty
Noisy air pump	1. Incorrect belt tension	Adjust belt tension
	2. Pulleys damaged, loose or misaligned	Tighten loose pulleys, renew damaged pulleys
	3. Air pump failing or seizing	Test air pump, service or renew if faulty

ENGINE SPEED	TEST	COMPONENT CONDITION	READ/OBSERVE
START (cranking)	Cranking voltage	Battery; starting system	Voltmeter
	Cranking coil output	Coil; ign. primary circuit	Scope trace
	Cranking vacuum	Engine	Vacuum gauge
	Positive crankcase ventilation	Crankcase emission equipment	Vacuum gauge
IDLING	Idle speed	Carburetter idle setting	Tachometer
	Dwell	Distributor/drive; points	Dwell meter; scope
	Initial timing	Spark timing setting	Timing light
	Fuel mixture	Carburetter setting	Exhaust gas analyser
	Manifold vacuum	Engine idle efficiency	Vacuum gauge
CRUISE (1,000 r.p.m.)	Dwell variation	Distributor mechanical	Dwell meter
	Coil polarity	Ignition circuit polarity	Scope trace
	Cam lobe accuracy	Distributor cam	Scope trace
	Secondary circuit	Plugs; leads; cap; rotor	Scope trace
	Coil and condenser condition	Coil windings; condenser	Scope trace
	Breaker point condition	Points closing/opening/bounce	Scope trace
	Spark plug firing voltage	Fuel mixture; compression; plug/rotor gaps	Scope trace
	Fuel mixture	Carburetter	Exhaust gas analyser
	Engine/cylinder balance/power drop	Cylinder compression	Tachometer (150 r.p.m. scale)
ACCELERATE	Spark plugs under load	Spark plugs	Scope trace
	Carburetter open/close action	Carburetter	Exhaust gas analyser
TURNPIKE (2,500 r.p.m.)	Timing advance	Distributor mech./vacuum advance	Timing light/advance meter
	Maximum coil output	Coil; condenser; ignition primary	Scope trace
	Secondary circuit insulation	H.T. cables, cap, rotor	Scope trace
	Charging voltage	Regulator; cut-out	Voltmeter
	Fuel mixture	Air cleaner, carburetter	Exhaust gas analyser
	Exhaust restriction	Exhaust system	Vacuum gauge

CORRECT READINGS	CHECK SEQUENCE—FAULT LOCATION	
9·6 volts minimum at the battery	Battery—starter motor—connections/cables—dynamo/alternator—regulator	
17 KV. minimum	Ignition coil	Pattern 1
10—15 in. Hg even pulse	Hoses and connections—Valve rocker clearance—Gulp valve—Servo (if fitted)—Inlet manifold leaks—Valves or seats—Piston rings	
6–10 in. Hg	Oil filler cap—Pipes and connections—Emission valve—Oil separator	
See 'TUNING DATA'	Carburetter adjustment—Hoses and connections—Gulp valve—Servo (if fitted)—Carburetter limit valve or mechanical condition	
4-cyl. : 57 to 63°; 6-cyl. : 34 to 37°. See pattern 1	Breaker points—Distributor and drive mechanical condition	
See 'TUNING DATA'	Distributor adjustment	
See 'TUNING DATA'	Carburetter adjustment—Hoses and connections—Gulp valve—Crankcase emission valve—Servo (if fitted)—Carburetter limit valve or mechanical condition—Air pump—Check valve—Spark plugs	Pattern 2
18 to 20 in. Hg	Hoses and connections—Gulp valve—Inlet manifold leaks—carburetter limit valve—Valves or seats—Piston rings	
Variation of 2° maximum	Distributor and drive mechanical condition	
See Pattern 2	Ignition circuit connections—Ignition coil	
2° max. variation. See pattern 3	Distributor mechanical condition (cam)	
Standard pattern	Spark plugs and leads—Breaker points—Carburetter adjustment—Hoses and connections—Gulp valve—Servo (if fitted)	Pattern 3
See Pattern 4	Ignition coil—Condenser	
See Pattern 1 (inset)	Breaker points—Condenser	
See Pattern 5; voltage 6—10 kV	Spark plugs and leads—Breaker points—Distributor cap and rotor—Carburetter adjustment—Hoses and connections—Gulp valve—Servo (if fitted)	
See 'TUNING DATA'	Carburetter adjustment—Hoses and connections—Gulp valve—Servo (if fitted)—Crankcase emission valve—Air pump—Check valve—Injectors	Pattern 4
Max. variation/cylinder 40 r.p.m.	Valve rocker clearance—Valves and seats—Piston rings	
See Pattern 6; 10 kV/plug maximum	Spark plugs and leads—Carburetter adjustment—Hoses and connections—Gulp valve—Servo (if fitted)	
Initial rich, lean off at throttle closure	Carburetter limit valve and mechanical condition—Hoses and connections—Gulp valve—Air pump	
See 'TUNING DATA'	Distributor mechanical condition, vacuum unit, centrifugal weights and springs	Pattern 5
Standard pattern; minimum reserve 2/3 more than requirement	Ignition coil—H.T. circuit insulation	
Standard pattern	H.T. leads—Distributor cap and rotor	
14·5 volts; steady reading	Cut-out—Voltage regulator—Dynamo/Alternator	
See 'TUNING DATA'	Hoses and connections—Carburetter adjustment—Air cleaners—Gulp valve—Air pump—Check valve—Injectors	
No variation in reading at constant speed for 10 sec.	Exhaust system	Pattern 6

EXHAUST EMISSION CONTROL

DESCRIPTION

Air is pressure-fed from an air pump through an injection manifold to the cylinder head exhaust port of each cylinder. The check valve in the air delivery pipe prevents blow-back from high pressure exhaust gases. The pump also supplies air through a gulp valve to the inlet manifold to provide air during conditions of deceleration and engine over-run.

Air Pump

The rotary vane type air pump is mounted on the front of the cylinder head and is belt driven from the water pump pulley. Air is drawn into the pump through a dry-type renewable element

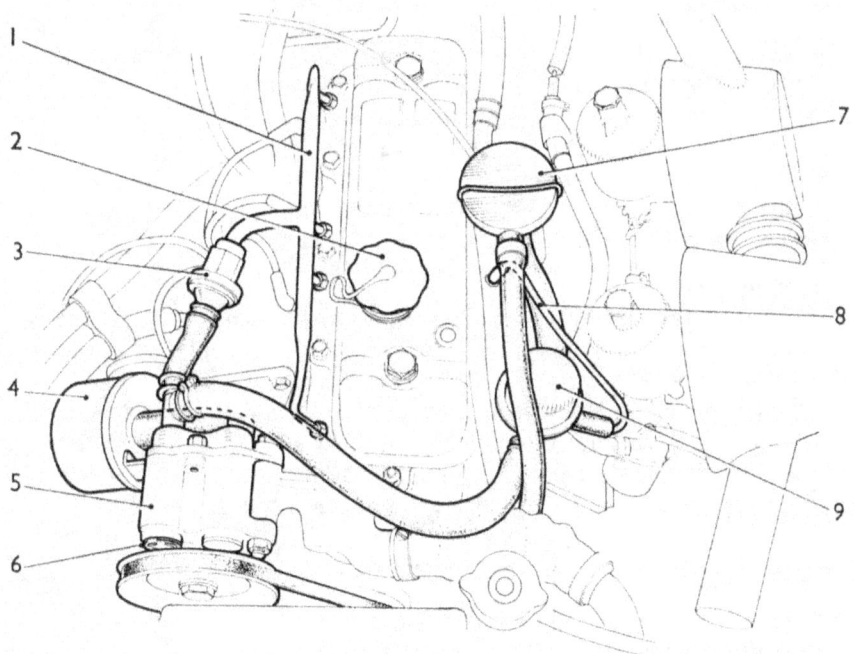

1. Air manifold.
2. Filtered oil filler cap.
3. Check valve.
4. Emission air cleaner.
5. Air pump.
6. Relief valve.
7. Crankcase emission valve.
8. Vacuum sensing tube.
9. Gulp valve.

Exhaust emission control

filter. A relief valve in the pump discharge port allows excess air pressure at high engine speeds to discharge to the atmosphere.

Check Valve

The check valve's function is to protect the pump from the backflow of exhaust gases. It is fitted in the pump discharge line to the injection manifold. The valve shuts if the air pressure ceases while the engine is running; i.e., if the pump drive belt should break.

Gulp Valve

The gulp valve, fitted in the pump discharge line to the inlet manifold, controls the flow of air for leaning-off the rich air/fuel mixture present in the inlet manifold immediately following throttle closure after running at full throttle opening, otherwise known as engine over-run.

A sensing pipe connected between the inlet manifold and the gulp valve transmits manifold vacuum directly to the underside of the diaphragm and through a bleed hole to the upper side. Sudden increases in manifold vacuum which occur immediately following throttle closure act on the underside of the diaphragm which opens the valve and admits air to the inlet manifold. The bleed hole allows the differences in vacuum acting on the diaphragm to equalize and the valve closes.

On some engines a restrictor is fitted in the air pump discharge connection to the gulp valve, which prevents surging when the gulp valve is operating.

Carburetter

The carburetters are manufactured to a special exhaust emission control specification and are tuned to give optimum engine performance with maximum emission control.

A limit valve is incorporated in the carburetter throttle disc which limits the inlet manifold vacuum to a maximum of 20.5 in. Hg, ensuring that under conditions of high inlet-manifold vacuum the mixture entering the cylinders is at a combustible ratio.

AIR PUMP

Drive Belt Tensioning

With proper tensioning, a total deflection of $\frac{1}{2}$ in., using moderate hand pressure, should be possible at the midway point of the longest belt run between the pulleys. To tension the belt:
    (1) Loosen the air pump mounting bolt and adjusting link bolts as shown in the illustration.
    (2) Using hand pressure only, pull the pump in the required direction until the correct tension is obtained.
    (3) Tighten the mounting and adjusting bolts to a torque figure of 10 ft. lbs.

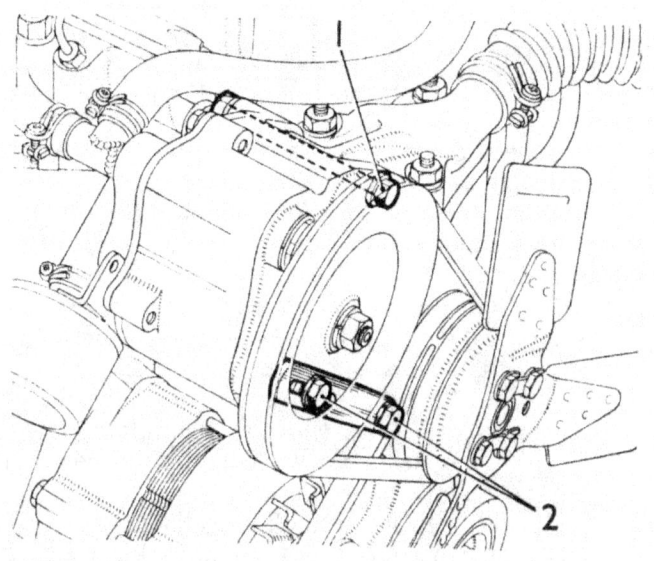

1. Pump mounting bolt.   2. Adjusting link bolts.

Drive belt tensioning

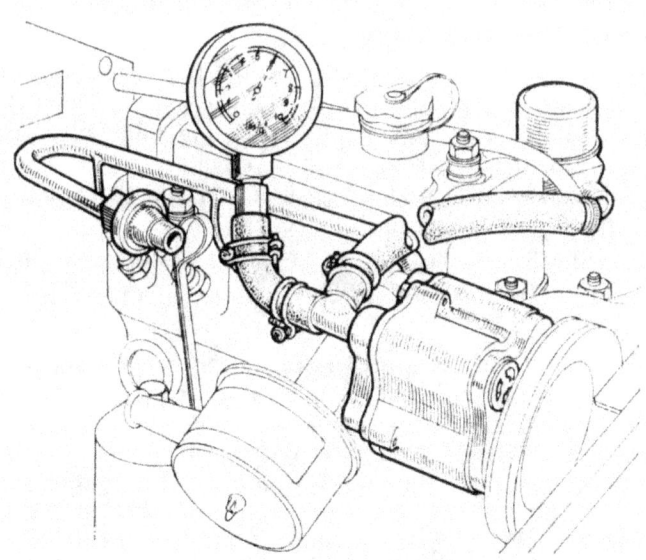

The pressure gauge connected

Air pump testing

Testing
(1) Check the drive belt for correct tensioning.
(2) Connect a tachometer to the engine in accordance with the instrument-maker's instructions.
(3) Disconnect the gulp valve air supply hose at the gulp valve and securely plug the valve.
(4) Disconnect the air manifold supply hose at the check valve, and connect a pressure gauge to the hose (see illustration).
(5) Run the engine at the air pump test speed given in 'General Data'– see TUNING DATA: a gauge reading of not less than 3 psi should be registered.
    (a) If the correct reading is not obtained, remove, dismantle and clean the pump air cleaner. Reassemble using a new element, refit the air cleaner, and repeat the test.
    (b) If the reading is still unsatisfactory, check the relief valve for leakage. Renew the relief valve if faulty and repeat the test.
    (c) If a satisfactory reading is still unobtainable, remove and have the air pump serviced.
(6) Increase the engine speed to 3,000 rpm. When a gauge reading of between 4 and 5 psi is registered, the relief valve should operate. If the relief valve fails to function, remove the pump and renew the relief valve.

Removal
(1) Disconnect the air hoses from the pump connections and remove the air cleaner.
(2) Loosen the mounting and adjusting link bolts and slip the belt drive from the pump pulley.
(3) Remove the top adjusting link bolt and the nut securing the pump mounting bolt.
(4) Support the pump, withdraw the mounting bolt, then lift the pump from the engine.

Replacement
(1) Position the pump in the mounting bracket then fit, but do not tighten, the pump mounting bolt.
(2) Replace, but do not tighten, the adjusting link bolt.
(3) Fit and tension the drive belt.
(4) Reconnect the hoses and refit the air cleaner.

Relief Valve Replacement
(1) Remove the air pump.
(2) Remove the pump pulley.
(3) Place a ½ in. diameter soft metal drift through the pump discharge connection so that it register against the relief valve, then drive the valve from the pump.

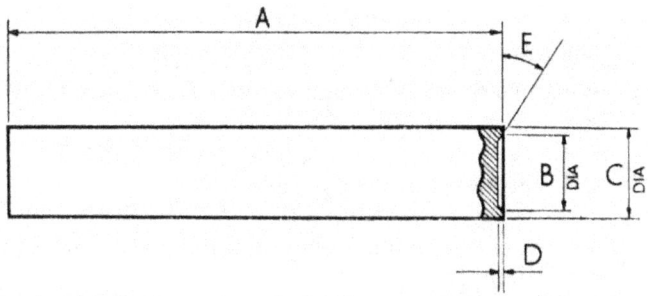

The dimensions of the relief valve replacing tool

A = 5 in.   B = ·986 in.   C = 1·062 in.
D = ·05 in.   E = 30°.

Relief valve tool

(4) Fit a new copper seating washer to the new relief valve and place the valve into the pump body.
(5) Using a tool made to the dimensions shown in the illustration, drive the valve into the pump body until the copper seating washer is held firmly, but not compressed, between the valve and the pump body.
(5) Refit the pulley, then replace the air pump.

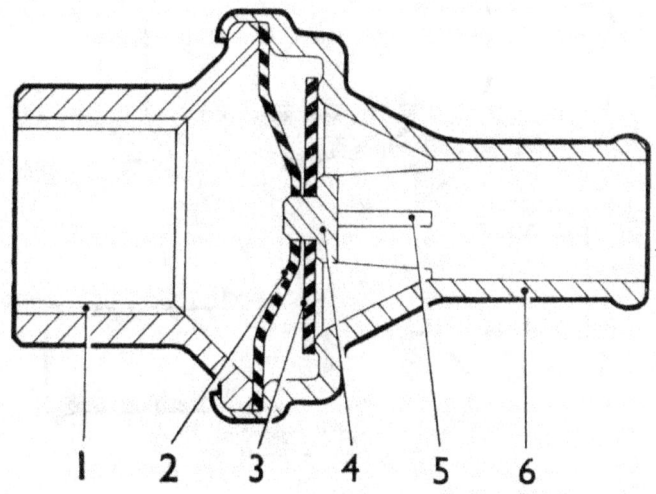

A section through the check valve

1. Air manifold connection.   4. Valve pilot.
2. Diaphragm.   5. Guides.
3. Valve.   6. Air supply connection.

Check valve

CHECK VALVE

Removal
(1) Disconnect the air supply hose from the check valve connection.
(2) Hold the air manifold connection to prevent it twisting and unscrew the check valve.

Testing
(1) Blow with the mouth through the valve, in turn from each connection.
   Note: Never use the high-pressure air hose for this test.
(2) Air should pass through the valve when blown from the air supply hose connection.
(3) Should air pass through when blown from the air manifold connection, replace the check valve.

Replacement
(1) Hold the air manifold connection to prevent it twisting, then screw in and tighten the check valve.
(2) Reconnect the air supply hose to the check valve.

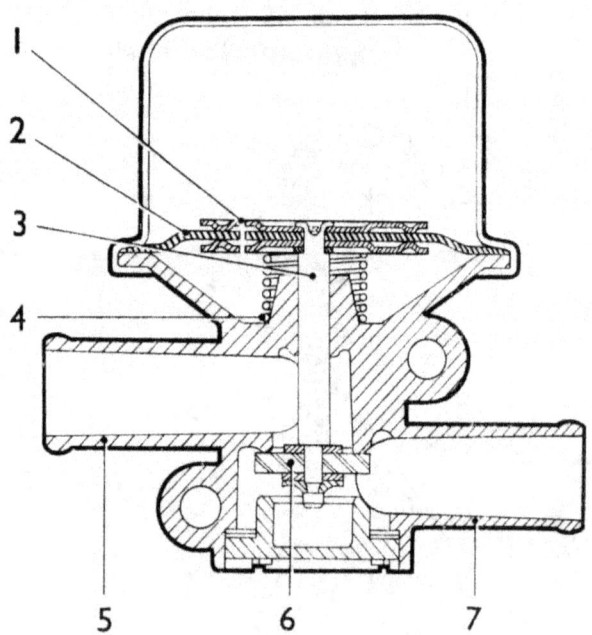

A section through the gulp valve

1. Metering balance orifice.
2. Diaphragm.
3. Valve spindle.
4. Return spring.
5. Inlet manifold hose connection.
6. Valve.
7. Air pump hose connection.

Gulp valve

GULP VALVE

Testing
(1) Disconnect the air supply hose at the gulp valve, then securely plug the disconnected hose end.
(2) Connect a vacuum gauge to the air supply connection of the gulp valve.
(3) Run the engine at idling speed and at operational temperature.
(4) A zero vacuum reading should be registered on the gauge indicating that the valve is seating correctly. If a vacuum is registered, replace the gulp valve.
(5) Operate the throttle from closed to open in rapid succession; The gauge should register a vacuum, then return slowly to zero. Repeat the test several times observing the gauge reaction; if the gauge fails to respond as above, renew the gulp valve.

Removal and Replacement
(1) Disconnect the air hoses.
(2) Unscrew the mounting screw and remove the gulp valve.
(3) To replace, reverse the removal procedure.

CARBURETTERS

The carburetters are adjusted and tuned to give optimum engine performance with efficient engine emission control. Adjustments to the carburetter settings must ONLY be performed by a licensed Pollution Control Service Station.

CRANKCASE EMISSION CONTROL

Refer to the ENGINE chapter in Section II for the description and the testing and servicing procedures.

NOTES

WIRING DIAGRAMS

(ALL MODELS)

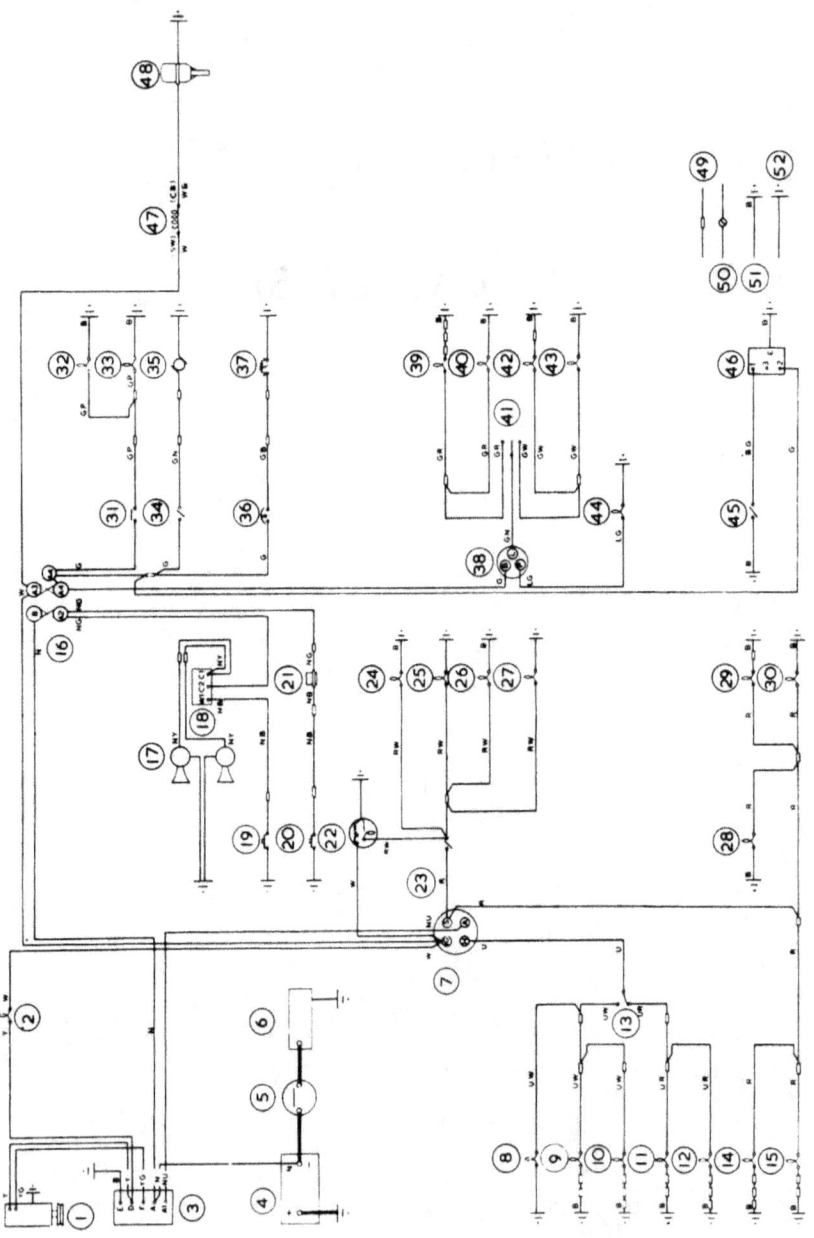

'Sprite' I

'Sprite' I

Key to 'Sprite' I: 1 Generator   2 Ignition warning light   3 Control box   4 12-volt battery   5 Starter switch
6 Starter motor   7 Lighting and ignition switch   8 Main beam warning light   9 Righthand headlamp main beam
10 Lefthand headlamp main beam   11 Lefthand headlamp dip beam   12 Righthand headlamp dip beam   13 Dipper switch
14 Lefthand sidelamp   15 Righthand sidelamp   16 Fuse unit   17 Connections for twin windtone horns (when fitted)
18 Horn relay   19 Horn push   20 Horn push   21 Horn   22 Cigar lighter and illumination   23 Panel light switch   24 Panel light
25 Speedometer light   26 Panel light   27 Tachometer light (when fitted)   28 Righthand tail lamp   29 Number plate lamp
30 Lefthand tail lamp   31 Stop lamp switch   32 Righthand stop lamp   33 Lefthand stop lamp   34 Heater switch (when fitted)
35 Heater motor (when fitted)   36 Fuel gauge   37 Fuel gauge tank unit   38 Flasher unit   39 Lefthand front flasher
40 Lefthand rear flasher   41 Flasher switch   42 Righthand rear flasher   43 Righthand front flasher   44 Flasher warning light
45 Windshield switch   46 Windshield wipers   47 Ignition coil   48 Distributor   49 Snap connectors
50 Terminal blocks or junction box   51 Earth connections made via cable or   52 Via fixing bolts

Cable Colour Code   B Black   U Blue   N Brown   G Green   P Purple   R Red   S Slate   W White   Y Yellow
L Light   D Dark   M Medium
When a cable has two colour code letters the first denotes the main colour and the second denotes the tracer colour

293

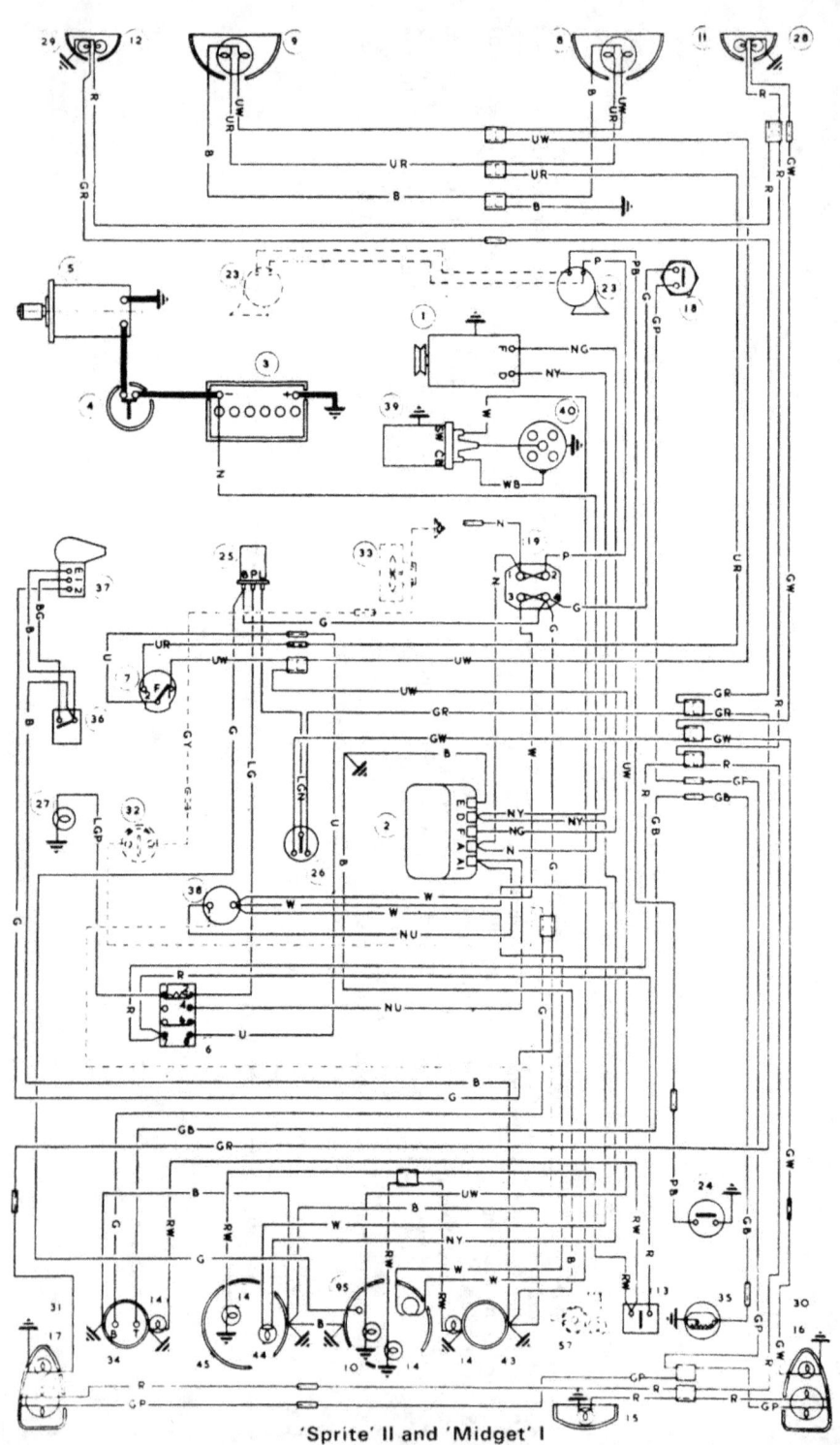

'Sprite' II and 'Midget' I

'Sprite' II and 'Midget' I

Key to 'Sprite' II: 1 Dynamo 2 Control box 3 Battery—12-volt 4 Starter switch 5 Starter motor 6 Lighting switch
7 Headlamp dip switch 8 Headlamp—righthand 9 Headlamp—lefthand 10 Main-beam warning lamp 11 Sidelamp—righthand
12 Sidelamp—lefthand 13 Panel lamps switch 14 Panel lamps 15 Number-plate illumination lamp 16 Stop and tail lamp—
righthand 17 Stop and tail lamp—lefthand 18 Stop lamp switch 19 Fuse unit 23 Horn (twin horns when fitted) *
24 Horn-push 25 Flasher unit 26 Direction indicator switch 27 Direction indicator warning lamp 28 Front flasher lamp—
righthand 29 Front flasher lamp—lefthand 30 Rear flasher lamp—righthand 31 Rear flasher lamp—lefthand
32 Heater or fresh-air motor switch * 33 Heater or fresh-air motor * 34 Fuel gauge 35 Fuel gauge tank unit
36 Windscreen wiper switch 37 Windscreen wiper motor 38 Ignition switch 39 Ignition coil 40 Distributor
43 Oil pressure gauge 44 Ignition warning lamp 45 Speedometer 57 Cigar-lighter * 95 Tachometer (impulse) (later cars)
Note: All items marked (*) fitted as optional extras—circuits shown dotted

295

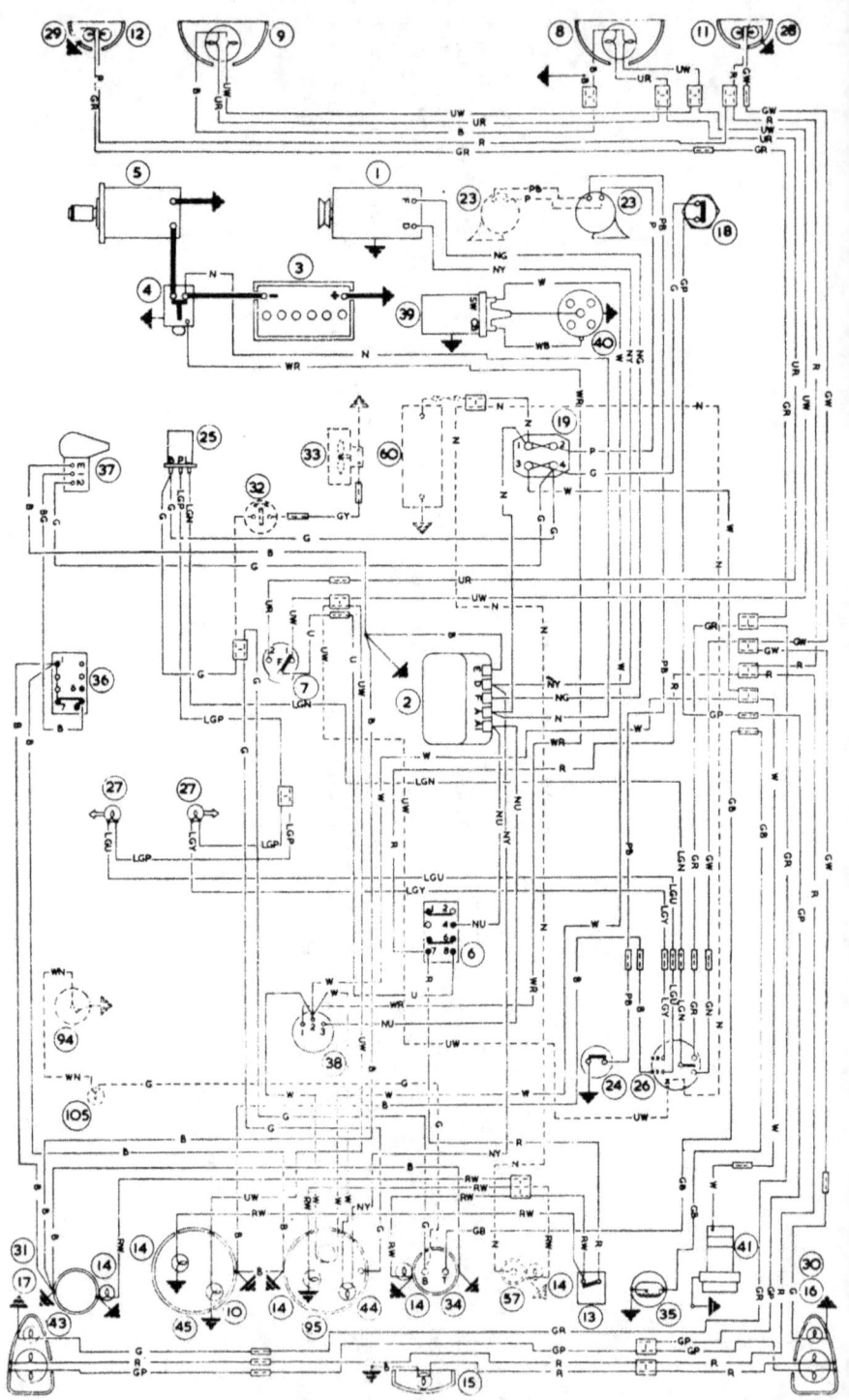

'Sprites' III and IV, 'Midgets' II and III

'Sprites' III and IV, 'Midgets' II and III

Key to 'Sprites' III: 1 Dynamo 2 Control box 3 Battery (12-volt) 4 Starter solenoid 5 Starter motor 6 Lighting switch 7 Headlight dip switch 8 Righthand headlamp 9 Lefthand headlamp 10 Main-beam warning light 11 Righthand sidelamp 12 Lefthand sidelamp 13 Panel light switch 14 Panel lights 15 Number-plate illumination lamp 16 Righthand stop and tail lamp 17 Lefthand stop and tail lamp 18 Stop light switch 19 Fuse unit (35 amps) 23 Horn (twin horns when fitted) 24 Horn-push 25 Flasher unit 26 Direction indicator switch 27 Direction indicator warning lights 28 Righthand front flasher lamp 29 Lefthand front flasher lamp 30 Righthand rear flasher lamp 31 Lefthand rear flasher lamp 32 Heater or fresh-air motor switch (when fitted) 33 Heater or fresh-air motor when fitted) 34 Fuel gauge 35 Fuel gauge tank unit 36 Windscreen wiper switch 37 Windscreen wiper motor 38 Ignition/starter switch 39 Ignition coil 40 Distributor 41 Fuel pump 43 Oil pressure gauge 44 Ignition warning light 45 Speedometer 57 Cigar lighter (illuminated) 60 Radio 94 Oil filter switch 95 Tachometer 105 Lubrication warning light

Cable Colour Code N Brown U Blue R Red P Purple G Green LG Light Green W White Y Yellow B Black
When a cable has two colour code letters the first denotes the main colour and the second denotes the tracer colour

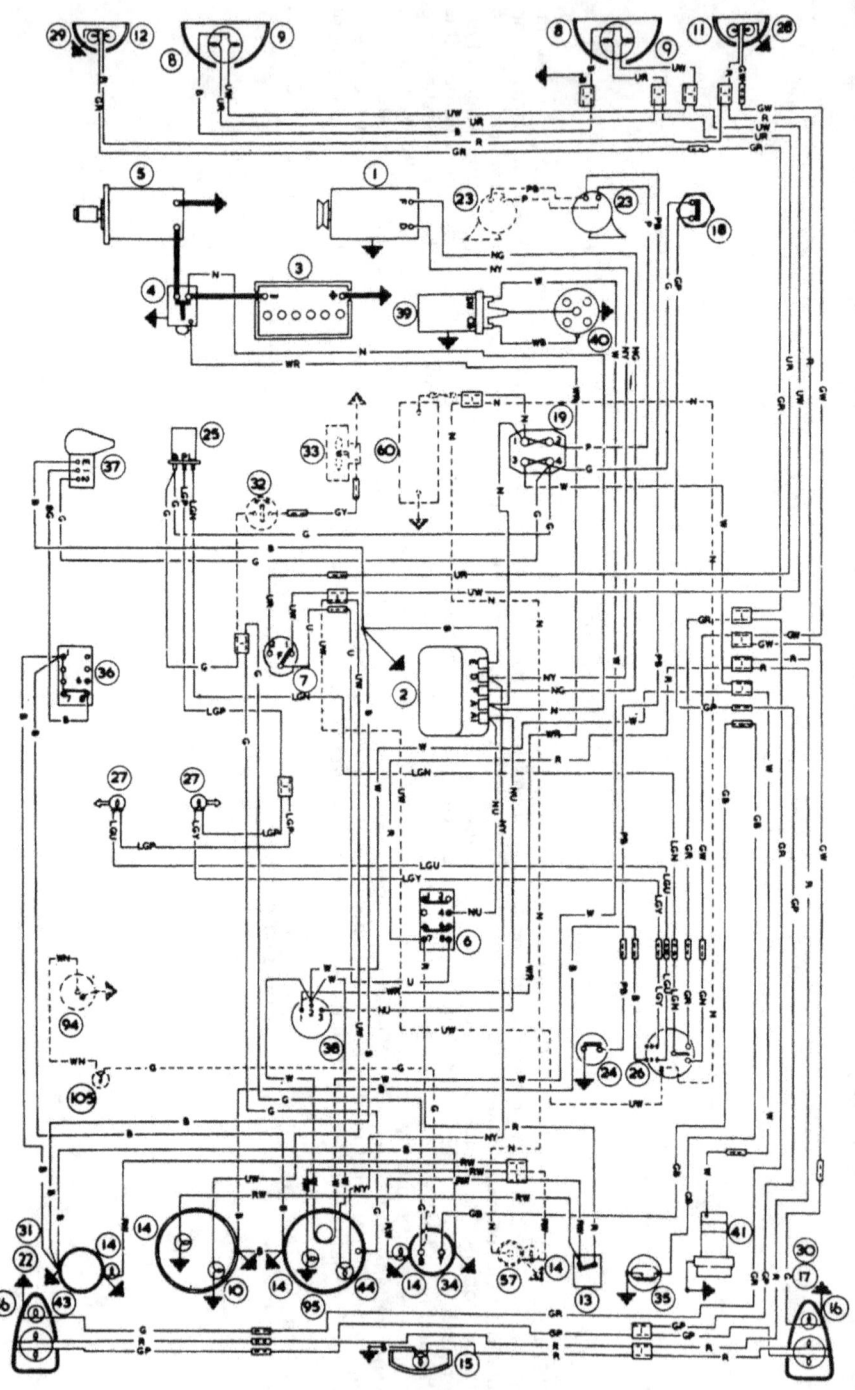

Midget III, Sprite IV, positive earth (up to 1967)

Midget III, Sprite IV, positive earth (up to 1967)

Key to Sprite IV: 1 Dynamo/alternator 2 Control box 3 Battery 4 Starter solenoid 5 Starter motor 6 Lighting switch 7 Headlamp dip switch 8 Headlamp dip beam 9 Headlamp main beam 10 Headlamp main beam warning lamp 11 Righthand parking lamp 12 Lefthand parking lamp 13 Panel lamp switch 14 Panel lamps 15 Number plate illumination lamp 16 Stop lamp 17 Righthand tail lamp 18 Stop lamp switch 19 Fuse unit 20 Interior courtesy lamp 21 Interior courtesy lamp door switch 22 Lefthand tail lamp 23 Horns 24 Horn push 25 Flasher unit 26 Direction indicator switch 27 Direction indicator warning lamp 28 Righthand front flasher lamp 29 Lefthand front flasher lamp 30 Righthand rear flasher lamp 31 Lefthand rear flasher lamp 32 Heater or fresh air motor switch 33 Heater or fresh air motor 34 Fuel gauge 35 Fuel gauge tank unit 36 Windscreen wiper switch 37 Windscreen wiper motor 38 Ignition/starter switch 39 Ignition coil 40 Distributor 41 Fuel pump 43 Oil pressure gauge 44 Ignition warning lamp 45 Headlamp flasher switch 46 Coolant temperature gauge 49 Reverse lamp switch 50 Reverse lamp 57 Cigar lighter, illuminated 60 Radio 64 Bi-metal instrument voltage stabiliser 65 Luggage compartment lamp switch 66 Luggage compartment lamp 67 Line fuse 77 Windscreen washer pump 82 Switch illumination lamp 94 Oil filter switch 95 Tachometer 105 Oil filter warning lamp 118 Combined windscreen washer and wiper switch 152 Hazard warning lamp 153 Hazard warning switch 154 Hazard warning flasher unit 159 Brake pressure warning lamp and lamp test push 160 Brake pressure failure switch 168 Ignition key audible warning buzzer 169 Ignition key audible warning door switch 170 Righthand front side marker lamp 171 Lefthand front side marker lamp 172 Righthand rear side marker lamp 173 Lefthand rear side marker lamp 198 Driver's seat belt buckle switch 199 Passenger's seat belt buckle switch 200 Passenger seat switch 201 Seat belt warning gearbox switch 202 'Fasten belts' warning light 203 Line diode 211 Heater control illumination bulb

Key to colour code: **N** Brown **U** Blue **R** Red **P** Purple **G** Green **LG** Light green **W** White **Y** Yellow **B** Black **K** Pink **O** Orange **S** Slate

When a cable has two colour code letters the first denotes the main colour and the second denotes the tracer colour

NOTE: COMPONENT IDENTIFICATION AND WIRE COLOUR CODE SHOWN ABOVE APPLIES TO ALL OF THE FOLLOWING WIRING DIAGRAMS

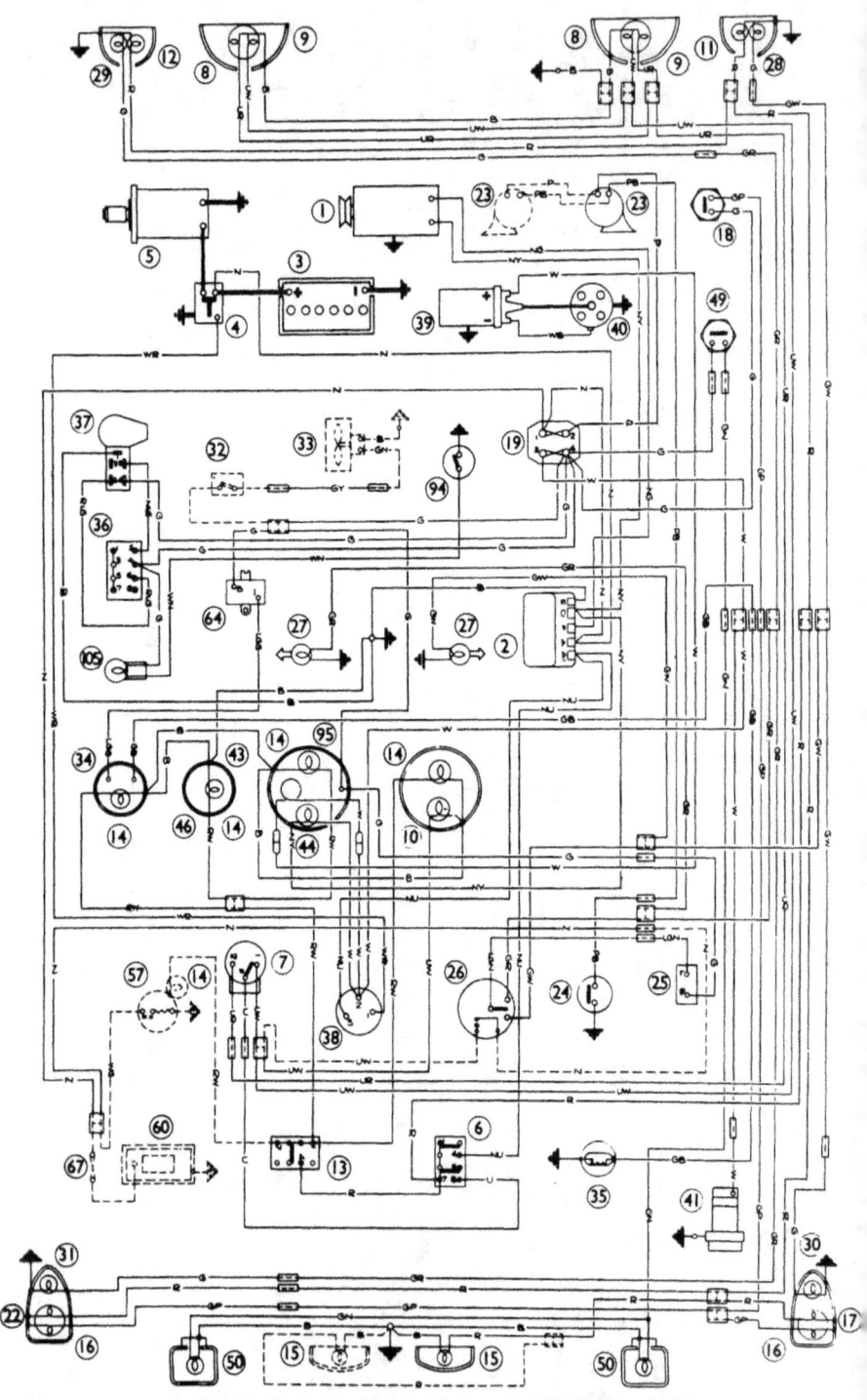

Midget III, Sprite IV, negative earth, G-AN4 60460 to 74885 and H-AN9-72041 to 85286 (1967-69) - See page 299 for KEY

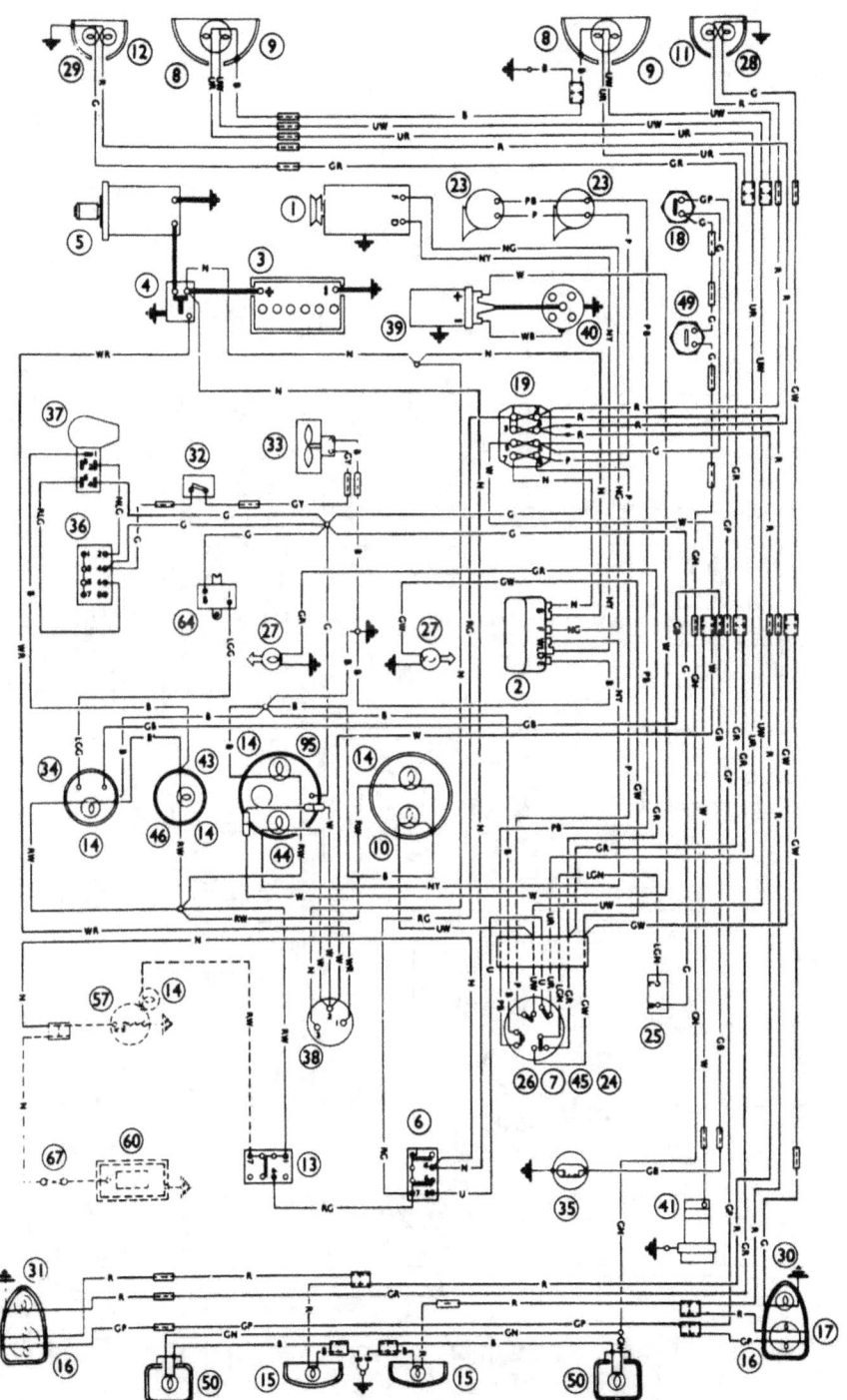

Midget III, Sprite IV, negative earth, G-AN4 and G-AN5-74886 to 89514
and H-AN10-85287 to 86302 (1969-70) - See page 299 for KEY

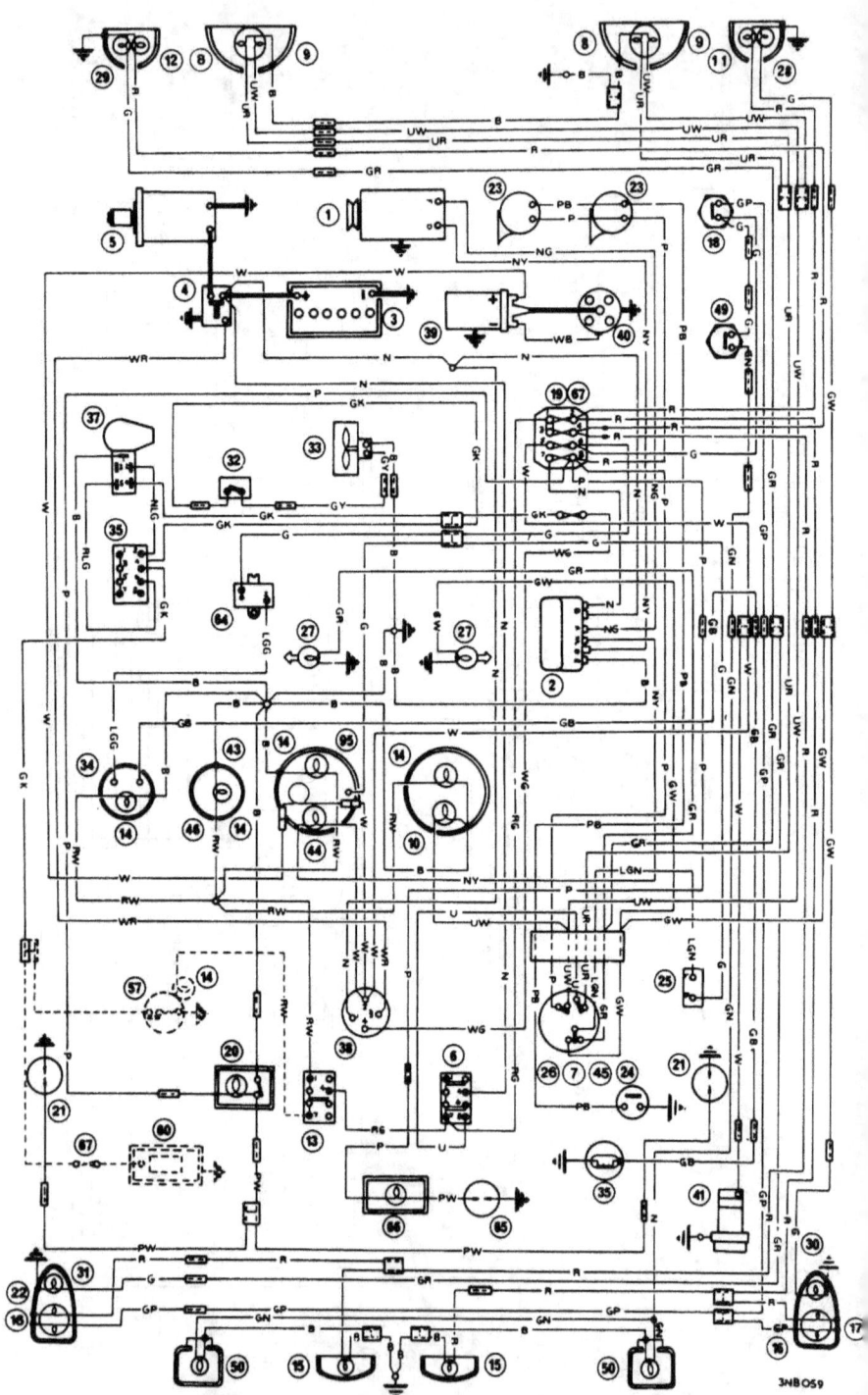

Midget III, Sprite IV, negative earth, G-AN5 89515 to 105500 and H-AN10-86303 on (1970-71) - See page 299 for KEY

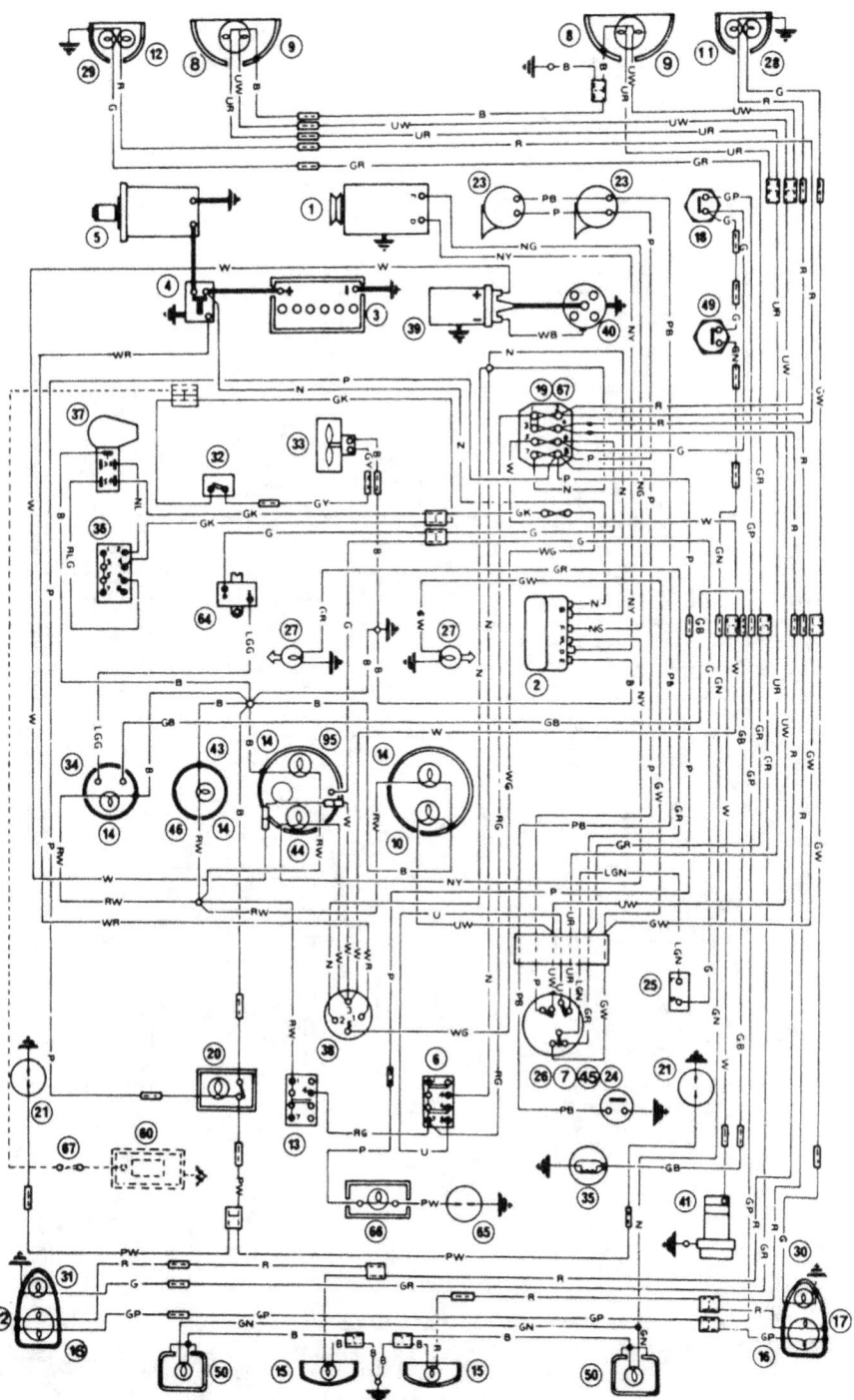

Midget III, negative earth, G-AN5-105501 to 128262 (1971-73) - See page 299 for KEY

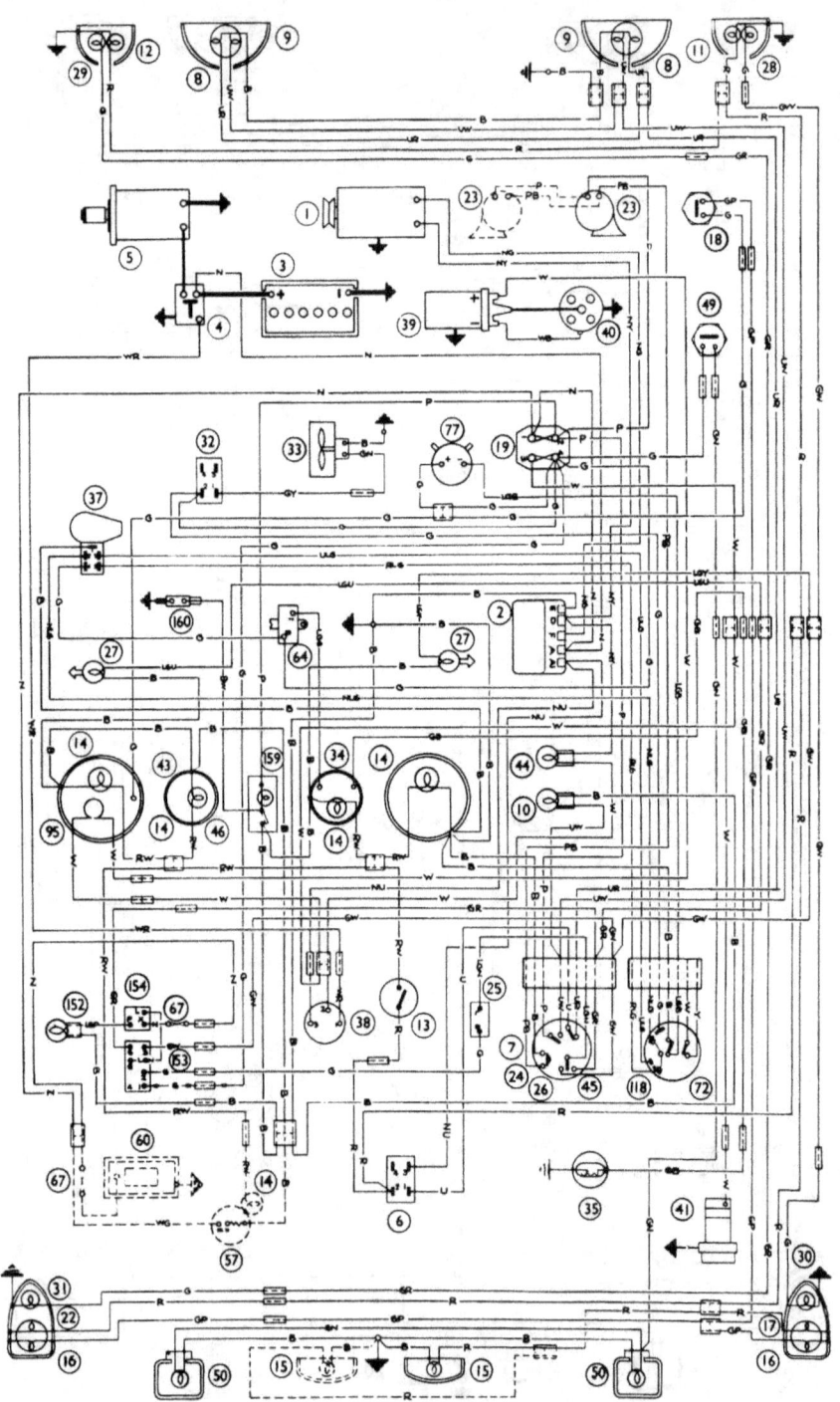

Midget III, Sprite IV, North America, negative earth, G-AN4-60460 to 66225 and HAN9-72041 to 77590 (1967-68) - See page 299 for KEY

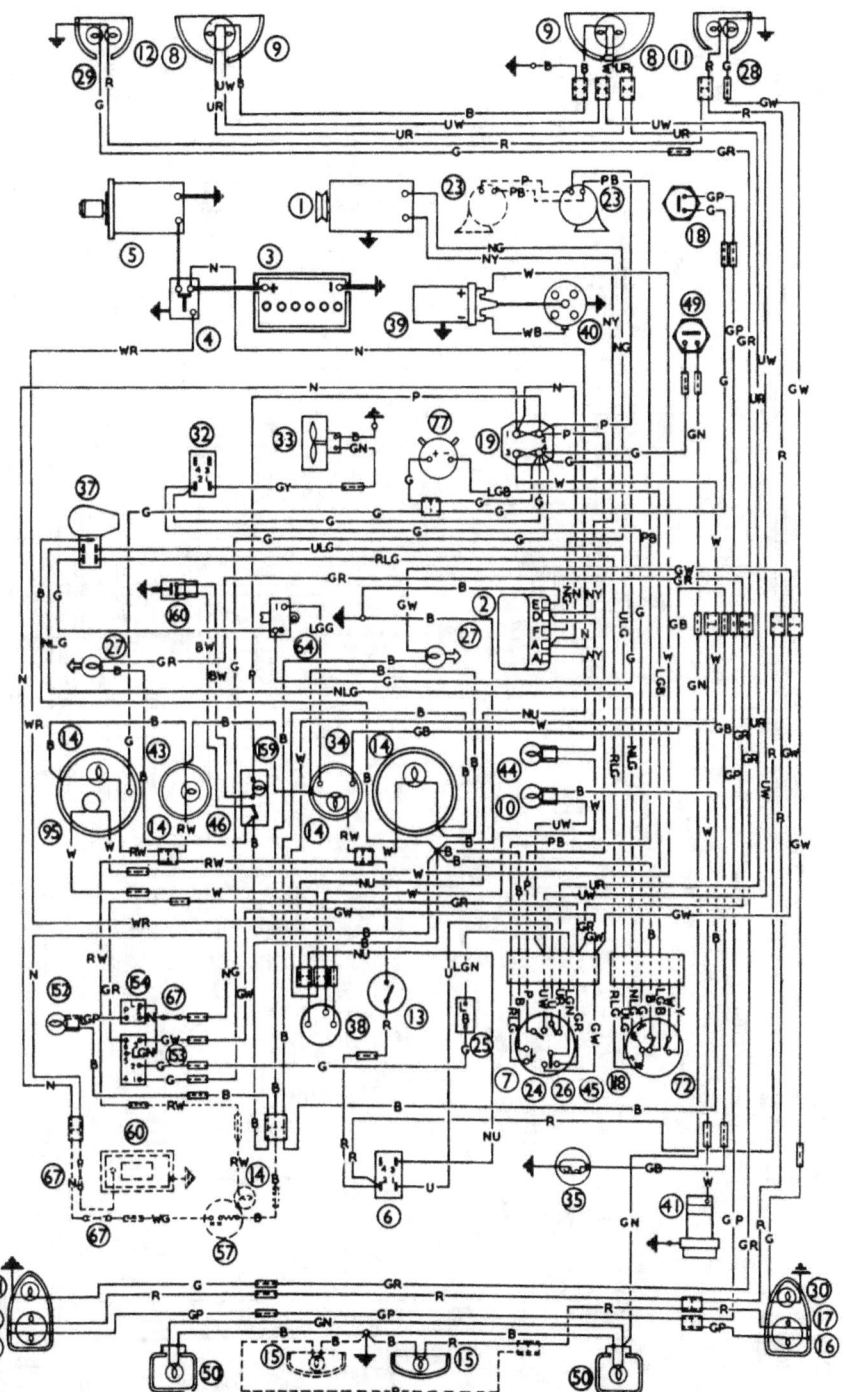

Midget III, Sprite IV, North America, negative earth, G-AN4-66226 to 74885 and H-AN9-77591 on (1968-69) - See page 299 for KEY

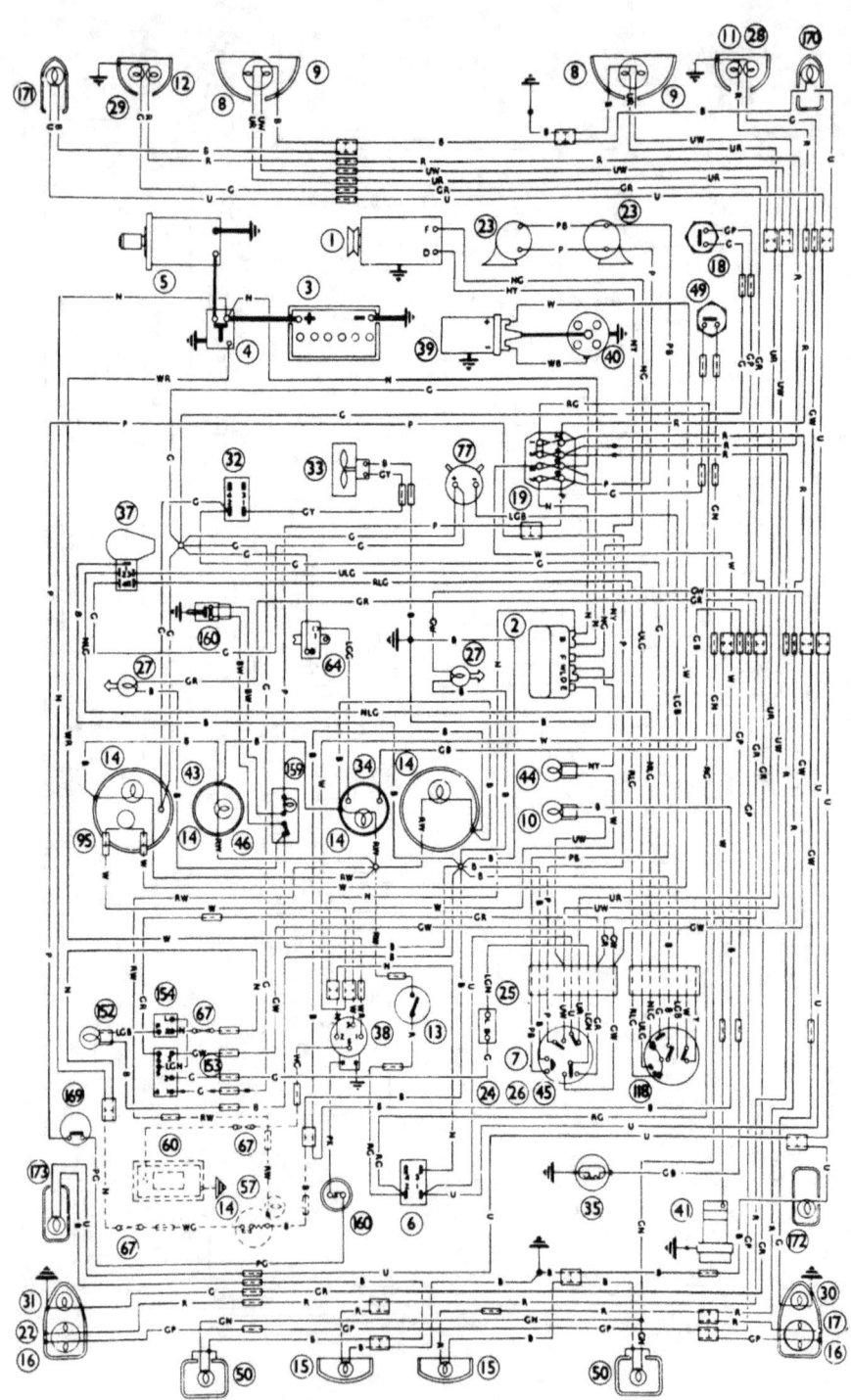

Midget III, North America, negative earth, G-AN4 and G-AN5-74886 to 89514 (1969-70) - See page 299 for KEY

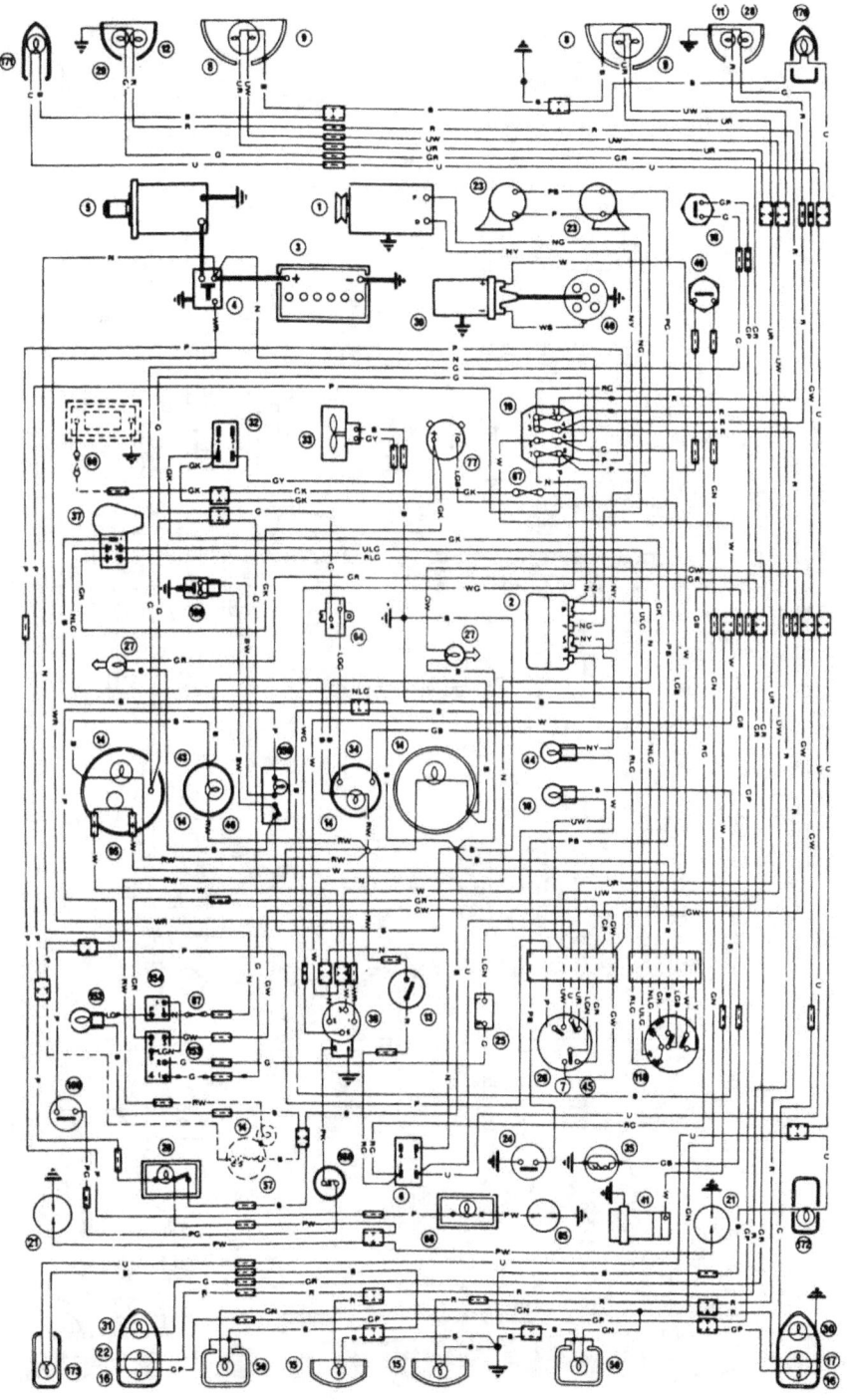

Midget III, North America, negative earth, G-AN5-89515 to 105500 (1970-71)
See page 299 for KEY

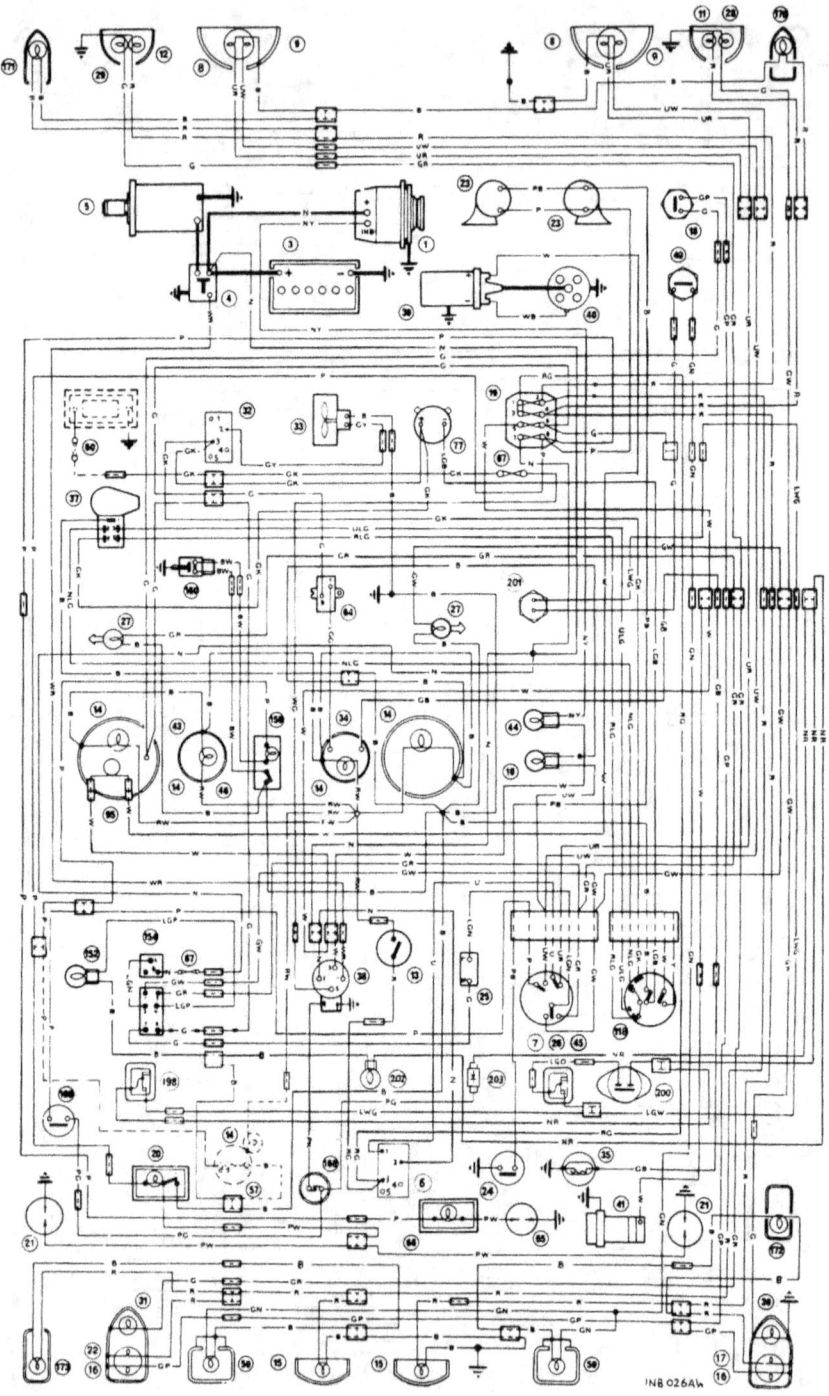

Midget III, North America, negative earth, G-AN5-105501 to 123730 (1971-72)
See page 299 for KEY

Sequential seat belt system

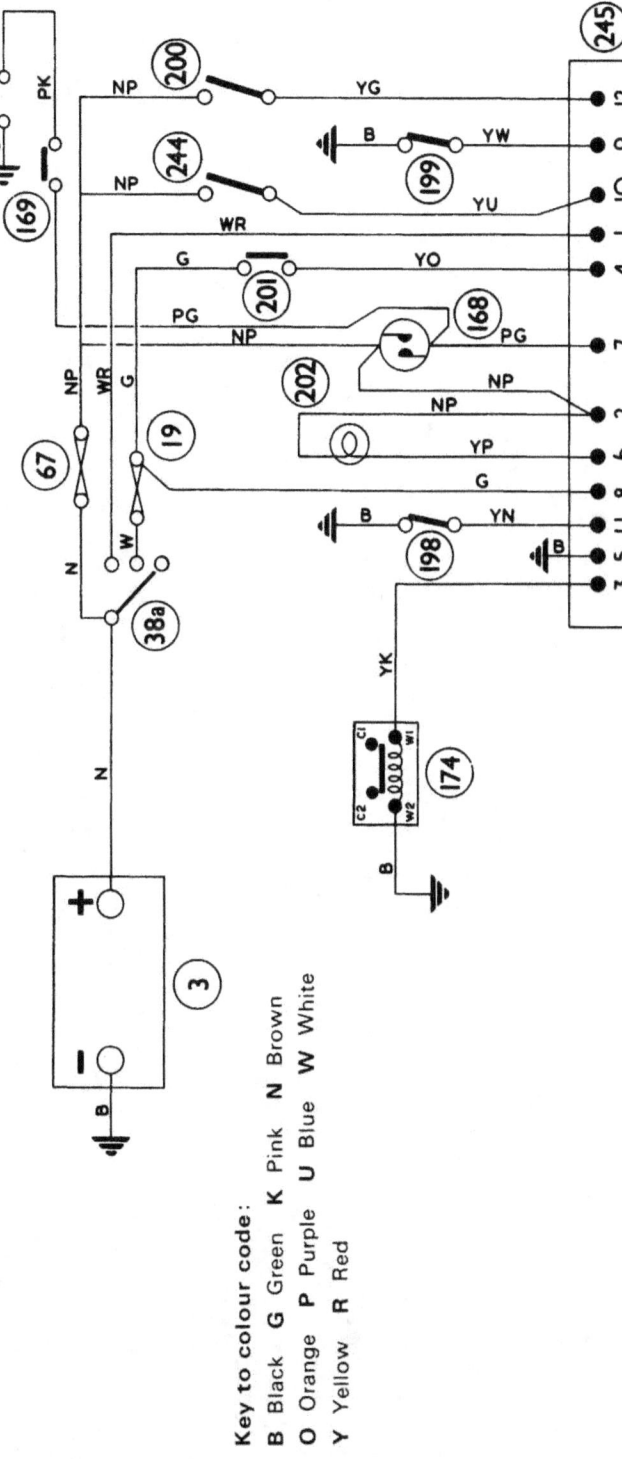

Key to colour code:
B Black G Green K Pink N Brown
O Orange P Purple U Blue W White
Y Yellow R Red

Key–seat belt system: 3 Battery 19 Fuse, 35 amps (connecting fuse box terminals 5 and 6) 38a Ignition/starter switch 38b Ignition key switch 67 Line fuse (500 milliamp) 168 Warning buzzer 169 Warning buzzer door switch 174 Starter motor relay 198 Driver's seat belt switch (normally closed) 199 Passenger's seat belt switch (normally closed) 200 Passenger's seat switch (normally open) 201 Gearbox switch (closed in gear) 202 'Fasten belts' warning lamp 244 Driver's seat switch (normally open) 245 System control unit

NOTES

INCREASING POWER

&

PERFORMANCE

Photo by Bill Norcross

INCREASING POWER AND PERFORMANCE

Before considering the steps necessary to derive increased power and performance from the BMC Sprites and Midgets, it is well to reflect on the indisputable fact that one must begin with good raw materials in order to have a good finished product. It may seem elementary to admonish the owner in this fashion, but the number of drivers who either fit high-performance equipment to unsound engines or who demand that the process be cut short of perfection is amazingly high.

Seldom does the new owner dash away from the showroom directly to his home workbench or to a specialist's shop where the car is fitted with all the modifications. Generally, it is after the fuzz has been well rubbed off that some decision is made to strive for a little more performance. And, here it is that the fat hits the fire. An automobile with 20,000 miles (32,000 km.) on the odometer which has had no service beyond major tune ups (as is ordinary) is well on its way to becoming tired. In normal service, another 10,000 miles or so can be expected before bearings need replacement and, if one will tolerate a loss of power, before even the valves require grinding.

However, to deem such an engine with 20,000 miles of service behind it suitable for modification is to practically guarantee that it will not complete the next ten thousand.

The chassis, too, is bound to be far from pristine and no detail should be overlooked in restoring it to original if there is any promise of competition or hard driving.

Therefore, the first step along the path to power is the admonition so many times expressed, yet so often disbelieved because it is so simple: **Bring everything up to stock!**

In sports car racing under rigidly enforced regulations, there are always a number of cars which consistently outperform their identical twins. Often these winners are "protested" by other entrants who believe that the rules have been subverted. But, in nearly 100% of the cases, the vehicles are, indeed, "stock". This very adherence to the letter of the specifications is the secret.

Because of manufacturing tolerances, even selective assembly, were it practiced wholly, would result in a perfect car only once in a million times. But rest assured, that car would take the measure of any other unit coming off the assembly line.

This is not to imply that there can be no improvement on the manufacturer's design or workmanship, far from it, but is a reminder that the builder has set up a great many specifications to which we can hew without doubt. In the former scheme of things with Club racing where no improving the breed was permitted at all, establishing these specifications within the engine and chassis was the only way to secure any advantage . . . to create the one-in-a-million vehicle, in effect.

The past tense is used in this connection because the major sanctioning organizations in the United States have announced that with this 1963 season a certain amount of breed improving will be admitted. To those who do not plan to compete in circuit events, this may seem of less than passing interest, but actually, here is where the keenest talents will be focused and from these efforts will come the moderate modifications which result in a great deal of performance.

Such modifications have been permitted for a number of seasons in Southern California . . . the home of speed shops and hot rods . . . and the racing Sprites from Los Angeles and environs have amazed onlookers with their ability to trounce Alfa Romeos, MGs and other vehicles of much greater horsepower rating and cost. These cars were well along in development when this country got its first look at a "real" racing Sprite — that is to say, the competition cars which Donald Healey brought to Sebring in 1959 — but then the factory modifications were well examined by the local experimenters and improved upon in many cases. I had the pleasure of becoming intimately acquainted with the Sprite team at Sebring and of doing one of the longest road tests ever put upon a racing car when Charles Weber and I drove two of the BMC team vehicles to Los Angeles following the race.

Beginning with that close association, Sprite developments have never ceased to interest me and I have fleshed out my own experience with those of the top mechanics who specialize in small engines and those of the drivers who seem to agree on the best methods to use in making the car handle. These opinions are relayed herein.

After this small diversion, let us drift back to the original premise: **Begin with a sound automobile.** If your car has a number of miles showing on the odometer it may be either "just broken in", or broken up. Whatever the condition, have a try at simulating ideal specs.

In reference to **ultimate development** of the engine, it is, of course, necessary to completely disassemble the unit and perform some machine work to establish these truths. Take the cylinder head for instance; here the combustion chambers must be equalized absolutely. The deck height of the pistons must be established exactly and the mating surfaces of the head and block made parallel. A parallel relationship between block surface and crankshaft centerline is also a requirement. All of which calls for align boring of mainbearing webs, surface milling or grinding of the block and careful spot grinding of the combustion chambers.

If your budget will not encompass these machine shop operations, then, you must, by necessity, make do with less precision. But, be assured that the healthiest and longest-lived engines will have been stripped to the bare block and worked as though they were rough castings.

This may sound discouraging, but it does not imply that nothing can be done. All of us sometimes settle for less than the very best. You should not settle for less than a first class valve job before beginning to work on the engine, however. Even assuming that your vehicle is straight from the works and that the preservative has scarcely been removed from the brightwork, do a valve job.

We are assuming that no other mechanical portion of the engine requires attention, that it is sound and in good order. We are also assuming that you have taken advantage of the small, non-mechanical aids to sharp tuning such as using 10-30 oil, rather than a straight 20 or 30 weight. Presumably you have also run a molybdenum di-sulfide oil additive for one oil change period, freed up all moving parts, wheel bearings, U-joints, etc., and are using Castrol 'R' in the gearbox (30 wt. for colder climates, 40 for hotter areas). A wide range lubricant such as Kendall SCL (80/90) should be in the differential and wheel alignment should be exact. A Lucas sport coil can also be fitted to ensure adequate spark at high rpm.

At this juncture, then, you are ready to begin physical improvements.

NOTE: Consult the latest competition regulations before making any alterations to the engine or chassis. This especially applies to SCCA events.

Since it is such a simple matter to remove the cylinder head, take it off and perform the following operations: (Refer to appropriate section for details).

(1) Remove valves and valve springs, rocker arms and shaft.
(2) Establish the length of the valves from head to tip of stem as being identical by grinding the stems to agree with the shortest individual valve.
(3) Check the stem-to-guide clearance and establish it at the maximum recommended by the factory: .0025" inlet; .003" exhaust. If you do not have access to the necessary micrometers, a rule of thumb is that the valves should drop freely through the guides of their own weight. Excessive clearance, naturally, results in greater oil consumption, smoking and the like. If you are in doubt, take the head to an automotive machine shop and have the parts in question measured.
(4) Check the springs (or have them checked) for equal length and tension. Throw away the weak sisters and obtain new ones. If you have a Sprite, obtain Mark II springs (88 lbs. closed).
(5) Grind the valves. If you take the head to a shop to have the grinding done by machine, nonetheless hand lap the individual valves into their seats to a 1° interference fit. Another rule of thumb: When you drop the valve onto its seat from half stem height, it should be a trifle resistive to being pulled off the seat, as though it wants to stick.

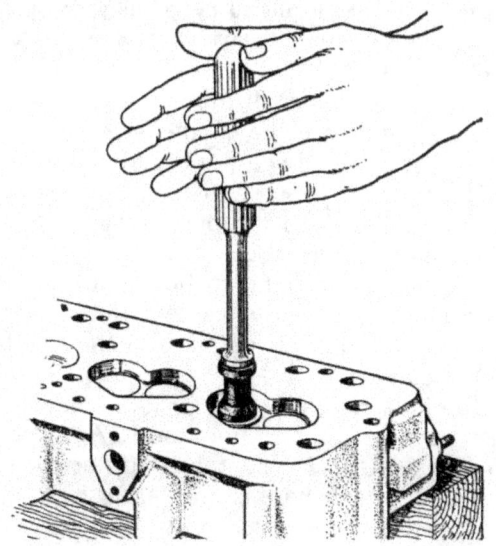

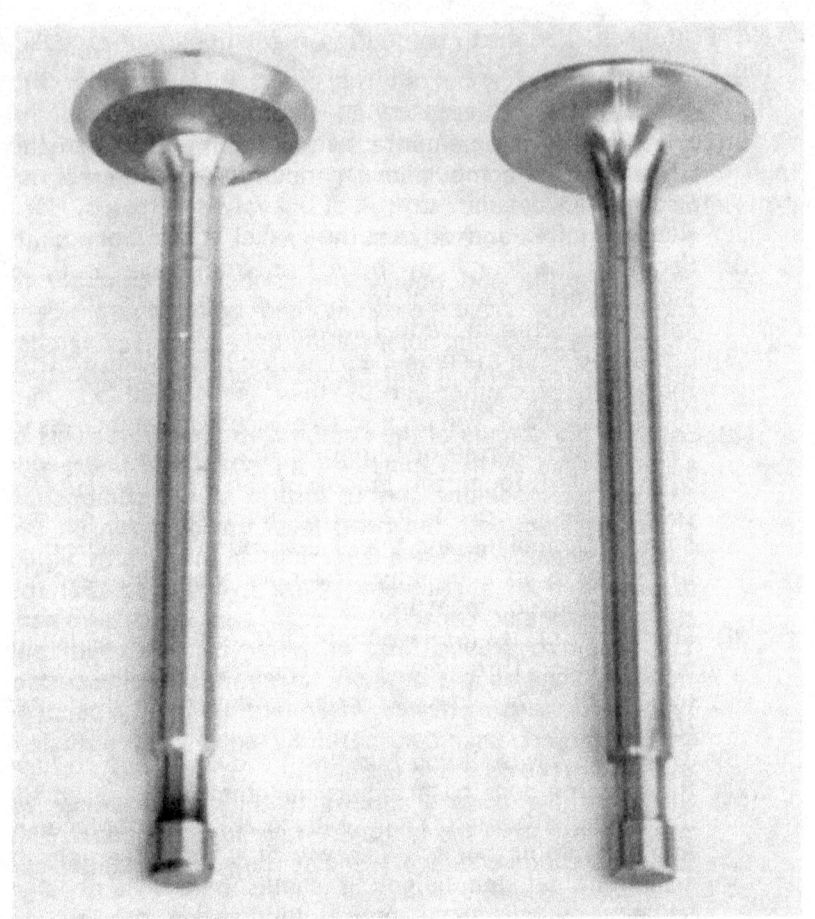

Optional valve, right, has been lightened by grinding and polishing. Stem is blended into head which has been thinned. Improved gas flow and lighter reciprocating weight are the benefits.

At this point you can re-install the valves and rocker assembly, replace the head and tune the engine — with a close to Zero dollar expenditure. However, if you want to spend a few dollars, if you find it necessary to have some of the above work done in a shop or if you have access to a flexible-shaft grinder, the following operations should be performed:

(1) For the Sprite, bring it up to Mk. II valve specifications by reaming out the inlet valve seats to accommodate the 1.156" Mk. II inlet valve, an over-the-counter part at any BMC dealer.

(1A) Obtain optional valves (part #Q 2494 inlet and Q 2495 exhaust. Or, larger valves from the 1275 cc engine can be used (part #12G 941 for intake and part #12G 1322 for exhaust). Note that there is a different method of holding these valves to the spring, so use split cotters 88G 459.

These valves should be polished and lightened (refer to photo). This is about all the combustion chamber will stand, and it is necessary to carefully rout around the valves to provide clearance between valve head and the sidewall of the combustion chamber so that flow will not be impaired and the purpose of big valves defeated. However, do not enlarge such that the gasket is overlapped.

(2) Carefully grind and polish the combustion chamber to eliminate any valve pocketing and break sharp edges around the sparkplug hole. (Study the accompanying photos.) Use restraint, it will be necessary to grind further to equalize the chambers.

(3) Equalize the volume of the combustion chambers. This is accomplished by first, plugging the sparkplug holes with soft wax or modelling clay to form a closed combustion chamber. Then with the head level upside down on the bench, carefully fill each chamber, in turn, with liquid dispensed from a graduated glass cylinder so that the cubic centimeter capacity of each can be determined. Engine oil, hydraulic fluid or water can be used, any liquid, as long as it is possible to read the level accurately in the dispensing device. After determining the capacity of the **largest** chamber, carefully polish out sufficient metal from the others to equal it.

(4) Grind out the ports according to the line drawings reprinted here from the factory's stage tuning manual. This is the condition of Stage 5.

In performing this grinding operation, take care that the port is not shifted. That is, remove an equal amount from both sides of the port wall because the wall is fairly thin at one point.

(5) Update the Sprite by fitting inlet manifold Part #Q 2344 (same as MK II) and two SU H-2 carburetors.

(6) Match the manifold ports with the head ports by grinding as necessary to ensure a smooth gas flow.

The optional 1½" SU carburetors can be installed, of course, but unless you are prepared to go considerably further with modifications, they will not represent a good investment.

(7) Have the block-mating surface of the head milled .030" to establish its true condition and to restore the compression ratio lost by the cleaning up process in the combustion chambers.

You can now install the rocker assembly and valves, refit the head to the block and be reasonably assured that it is about as efficient a unit as possible.

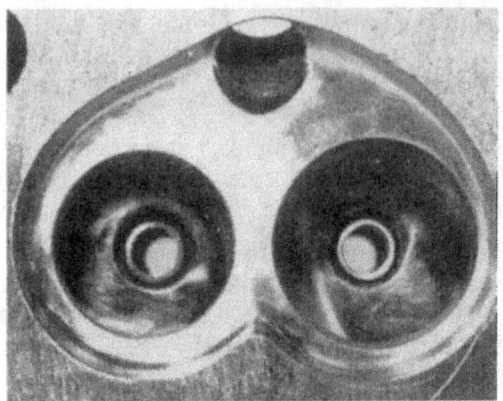

Ported and partially polished, the head is yet to be domed. Notice the chamber configuration. Bronze guides are flush.

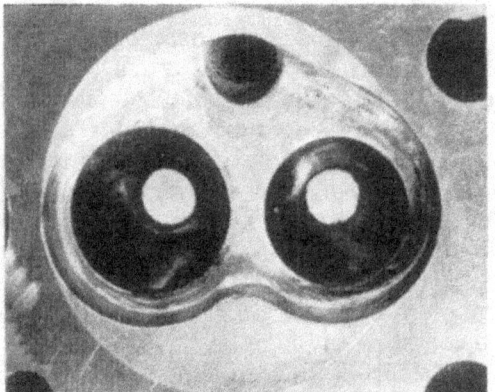

With the head surface-milled .090-in., the chamber is domed to provide piston clearance. Compression will be 13-to-1.

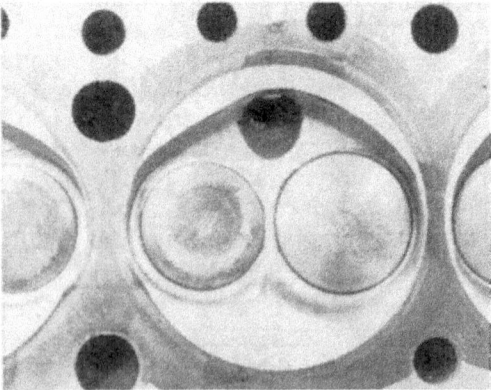

Intake valves of 1-9/32 inch, exhaust valves of 1-5/32-inch diameters are installed, then numbered to match seats.

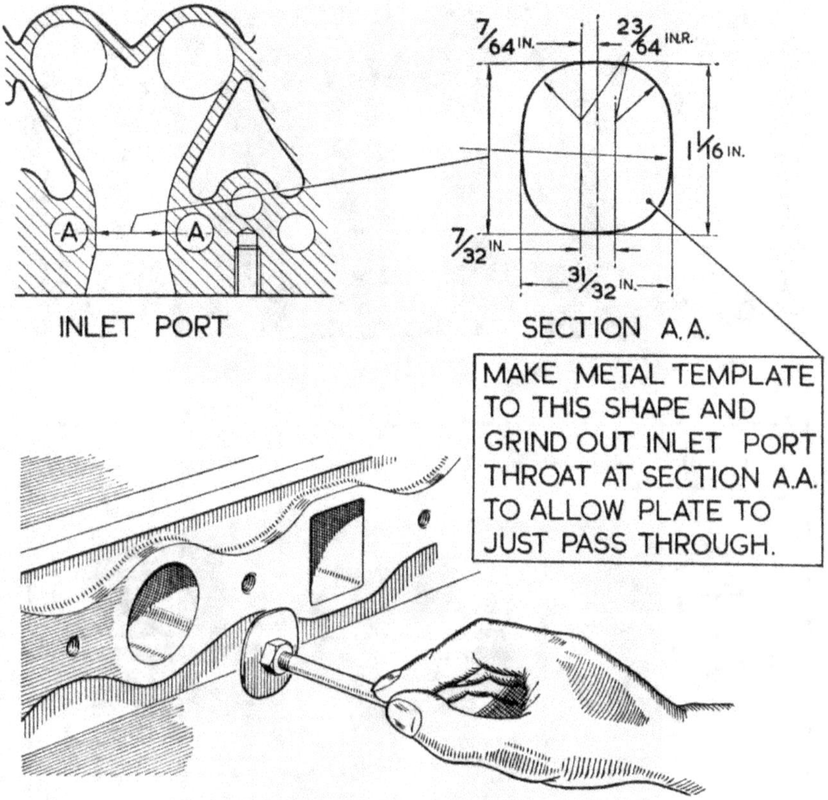

Fig. 1. Inlet port template.

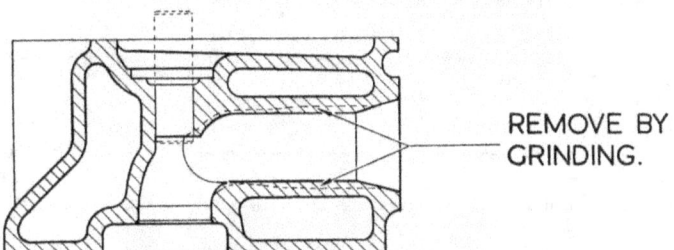

Fig. 2. Section through the inlet port.

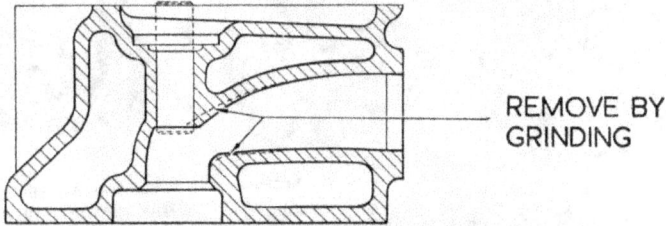

Fig. 3. Section through the exhaust port.

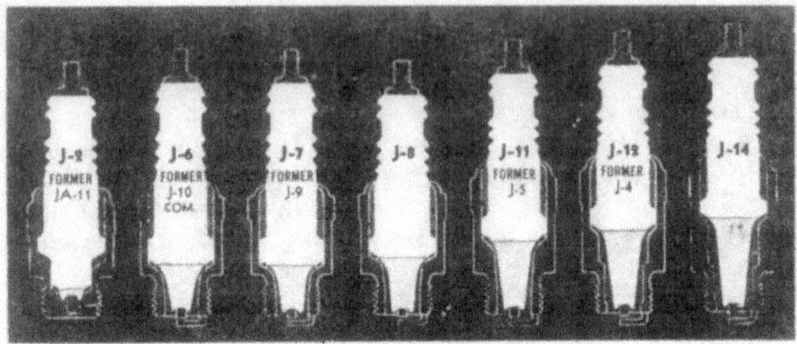

—*Heat range of Champion spark plugs. The plug on the left is the coldest, the one on the right, the hottest.*

PROPER HEAT RANGE APPLICATION after appreciable operation, is shown below:

REGULAR FUELS

Rusty brown to grayish tan powdery deposit on firing end of plug; normal degree of electrode erosion.

LEADED FUELS

White powdery or yellowish glazed deposit on firing end of plug; normal degree of electrode erosion.

NOTE: Deposits characteristic of leaded fuels, sometimes called "encrustments", do not interfere materially with spark plug operation, and should merely be cleaned off at regular service intervals.

WORN-OUT PLUG

Caused by normal service beyond life of plug. Spark plugs should be replaced every 10,000 miles for maximum economy and performance.

PLUGS TOO HOT FOR THE TYPE OF SERVICE GENERALLY APPEAR AS FOLLOWS:

PLUGS TOO COLD for the type of service are shown below:

OIL FOULED

Wet, sludgy deposit on firing end of plug; negligible degree of electrode erosion.

GAS FOULED

Dry, fluffy deposit on firing end of plug; minor degree of electrode erosion.

White, burned or blistered insulator nose; badly burned and corroded electrodes.

Horsepower will have been increased notably in the upper range through these modifications and you will still have relatively unchanged low speed characteristics if carburetor tuning is carried out thoroughly.

A bit more richness than that which is tolerable for economy can be employed in setting up the carburetors. The great latitude of the SU jet needles makes it generally possible to obtain it without deviating from the normal needles. Richness in the upper range is most desirable if hard driving is contemplated and the policy of most tuners is to richen until the sparkplugs begin to reflect the condition in a definite manner.

If you are not familiar with the method of reading sparkplugs, consult the accompanying chart to re-acquaint yourself with the tip appearances which reflect various conditions. The proper method of taking a plug check for the tuner who is preparing a car for the street, is to warm up the engine, then switch to a new set of plugs of the designated heat range. Use a torque wrench to make sure the gasket is properly crushed. Drive the car away smartly and take it for a run where it is possible to keep the engine in the power range (3,000 & up) for most of the time. Five miles is not too far . . . the equivalent of three laps on most circuits, in other words. Coast it in with the engine running at 3,000 rpm, flick off the ignition switch and close the throttle simultaneously. Thus the plugs will not have been accidentally fouled by slow running and their true reading obscured.

A note of caution on a recent development: It has been noted that the new Autolite plugs do not show the light tan insulator characteristic of correct mixture and heat range. Rather, they remain white, even after prolonged use. The only discernible change when mixture is correct is a slight bluing of the center electrode tip. A full rich mixture, one which can easily be tolerated is denoted by a fine black line such as might be drawn by a pencil, forming at bottom of the porcelain. Overly rich results in a discoloration of the porcelain. Autolite AG 22 is the normal heat range for this engine, AG 32 the next colder range, such as might be used in competition or with a more modified engine supporting higher compression. (Equivalent to N5 and N3 Champion designations.)

If additional richness in the upper range obtained by dropping the normal needle results in an intolerable rich condition for slow running and where much traffic driving is encountered, it may be wise to install a platinum tip plug (such as Lodge, or NGK) with a wider heat range to cater to this operational pattern. Selecting jet needles with a sharper taper near the tip but with the same butt measurements is another solution.

"Making a needle" is a much heard phrase, wherein the amateur mechanic tapers the jet needle to his own specifications to attain a mixture he deems advisable. This procedure smacks of a great deal of effrontery when it is considered how much research has been carried out by the SU carburetor concern over the past half-century to establish the needle contours listed in their catalog but with an engine dynamometer as a research tool, you can alter needles to change the fuel/air ratio at any point along the curve. If the needle which appears to be most suitable does not happen to be available, it is possible to reshape it to one designated in the catalog, or by the cut-and-try method. Needless to say this is not recommended procedure for the novice.

Having completed the work on the cylinder head, the owner who wants to extract the most power without going into a complete disassembly process will fit the optional dual exhaust system consisting of a manifold and down pipe (Part #AHA5448) a second exhaust pipe (AHA 5449), silencer (muffler) (AHA 98) and the necessary clips to support the second pipe (AHA 5450).

This set up actually does more for the engine than most such kits. The normal manifold is pretty restrictive and has the added disadvantage of over-scavenging the center pair of cylinders which share a siamese port.

If the option is not easily obtainable locally, try those firms listed in this section which stock a good supply of competition parts, or your neighborhood muffler shop can probably fabricate a unit using the photo as a guide if it has had no previous experience with this engine.

To proceed from this point requires removal of the engine from the chassis. Depending on how much the owner wishes to spend, how extensive his ability as a mechanic or his access to machining equipment, the A series engine can be modified to almost any degree resulting in up to 95 horsepower at 7,000 rpm! At least this is the rating attained by the 1100 cc units developed by Joe Huffaker at the Competition Department of BMC in San Francisco.

Huffaker has probably spent more time in experimenting with the A series engine than anyone in the United States . . . and has the results to show for it.

BMC, active in Formula Jr. racing since its inception, has had considerable success with the A series engine against its popular Ford counterpart which actually has a superior head design and a more modern bore-stroke ratio to begin with. Again this is because of meticulous attention to detail and a willingness to "take a chance on the untried", as Huffaker says.

Chick Vandagriff, of Hollywood Sports Cars who supports BMC product racing to the hilt in his area has another premise which should be crocheted into a wall motto for every garage: "Never take anything for granted". (In his shop only one mechanic works on each engine brought in for overhaul or modification. In this way there is never an opportunity to utter the ghastly phrase: "I thought somebody else did it".)

So, be guided by the experience of others but never assume that because someone says it's so that it is so, or that it cannot be done.

Relating this to the A engine, the maximum factory sanctioned overbore is .040" resulting in a cylinder diameter of 2.518", somewhat short of the 1100 ccs permitted under Formula Jr. rules. So, Huffaker bores out the block to 2.75" then sleeves the bore down again to 2.65". With the stock 3" stroke this gives a displacement of 1096 ccs. The fact that the overboring runs right out of wall and into the water jacket at times does not disturb Huffaker nor make the sleeve job less successful. This is the best way to get maximum displacement . . . which in turn means maximum power.

Note: If you are oriented toward club racing, then .030" overbore is the limit if you want to stay in the displacement class.

Pistons for the big 2.65 bore are available from BMC, San Francisco, but they are domed, which requires a milling job on the heads. Presumably matching heads are also for sale, although at this time only complete engines have been sold.

Optional 9.3 to 1 compression ratio piston is flat top compared with dished normal Sprite 8.3 to 1 type.

If you prefer to bore to some intermediate diameter or refrain from using the domed BMC pistons, proprietary pistons are to be had in any dimension. For example Jahns Quality Piston Co., Los Angeles, manufactures standard compression (8.3 to 1) 9 to 1 and 11 to 1 pistons in any bore size you may wish to specify. The charge for this custom service is $1.00 above the regular price per piston. Part # is 273-H on these pistons.

Optional pistons from the factory with 9.3 to 1 ratio (Part #2A 946) make some difference in the Sprite, to be sure, but if you are going into a complete tear down anyway, it is more rewarding to fit the 11 to 1 ratio in standard bore or oversize. The Jahns pistons are grooved for two 3/32" compression rings and one 5/32" oil ring. These are American sizes which makes the selection of rings somewhat easier and more convenient . . . that is to say, a wide range of types is to be found in almost any neighborhood parts house. When installing any pistons, check their height in relation to the block at top dead center and be sure they are identical.

The disassembly process gives the owner a chance to determine if critical dimensions and clearances in his engine are correct and to restore them to specification. Depending on the use to which he expects to put the engine, he should also spend some time and money making sure the block is correctly finish-machined. As mentioned in the introductory part of this section, the best engines have been treated as though they had been taken off the assembly line before finish machining: "Don't take anything for granted".

If your plan is to place the engine under extreme stress, as in racing, the crankshaft should be magnafluxed to determine if there are any hidden flaws which would result in fracture. If it is sound, have it shot-peened, the main and rod journals polished to .001" under minimum and micro-finished.

Connecting rods should also be lightened and polished as well as shot-peened after magnafluxing. These two components are the weak link in the A Series chain. Not too weak, if proper attention is paid to rev limits, oil pressure and temperature, but capable of giving trouble if unattended to.

Balancing of the assembly by first equalizing rod and piston weights, then balancing the crank statically and dynamically, with and without flywheel and clutch, is mandatory.

The Sprite-Midget flywheel can stand a considerable reduction in weight which contributes mightily toward acceleration and top end performance. An optional flywheel (Part #Q 2348) has long been listed in the catalog but few if any ever reached these shores. You might try. Or, you can ship your flywheel and clutch to Weber Speed Equipment Co., Santa Ana, California, who specialize in removing excess poundage from the flywheel. Here it will also be faced on the same type of machine as used by the works and balanced with the clutch which will, in the meantime, have been beefed up with stiffer springs or additional springs. The cost for this worthwhile improvement runs around $30.00.

Increased power, naturally means more work for the clutch and the beefed up type or the factory competition model (Q 2349) is a requirement for any modified engine.

In re-assembling the engine, establish more clearance between piston and wall by honing out the bore. .005" is generally accepted as sufficient for the stock diameter. Makers of pistons will recommend clearances for their products.

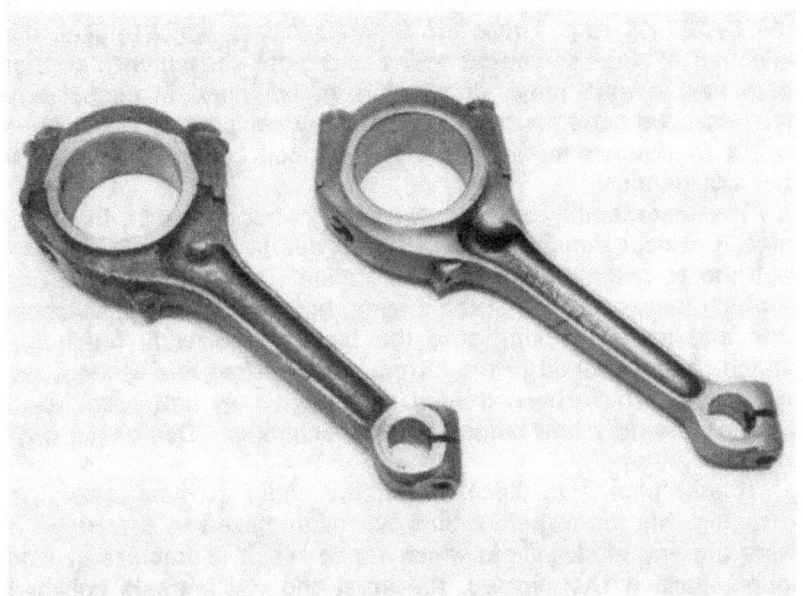

Relatively heavy connecting rods should be lightened and polished, shot-peened and magnafluxed if competition with "full house" engine is contemplated.

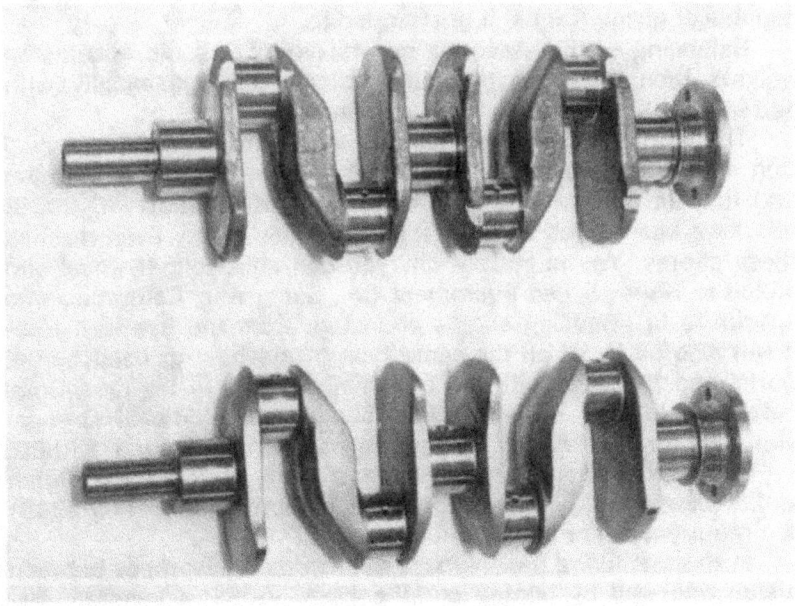

Same treatment is accorded to crankshaft as connecting rods. In addition to lightening and strengthening, perfect balance is a necessity.

Lightened and balanced flywheel has material taken from both faces. Beefed up competition clutch has nine springs in place of six found on normal part.

The subject of a camshaft is tricky. We can do no better than reprint a segment of a survey which I made for SPORTS CAR GRAPHIC and advise the owner to think well on what he expects from his engine before purchasing.

In presenting this camshaft discussion, however, it might be well to point out that the successful racing Sprites on the West Coast have retreated somewhat from the high revving plateau that they strove for at one time. Whereas the winning cars in the past were being turned to 7500 rpm consistently, the aim now is to peak at 6500 rpm and limit the engine to that figure. Longevity is the reward and finishing more races the pay off. "You can't win if you don't finish" is an old but true gibe. Keeping the tachometer from twisting off the dial is now considered extremely important.

In Formula Jr. or where a teardown after each race is possible, then ultra-high revs can be tolerated with the full knowledge that you are on the ragged edge. For the street, of course, a 6,500 rpm limit is extremely sensible.

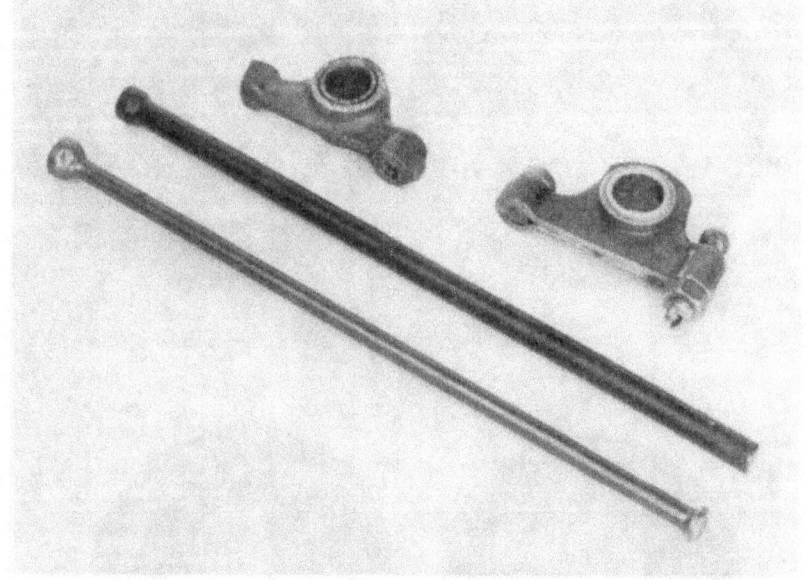

Owners of late model Sprites and Midgets may prefer to substitute lightened forged rocker arms from earlier engine for pressed steel type. Light pushrods are sold by many cam grinders.

Employing a camshaft which alters the torque-horsepower curve to peak at a lower figure is the answer, of course. Changing rear end gearing to comply with this nex maximum has been one of the other speed secrets of the winning cars. Differential assemblies, as well as ring and pinion sets, are offered by the factory ranging from 3.73 to 5.375. Choosing the right one is, once more,

AUSTIN HEALEY SPRITE

Cam	Duration					Lift @ Lash	Notes
Factory stock incl. 1961	230	5	45	40	10	.280" @ .019"	Good for economy. Low end satisfactory with improved engine.
Factory Mk II	230 in. 252 ex.	5	45	51	21	.312" @ .021"	Better top & increased power through full range with factory-improved engine. Good street cam for fully improved engine.
Factory option Part #2A. 948	252	16	56	51	21	.310" @ .015"	Street-competition. Idle rough, low end sacrifice. HD springs required.
Factory option Part #Q 2629	280	20	80	50	50	.380" @ .015"	Competition. Long course. Still drivable on street. Rough idle & poor low end torque. HD springs required.
Potvin X95	278	31	67	70	28	.411" @ .014"	Competition-street. Moderate engine improvement required. Kit not necessary.
Potvin X 105	280	30	70	70	30	.411" @ .015"	Competition. Improved engine mandatory. Strong from 3,000 up. Kit not required.
Weber "Full Race" CTS	263	25	58	58	25	.330" @ .019"	Competition-street. Idle tolerable, 6500 rpm with good power. Improved engine, required.
Howard A-11	252	17	55	55	17	.324" @ .014" in. .016" ex.	Comes in at 2300 with slightly rough idle. Strong to 7200 rpm.
Howard A-11A	261	20	61	61	20	.330" @ .017" in. .020" ex.	Competition cam with good mid-range and a top end to 7400 rpm.
Howard A-16B	264	22	62	62	22	.330" @ .017" in. .020" ex.	3800-8000 rpm range. Strictly a track cam used with modified engine.
Isky MM-3	252	16	56	56	16	.320" @ .012" in. .014" ex.	Street-competition. Low end impaired but strong acceleration over 3000. Improve engine, kit advised. Springs req.
Isky MM-32	257 in. 260 ex.	18	59	60	20	.325" @ .016" in. .019" ex.	Competition-street. Rough idle. Power comes on at 3500. Rev limit 7500 with improved engine. Kit required.
Isky MM-55	260	20	60	60	20	.325" @ .016" in. .019" ex.	Competition-Form. Jr. Range: 4000 to 8000. Improved engine, kit required.
Racer Brown 244-A	295	40	75	79	36	.370" @ .017"	Competition-Form Jr. Fast course. Improved engine only. Kit advised.
Racer Brown 268-A	276	26	70	74	22	.415" @ .017"	Competition. Hi lift for hi revs. Better mid range than 244-A. Improved engine and kit required.
BMC-Winfield 1000	308	46	82	82	46	.360" @ .019"	Competition-Form Jr. Top end good. Improved engine necessary.
BMC-Winfield 1100	316	50	86	86	50	.366" @ .019"	Competition-Jr. comes on at 4500, peak 6800, limit 8200 in fully improved engine.

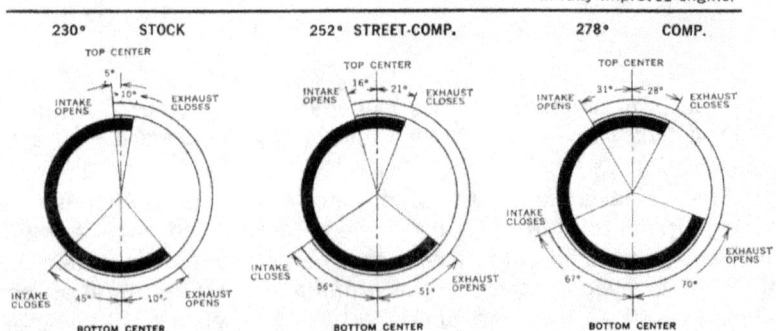

Duration picture of three cams, above, easily illustrates difference in various grinds to obtain a specific type of power.

a matter of application. However, for competition, a close-ratio gearbox, is a must for the Sprite. The Mk. II box, with its ratios of 3.2 (1st) 1.91 (2nd) 1.35 (3rd) and 1.0 to 1 is fine. The option (Q 2354) offered for earlier Sprites was practically identical at: 3.0, 1.99, 1.35 and 1.0.

The factory's limited slip differential (HAC 23) will be found in competition cars, almost without exception.

Back to the engine.

It is best to install the latest type oil pump. A modified distributor has been catalogued, but most owners merely take the standard part to an ignition specialist and have him re-work the advance curve so that full advance is achieved about 500 rpm sooner. A total of 18° to 20° advance, static and dynamic, is considered about right for the improved engine. This can vary from powerplant to powerplant, so use it as a guide.

In reworking the valve train for more action, you may wish to substitute the older forged rocker arms for the newer pressed steel type after having suitably ground and polished them to a aluminum weight. With some camshafts, the grinders recommend lightened pushrods and tappets, either of their own manufacture or altered by the owner. Tappets can be drilled (see photo) to remove weight, but be careful not to alter the diameter, score the sidewalls or leave any burrs. Valve springs should be selected as per the cam grinder's directions. The factory, as usual, lists springs, collars and keepers for their cam kit, (see list) and there is no point in not using it. However, the factory cam has been surpassed for all-out power, at least, by nearly all the U.S. grinders and buying springs from them is a simpler matter.

Stock valve spring and tappet (center) are flanked by heavy duty dual spring and drilled tappet.

In setting the engine up for competition, finally, it almost goes without saying that the owner will either blank off the coolant thermostat with a sleeve (Part #11G.176) or leave it out entirely to lesson water flow restrictions. The cold air box for the carburetors is a sound idea, but one can be manufactured in the home workshop with less effort than ordering one from your friendly BMC dealer. The oil cooler which was formerly catalogued is not available, apparently, but BMC still vends a cooler for the MGA and Healey, so if you are determined to have one, it can be installed. The large sump for Sprites (Q 2341) is a good investment. Baffling the sump to hold more oil around the pump pickup in spite of hard deceleration or sharp turns has been gone into by some mechanics, but the value cannot be readily assayed. Like the cooler, it could well be valuable insurance.

With little more, if anything, to be done with the power train, the competition minded individual will turn to the chassis.

Here, it is all suspension. The Sprite and Midget suffer from a softness of springing in factory form and the works has endeavored to correct this by making available optional springs. They, like many small-demand items are not in plentiful supply on this side of the Atlantic, but those who have obtained the parts are extremely enthusiastic. As far as is known at this time, the Sprite of George Cheney, Cal Club Champion in 1961, is the only competition car fully set up with factory options. Front springs (Q 2334), rear springs (Q 2335) (as described in the suspension section) anti roll bar (Q 2315) and the optional shock absorber valves (Q 2325 front, Q 2333 rear) comprise this factory kit. George's car seems to handle as near perfect as it is possible to get with a Sprite but he has yet to try the Armstrong adjustable shock absorbers (rear only) which are replacement parts on the MK II and Midget. These lever type shocks are a duplicate of the stock dampers in appearance, except for a micrometer adjusting cam on the exterior. It is not necessary to disconnect the shocks in order to change the adjustment. Armstrong Part #7401 ADJ is the identification. Bill Corey, Pasadena, California is the source.

As far as brakes are concerned, the options run the gamut from 8" front drums, as used on the Austin A-40 (Part #Q 2353) through Alfin drums (Q 2491) to disc brakes and their concomitant wire wheels (Q 2431 for the set). The 8" are a distinct improvement, the Alfins are extremely good and the discs transform the car. Prior to this time, such conversions upped the older Sprite from Class H, if it had been so classified, to Class G, arbitrarily. What will happen under the new regulations remains to be seen.

In the event you want to stay Class H (and the rules stay as they are) by all means have the 7" brake shoes re-fitted with Metalik brake linings. These linings are a great development for both street and competition, eliminating fade and giving a smoother, grab free stop. They are to be had in many shops all over the country, but, for one Bill Corey will exchange brake shoes with you or apply the lining to your shoes.

There are two S.U. electric fuel pumps suitable for the Sprite; low volume (AUA 50 HP) and hi volume (AUA 57 HP). Either of these is to be preferred to the mechanical AC with which the car is equipped because they are not affected by engine speed and are not subject to vapor locking. The bigger fuel tank (Q 2336) may be of some value in certain instances, but they are rare.

A quick-opening gas cap and a racing windscreen are the final works options, for the man who must have everything.

FACTORY OPTION PARTS LIST

ENGINE ITEM	PART NO.
1¼" carbs (pair)	Q.2343
Manifold for 1¼" carb	Q.2344
Heavy inner & outer valve springs, etc.	
Spl. exh. manifold	AHA.5448
Competition Con. Rod	Q.2346
Dual exh. system (Stage 5)	
Front manifold	AHA.5448
Exh. pipe	AHA.5449
Silencer	ARA.98
Clips (2)	AHA.5450
Exh. valve (KE 965 material)	AEA.400
High comp. pistons 9.3:1 flat top	2A.946
High lift cam	2A.948 or Q.2629 (See Cam List)
Distr. for HL cam	40656 Lucas
Crankshaft	AEA.406- AEA.440 64.87
Comp. clutch	Q.2349
HD clutch	AET.31
Thermostat blanking sleeve	116.176

SUSPENSION:	
Wire wheels & disc brake conv. set	Q.2431
Alfin brake drums	Q.2332
8" front brake conv. set (Late A-40)	Q.2353
Anti-roll bar	Q.2315
Front SA valves	Q.2325
Rear SA valves	Q.2333
Stiff front springs	Q.2334
Stiff rear springs	Q.2335
Wire wheel	Q.2425

OTHER EQUIPMENT	
Close ratio box	Q.2354
Close ratio gears	
Electric fuel pump	AUA.50 HP, low volume AUA.57 HP, high volume
Racing Screen	Q.2309
Large cap. fuel tank	Q.2336
Quick action filler cap	HS.7972 or Q.2485

FACTORY OPTION PARTS LIST

REAR END RATIOS:
Compl. diff. assemblies
   5.375 ratio
   4.55 ratio   ATA.7073
   3.73 ratio   ATA.7093
Crown & pinion   ATA.7293
   5.375   ATA.7040
   4.375   C4-110
   4.55   8G7129
   3.73   ATA.7240
   (Nose Piece ATA. 7167 must be used
   for this ratio.)
Speedometer heads

    In carrying out any modifications to the car along these lines, always keep in mind that no detail should be overlooked. For instance, if you replace the gear set in the differential, and want to have an accurate speedometer, you must also change the speedometer head. Elementary, but an unaccountable number of owners never ask for the speedometer parts when buying ring and pinion sets.

    Otherwise, it is a check and re-check affair. By following the detailed instructions in this book on disassembly, repair and assembly of the automobile's components, you know that you are being guided by an experienced hand. However, do not suspend your own judgment. Misprints are possible, indeed found, in factory shop manuals. Writers, editors and printers are only human. So, proceed carefully, trying and testing as you go. The carpenter's rule: "Measure twice before you cut it once" is still valid.

PERFORMANCE DATA JUDSON MODEL SP SUPERCHARGER ON STOCK A-H SPRITE

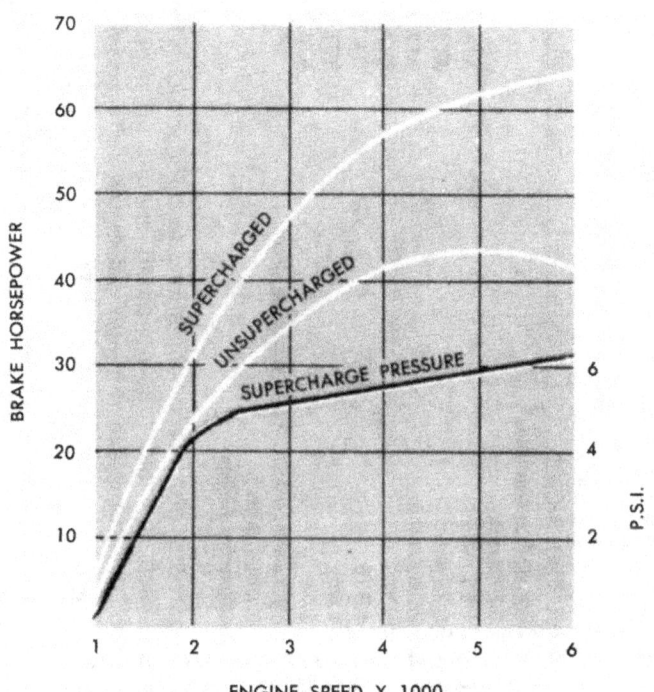

45% MORE H.P.

Acceleration in seconds:	UNSUPER-CHARGED	SUPER-CHARGED
0-40	9	7
0-50	14	9
0-60	21	12
0-70	36	19
30-50	10	6
45-60	11	6
Top speed	78	94
Cruising speed	60-65	75-80
Fuel Consumption (mpg)	29/38	28/35
BHP @ 5000 RPM	42.5	61
Fuel Air Ratio	75%	75%
Wt/ Power Ratio	42	29
Noise Level (Decibels)	49	49

SUPERCHARGING

To realize a decent increase in power without going into a disassembly process, but by spending a moderate amount of money ($169.50) the application of a low-pressure supercharger seems to be the answer. The Judson, a rotary vane type delivering about 6 lbs. of boost at maximum, has an excellent record for reliability and service. It raises horsepower to approximately 65 hp on the 46 hp engine. Blown engines, on the whole, are no less dependable than unblown and require no more maintenance other than checking the oil level in the lubricator. Since consumption of lubricant is approximately 1 quart every 800 to 1,000 miles, this imposes no hardship on the owner who gives nominal attention to his engine.

To give a rather complete idea of the normal supercharger installation, or for the benefit of the Sprite owner who may purchase a used blower unit, we are including a step-by-step description of the fitting sequence.
  (1) Disconnect gas line, vacuum advance line, choke control and throttle control from carburetors. Remove carburetors, heat shield and intake manifold from engine. Replace original heat shield bolt that clamps breather tube to crankcase. Remove gas line completely by disconnecting from fuel pump. (See Fuel System Section.)
  (2) Remove radiator.
  (3) Unscrew bolt from end of crankshaft located in center of crankshaft pulley. To remove this bolt it is necessary to straighten the locking washer under the head of the

bolt so that the bolt can turn. If bolt is too tight to remove by wrench, it can be broken loose by using a chisel on the side of the hex. Original crankshaft pulley is not removed from the engine.

(4) Place aluminum crankshaft pulley furnished with supercharger kit on front of original pulley making sure that shoulder is inserted in bore of original pulley and rivets line up with holes in aluminum pulley. Replace original flat lockwasher and bolt on crankshaft. Rebend one side of flat locking washer against bolt head and punch other side of washer into hole of aluminum pulley. This locks the pulley onto the crankshaft.

(5) Replace radiator.

(6) The flexible fuel line is installed by removing the fuel pump end of the original fuel line as shown in the sketch below. This short section of the original fuel line is then

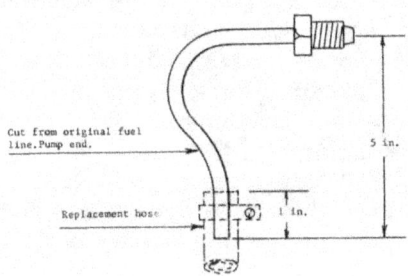

335

inserted approximately 1" into the flexible gas line furnished and clamped with one of the hose clamps removed from the original carburetor hose.

(7) Place lubricator in position as shown in photo. Container should rest against throttle tube support and brake cylinder angle. Use mounting plate on bottom of lubricator as template and drill two ⅛" holes. Fasten lubricator with two self tapping screws furnished with kit.

(8) Remove original throttle cable clamp from the SU carburetor throttle bar and insert in the throttle arm of the carburetor furnished with kit. Insert throttle cable clamp through inside hole as shown in photo. One washer goes between hex and throttle arm and two washers between throttle arm and cotter pin.

(9) Fasten supercharger to engine using original nuts and washers that held manifold to engine. Make sure that center support bolt is backed off free of exhaust manifold plate before tightening nuts securely. Screw down center support bolt until resting on exhaust manifold with just enough tension to support supercharger but not enough to pry on manifold. Lock center support bolt in position with nut.
(10) Fasten heater tube with one original clamp as shown in photo. Use original bolt and washer.
(11) To install front support brace, remove nut and washer from upper stud on rubber engine mount. Place end of brace with hole on stud. Replace washer and nut firmly on engine support but do not tighten.
(12) Remove loose bolt with washer from front of supercharger and place through slotted end of support brace.
(13) Fasten front support securely by tightening nut on engine support stud and bolt on supercharger.
(14) Re-position water hose by using wire clip around support brace and hose as shown in photo. This prevents belt from rubbing on hose.

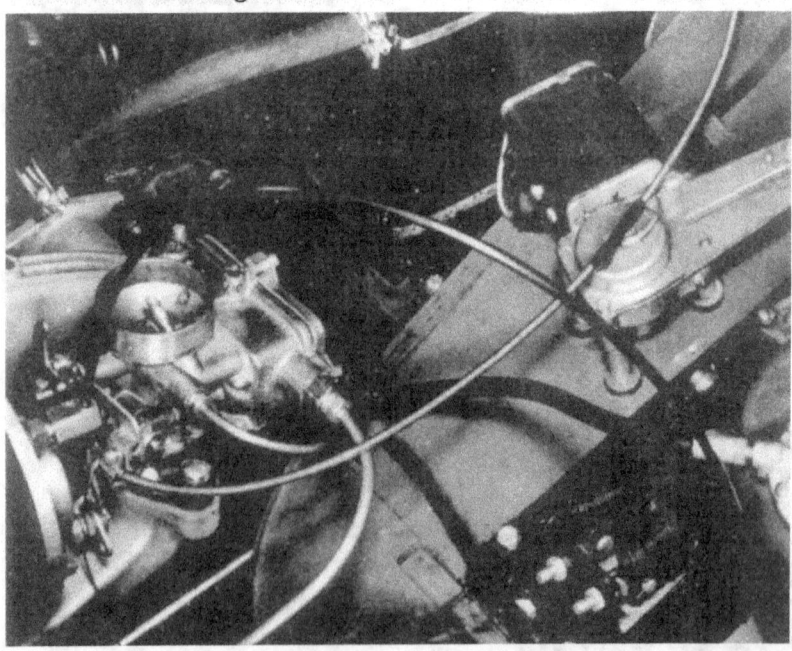

(15) Remove 5" from carburetor end of original vacuum advance line. This should be done by scoring tube with file and breaking (cutting with cutters will close hole). Insert original vacuum advance line into hose on end of extension furnished with kit. Original line should be in-

serted in hose as far as possible. Remove small tube fitting from vacuum connection on carburetor, insert on copper line and connect to carburetor pushing tube into carburetor connection as far as possible.

(16) Bend fuel line as shown in photo and connect to carburetor. Tighten fitting on carburetor and fuel pump.

(17) Connect choke wire to carburetor making sure that the choke button is pushed in completely on the dash panel and that the choke butterfly on the carburetor is fully open. Choke sheath is clamped on carburetor as shown.

Choke wire goes through brass fitting on carburetor and is clamped by screw. Friction tape should be wrapped around the choke sheath where it passes over the windshield wiper motor. This will insulate the choke control from the windshield wiper motor wire terminal.

(18) Push throttle cable through extension bolt on rear of supercharger. Feed cable through original clamp that has been inserted on carburetor arm. Pull cable down making sure sheath is securely bottomed in fitting below lubricator and in extension bolt on back of supercharger. Before tightening clamp for throttle cable, bend cable assembly down flat against fender. Tighten clamp on carburetor. If cable is not bent down against fender before tightening clamp, the engine will speed up when hood is closed.

(19) Connect oil line to lubricator and to the fitting on the intake manifold directly under the carburetor.

(20) Drop idler bracket down by loosening clamping bolt until idler pulley rests on shock absorber.
(21) Place belt over crankshaft pulley and pulley on supercharger. Pull idler pulley tightly against belt and tighten clamping bolt on idler bracket making sure that idler pulley is in line with the other two pulleys and that the idler bracket is not in contact with pulley on supercharger.
(22) Bend fan blades forward slightly until there is 5/16" to 3/8" clearance between blades and supercharger belt.
(23) Place air cleaner on carburetor and fasten original hose from valve cover to connection on air cleaner using original clamp. Secure air cleaner to carburetor by tightening clamp on bottom of air cleaner with screwdriver.
(24) Refill radiator.
(25) Fill the automatic lubricator with No. 10 HD (detergent) motor oil. The engine must not be started unless the lubricator is connected and filled with oil. The lubricator tank has a capacity of 1½ qts.
(26) Fill float chamber of carburetor by pumping lever on side of fuel pump and start the engine. As soon as the engine is running, adjust the lubricator as per instructions under lubrication. After engine is warm, set idle mixture on carburetor. Adjust back and forth until a smooth idle is obtained. The idle speed adjustment screw is spring loaded and located on the throttle arm of the carburetor. With pliers set idle speed at approximately 800 RPM.

SUPERCHARGED ENGINE TUNE-UP DATA

Valve Clearance

The stock valve is recommended. Check to make sure that both intake and exhaust valves have a clearance of .012.

Head Bolts

Tightness of head bolts should be checked to 40 ft. lbs. starting from center bolts and working out.

Spark Plugs

Remove the spark plugs and examine for wear and corrosion. If spark plugs are not in good condition they should be replaced. Use Champion N-5 spark plug, gapped at .020 to .022. Tighten to 30 ft. lbs.

Ignition Point Setting

Stock gap of .014 to .016 is recommended (54 to 57 degrees if set with cam dwell indicator).

Ignition Timing

The stock ignition timing setting of 5 degrees before top dead center is recommended. If additional retard is required because of available fuel or carbon deposits, it can be obtained with the knurled screw on the side of the distributor.

Carburetor

The carburetor furnished with the supercharger has fixed jets and has been specifically set up for the supercharged Sprite. It provides the correct fuel-air ratio throughout the entire speed range of the engine. The only adjustment provided for on this carburetor is for the idle mixture and idle speed.

A flat spot will be encountered at slow speeds or on acceleration if the idle mixture is too lean. The idle adjusting needle valve (brass screw) should be unscrewed until engine slows down appreciably, then the throttle adjusting screw screwed in to provide correct idle speed.

OPERATIONAL DATA

Lubricator Adjustment

(Lubrication is very important). To adjust the lubricator proceed as follows: Start the engine. The small knurled knob on the very top (under protecting cap) should be unscrewed a half-turn to get the oil flowing and then adjusted with your fingers until the lubricator is putting out approximately one drop of oil every four to five seconds at idle. This can be timed through the small window on the lubricator. Screw clockwise to decrease the amount of oil consumption. Oil consumption should run one quart of oil every 800 to 1,000 miles and the oil level should be checked occasionally so that you do not run out of lubricant. Engine and lubricator should be warm while adjustments are being made. The adjustment should be checked after the first one hundred miles. The oil from the automatic lubricator is to oil the bore of the supercharger housing and also acts as an upper cylinder lubricant. The two main rotor bearings of the supercharger are greased and sealed at the factory. **Use any good grade of SAE No. 10 detergent motor oil.** Do not use an upper cylinder lubricant as most top oils are primarily a cleaner and not a lubricant. Do not use a multiple viscosity oil. In making a long descent from high altitudes it is advisable to open the throttle occasionally to insure adequate lubrication because of the high vacuum. The lubricator should be adjusted and left alone as any variance that will occur at idle will be slight under actual operation and is averaged out over the vacuum range of the engine.

Fuel

Premium grade or high octane gasoline is recommended on the supercharged engine. Super premium fuels are not necessary.

Break-In-Period

No breaking-in-period is required for the Judson Supercharger. We do, however, recommend that the engine be run slowly or at idle for at least fifteen minutes before placing the engine or supercharger under load.

Noise

The supercharger may sound noisy when it is first started or within the first half hour of operation. This noise is nothing to be concerned about and will disappear completely within the first 20 to 40 miles of hard driving. A slight clicking noise sometimes at idle or after backing off of the throttle after a hard run is characteristic of a vane type supercharger.

Belt Replacement

In case of drive belt breakage the supercharger will cease functioning but the engine will continue to operate. The drive belt is a standard size and can be purchased from any automotive jobber under Gates number 8209 or from your Chevrolet dealer and is the same belt as used on the Chevrolet 6 cylinder (1955-1956. w/H.D.

Temperature

Because the supercharger is scavenging the hot gasses from the cylinders, the Sprite engine has a tendency to operate colder when supercharged. In cold climates we recommend replacing the 164 degree water thermostat with a 180 degree water thermostat. This replacement water thermostat can be purchased at your local Chevrolet dealer as Water Thermostat No. 3133698, Type 108, 180 degrees.

As on the unsupercharged Sprite, a section of the radiator should be blocked off in freezing temperatures in order to raise the temperature of the engine compartment and the temperature of the charge entering the carburetor. A flat spot will be encountered on acceleration if the water temperature or the temperature of the air in the engine compartment is too low.

Supercharger Pressure

A supercharger gauge is available as an accessory for the Judson Supercharger. Gauge matches other instruments on Sprite dash panel and reads both manifold vacuum and pressure. The Judson Supercharger replaces the vacuum in the manifold with a pressure in proportion to the load placed on the engine. There is always a vacuum in the manifold when the engine is at idle or when the engine is not under load. The vacuum in the manifold is replaced with a pressure as the throttle is opened and the engine is placed under load. Highest boost pressures are obtained under full throttle operation when accelerating or going up an incline. Pressure will vary according to condition of engine, altitude, speed, humidity and engine load. Maximum manifold pressure, because of these conditions, will vary between 5 to 7 pounds. Even when the engine is not operating with a manifold pressure at idle or when there is no load on the engine, the efficiency of the engine has been increased due to the improvement in volumetric efficiency. There is a direct relationship between fuel consumption and manifold boost pressure as the horsepower available increases with the boost pressure. When you do not use the additional power afforded by the supercharger by pushing the engine, you do not pay for it through increased fuel consumption.

ITEMS TO CHECK FOR LACK OF PERFORMANCE
Installation of Supercharger

It is very important that the instructions be followed exactly in installing the supercharger on the engine. Mistakes usually made: throttle cable improperly adjusted not allowing throttle on carburetor to open or close completely. Sheath for throttle cable must be seated in extension bolt on back of supercharger and also seated in chassis fitting below lubricator. The throttle on the carburetor must be completely open when the accelerator pedal is fully depressed. Choke butterfly in throat of carburetor should be fully open when choke button on dash panel is pushed in completely. If center support bolt located on supercharger manifold is screwed in too far it will pry the manifold away from the side of the engine causing a leak resulting in a rough idle and poor performance. Support bolt should be tight enough to support the weight of the supercharger.

Engine

Maximum performance after supercharging is a function of engine condition and tuning. Engine deficiencies often unnoticed before supercharging sometimes prevent the increased performance that can be expected from the supercharged engine. Because of this the supercharger will often be blamed for poor performance when such is not the case. If the installation has been made in accordance with the instructions and the performance is poor it is usually due to a leak in the induction system, improper valve clearance or a faulty ignition system.

The ignition system on the supercharged engine should be in good condition and properly adjusted, incorrect timing and point setting as well as faulty plugs or ignition wiring affects performance considerably and contributes to poor performance. See installation data for timing, point and plug setting. If poor performance cannot be attributed to any of the above after a thorough checking it can be assumed that the trouble is of an internal mechanical nature and the engine itself should be checked by a competent mechanic. Best performance for dependability is obtained from the stock engine. We do not recommend increasing the compression ratio, the use of a special cam or making any other basic modifications on the supercharged engine.

COMPETITION & MODIFICATION EQUIPMENT SUPPLIERS

Here are a few of the firms which have become sources either for factory competition parts or proprietary items in the United States. It is not intended as an index of suppliers, merely a listing of a few companies who have been readily available to West Coast enthusiasts. Consult your favorite enthusiast's periodical for advertising which will direct you to others.

ARROW MOTORS, 912 N. Long Beach Blvd., Compton, Calif. 90221
Complete line of factory parts. Competition parts, factory & proprietary.

BILL COREY, 140 W. Union St., Pasadena, Calif.
Judson Superchargers, Metalik brake linings, engine rebuilding, chassis dynamometer tuning.

HOLLYWOOD SPORTS CARS
5766 Hollywood Blvd., Hollywood, Calif.
Factory competition parts, engine modifications.

JUDSON MFG. CO., Consohocken, Pennsylvania
Superchargers.

BRITISH MOTOR CARS, COMPETITION DEPARTMENT
1200 Van Ness Ave., San Francisco, Calif.
Competition parts, factory & proprietary. Engine modifications.

WEBER SPEED EQUIPMENT CO., 310 S. Center, Santa Ana, Calif.
Camshafts, flywheel & clutch modifications.

SHOEFER TIRES, INC., 901 S. Hanover St., Baltimore, Md.
Speedwell of England speed equipment.

HANK THORPE, INC., COMPETITION DEPARTMENT
P.O. Box 201, 200 Woodbridge Ave., Edison, N.J., 08817
Competition parts, Mini-lite wheels.

BAUGH AXLE SERVICE
50155 Gravel Ridge Rd., Utica, Mich. 48087
Limited slip differentials.

Many photos and the cam chart in the foregoing chapter were reprinted through the courtesy of Sports Car Graphic magazine where they appeared in various issues.

www.ingramcontent.com/pod-product-compliance
Lightning Source LLC
Chambersburg PA
CBHW071954220426
43662CB00009B/1127